Dreams of Empire

Napoleon Bonaparte in 1792, aged 23

Dreams of Empire

Napoleon and the first world war
1792-1815

PAUL FREGOSI

A BIRCH LANE PRESS BOOK
PUBLISHED BY CAROL PUBLISHING GROUP

First Carol Publishing Group Edition 1990

A Birch Lane Press Book
Published by Carol Publishing Group

Editorial Offices   Sales & Distribution Offices
600 Madison Avenue   120 Enterprise Avenue
New York, NY 10022   Secaucus, NJ 07094

In Canada: Musson Book Company
A division of General Publishing Co. Limited
Don Mills, Ontario

Published in Great Britain by Hutchinson, 1989

Queries regarding rights and permissions
should be addressed to: Carol Publishing Group,
600 Madison Avenue, New York, NY 10022

Manufactured in the United States of America
10 9 8 7 6 5 4 3 2 1

Library of Congress Cataloging-in-Publication Data

Fregosi, Paul.
      Dreams of empire : Napoleon and the first world war, 1792-1815 /
   Paul Fregosi.
         p.   cm.
      "A Birch Lane Press book."
      Includes bibliographical references and index.
      ISBN 1-55972-036-0 : $21.95
         1. Napoleon I. Emperor of the French, 1769-1821--Influence.
   2. France--Colonies--History--19th century. 3. France--History,
   Military--1789-1815. 4. Napoleonic Wars, 1800-1814--Campaigns.
   I. Title.
   DC202.8.F74   1990
   940.2'7--dc20   90-40631
                                                         CIP

I dedicate this book

To Maria, Fatima they call her in Brazil,
our two little girls Lindsey and Isabelle,
and to Eva who is not so little

To the dear memory of Olive, never forgotten

To our son, Edouard

To our granddaughter Olivia, and to Jutta

To Charles and Hélène Ciccolini, to their
progeny and to their progeny's progeny

To my wartime comrades of the Free French Naval
Forces and of the French Navy

and, most aptly,

To the memory of my Corsican father and of my
English mother

Contents

7

PART TWO
The Peace of Amiens 1801-1803

PART THREE
The Napoleonic Wars 1803-1814

PART FOUR

The War of 1812

PART FIVE

The Hundred Days of 1815

Epilogue

Acknowledgements

My thanks for their help in a variety of so many ways in the preparation and writing of this book go to Hervé Meslin, Sam Morris, Jacques and Michèle Jouines, Graham Greene, John Curran, Roland de la Poype, 'Groke' Jowitt, Dr Antonio Luis Vale, René Ponthus, Yves St Jacob, Nissim Marshall, Paul and Marie-Louise Martin, Rubens de Azevedo, Brian and Jane Meadows, Ted Morrisby, Werner Lüderitz, the Bruneaus and the Brulets, G. M. Schulten of the Dutch army historical service, to the staff of the Bibliothèque Nationale in Paris, of the British Museum Library in London, of the Mitchell and New South Wales public libraries in Sydney, of the Bibliothèque Municipale in Antibes and of the New York Public Library, to my wife and children for their patience and understanding when I invariably came late to the table for lunch and dinner, and to Giovanni, Bruce, Céline and Christine for never grumbling when my printer would wake them at three o'clock in the morning in dear old Double Bay, Sydney.

'In retrospect the Napoleonic adventure in France seems surprisingly devoid of permanent political effects: the map of Europe is not all that different before and after. But there is no denying the importance of the Napoleonic wars to the rest of the world.'

COLIN MCEVEDY in *The Penguin Atlas of Modern History*

'It would perhaps have been more appropriate to label these two decades culminating in Waterloo the "First World War" than to so name the brief struggle of a hundred years later.'

ALISTAIRE HORNE in the preface to
Napoleon, Master of Europe 1805-1807

List of Maps

Illustration Credits

The publishers would like to thank all those listed below for kindly allowing us to reproduce illustrations in this volume.

Frontispiece – The Mansell Collection: page 56 – Mary Evans Picture Library: page 78 – The Mansell Collection: page 155 – The Bridgeman Art Library: page 175 – National Maritime Museum, Greenwich: page 195 – The Bridgeman Art Library: page 200 – Mary Evans Picture Library: page 228 – The Bridgeman Art Library: page 236 – Mary Evans Picture Library: page 342 – Rowlandson: page 253 – The Bridgeman Art Library: page 261 – Mary Evans Picture Library: page 264 – The Bridgeman Art Library: page 273 – National Maritime Museum, Greenwich: page 304 – National Maritime Museum, Greenwich: page 317 – National Maritime Museum, Greenwich: page 323 – National Maritime Museum, Greenwich: page 326 – Hulton Picture Library: page 354 – Hulton Picture Library.

Preface

As a schoolboy in France and England I knew, of course, of Austerlitz and Wagram and Waterloo and Trafalgar and Marengo; but I knew nothing until at least a quarter of a century later of the siege of Fort Cornelis in Java, nor of the Battle of Blueberg in the Cape colony of South Africa, nor of the attack on Crête-à-Pierrot in Haiti, nor of the Battle of Grand Port off Mauritius, nor of Commodore Blankett's bombardment of the Red Sea port of Kosseir, nor of the abominations of Victor Hugues in Guadeloupe, nor of General Beresford's capture of Buenos Aires and of Captain Jacques de Linier's recapture of it six weeks later. I had never heard of Admiral Duckworth's foray in the Dardanelles, nor of the French 'partisan' General Pierre Perron in India, nor of the British attack on Delhi defended (badly) by the scoundrelly General Bourquien against the brutal General Lake. I knew nothing of Admiral Sir Home Riggs Popham's piratical South American schemes, Wellington's command of a Venezuelan expedition, Commodore Sir Sidney Smith's fighting presence at Saint-John-of-Acre (that, Napoleon Bonaparte said, made him miss his destiny), nor of General Amable Humbert's invasion of Ireland with one thousand French infantry and cavalry nor of his role, later, at the Battle of New Orleans.

I knew, of course, of General Bonaparte's Egyptian expedition and, slightly, of Toussaint L'Ouverture's struggle for the independence of Haiti, but I did not know that more British died in six years of warfare in the West Indies than in six years of campaigning in Spain and Portugal during the Peninsular War, nor that it was in the West Indies, in the island of Martinique, in 1809, that the British captured their first 'eagle', the battle standard that Napoleon's soldiers, hankering for glory, always carried with them into battle.

It became clear, after a considerable amount of reading, of piecing together seemingly inconsequential and disparate items of historical information, that there were two wars underway at the same time: one was for the mastery of Europe, the other for the mastery of the world – or at least a large part of it. That is what Napoleon Bonaparte's Indian and American dreams were all about, as well as the more realistic British colonial and imperial ambitions. Russia, Austria and Prussia figured more prominently than did Britain in the fighting in Europe but overseas Britain was France's main, and often sole, enemy.

The two wars merged tactically sometimes, on the island fringes of Europe, notably in eastward-looking Malta and Corfu. But they remained quite distinct, although they inevitably affected each other, and the combatants, notably the sailors, passed from one war to the other according to the needs of their service.

This narrative is not only an account of the campaigns in these more distant regions but even more of the men who fought in them. For war is, above all, a human experience, a matter of courage and cowardice, of terror, chivalry, violence, death or survival. Inevitably, because of the nature of the conflict, most of these warriors were British or French. But they did not always fight alone. Many others were drawn into the conflict: the Spaniards, the Dutch and the Portuguese, for they were old actors on the colonial scene; the Russians, spurred by primeval urges which drove them east all the way to Alaska and south towards India and the Black Sea; the Turks, whose moribund, disintegrating Ottoman Empire was the potential prey of half a dozen rival powers; the Americans, independent since only a dozen years but ready soon to conceal their own brand of imperialism under the cloak of that 'manifest destiny' which the super-patriotic American press and politicians extolled less than half a century later. There were also Indonesians, Malays and Filipinos, Brazilians, Argentinians, Uruguayans and Venezuelans, Egyptians, Arabians and Arabs, Indians, Boers, Maltese, Greeks, Haitians and Irishmen, West Indians and West Africans, Hottentots and Mozambicans, all caught up at one time or another in the fray, sometimes for years. The wars of the French Revolution and Empire were truly a world war.

Two battles on continental Europe find a place in this book. The battle for the port of Toulon, at the western end of the French Riviera, is one; Waterloo is the other. The British probably had plans to turn Toulon into another colony, a second Mediterranean base like Gibraltar. Toulon, anyway, is where Napoleon Bonaparte, a captain when he arrived there in September 1793 and a general when he left three months later, first showed he was a great soldier and a man whom history would have to take into account.

Toulon was the reveille. Waterloo was the last post.

Thousands of books have been written about the European part of the conflict. The immensity of the fighting in Europe overshadowed what was happening in the rest of the world. To this day most people consider the Napoleonic wars a European struggle, and little has been written about the other war – the war overseas, the war for colonies and for empires. Yet it is a story worth the telling. For while Europe went largely back in 1815 to what it had been in 1792, the war for empires changed the course of human history. From it emerged a new, vast British Empire which – in spite of the recent loss of its thirteen American colonies – would cover a quarter of the globe, and a France still strong enough to invade and occupy Algeria some fifteen years later. And from those lost thirteen British colonies in North America grew an immense transcontinental empire which would soon reach the Pacific and sweep across the seas.

Prologue

CHAPTER ONE

Prelude and Panorama

THE GREAT WAR 1792-1815

Waterloo was not the last battle in the Napoleonic Wars. The final duel was fought thousands of miles away, across the Atlantic, on the beaches and green hills of Guadeloupe, on August 10, 1815. It is not the monuments on Waterloo but the resting places on that Caribbean island of the French and British soldiers killed nearly two months later that mark the end of the long conflict.

Admittedly Guadeloupe was only a post-scriptum after Waterloo. But the consigning of this West Indian episode to total oblivion is in line with our selective and totally Europe-orientated approach to the Napoleonic Wars.

Yet the overseas campaigns, which began in 1793, form an important part of the political, imperial, commercial, military and maritime rivalry that had stamped Anglo-French relations for seven hundred previous years. They also engulfed the Spanish and Dutch colonial empires and transformed and enlarged the United States of America which became involved on the sidelines as a co-belligerent – but never anyone's ally – in the conflict, first in a naval war against France (1798-1801), then against Britain in the misnamed War of 1812, which actually lasted until 1815.

The United States came out, in fact, as a major beneficiary of the Anglo-French conflict. For, faced by Britain's mastery of the seas, Napoleon felt he could not defend the huge, sprawling French territory of Louisiana, which included wholly or in part thirteen of today's forty-eight continental states, and sold it to President Jefferson, thus doubling the size of the United States overnight. The British Empire, however, was the more direct winner of the Napoleonic Wars. It, too, doubled in size and became, for a century and a half, the Empire upon which the sun never set.

It is one of the ironies of history that, in his endeavours to achieve French domination in the world, Napoleon Bonaparte became the architect of British – and subsequent American – global greatness.

In the very early stages of this great war, the future emperor of the French was a very minor figure indeed. In 1792, when France went to war against Austria and Prussia, he was just a junior artillery lieutenant, not yet twenty-three, only a few years out of the military college in Brienne. He was sallow-faced, awkward in his movements, ill at ease with women, and his long, greasy hair fell in untidy locks over his dandruff-covered shoulders. He was poor and he looked it in a threadbare uniform worn away at the elbows. When he was in Paris, a friend of his mother from Corsica, Madame Permont, the wife of a French official who had moved with her husband from the island to the French capital, often invited the hungry young officer home to supper. Her daughter, the mischievous Laure, thought young Bonaparte looked so ridiculous with his thin legs in wide-topped, knee-length, down-at-heels boots that she called him 'Puss-in-Boots', a sobriquet which he particularly disliked.

In those days the future ruler of France was not yet fully integrated into his French nationality. It is even said that he had tried a few years before to join the British navy as a midshipman. A Corsican nationalist, he brooded over the fate of his native island sold by Genoa to France in 1768, the year before his birth, and he longed to see it become independent. Corsica, he felt, was despised by the French as a conquered land and a mere colony. 'My countrymen, in chains, kiss the hands of those who oppress them. . . . Corsicans were able by following all the laws of justice to shake off the Genoese yoke, and they can do the same with the French one,' he wrote passionately of his island home.

Yet Napoleon Bonaparte was serving as an officer in the French army when, in 1792, volunteers singing 'La Marseillaise', the new battle song, were marching to the eastern and northern frontiers to meet the coming onslaught. Because of his alien loyalties perhaps, none of this martial activity stirred young Lieutenant Bonaparte. He simply requested, and obtained, leave to escort his sister Elisa, who had just finished her studies, home to Corsica. There he plunged into local politics.

Britain, which was to become his main enemy for more than twenty years, was not yet then in the war. Along with Spain, Holland and Portugal – curiously, the only other countries with vast colonial empires – Britain was only drawn into the conflict on February 1, 1793, a few days after the execution of Louis XVI, when France declared war on her. It was a sailor, with naturally enough a world view of strategy, who was to suggest to the French the global dimensions a conflict with Britain might assume. Admiral Armand Kersaint would assert, with a certainty that his distinguished services seemed to justify, that Britain was vulnerable and that she could be hit and defeated in two places in the world: Ireland and India. It was a message that was to be remembered later.

Perhaps Kersaint – who was to be guillotined in December 1793, during the Terror – failed to recognise that the sea and the British navy stood between France and these objectives. Or perhaps he was over-confident. After all, a dozen years ago he had fought and defeated the British not once but several times. As a frigate captain during the American War of Independence he had captured in the West Indies two British frigates, HMS *Ceres* and HMS *Lively,* and later a corvette, and he had also taken part in the capture of British-held Essequibo and Berbice in Guyana.

But, unknown to Kersaint, this was a new Britain that France was now facing. From the moment she entered the war she became the steadfast leader, inspirer and, particularly, paymaster of every coalition that was formed by the panic-stricken royal houses of Europe to fight, first against the tattered but ardent young armies of the Republic, then against the disciplined, formidable Grand Army of the Emperor Napoleon.

It is a conflict that historians have divided into two parts: the Wars of the French Revolution, from 1792 to 1801, and the Wars of the French Empire, from 1803 to 1815, with an uneasy two-year truce, the Peace of Amiens, in between. During these two decades Britain and France, who had been at each other's throat since 1066, clashed not only on the battlefields of Europe but also in Africa, north, west and south; in the Americas; in the Middle East; on the Asian mainland and in Indonesia and the Philippines; and, at sea, in the Mediterranean and in the Atlantic and Indian Oceans and even in the South China Sea.

In the century that followed, British historians and the British public called it The Great War. It was also the first world war.

ALL THE WORLD'S A STAGE

Since Europe was massively engulfed by the wars both of the French Revolution and of the French Empire and since most European countries, or at least their royal families, were frightened out of their wits for more than twenty years, it is on Europe that the attention of historians of this epoch has always been concentrated.

Such men were mainly Europeans, anyway, with a natural native tendency to stress the Old World. But there is an additional reason for their attitude. The titanic struggle under way in Europe eclipsed every-

thing else that was happening in the world. Europe felt directly and intensely the immediate consequences of the colossal tremors that spread
out from Paris. But even so, it was the outside world that would be
more profoundly transformed.

On the eve of the Revolution, in terms of population and of political
power, France was the leading nation in Europe. Or perhaps where
power was concerned, she and Britain were neck and neck. For Britain
already reigned over the world's largest growing empire overseas. And
she was to expand her possessions considerably during the next two
decades, the years covered by this book, doubling the area of her
realms and increasing their number from twenty-six to forty-three.

In the late eighteenth century, however, France was one of the giants
of the world. Her population on the outbreak of the Revolution was
around twenty-eight million, only a few million less than that of
Russia, in those days a largely ineffective land mass far away to the east.
France also had as large a population as the powerful but largely land-
locked multi-national Austrian Empire which extended over much of
central and eastern Europe, with just a strip of territory bordering the
Adriatic. France's population greatly outnumbered that of the other
European colonial powers: Britain with fifteen million inhabitants;
Spain with nine million; Portugal with two and a half million; the
Netherlands with two million.

Europe was then, even more than today, a hotchpotch of national-
ities and independent states. There were about seventeen million Germans. Prussia, the leading German state, accounted for seven million
of them. The rest were split up into a multitude of small principalities
such as Hesse, Brunswick and Hanover, the latter allied to the British
Crown, which provided a large pool of mercenaries to the British
army, on a strictly cash basis.

Tiny, poverty-stricken Switzerland provided mainly cannon-fodder
to the richer countries. With a population of only around one and a half
million, she managed to send regiments of highly trained soldiers to
fight on battlefields all over the world.

The Polish people, eight million of them, were another great source
of military manpower. But her mercenaries, almost to a man, only
fought for France. Polish soldiers, with the heroism that has always
marked their nation, fought on every European battlefield and in
Egypt and Haiti too.

Italy, original home of the Bonapartes before the family migrated to
Corsica in the early sixteenth century, was a collection of small states
and duchies and republics and kingdoms. The two most important
were the Kingdom of the Two Sicilies (capital Naples) – where in 1792
Lady Hamilton's husband was British ambassador – which covered
much of southern Italy as well as Sicily itself, and the Kingdom of
Sardinia. Sardinia also extended well outside the island of that name

and included, on the mainland, Piedmont and Savoy. Its capital was Turin. Milan, not far away, was the capital of Lombardy, then under Austrian rule. The Pope, in Rome, was the master of a large slice of central Italy. A handful of dukes and doges ruled over Venice, Genoa, Florence, Pisa and various other city-states. Venice, a minor colonial power, owned Corfu and the Ionian islands, off Greece and Albania. The whole Italian ensemble had a population of around eighteen million talkative and talented inhabitants.

The Turkish, or Ottoman, Empire with which Britain and France occasionally and untidily clashed, sprawled like a half-dead octopus over large areas of southeastern Europe, western Asia and northern Africa. Ruled from the Supreme Porte imperial court at Istanbul, then known as Constantinople, it had a population, alternatively lethargic and turbulent, of about twenty-five million. Some five million of them were Europeans from the Balkans: Greeks, Bulgarians, Serbs, Bosnians, Macedonians, Montenegrins and Albanians.

The fifteen million inhabitants of the British Isles, about half the size of France in area, included five million in Ireland. Constitutionally part of the United Kingdom, Ireland was in fact a colony and provided England with famished labourers and many of her soldiers and sailors, often of doubtful loyalty and quite eager to serve in enemy ranks when captured by the French. The British population also included some one million in Scotland, where Britain recruited many of her army officers from the impoverished gentry.

In the faraway Pacific, a few hundred British convicts, soldiers and free settlers, in what is today the city of Sydney, were laying the foundations of the future Commonwealth of Australia. Britain was also established among the Windward and Leeward Islands.

The Indian subcontinent, today's India, Pakistan, Nepal and Bangladesh, supported a population of a hundred and eighty million, mainly Hindus and Muslims, spread out in various states, only a small proportion of which were then under British rule.

Indonesia, then known as the Dutch East Indies, had a population of twelve million people, the nearby Spanish-ruled Philippines had just over two million.

China, to be described by Napoleon as a sleeping giant, with about three hundred million people, considered itself the centre of the world. Arrogant and weak in spite of its huge population, it was doomed to become a victim to encroaching Russians, Japanese, British, French, Portuguese and Americans.

The Japanese, belligerently insular in their nearby flotilla of islands, had a population of twenty-eight million.

Africa, forbidding and frightening, was then truly the Dark Continent, unknown, virtually untouched except on the edges. Part of Muslim North Africa was nominally within the Ottoman Empire.

There were a few trading posts and colonies on the West Coast of
Africa, mainly British, French, Spanish and Portuguese, mostly engaged in the traffic of black slaves. The Arabs were the main slave
traders on the East Coast. The Dutch colony at the Cape of Good
Hope was not only a port-of-call and supply base for ships sailing from
Europe to the Far East, India and New South Wales. Because of its
mild climate, it was already becoming a colony of settlement and its
wines were already appreciated by those who had the good fortune to
drink them. It had a small white population of around twenty thousand souls, most of them of Dutch, German and French Huguenot
origin.

The United States of America, its frontiers already moving west and
south into Ohio, Kentucky, Tennessee, Alabama and Mississippi, had
been independent for only a dozen or so years. Its population of five
million was not yet fully aware of that 'manifest destiny' which was to
drive the upcoming generations of Americans all over the continent,
conquering all who opposed their acquisitive fury. Across the border
to the north, Britain still stood guard over two hundred thousand
Canadians, most of whom were of French stock.

In Latin America, the demographic picture was then also very different from today's. In the Spanish Viceroyalty of La Plata, the whole
region accounted for about 350,000 men, women and children, with a
considerable proportion of Negroes and Indians. The town of Buenos
Aires, the capital of today's Argentina, had a population of forty thousand, as did Montevideo, on the other side of the River Plate, now the
capital of Uruguay. Across the Andes, Chile boasted a population of
around 800,000. The giant Portuguese colony of Brazil had two
million inhabitants – not counting a probable few hundred thousand
primitive Indians in the forests – many of them black slaves from
Africa. Venezuela, Colombia and Ecuador, then joined in the Vice-
royalty of New Granada, with about two and a half million people,
while the Viceroyalty of Peru accounted for another one and a half
million.

But it was the Viceroyalty of New Spain, stretching from the
isthmus of Panama all the way north to California and what are today's
western states of the USA, that was Spain's proudest possession in the
New World. Some seven million people probably lived in this dominion, five million of them within the borders of the modern country of
Mexico. The northern borders of New Spain were rather vague, but
they embraced the French-speaking Captaincy of Louisiana, capital
New Orleans, which had a population of forty thousand Frenchmen
and French Creoles (white Frenchmen born in the territory),
Spaniards and blacks, with a sprinkling of Americans, known locally as
'Kentiks' as so many of them were from Kentucky.

And finally, the nearby West Indies were largely divided among the

Spaniards, British and French. Haiti, then known as Saint-Domingue, was the jewel of the French colonial empire.

Of the French colonial possessions Haiti was by far the richest. With eight thousand plantations, it monopolised two-thirds of France's overseas trade and supplied most of the sugar, coffee, cotton and indigo consumed in continental Europe. Fifteen hundred merchant ships called in Haiti every year, more than in Marseille, France's chief port. No less than sixteen factories in Bordeaux refined the sugar from Haiti, turning it into fine rum. The territory was a vast and highly successful business enterprise that made huge fortunes for the merchant dynasties of Marseille, Nantes and Bordeaux, and for many of the country's landowning, aristocractic families – including that of the future empress of the French, Napoleon's Creole first wife, the gracious and vivacious Josephine, born in Martinique.

The population of Haiti consisted of forty thousand whites, thirty-eight thousand free mulattos and blacks, and half a million black slaves. The colony wasn't only prosperous. It was also a boiling cauldron of racial, political and class conflicts in which everybody hated and despised everybody else with an intensity, insensitivity and intolerance unexpected on the part of a people as civilised as the French but which they have often shown throughout their turbulent history.

Whites, mulattos and blacks loathed each other, the poor whites couldn't stand the rich whites, the rich whites despised the poor whites, the middle-class whites were jealous of the aristocratic whites, the whites born in France looked down upon the locally-born whites, mulattos envied the whites, despised the blacks and were despised by the whites; free Negroes brutalised those who were still slaves, Haitian-born blacks regarded those from Africa as savages. Everyone – quite rightly – lived in terror of everyone else. The blacks, their lives depending on their master's whim, worked in the plantations sixteen hours a day and sharpened their machetes, awaiting the day of revenge. It was a country ruled by fear, torture, the lash and the noose. God was obviously looking the other way. Haiti was hell. But Haiti was rich.

Haiti was the pride of colonial France. The rest of her overseas empire consisted of disparate bits and pieces scattered across the globe.

On the eve of the Revolution, the once magnificent French Empire in the Americas was made up of only a few leftovers. In the Caribbean, in addition to Haiti, France only ruled over a few small islands in the Antilles: Martinique, St Lucia, Guadeloupe, Tobago (captured from the British a few years previously), and some tiny specks here and there, such as Désirade, Marie Galante and Les Saintes. On the South American mainland, France was present in only one territory, Guyana (capital Cayenne), wedged between Brazil and the British and Dutch Guyanas. In North America the French flag still flew defiantly over St Pierre and Miquelon (eight square miles), a fishing settlement consisting of two small and bleak, storm-battered islands off the coast of Newfoundland.

These remnants were all that was left of France's American empire. Canada and Louisiana had been lost a quarter of a century before: Canada when Wolfe defeated Montcalm on the Plains of Abraham, Louisiana given away as a present soon afterwards by Louis XV of France to his Spanish Bourbon cousins to console them for the loss of Florida to the British (the Spaniards took it back a few years later).

France owned a few more islands, bases and trading posts across the globe. They were as much the sad relics of thwarted colonial ambitions as hopeful steppingstones to new adventures and conquests: Pondicherry and a handful of other small settlements in India; Gorée and St Louis on the West African coast, the foundations of the future colony of Senegal; Mauritius, Réunion and the Seychelles in the Indian Ocean.

It wasn't a great colonial empire. Including Haiti, it was perhaps as large as France itself.

The British Empire, on the other hand, the empire that Napoleon hoped to conquer, was far more impressive. First of all, it was sixty times larger. The loss of the American colonies a few years earlier had not dampened British enthusiasm for distant endeavours. Canada, virtually empty, stretched away to the north and west, a happy hunting ground for the fur trappers of the Hudson's Bay and North West companies and for the French Canadian *coureurs des bois*, the fur trappers and traders of French origin who spent most of their life in the forests. The circle of British possessions in the western hemisphere was completed by Newfoundland, Britain's oldest colonial possession, Bermuda, Belize in Central America, British Guyana in South America, the Bahamas off Florida, Jamaica, the Barbados, Antigua, St Vincent, St Kitts-Nevis, Grenada, Montserrat and Dominica in the Caribbean, and the disputed (with Spain) desolate and unoccupied Falkland Islands not far from the Antarctic.

In India, where the Englishman Clive had defeated the Frenchman Dupleix forty years previously, Britain (through the East India Company) ruled over Bengal, the territory of the northern Sarkars, along the northeast coast, and held outposts in Bombay and Madras. The rest of the country was the tumultuous breeding ground of continually warring Hindu and Muslim dynasties, often encumbered with huge armies led by foreign – mainly French – mercenaries in the service of resplendent rajahs, sultans and nawabs. The wily traders of the Company, and French and British government agents, were active throughout the subcontinent, trickily making their way through a maze of

Oriental intrigue in the hope of earning more profits for their share holders at home or of gaining territorial sovereignty or advantages for their respective countries.

To the southeast, down in the Pacific, Australia was just starting to be colonised by the British, not only to supply a new dumping ground for convicts in replacement for the lost American colonies, but also to become a bastion of British power in the antipodes. In West Africa, Gambia had already slipped into the British orbit and so had Sierre Leone, a colony founded for freed slaves. In the south Atlantic, the grim island of St Helena also flew the Union Jack.

Nearer home the colonising instinct of the British was also strong. Early in the eighteenth century they had occupied on Spanish soil the fortress of Gibraltar. The Rock of Gibraltar became, for the British, a symbol of their might and has remained so, a strange memorial today to the power that once was. But in the two preceding centuries it stood as an insolent reminder to the people of Europe that they were all accessible to Britain.

After this rapid survey of the French and British colonial empires a glimpse of the other overseas empires is in order. These were essentially the Dutch, Spanish and Portuguese. We could also, almost legitimately, add Turkey, with its capital Constantinople a stone's throw away across the Bosphorus from its vast Asian hinterland. Its empire of a thousand and one nights was a strange and picturesque agglomeration of peoples from Arabia, the Near and Middle East, Egypt and North Africa, southeastern Europe and the islands of the Aegean Sea. Russia should be mentioned also, although the main thrust of its colonialism was essentially aimed at the adjoining continental land mass, beyond the Urals to Siberia in the east, and southward to the Muslim lands of Tashkent and Bukhara. Russia's perennial Indian ambitions, however, were already apparent in the mad dreams of Tsar Paul I. They were fed and encouraged by Napoleon's own Indian visions. And Russia, for a while, also had designs in America. But the Russians went out there on their own, on the west side of the continent, far from the scene of the conflicts in which France, Britain and the United States were involved. By 1804 they had founded a fur-trading station at Sitka, in Alaska, and eight years later built the Fort Ross stockade near San Francisco. The local Russian River recalls their former presence there.

After some unpleasantness with the Mexicans, the Russians abandoned northern California thirty years later and, in 1867, sold Alaska to the United States for seven million dollars – a great bargain for the Americans.

Which country – with its colonies – was allied with which during the entire conflict was frequently confusing. Only Britain, and to a large extent Portugal, were steadfast in their opposition, first to Republican then to Imperial France. The others wavered according to their fluctuating interests, and to the way the winds of war blew.

The poor Spaniards in particular turned and twisted with the wind. After abandoning the British (so did the Dutch, more or less at the same time), giving up their colony of Santo Domingo in exchange for French-occupied areas of Spain, and then exchanging Louisiana in 1801 for the French-held Italian Duchy of Parma, they joined the French for just long enough to get their fleet trounced, along with France's, by Nelson at Trafalgar. Finally, outraged at Napoleon's efforts to unseat their king and place his brother Joseph on the throne, the Spaniards turned against their French protectors in 1808 and called in the British. Thus began the Peninsular War and Wellington's rise to fame.

But not only Spain and Holland changed sides during these wars. Russia, Sweden, Austria, Turkey, Prussia and a multitude of small German states also switched allies at various times. The situation led sometimes to some curious fighting. In 1807 Admiral Duckworth forced the Dardanelles to confront the Turks and later that year a Turkish fleet under Pasha Seid-Ali was shattered off Lemnos in the Aegean by a Russian squadron led by Admiral Senavin. (So outraged was the Ottoman admiral at the poor performance of some of his ships that he summoned three unfortunate captains to his flagship and had them strangled on the spot.) Normally Britain should have cheered this Russian victory, for Turkey was the common enemy of both British and Slavs. But Britain and Russia had in fact just gone to war, so when some of the victorious Russian vessels, sailing back to the Baltic, put into French-occupied Lisbon, the British then blockaded them. Other British warships, allied to a Swedish flotilla, pounced upon and defeated another Russian squadron in the Baltic, led by Admiral Chanichef. (Chanichef, disgraced, was luckier than the beaten Turkish captains of Lemnos. The Tsar simply demoted him from his rank of admiral to that of ordinary seaman.)

All in all, it must have been difficult sometimes for the various belligerents to know why and whom they were fighting. Few can have been more confused than the Dutch. Holland, under the Stadholder William V, a member of the traditional ruling house of Orange-Nassau, originally came into the war alongside Britain. But she was very divided in her sentiments. The powerful so-called Patriot Party supported the French. William V was pro-British. Beaten by the French, whose cavalry captured a large part of the Dutch fleet iced up in the frozen Texel, the Stadholder fled to exile in London. Holland then dumped England, joined France and became the Batavian Republic.

In 1806 Napoleon decided to make his brother Louis King of Holland and the Batavian Republic became a kingdom which endured until Louis, resentful at being Napoleon's puppet, abdicated his throne in 1810. Furious at his brother's royal defection, Napoleon annexed Holland and made it part of France. Dutchmen became Frenchmen and Dutch colonies French.

In fact Java was then the only Dutch colony still unoccupied by the British. At one time the Dutch had reigned over a colonial empire fifteen times larger than the French, composed of valuable titbits which had made the fortune of many Amsterdam merchants: Ceylon (Sri Lanka); Java; the Cape of Good Hope province; the Spice Islands, as the Moluccan islands were known; Malacca in the Malayan peninsula; a number of small islands in the Caribbean, including Saba and St Martin; Guyana on the South American mainland and Curaçao off. But the British had snapped all these up, one by one.

The Portuguese colonial empire, on the other hand, was almost as big as Britain's. Brazil was its *pièce de résistance*. The remaining Portuguese colonies were a motley assortment of far-flung islands and bits of territory, reminiscent of the French colonial empire but considerably older, for the Portuguese had been pioneer maritime explorers and their first overseas territory, Madeira, was discovered in 1418. In addition to immense Brazil, the Portuguese colonial empire was made up of Goa, Damao and Diu on the west coast of India; Timor, in the Indonesian archipelago; Macao, a trading post near Canton leased from the Chinese emperor; various establishments on the west and east coasts of Africa, including Mozambique and Luanda, site of the present capital of Angola. The Atlantic islands of Madeira, the Azores and Cape Verde completed the Lusitanian domain.

The largest empire of all was that of Spain, at least one and a half times as large as Britain's, nearly a hundred times vaster than France's. It covered a large part of South, Central and North America, all the way from Cape Horn in the south to the Canadian prairies in the north. Because of its wealth, size and populations, and its numerous flourishing cities, it should have been the most prosperous. But it was just too big for Spain to manage and was on the brink of disintegrating.

Half South America was Spanish, the other half Brazil and the Guyanas. The status of the Falkland Islands, disputed between Spain, France and Britain, was unclear but Spain probably had the best title.

With the exception of British Belize, all of Central America was also Spanish. Spain ruled over old Mexico and, somewhat tenuously, over what are today very roughly the states of New Mexico, Texas, Arizona and California, as well as Florida, recovered from the British in 1783. Louisiana, administered as a Captaincy and Spanish for a few more years before reverting to France, probably comprised most of what are today the states of Louisiana, Arkansas, Oklahoma, Missouri, Kansas, Iowa, Minnesota, North and South Dakota, Nebraska, Montana, Wyoming, Colorado, and even Oregon and Washington.

The crimson and gold flag of Spain also flew over the large Caribbean islands of Cuba, Puerto Rico and Trinidad, and over the eastern two thirds of Hispaniola, Santo Domingo while, outside of the Americas, the main Spanish dominion was the Philippine Islands, capital Manila. The Pacific island of Guam was Spanish, as were the Marianas, the Carolines, and the Canaries and Fernando Po in the Atlantic. Included in the Spanish hemicycle around the world were a few forts and trading posts on the West African coast.

At the time of the French Revolution, American imperialism was still unborn. 'The frontier', a vague term which in those days meant Ohio, Indiana, Tennessee and Kentucky, marked the limit of American territorial ambitions. The first exponent of imperialism overseas would be Captain David Porter who, during the War of 1812, commanded the 32-gun frigate, USS *Essex,* on her extended cruise in the Pacific Ocean. This imperialist beginning was very modest indeed. Porter sailed his ship around the Horn, captured a number of whalermen and called at the Marquesas Islands where he claimed and occupied Nuku-Hiva for his country and renamed it Madison Island. The name didn't last and neither did the claim. The Marquesas have been French for nearly one hundred and fifty years.

Two other small colonial powers should be mentioned: Denmark and Sweden. Denmark ruled the large but cold and barren northern dominions of Greenland and Iceland, and one small island in the North Sea, Heligoland, which Britain later took, turned into a colony and traded with Germany for Zanzibar.

Denmark also had a small stake in the tropics – the islands of St Croix, St John and St Thomas which placed it on the fringes of the Franco-British contest in the West Indies – and a trading establishment in India, at Trinquebar on the Coromandel coast. However, when Denmark came into the war on the French side, the British took Trinquebar over and from that time Denmark confined its colonial business ventures to codfish and sealskins from Greenland and Iceland.

Sweden had one colony, St Batholomew in the West Indies. But it figured only very fleetingly in the war and no fighting took place there at all. Sweden, anyway, was only a very minor participant in these wars. They marked her deeply, nevertheless: her kings are descendants of Bernadotte, one of Napoleon's marshals who charmed the Swedes into calling him to their throne.

SUGAR, SLAVES AND RACISM

Colony collecting was both a fashionable and a profitable European national pastime in the eighteenth century. France before the Revolution, was one of the least successful entrants in the colonial chase. Britain had supplanted her in India and Canada, and Spain had taken her place in Louisiana. But when the French Revolution broke out, at first the French just wanted to retain what little inheritance they had, and perhaps win back the lands they had lost. They did not crave the colonies of others.

It was General Bonaparte himself, in association with Talleyrand, the French Foreign Minister, who first brought a heavy touch of colonial imperialism to the French revolutionary scene when, in 1797, he took Corfu and the Ionian Islands from Venice, occupied Malta and invaded Egypt the next year.

In the early days of the Revolution, however, rather than fighting to take other people's colonies, France, under the influence of the abolitionist Abbé Raynal, had been trying to eradicate slavery from her own. 'The slave, an instrument in the hands of wickedness, is less than a dog,' the Abbé had written more than twenty years previously, in his *Philosophical and Political History of the Establishment and Commerce of the European in the Two Indies.* He had gone on to plead for 'natural liberty' which, he said, was 'the right which nature has given to everyone to dispose of himself according to his will.' It sounds innocuous today, but it had been more than daring at the court of Louis XV: it had been downright subversive.

In spite of its heavy, unwieldy title, its highly emotional tone and its many inaccuracies, the book ran into no less than forty editions before the French Revolution, was translated into several languages and, according to some historians, had a major influence on the Revolution itself. It certainly inspired the Haitian slave Toussaint L'Ouverture, the coachman of a kindly and considerate planter who lent him the book, to lead his black countrymen in their fight for freedom.

Raynal seemed to triumph in 1794, just a few days before the blue, white and red Tricolour became the flag of France, when the Paris Assembly on February 4 abolished slavery in the French colonies. But the victory was a very muted one. Although the abolition applied technically to all French colonies, for reasons of politics, business or war it was in fact only very selectively implemented. It became law in Guyana, in Haiti and in Guadeloupe. It was not carried out in Martinique, occupied by the British, nor, because of opposition from merchants, planters and businessmen, in the Indian Ocean islands of Mauritius and Réunion, nor in Senegal, although they were all under direct French Republican rule. And anyway, when he became First Consul in 1799, one of General Bonaparte's first cares was to announce, in deliberately vague words, the forthcoming reinstatement in the French colonies of 'the regime under which they had always prospered since their beginnings'. It was an indication of his intention to restore slavery, the regime under which the planters had prospered.

The reintroduction of slavery is one of Napoleon Bonaparte's least known and most unattractive actions. Many instances exist of his contempt for people of colour. He strongly opposed the promotion of coloured men to a high military rank and swore to tear off the officers'

epaulettes from those he scornfully called 'these gilded Africans' who
had received their commissions during the French Revolution. He sent
General Richepanse to Guadeloupe and General Leclerc to Haiti, both
with large armies, to restore slavery, to make slaves again of men and
women who had been freed eight years previously, to force them back
to their old masters, their plantations and their chains. It was one of his
most iniquitous deeds.

As soon as the preliminaries of the Peace of Amiens with Britain
were signed on October 7, 1801, Bonaparte ordered the governors of
the French islands in the West Indies and the Indian Ocean to inform
planters they need have no fear their slaves would be freed. Admiral
Decrès, the newly-appointed minister of the navy and colonies, went
further and asked that the law giving the slaves their freedom should be
axed immediately.

'I am too French to be cosmopolitan. ... I want slaves in our
colonies. Liberty is a food for which Negro stomachs are not yet
ready,' Decrès wrote in his report to First Consul Bonaparte.

Under the pressure of colonial business interests, the parliament in
Paris voted in favour of the re-establishment of slavery in the French
colonies by two hundred and eleven votes to sixty. Money, once again,
as so often in the course of human history, had proved stronger than
justice.

Nowhere had abolition, when first announced, been greeted more
deliriously than in Guadeloupe where the new governor, Victor
Hugues, arrived on June 2, 1794 with a portable guillotine and 1,153
eager, young Republican soldiers. Hugues landed on an island recently
occupied by the British, attacked them immediately, proclaimed freedom for the slaves and went on, with the aid of these newly-freed men,
to chase out the British army, several times larger than his own.

Hugues may have been a corrupt and sadistic scoundrel but he was
also an energetic, courageous and even inspiring leader, and he found
among the freed black slaves an army of enthusiastic supporters. They
were eager to take the message of Liberty–Equality–Fraternity at the
point of a gun to the nearby British islands where slavery continued
undisturbed and the planters there, fed by stories from Royalists who
had escaped from Guadeloupe, lived for many years in terror of black
or native Carib revolts, of the vengeful Victor Hugues, and of his portable guillotine.

Planters in the West Indies were usually sugar men. Sugar was big
business. The West Indian campaign in the 1790s not only involved
fighting with guns and swords. The basic conflict was economic.
Through their blockade, the British cut off the French West Indies
from markets in France and in the rest of continental Europe, and from
the United States. So, to survive, Guadeloupe, under Hugues, resorted
to unbridled and highly profitable privateering in which British and

Americans were lumped together as the common English-speaking enemy.

In Europe, however, British mastery of the sea meant that tropical products were all in short supply during the war. A pound of sugar cost nine times more in Paris than in London. Coffee and tobacco were rare items. The French tried to smoke cabbage leaves but French cabbages just didn't have that Virginia tobacco flavour. They brewed oak acorns instead of coffee beans but found the mixture undrinkable. To replace sugar, chemists experimented with the European beets, and this time however they triumphed. They found a new source of sweetener to replace sugar cane and sugar beet remains to this day one of France's main crops.

Now may be the right place to clarify Napoleon's views about colonialism. 'The colonial system such as we have known it is finished for everybody,' he said in St Helena. He was right in the case of Spain who lost most of her empire during the next twenty years, but he was out by about one hundred and fifty years for everybody else. The colonial system, in fact, grew immensely during the nineteenth century, notably in Africa and Southeast Asia, and only finally collapsed when 'the winds of change' blew over these regions after World War II.

Napoleon believed Britain should bring about 'a more advantageous political combination' with her colonies, foreseeing the creation of the 'dominion' system which Britain instituted nearly a century later in Canada, Australia, South Africa, India and New Zealand but had so conspicuously failed to do with the thirteen American colonies. 'England ought to anticipate a kind of emancipation for her colonies, for she is bound to lose a large number of them in time, and it is up to her to take advantage of the present in order to make sure of securing new ties and more favourable relationships with them,' he said.

Napoleon's early ideas on colonialism had been influenced by Josephine, his Creole wife from Martinique, whose family had owned vast estates in the West Indies, and by her friends from that part of the world. They all favoured close ties between the colonies and the mother country which furnished them with a market for their products and financial and military backing when required, and they nearly all supported slavery which provided them with cheap labour.

Napoleon, who was usually ready to admit if he had been wrong (after enough time had elapsed), when in St Helena described the expedition he had sent to Haiti to fight against the rebellious blacks as 'one of the greatest follies of which I was ever guilty'. He blamed the moneyed people of the colonies for the policies he followed. 'I was continually beset with applications from proprietors of estates, merchants and others,' he explained. Even if the French had won in Haiti, he added, the only people who would have gained anything would have been wealthy plantation owners and businessmen.

Napoleon must have had a bad conscience over his reinstatement of slavery. Only eight days after reaching Paris, after his escape from Elba, in 1815, although pressed and threatened on all sides, he found the time to sign a decree on March 28 outlawing the slave trade. Perhaps he had become aware, in the intervening years, of all that slavery implied.

It is necessary to understand the ferocity of slavery in order to understand the ferocity of the subsequent fighting in the slave islands. In Haiti, where slaves were particularly badly treated, their owners could do almost anything they liked with them. A white planter, Monsieur Lejeune, thought his slaves were trying to poison him. He had the feet of two black women placed over a fire and roasted to make them confess. A wealthy white woman ordered her cook thrown into a fire for spoiling the meal when she had important guests – whom she had wanted to impress – to dinner. Recalcitrant or rebellious slaves could be castrated, or thrown into a cesspool to drown in human faeces, or boiled alive in bubbling vats of sugar. A punishment regarded as particularly amusing was to ram gunpowder up the backside of a slave, then to light it and blow him up.

Murder and torture were not, alas, isolated incidents confined to Haiti. Hundreds, probably thousands, of cases are on record, in all the West Indian islands, British, French and Spanish. A slave who ran away in Jamaica was punished with death when caught. In the Barbados a master had the right to cut off the arms and the legs of his slaves. But it was forbidden to dismember a slave if he belonged to someone else: it was against the rights of private property, and the guilty party could be sued in a civil – not criminal – action. In Tobago, in 1798, a white man stabbed and killed a Negro slave. The murderer was tried and acquitted for lack of evidence for the only witnesses were blacks, and the evidence of a slave was not admitted in court. In 1801, a law passed in the island of St Vincent to discourage kind owners from emancipating their slaves required them to pay a £300 manumission tax on every male slave freed and £200 on every female.

In the island of Nevis, in 1811, a planter named Huggins had thirty-two of his slaves publicly flogged with heavy whips in the marketplace of Charlestown. Their crime was to have hidden themselves to avoid carrying dung into the fields at night. Among the women victims, one received 212 lashes, another 291. One man was given 365. The local House of Assembly considered that Huggins had really gone too far this time – he was renowned for his brutality – and passed a resolution stigmatising him for 'an act of barbarity altogether unprecedented in Nevis'. Huggins was tried and acquitted. But the printer of the *St Christopher Gazette*, the local newspaper, was prosecuted and fined for libel for publishing the original House resolution. One of the flogged women died soon afterwards. The coroner decided that the slave woman had died 'by the visitation of God, in a natural way'. Since God was responsible for her death there was nothing more to say.

Racial discrimination, in a much less violent form, was also part of the social order of the day. Lord Wellington, when serving in India, refused to allow half-caste officers to join his regiment and expressed his strong disapproval of the British agent in Hyderabad for living with a mistress, not on moral grounds but because she was an Indian, albeit a high-caste princess.

Racism, we must not forget, is not specifically a white man's malady. It is one of the universal aberrations of mankind. Yet different cultures, different races, different ways of life, of cooking, of trying to reach God, different colours of skins, all exist and flourish. Variety, the proverb says, is the spice of life. It is something to be enjoyed, not something to be cursed and condemned.

THE INDIAN DREAM OF A CORSICAN OFFICER

The massive, glittering career of Napoleon in Europe so completely overshadows all that happened elsewhere in the world that we forget his greatest ambition had not been to become Emperor of the French and conqueror of Europe but to be Emperor of the East and conqueror of India. Alexander the Great was his hero, not Charlemagne.

When he was a youth Napoleon was totally uninterested in Europe – apart from, of course, his native Corsica. 'A molehill,' he disparaged Europe. 'Only in the East, where six hundred million people live, have there been great empires and great chances,' he told his friend and future secretary Bourrienne when both were junior officers in Paris. 'It is in the East that I must seek fame. All great fame comes from there.'

The East was his obsession when, a general of twenty-eight, he defeated the Austrians and Piedmontese, conquered Italy and forced Venice to give up its sovereignty over the Ionian Islands, lying off the Albanian and Greek shores, on the edge of the Ottoman Empire.

The position of these islands on the fringes of the East gave them great strategic importance.

'The islands of Corfu, Zante and Cephalonia are more valuable to us than the whole of Italy,' the victorious general, proud of his diplomatic coup, rejoiced in the report he wrote from the conquered Italian peninsula to the Directory, the five-man group that was governing France since the execution of Robespierre on July 28, 1794. 'The Turkish Empire is crumbling. Possession of these islands will enable us either to give it our support, to the extent this is possible, or to take our share of it.' Bonaparte understood geopolitics a century before the term was even coined. 'A great maxim of the [French] Republic ought to be henceforth never to abandon Corfu, Zante, etc,' he stressed.

No one believed the Ottoman Empire could survive as an entity much longer. 'The Eastern Question', as the death-rattle of Turkey and its empire was euphemistically called, was one of the major pre-occupations of the great chanceries of Europe, all busily scheming who should get which bit of the doomed imperial domain. In fact, its demise did not occur until more than a century later.

On his return from Italy, General Bonaparte was offered the command of the so-called 'Army of England' being readied in northern France and Flanders for an invasion of the British Isles. He chose instead to invade the Turkish province of Egypt. 'To destroy England we must seize Egypt,' he wrote to the Directory. His thoughts, however, were already soaring beyond the Nile, beyond the Euphrates, beyond the Indus even, to the Ganges, the sacred River of the Hindus which flowed across the northern plains of India, into the Bay of Bengal, where British and French ships still clashed from time to time.

Plans for an invasion of India were already weaving through his fertile brain. Britain could not be invaded while the British navy was on guard in the Channel. 'Then we must undertake an eastern expedition that would menace her trade with India.'

These proposals to threaten British trade were a smoke screen to obscure his own imperial predilections. 'The vision of the Tricolour floating above the minarets of Cairo and the palaces of the Great Mogul of Delhi fascinated a mind in which the mysticism of the south was curiously blent with the practicability and passion for details that characterise the northern races,' was how British historian J. H. Rose explained these motivations in his *Life of Napoleon I*. Written more than eighty years ago this is still one of the most readable biographies of the Emperor ever published. One can query the writer's reference to Napoleon's 'mysticism'. Bonaparte was certainly a dreamer. But a mystic, never! He did possess in full, however, 'practicability and passion for details'. These were his great strengths.

The dreamer was the man who conjured up visions of India, of spires and minarets and turbans and elephants and palaces. The practical man was the one who, on his way to Egypt (an amazing enterprise in itself), was already calculating which would be the best route onward to India: overland through what are today Israel, Jordan, Iraq, Iran, Afghanistan and Pakistan, or by sea from a Red Sea port, Suez or Kosseir, over the Indian Ocean to Mangalore, in the realm of Tipoo Sahib, Sultan of Mysore.

The dreamer took over completely, at least for a while, after he defeated the Mamelukes at the Battle of the Pyramids, and occupied Cairo, one of the great capitals of the exotic Muslim world. 'I felt the earth flee from beneath me, as if I were being carried to the sky,' he reminisced twenty years later on St Helena.

These were not the nostalgic reminiscences of a middle-aged man, beaten and bitter, evoking a past that never was. The exiled, lonely

Emperor was remembering the immense elation he had once experienced as a romantic conqueror when all seemed possible under a
desert sky and the world was his to take. Egypt, he once told Josephine's friend, Madame de Remusat, was 'the most beautiful time of
my life because it was the most ideal. I saw myself marching into Asia
. . . riding an elephant, a turban on my head, attacking the power of
England in India.'

Bonaparte in Egypt was still in his twenties and there was, of course,
an element of fantasy in his romantic ambitions. But this impression
comes mainly because he failed, in this instance, to realise his vision.
But wasn't Napoleon Bonaparte's whole life story, starting with his
birthplace and with his name of such unforgettable and unusual resonance, just one outlandish adventure that would sound unbelievable
if it hadn't, in fact, happened?

SHIPS, SAILORS AND THE SEA

At sea the war was worldwide. In spite of the tight British blockade of
battleships and frigates around the French coast, French ships did
manage to slip through the cordon to harass their enemies in the
Atlantic, the Caribbean and, particularly, the Indian Ocean. Even so,
their efforts often ended disastrously. The French naval record in these
wars makes depressing reading. They lost one engagement after
another to the British, of which the battles of the Nile and of Trafalgar
are the two best known.

The French navy, with the exception of a handful of French frigates
in the Indian Ocean, may have been remarkably unsuccessful in its encounters with the enemy but the French privateers, or 'corsaires' to
give them their more attractive French name, were considerably more
fortunate. So, to begin this section more cheerfully for the French,
we'll start by recounting the most famous exploit of the most illus-
trious corsair of them all, Robert Surcouf, of St Malo: the capture by
boarding of a heavily-armed East Indiaman, the *Kent,* in October 1800.

Surcouf operated mainly in the Indian Ocean, with his base on the
island of Mauritius, or Ile-de-France, as it was then known, and the encounter between the two ships took place in the Bay of Bengal.

The *Kent,* commanded by Captain Rivington, carried thirty-eight
guns and was defended by four hundred men, including not only its
crew and male military passengers but also the crew of another Indiaman which had caught fire and sunk on the voyage out to India. All
those on board had been rescued by Rivington.

Surcouf's ship, a converted merchantman, the 18-gun *Confiance,*
was in the middle of a most rewarding 'cruise', as these privateer forays
were known. In a few weeks, he had captured fourteen prizes, some
of them large Indiamen. Most had been sent with prize crews to

Ile-de-France, and the *Confiance*'s normal crew of more than two hundred was down to one hundred and twenty.

The fight lasted two hours. Surcouf brought his ship alongside the *Kent* and his men scrambled aboard and took the Indiaman over. Captain Rivington, mortally wounded and, anticipating Captain Lawrence of the American frigate USS *Chesapeake* in a much later battle, in the War of 1812, died with the order 'Don't give up the ship'. (Actually, British and more formal, Rivington said: 'Do not give up the ship.')

In neither case were the orders of the dying captains obeyed. Both ships surrendered. The *Kent* had a senior British army officer on board, General St John, on his way to a new posting in India. He had carefully stayed below decks during the fighting and was made a prisoner. So, most courteously, was his wife, a German aristocrat, and several other lady passengers. Surcouf, a gentleman, albeit a French one, told the terrified ladies to remain in the cabins and posted armed sentries in front of the doors to save them from what later Victorians were to call a fate worse than death.

The depredations of the French corsairs, although they did not affect the outcome of the war, caused considerable losses to British shipping. During the first four years of the war, from 1793 to 1797, the British lost 2,266 ships to these commerce raiders.

The Caribbean was another favourite haunt of French privateers, largely organised by the notorious Victor Hugues, who first governed Guadeloupe and then French Guyana. Hugues granted letters-of-marque – which authorised merchant ships to carry guns and attack shipping – to practically any French-registered vessel, even grubby little island trading schooners, and made a fortune from their activities. A very incomplete list of corsairs based in Guadeloupe in the mid-1790s gives the names of sixty-two ships, and Hugues would have got his cut on the activities of most of them.

The British were not the corsairs' only victims. American ships were among their favourite targets. The vituperative Hugues made little distinction between the British and the Americans. 'At the siege of St Lucia there were more than thirty [American] vessels chartered to carry troops and ammunition for the British. When the British army was assembling in the Barbados, there were more than eighty American ships taking them supplies,' he wrote in an angry letter to the revolutionary government in Paris, anxious lest his freebooting activities might provoke the United States into war with France (they did in 1798).

'The American name evokes here [in Guadeloupe] only contempt and horror,' he went on in the style of invective favoured by the French revolutionaries. 'The infamous deeds which they have carried out in this region against the French, their meaness and servility towards the British nation have brought them their due ... should the French Republic not remind that perfidious nation that we spent freely of our blood and treasure so that it could be free?'

The independent-minded Hugues then drew up a decree on March 5, 1797 giving French naval vessels and privateers the right 'to capture and bring into ports of the French Republic all neutral vessels bound for the islands occupied by the British or by French Royalists.'

'Any vessel commissioned to sail to these ports will be considered a pirate,' he continued, 'and the crews judged and punished as such.'

When the horrified Directory heard of this decree, they annulled it immediately. As it had originally been worded, it would have given the bloodthirsty Hugues the opportunity of hanging or perhaps even cutting off the head (for Hugues was very attached to his guillotine) of every captured seaman.

In 1797, the year of Hugues's decree, three hundred and thirty-six American ships were captured by French privateers, mostly in and around Hugues's own Caribbean fief. In all, during the three years of Directory rule, eight hundred and thirty-four captured American vessels were taken into French ports. Washington sent a three-man mission to Paris to negotiate a settlement of the quarrel with the French. But they returned in disgust after the French Foreign Minister, Charles Maurice de Talleyrand-Périgord, to give him his full name, demanded a bribe of $250,000 as a preliminary sweetener to the discussions.

This demand must have particularly outraged the Americans as Talleyrand had only returned a couple of years before from a long stay as a refugee in the United States. Fearing for his powdered, peruked head, he had departed first to England, then to North America where, dabbling in local real estate in Philadelphia, he had sat out the bloody two years of the Terror.

In 1798, its patience exhausted, the United States Government ordered its naval vessels to attack on sight any armed French ship, which meant nearly every boat flying the French flag, for practically all French merchantmen in those days, even the smallest and dirtiest schooner in the West Indies, carried at least a gun or two. It was not quite war, but nearly. American historians usually refer to it as the Quasi-War with France, or as the Naval War with France, since there was no fighting on land at all. Nor, to be precise, was there much fighting at sea either. The major contest took place between two frigates, the 38-gun USS *Constellation*, and the French 36-gun *L'Insurgente*. It was an American victory.

Mercifully, all the belligerents were often willing to put the war aside for a while if the demands of common humanity required it. Today, when ruthless competing ideologies and horrendous new weapons have wiped out all forms of humanity and even common sense from warfare, we can only salute those days when chivalry was still practised in the fighting. This was particularly true among sailors.

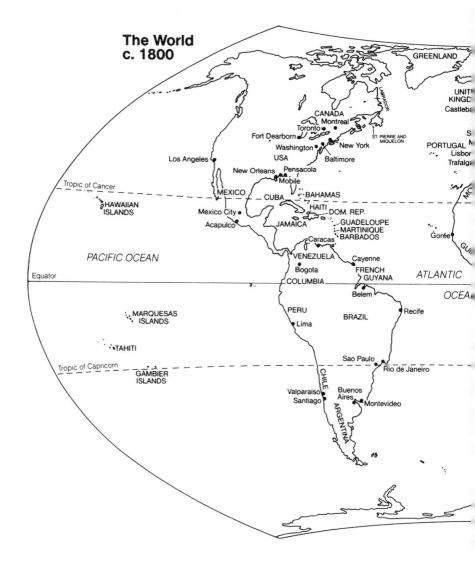

The World
c. 1800

The British learnt that Empress Josephine, Napoleon's wife, who loved flowers, wished to turn the garden of her estate at Malmaison – where she grew over a hundred varieties of roses – into a showpiece of exotic blooms. Could anything have been more chivalrous than the order the Lords of the Admiralty sent to His Majesty's captains and all ships at sea, that all plants and packages of seeds addressed to the Empress of the French found on captured vessels were to be forwarded to her without delay?

When HMS *Blenheim*, carrying the flag of Admiral Sir Thomas Troubridge, disappeared in a gale in the Indian Ocean somewhere between Madagascar and Mauritius, Governor Decaen in Mauritius gave the searching British vessels all the help he could command, ordered the French ships in the vicinity to be on the lookout for the missing vessel, sent reports to the British authorities in Cape Town, allowed a British frigate, commanded by Troubridge's son, to sail into a Mauritian port under flag of truce, and gave him pieces of washed up wreckage in the hope it might help him to identify his father's ship.

Civilised conduct broke down sometimes during the Napoleonic Wars, but the old traditions of gallantry, on and off the battlefield, usually prevailed. This was so, even during the French Revolutionary period, when an immense ideological gap – much greater than that today between the USA and the USSR – separated the two sides.

Just the same, it must have required the maximum of discipline for the stuffy British to extend to defeated French Republican foes (who had committed the unspeakable crime of cutting off their king's head) the courtesies and hospitality that the rules of war and good manners demanded, and to treat as gentlemen the captured French Republican officers some of whom, before joining the army, had been stable lads, innkeepers or rabbit-skin salesmen, and who didn't even know how to hold their knives and forks properly at table.

The prissy Lady Elliot, wife of the British Viceroy of Corsica when, under the name of the Anglo-Corsican Kingdom, the island became a virtual British colony for a few years in the mid-1790s, had on one occasion to entertain some captured French naval officers. She found it a great ordeal.

'We had to dinner the two captains of the *Ça Ira* (and the *Censeur*),' she wrote to a friend. 'To describe their appearance is impossible. . . . Their filth was shocking. I was so filled with horror and astonishment that I sat perfectly silent for two hours.'

Lady Elliot notwithstanding, there were, however, many displays of mutual sympathy and even friendship between the officers of the two warring nations. In spite of their differing temperaments, they often found much to like in each other, even if it was only their mutual courage. Many British officers, like so many of the British upper class, found France a congenial country. Admiral Sir Sidney Smith, for instance, went to live in Paris when the war was over and when he died in 1840 one of the pallbearers at his funeral was Admiral Jacques Bergeret who, as a frigate captain, had fought the British off the Lizard, in the Atlantic, in the Mediterranean and in the Indian Ocean.

The francophile attitude of many British officers inevitably implied a liking for the French as well as for their country. Nelson, the product of a mingy middle class, was the exception. He loathed the French whom he habitually described as 'villains'. But where foreigners were concerned, Nelson was paranoid. He despised the Spaniards, Italy was a country of 'fiddlers and poets, whores and scoundrels', and he even looked down upon the Irish (they were 'vagabonds') although they were technically British and many served in the navy. As for Napoleon Bonaparte, to Nelson he was 'that animal'. Nelson was typically English: in the best way by his courage and endurance, in the worst way by his insularity.

Excluded from Nelson's rabid xenophobia were the Danes. He addressed them as 'Brothers of Englishmen' when he summoned them to surrender at Copenhagen in 1801. For Nelson that must have been the ultimate in praise. The consideration he showed towards these Scandinavians was perhaps because, like many East Anglians, Nelson was a descendant of Vikings – his forbears were Danish and bore the name of Nielsen.

But whatever his faults, Nelson was a born leader of men, brave to the point of folly, one of the greatest fighting sailors and naval tacticians the world has ever known. So all must be forgiven him, for men of his daring and genius have been few in history.

Forgetting the French-hating Nelson, one recalls with pleasure the kindness and courtesy that took over between British and French adversaries at the inevitable moment when one of them was down. The Canadian Sir Benjamin Hallowell, when forced to surrender to Admiral Honoré Ganteaume, while in command of a convoy off Malta, was treated with such hospitality, consideration and sympathy that a few years later, after the Battle of Trafalgar, as a token of gratitude for 'the civility' Ganteaume and his officers had shown him, Hallowell sent the captured Captain Infernet, of the French ship-of-the-line *Intrépide*, 'two dozen shirts, stockings, a bed, and some cloth to make a coat, and a draft for £100 to ease his captivity in England.'

Ships-of-the-line were the battleships of the period, so-called because they traditionally went into battle in line ahead, firing broadsides at the line of enemy ships sailing opposite, on a parallel course. They were two- or three-deckers, carrying usually sixty-four to one hundred and twenty guns.

Officers and seamen usually preferred, however, to serve in frigates. They were the workhorses and eyes of the fleet, usually carried twenty-four to forty-four guns, never joined in line of battle but often fought in single-ship actions against other frigates. Some particularly confident British frigate captains, thirsting for glory, were known to attack battleships. This was part of the John Bull syndrome, the theory once expressed by Nelson that one Englishman was worth three Frenchmen.

It is undeniable, however, that the French naval record during these wars was, to put it mildly, appalling.

The battle statistics speak for themselves: between 1793 and 1815, the French lost sixty ships-of-the-line and one hundred and seventy frigates in action against the Royal Navy, while British losses against the French during this same period amounted to six ships-of-the-line and eighteen frigates. For purposes of convenience, I have included among these battleship casualty figures a few fifty-gun warships that are in a class by themselves, not quite battleship and not quite frigate.

From a first-class fighting force in the previous century the French navy degenerated during the first years of the Revolution into an unholy rabble. The causes were many.

First of all, there was the Revolution itself. It had unleashed many forces, not all of which were inspired by the noble sentiments expressed by Thomas Paine's *The Rights of Man*, published in London in 1791. A spirit of mutiny in the army and navy, particularly the latter, was a natural concomitant of the social upheaval that demolished the structure of French society. Seamen would gather on the decks of their ships, elect their officers, sack those they didn't like, or beat them up, or denounce them to the tribunals – which was often the equivalent of a death sentence – or occasionally hang them.

Long before the 1797 Spithead and Nore mutinies in the British fleet, the French navy was undergoing its own much more violent traumas.

Many of the French naval officers were noblemen, or were at least more royalist in sentiment than republican. Unable to stomach the policies of the revolutionary government in Paris, the insults to the King and Queen, the growing calls for a Republic (which was proclaimed on September 21, 1792), and the increasing threats to their own lives or liberty, many fled abroad. During the first couple of years of the Revolution, the French navy lost no less than two-thirds of its officers to the guillotine, imprisonment or exile.

The loss of these trained and experienced officers was a disaster for the French navy and nation, but the revolutionary government in Paris did not regard their disappearance in that light at all. It was delighted to get rid of all those it regarded as politically unreliable. In the army, it had already replaced many of the royalist officers with politically sound privates and NCOs and turned young republican officers into colonels and generals in sometimes just a few weeks. Bonaparte had joined the siege of Toulon as a twenty-four-year-old captain in September 1793 and left it a general three months later. The army experiment, on the whole, had been a success, since the men chosen were often fervent, intelligent, and brave.

Working on the assumption that what was good for the army would also be good for the navy, the revolutionary government set out, with equal zest, to purge the fleet. Hundreds of seamen were promoted from the lower deck or brought in from the merchant service to command warships, largely on the basis of their political views. The result was catastrophic.

The navy was different from the army. Its officers had to be technicians and mathematicians as well as leaders of men. They had to be navigators as well as warriors, to know where they were on an empty sea with only the stars and the sun to guide them, how to use winds and currents, how to avoid shoals and reefs, how to handle sails, how to tack against the wind and at what moment during the rolling or tossing of a ship to give the order to fire so that the shots of a broadside didn't fall uselessly into the waves or soar equally uselessly into the sky.

The British consider as one of their great naval victories Admiral Lord Howe's defeat of the French on the Glorious First of June, in 1794. But some of the glory of the Glorious First of June vanishes when we remember that the French admiral in command, Louis Villaret-Joyeuse, had been a sub-lieutenant until the year before, that one of his two rear-admirals, Joseph-Marie Nielly, had been a sub-lieutenant until two years previously and the other, Françoise Bouvet de Précourt, a lieutenant until a few months ago. Only one of the captains commanding the French battleships had held that rank before the Revolution. Among the others, four had been lieutenants, two were previously sub-lieutenants, one a petty officer and one an able seaman. The remainder were former pilots, mates of merchant ships and masters of coastal vessels.

It was not only the officer corps of the French navy which had been gutted. The revolutionaries in Paris had disbanded the highly efficient and professional corps of seamen gunners, 5,400 trained specialists who were now accused of having become a privileged aristocracy of the sea. Forgetting that firing a gun from the heaving deck of a ship requires different training and reflexes from those of an artilleryman on land, the government ordered army gunners into the fleet. These men were not sailors, had no idea of the work aboard a ship, were often seasick and did not know how to aim a gun from a plunging and twisting deck. They simply helped to ensure a few more British victories at sea.

British naval gunners could fire two rounds every three minutes, often well-placed broadsides aimed at the hull that showered the between-decks with deadly jagged wooden splinters which usually assured a high casualty rate among the enemy crew. The French rate of fire was now half the British. They usually fired high, aiming for the masts. The purpose of this tactic, inspired by the predilection of the French for hand-to-hand fighting, was to bring down masts, sails and rigging in one inextricable mess and halt the vessel so that the French sailors, armed with cutlasses and transformed into soldiers, could then swarm aboard the disabled and helpless ship and take it. Boarding was the method of fighting which the corsairs, anxious to limit the damage on a future merchantman prize, usually favoured. It was a great idea, but against well-trained navy ships it rarely worked.

Many adventurous able-bodied seamen therefore preferred to sign on aboard privateers rather than serve in navy ships. Life was more exciting, and with luck and a bold captain they could always hope to earn a small fortune. Hence the constant and catastrophic shortage of trained seamen in the French navy.

The one-eyed French-Canadian, Admiral Pierre Martin, born in Nova Scotia in the days it was French and called Acadia, complained to the French Admiralty in 1795 that only four thousand five hundred of the twelve thousand men under his command had ever gone to sea. Nearly two-thirds of his sailors were landlubbers!

Here may be the right place to quote the British historian Sir William Laird Clowes, author of the many-volumed *History of the Royal Navy* published at the turn of this century.

'If the shooting of the French crew was wretched, the spirit and fiery courage of the French sailors – seamen we cannot call them – was above all reproach,' he wrote. But courage alone never won a battle at sea. Good seamanship and good gunnery were required. For most of the war, both were absent for too long from most of the French ships.

If gunnery standards were low at least decibel levels were high. A Dutch naval officer who took passage to Java on the French frigate *La Méduse* (whose later loss off the coast of Senegal made maritime history) was overwhelmed by all the noise around him.

'Everything, down to the minutest order, is carried out through trumpets, so that one single French frigate makes more noise than a Dutch squadron of fifty ships-of-the-line,' he wrote.

Even Napoleon Bonaparte, after his surrender in 1815, was startled by the quiet that reigned in Royal Navy vessels. On a French ship, he said, he could not hear himself speak.

'What I admire most about your ship is the extreme silence and orderly conduct of your men,' the Emperor confided to Captain Frederick Maitland of HMS *Bellerophon*, to whom he surrendered a few weeks after Waterloo and who was taking him across the Channel to Plymouth. 'On board a French ship everyone calls and gives orders, they gabble like so many geese.'

But of course Napoleon had rarely a good word to say about his navy, so often defeated. He could not help comparing it to his Grand Army, possibly the most formidable fighting force there has ever been.

There was nothing 'Grand' about the French navy. It was largely, with some notable exceptions, a ramshackle collection of fine ships and brave but untrained men, sometimes of uncertain loyalty, and often led by intimidated refugees from the guillotine. The French admirals were certainly more afraid of Napoleon's wrath than of the seemingly invincible ships of the Royal Navy, 'those far-distant, storm-beaten ships upon which the Grand Army never looked . . . [which] stood between it and the dominion of the world,' in the magnificent words of the American naval historian, Captain Alfred Mahan.

It will always remain a matter of controversy whether it was the navy that failed Napoleon or Napoleon who failed the navy. The French Emperor never did quite grasp the fact that ships could not be ordered to move around at sea to a strict timetable, as battalions can on land. But he was also badly served by his minister for the navy, the tortuous Admiral Denis Decrès, who held the post uninterruptedly from 1801 to 1814, and who apparently did his best to sabotage by his counsels many of Napoleon's plans, notably his India invasion projects. His reactions to nearly every proposal by the Emperor were negative.

So noticeably, in fact, that in 1808 when Napoleon was contemplating a two-pronged attack on Egypt and India by two combined army-navy expeditionary forces, one of twelve thousand men and the other of twenty thousand, he asked Decrès to send him a report, 'not to increase the difficulties,' he stressed, 'but to solve them.'

Decrès's allegiance was to the navy rather than to Napoleon. He was well aware of its weakness, particularly after the brutal purges of the Revolution, both in the quality of its seamen and the number of its ships.

In 1793, the year Britain and France went to war, the French navy possessed seventy-five ships-of-the-line to Britain's one hundred and fifteen. By 1813, after twenty years of war, the British navy had increased its battleship fleet to two hundred and seventeen, and she also had fifteen fourth-raters (ships of fifty guns) and two hundred and one frigates. France, that year, could line up one hundred and three battleships and fifty-five frigates. The numerical odds in Britain's favour had increased to more than two to one.

The Royal Navy, furthermore, was the only naval force present in strength on all the oceans of the world, with powerful shore stations and bases to back the ships at sea, often with senior admirals in command of these outposts. There were strong British squadrons stationed permanently in Barbados and Jamaica in the Caribbean, in Halifax in North America, in Freetown in West Africa, in Calcutta, Madras and Bombay in India, and in Gibraltar. Later, after their capture from the French and from the Dutch, Malta, Cape Town and Trincomalee in Sri Lanka were added to the list. But it was always in the West Indies that British naval power remained most present. In 1794, twelve British ships-of-the-line, twenty-one frigates, fifteen corvettes, sloops and other small vessels were permanently patrolling these tropical waters while the French could only count on the occasional man o' war breaking through the British blockade to bring supplies, men and ammunition to their isolated West Indian garrisons.

The sole permanent French overseas base was in Mauritius, and it only catered to the few frigates and privateers that roamed the Indian Ocean, the Arabian Sea and the Sunda Straits, harrying East Indiamen and coastal vessels around India, Burma, Malaya and Arabia – 'country ships' as these Asia-based merchantmen, often with Bombay Parsee owners, were known.

A British prisoner of war, Robert William Eastwick, captain of the captured country ship *Endeavour,* has left us vivid vignettes of life on board a warship of the French Republic in the Indian Ocean. His ship had been seized by the French frigate *Forte,* one of a squadron of four commanded by Admiral Pierre de Sercey.

'The discipline [on the *Forte*] was very slack,' reported Eastwick after his release. 'It was not at all unusual to see one of the foremast men, with his beef in his hands, eating it while walking the quarter-deck [traditionally reserved for officers], and claiming an equal right to it with the commanding officer. Nor was any scruple made of playing cards on the quarter-deck. The lieutenants generally came on deck with only trousers and an open shirt, often a check one, so that it was almost impossible to distinguish them [from the ordinary seamen].'

Several years later, in 1803, when First Consul Napoleon Bonaparte ruled over France, a new French squadron, the 74-gun *Marengo* and three frigates, under the orders of Admiral Linois, sailed into the Indian Ocean. This puny force was expected to cover the eastern seas from the Cape of Good Hope to the South China Sea, and had to face the India-based squadrons of British Admiral Peter Rainier, which consisted of eight ships-of-the-line and numerous frigates. But the atmosphere on the French ships remained light and hearty, if we are to believe another captured British sailor, Thomas Addison, who was a prisoner on the *Marengo.*

'We soon discovered the looseness of their discipline, officers and men meeting, hail well met,' he wrote. 'I frequently saw the ship's barber walking arm in arm with the captain, chatting intimately together on the quarter-deck.' One wonders what captain and barber could have been chatting about so intimately, but obviously jollity reigned among the officers and men of the *Marengo.* British gunnery put an end to it. Admiral Linois stayed two years in the East. He disgraced himself in the China Sea by fleeing from a twenty-six-ship East Indiamen tea convoy, taking it for a Royal Navy squadron and then, when on his way home in the Atlantic, mistook Admiral Sir John Borlase Warren's Royal Navy squadron for a merchant convoy, attacked it impetuously and lost the *Marengo* and his last frigate, both shot to pieces.

After Linois's departure, however, a trickle of frigates reinforced French naval forces in Mauritius and their subsequent fighting record is one of the best in the French navy. The Battle of Grand Port, in the offshore waters of Mauritius, was their own little Trafalgar.

Bad as the French naval battle statistics were in general, France's come-and-go allies did even worse, even the sturdy Dutch with their long maritime tradition. The British lost half a dozen minor vessels to the Dutch but sank or captured thirty of their ships-of-the-line and thirty-eight of their frigates. The Danes took just under a dozen small British vessels, corvettes, cutters and gunboats, the largest the 16-gun HMS *Seagull*, but lost twenty-four battleships and twenty-eight frigates.

The Turks, during their year (1807-8) of active war against Britain, lost one battleship, six frigates and various other smaller units without sinking even a British rowing boat. The Russians also lost a battleship and sundry minor craft to the British in 1808 but could not claim one single triumph, however small, in exchange.

The Spaniards, despised by all for their incompetence but who fought bravely and hopelessly, often with completely untrained crews that had never before gone to sea, lost twenty-one battleships and thirty frigates to the British and never managed to take or sink anything larger than a couple of 16-gun vessels.

The only navy that came out of the conflict against Britain with its laurels untarnished was the small and ardent United States Navy during the War of 1812. American frigates, meeting the British in battle, won at least as often as they lost. Even Lawrence's brave but dismal showing in the USS *Chesapeake* v. HMS *Shannon* engagement, with its (unheeded) call for no surrender, is seen by many Americans as a triumph of valour. Rightly so, for the gallant James Lawrence is much more appealing as a warrior than his popinjay victor, the arrogant Captain Philip Bowes Vere Broke.

The ocean was dangerous. Spain, Holland, France and the United States all found that out, for in all those years from 1793 to 1815 it was Britain and Britain alone that ruled the seas. And it was Britain's mastery of the sea that prevented the invasion of England by her enemies during the Napoleonic Wars. The seas were also the highway to the exotic East, to the Indies and to the Americas, to Botany Bay and to Africa – to a tropical world waiting to be conquered either for the Emperor Napoleon I and the House of Bonaparte or for King George III and the future House of Windsor.

PART ONE

The Wars of the
French Revolution
1792-1801

Napoleon Bonaparte and British Prime Minister William Pitt in 1805, carving up the world between them, Cartoon by James Gillray

CHAPTER TWO

The British Lion Miaows

THE GIBRALTAR THAT NEVER WAS
Toulon 1793

A Frenchman is inclined to regard the British occupation of Toulon in 1793 and the four months' siege that followed as just one episode – and not a major one, at that – in the long sequence of invasions and attacks that his country has endured. To him, there was nothing colonial about the fight for Toulon. But the British may well have reasoned differently when they seized this French seaport and naval base in the summer of 1793. They regarded its capture with discreet jubilation as a great promise for the future. Colonies were not solely a tropical enterprise for the British. Europe also provided its quota. Toulon, in mid-Mediterranean, could, like Gibraltar, become a new British stronghold in that strategically vital sea. Particularly as Gibraltar was several days' sail away, on the southern tip of Spain.

Throughout their history the British have shown a remarkable talent for seizing small territories, on or off the European coast. Not always so small either: they occupied about half of France during the Middle Ages and it took the French more than a century, from 1337 to 1453, to get rid of them. That conflict became known as the Hundred Years War.

British nibbling at Europe continued for nearly four hundred years and numerous bits of the continent and its offshore islands came under the rule of the English Crown: Calais, Dunkirk, Minorca, Corsica, Cyprus, Ireland, Gibraltar, Corfu and the other Ionian islands, Malta and Heligoland. We could add the Channel Islands except that they were part of the family heirloom that the Dukes of Normandy took with them when they crossed the Channel nine hundred years ago to become kings of England. So they are in a separate category and can happily and justly be viewed as a link of friendship between France and England.

Sometimes, in the course of their neighbourly intrusions, the English have stayed several hundred years. In Ireland and Gibraltar they haven't left yet. But if, unlike Spanish Gibraltar, French Toulon never became a British colony, thanks are mainly due to young Captain Napoleon Bonaparte, who began here his prodigious ascent to the top.

That summer of 1793 the south of France was seething with revolt against the *terroristes* in Paris who ruled France with a bloody hand under the dapper, well-dressed, fanatical and – by his own definition – virtuous lawyer, Maximilien Robespierre, one of the most sinister characters history has ever retched up. Invoking the loftiest ideals of Liberty, Equality and Fraternity, Robespierre had turned the guillotine into an everyday instrument of political action and had transformed Paris into an abattoir.

The foes of Robespierre were not only the Royalists. There were also Republicans who disagreed with him or his methods, notably the moderate Girondists, twenty-nine of whom had recently been arrested, most of whom were soon to have their heads cut off. Many of these came from the Bordeaux region and the surrounding Gironde department, hence their name. Lyon too was in revolt against Citizen Robespierre, so were Marseille, Avignon, Arles, and Aix-en-Provence, as well as Toulon.

Vice-Admiral Viscount Samuel Hood was hovering off the south of France blockading the French fleet in Toulon with his substantial squadron when, on August 22, two civilian envoys representing the people of Toulon came aboard his 100-gun flagship, HMS *Victory*, with a message from their fellow citizens. Would the British admiral kindly take over the town, the fortresses and the port of Toulon in the name of King Louis XVII, the eight-year-old son of the guillotined King? And would his lordship hold this small parcel of French territory in trust for the royal French child until he could regain the throne of his fathers?

Hood, a man of action, replied promptly in His Britannic Majesty's name that, yes, of course, his country would be delighted to hold Toulon in trust for His Most Christian Majesty King Louis XVII until the boy could take over his rightful throne.

More than one-third of the total French fleet, Hood knew, lay at anchor in Toulon harbour, its crews dangerously divided between those who backed the king and those who upheld the Republic. First, therefore, Hood sent one of his lieutenants, the young and debonair Edward Cooke, a fluent French speaker, to feel the pulse of opinion among naval personnel and civilians in Toulon. Cooke was escorted aboard by a royalist French officer from the Toulon fleet. His subsequent report was brief and to the point. The French navy might be split politically, but it remained firmly anti-British. The civilians ashore might be largely royalist in sentiment but even there the Republic had a large number of followers. Cooke himself had been arrested by republican partisans but immediately freed by a mob of local royalist citizens. In other words, the French were as volatile and as unreliable as ever. Hood, a no-nonsense type of Briton, decided to move in right away. Now was the time to win the war.

The British government in London had to be advised, of course, so he sent a fast frigate to England to inform the Prime Minister, William Pitt the Younger, of his new responsibilities in the Mediterranean. An arrogant old man – he was seventy – Hood knew very little about land-fighting but considered himself an expert on all the military arts. 'With five or six thousand good troops I should soon end the war,' he told Pitt.

But first, needing to make sure of enough men to carry out the operation in Toulon, he sent off a message to Britain's Spanish ally, Admiral Don Juan de Langara, who was blockading the southwest coast of France, asking for his support. Hood then ordered Captain Horatio Nelson, of the 64-gun HMS *Agamemnon,* to make full sail for Naples to request from the King of the Two Sicilies naval and army reinforcements.

Nelson made fast time to Naples and presented his request to the King through the British Ambassador, Sir William Hamilton, who unwisely introduced him to his pretty young wife Emma, the famed Lady Hamilton of romance and history. He obtained from the Neapolitan king assurances of the rapid dispatch to Toulon of seven thousand soldiers and three battleships. The naval squadron was to be commanded by Prince Francesco Caracciolo, an old admirer of the British who had fought in the Royal Navy against the French and the insurgents during the American Revolution. The Prince, now a venerable commodore of sixty-one, delighted at the prospect of helping once again his English friends, sailed to Toulon with his three 74s, the *Tandredi,* the *Guiscardo* and the *Samnita.*

Poor Prince Caracciolo! All his Anglophilia in no way served him in the end. Some years later, to please the Neapolitan royal family, Nelson had Caracciolo hanged from the yardarm of his own ship for taking part in a revolt against his king.

On August 27 Hood's British squadron sailed majestically into Toulon harbour to a noisy welcome by French Royalists. The procession of British men-'o-war was led by the frigate HMS *Tartar,* commanded by Captain Thomas Fremantle, the father of the yet unborn Charles Fremantle, the first man to hoist the Union Jack in Western Australia –

on the spot where the city of that name now stands.

Well in the van of the British naval force was also forty-seven-year-old the Honourable Keith Elphinstone, captain of HMS *Robust,* who will make repeated appearances in these pages. An elegant aristocrat and a brave sailor, but always slightly ineffective, Elphinstone was of noble Scottish lineage and was himself raised to the peerage in 1796 as Lord Keith (for defeating, without firing a shot, a Dutch squadron in South African waters – which in fact had never had the slightest intention of fighting him).

Having served ashore with a landing party at Charleston, South Carolina, during the American War of Independence, Elphinstone was regarded by Hood as expert in joint army-navy landing operations. On his arrival in Toulon, therefore, he was ordered to occupy Fort Lamalgue, on the eastern side of the harbour, as Hood set about neutralising the French ships, divided by rival factions, lying helpless in the harbour: thirty-one battleships and twenty-seven frigates and corvettes were at the British admiral's mercy. The French fleet was to be had for the picking.

Hood was soon joined by seventeen battleships from Langara's squadron, a mixed blessing since the Spaniards immediately made it clear that the fate and future distribution of the impotent French vessels would have to be a matter of joint decision, and not Admiral Hood's alone.

But Langara was otherwise a most cooperative ally and he landed several thousand troops, to be placed at the British admiral's disposal. Hood retained the supreme command of the allied forces in Toulon with Admiral Gravina, a southern Italian in Spanish service, as his deputy.

The British, so often contemptuous of Latins, surprisingly approved in the choice of Gravina, respected by all as a thorough professional, and the occupation went off without a hitch.

Understandably distrustful of the bulk of the French sailors in Toulon, Hood packed some five thousand of them into their four oldest and least battle-worthy ships and allowed them to sail away on parole as cartels to the French Atlantic ports of Brest, Lorient and Rochefort. (As cartels, they could not be attacked by any of the belligerents.) On arrival, many of these sailors were arrested as supposed royalists. Those who sailed to Rochefort were particularly badly treated. The officers were arrested on landing and put on trial for treason. They had the misfortune to be prosecuted by the nefarious Victor Hugues, soon to be appointed governor of Guadeloupe, who managed to send many of them to the guillotine.

Having secured his bases, Hood waited to see what the French would do. The wait was a short one. A French republican army of some ten thousand men, under General Jean-François Carteaux, moved up along the coast to meet him. On August 31, the vanguard of this army, about seven hundred and fifty men, clashed at Ollioules, a small village four miles northwest of Toulon, with a mixed Anglo-Spanish force of six hundred, commanded by Captain Keith Elphinstone. The French took the village and made it their headquarters for the next four months' siege of Toulon.

One of the French casualties in this brief but bloody Ollioules encounter was the officer in charge of the artillery, Major Elzéar Dommartin, hit in the shoulder by a musket ball and hospitalised. He was replaced a fortnight later by a morose, undistinguished, scruffy gunnery captain who happened to be passing by, escorting a convoy of military supplies from Avignon to the French army base at Nice. His name was Napoleon Bonaparte.

Bonaparte had returned to mainland France from Corsica only three months previously, bringing his widowed mother, brothers and sisters with him. Everything so far had gone against him. The Corsican patriots, whose cause he had at first espoused, had rejected him in favour of the old independence fighter, Pasquale Paoli. They had pillaged the family home in Ajaccio, threatened him with death and denounced him as a traitor. As for his combat experience, it was limited so far to a quick unsuccessful foray launched from Corsica against the small island of Santa Maddalena, off Sardinia. There was nothing yet in his background or outward appearance to hint at the genius which smouldered beneath.

Captain Bonaparte arrived on September 16 at Ollioules to take command of the army's meagre artillery, which consisted of sixteen pieces. General Carteaux had set up his headquarters at the nearby Chateau of Montauban. The town and harbour which the French had to recapture was a bustle of intense naval and military activity. In time the Allied land force fighting the French would grow to around 18,000: 2,000 British; 1,500 French Royalists; 7,000 Neapolitans; 6,000 Spaniards; and 2,000 Sardinians, among whom were troops from nearby Piedmont and from Savoy.

There were no clear lines of battle in the fighting for Toulon, but in fact the Allies had locked themselves in a trap, and Napoleon Bonaparte was quick to spot their predicament.

Toulon, main French naval base on the Mediterranean, was one of the most heavily defended strongpoints in France. It was ringed with fortifications and one of Hood's first actions had been to occupy most of the forts that surrounded the city and harbour, spread along the slopes of Mont Faron, a mountain overlooking the area from the north. Hood thus hoped to fight off French attacks from Carteaux's army on the west, and from a second force of about three thousand men, marching in from Nice. The commander of these troops, General Jean-François de la Poype, was particularly anxious to take the town – his

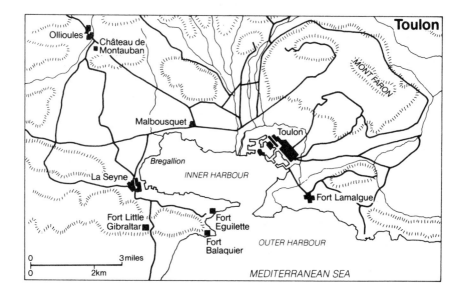

bride of a few days had been trapped in Toulon by Hood's unexpected arrival while she was at the hairdresser.

Toulon and its surroundings are situated on two bays, looking like a rough figure-of-eight and lying in an approximate north to south direction, with the southern bay opening to the sea. The northern bay, or inner harbour, about two miles wide and a mile across, is considerably smaller than the outer harbour and takes in, on its eastern shore, the town of Toulon.

The land separating the two circles of our figure-of-eight does not quite join, and the army that holds this narrow gullet controls Toulon. Fort Lamalgue, which Elphinstone had occupied the day of the British fleet's arrival, lay on a hill to the east of this passage, on a small peninsula jutting out into the harbour. A narrow stretch of water, little more than half-a-mile wide, separated this peninsula from another, called Le Caire, on the opposite side of the bay to the west.

On Le Caire were two forts close to each other, Fort Eguilette and Fort Balaquier, both overlooking the harbour. Obviously control of this piece of land was strategically essential.

The arrogant Hood at first failed to grasp this simple fact and Le Caire was left unattended. But young Captain Bonaparte, with an artilleryman's knack of spotting the most efficient place from which to blast the enemy, right away saw that the Le Caire peninsula was the key to a French victory. The best way to beat the Allies was to set up his guns there, fire on their ships, and burn them or force them out of the harbour.

General Carteaux was not enthusiastic about his underling's project, and delayed a decision. Carteaux was a former dragoon whose concept of military tactics was simply to charge ahead. His own plan was to take Toulon by storm, at the point of a few thousand bayonets.

The talents of this large, fat French general were minimal. Everyone in the French camp agreed that the best thing about their commander was his wife Catherine. Madame Carteaux, ten years younger than her husband and a magnificent, statuesque woman, always accompanied the general on his military postings. And everywhere they went, the couple took their own, huge double-bed. It was ceremoniously installed at the Chateau de Montauban, and from it General Carteaux then tried to direct the siege of Toulon – with the aid of Mme Carteaux who read his mail, corrected his orders and sometimes even signed them as 'Epouse Carteaux' ('Carteaux's wife'). All in all, it added a nice homely touch to the military operation.

A few days after taking over his duties, Bonaparte was introduced to a civilian commissioner from Paris, Paul Barras, a revolutionary as well known for his sexual debauchery as for his republican ideals. Impressed by Bonaparte's professional abilities, Barras backed his promotion on the spot from captain to major.

Over in the British camp in Toulon, some ten days before Bonaparte joined Carteaux's army, Colonel Mulgrave had arrived from Turin. He had been visiting the Piedmontese capital when news reached him of the British landing in the south of France. He immediately rushed to Toulon to offer his services to Hood and hopefully acquire some military glory.

Mulgrave symbolised the upper-class, well-bred Englishman of the pre-Regency period. An old Etonian, former ensign in the Foot Guards during the American War of Independence, Tory bigwig and Member of Parliament, fervent defender of slavery and friend of Pitt and anyone who counted, Mulgrave knew all the right people in the right places. The old boys' network was already a flourishing institution in Georgian England and Admiral Hood was glad to offer his friend the command of the British troops, with the acting rank of brigadier general.

Mulgrave was no genius but he had enough military knowledge and experience of land fighting to realise the topographical peril of the Allies. The British army chronicler, Sir John Fortescue tells us in his monumental *History of the British Army* that Mulgrave 'felt so uncertain of his safety that one of his first cares was to take such measures as he could for securing his retreat.'

Meanwhile Hood was having problems with his allies. Only the

Piedmontese soldiers were up to British standards, Hood felt. The Neapolitans, as far as he was concerned, were cowards, and the Spaniards villainous. But it was the French Royalists who were giving Hood the most concern.

Forgetting that no one in politics or war is to be trusted, the Royalists had rashly handed their town and navy to the British admiral for safekeeping. Now Hood and the British were masters of Toulon, and when Louis XVI's princely brother and, since the king's execution, Regent of France, the Count of Provence, wanted to visit this little liberated bit of France on the Mediterranean coast and meet his loyal subjects, he quickly ran into trouble. He had the support of the Spanish court, but in London Pitt's government was adamantly opposed to the visit. Secret instructions were sent to the British minister in Turin, where the Regent was staying, to do all in his power to dissuade him from making the trip. Just to make sure he didn't reach Toulon, the British government sent last-resort instructions to Hood to prevent him landing if he did arrive there.

In the face of a British barrage of objections and difficulties, the French Regent finally abandoned his project and crossed Toulon off his list of proposed journeys.

Instead of the French royal prince, Sir Gilbert Elliot arrived in Toulon from England, to become its civil commissioner. A Member of Parliament, the wily Sir Gilbert was a canny Scotsman, a man trusted with the highest affairs of state. He was soon to become Viceroy of Corsica and, years later, with the title of Lord Minto, Governor-General of India.

The precise nature of his functions as civil commissioner was never made clear but shortly after his arrival in the occupied French port, in a joint declaration with the British naval and military commanders, Elliot announced that the conditions under which the French Royalists had placed Toulon under British protection were to be changed: there was now no longer any question of simply holding the city in trust and handing it back to the French immediately the monarchy was restored.

The declaration, prepared in smooth, soothing language by the British cabinet in London, assured the good people of Toulon that Lord Hood's agreement concerning the young king would be respected, of course, but only after France had agreed to hand back to the Allies not only all the territories it had occupied but also pay a proper indemnity for damages caused. It would also have to provide the Allies with suitable guarantees for their security in the future.

Whatever the morality of the British statement, it did have one overwhelming effect: it gave Britain complete mastery over Toulon's future, for the new stipulations were so flexibly and loosely worded that they gave London the right, later, to impose whatever conditions, sanctions and indemnities it chose. Thus, the conditions had only to be made so harsh as to be rejected by the French, and a permanent British occupation of Toulon could be guaranteed.

The French Royalists in Toulon rightly felt they had been tricked. They had undoubtedly wished for the Republic's downfall, but they were patriotic Frenchmen and they had never intended to put the territorial integrity of their country in jeopardy. Yet that is what the London declaration did. In Fortescue's words, the British statement 'wrought untold mischief to the cause of the Allies.'

If Britain had managed to hold on to it, Toulon might very well have become another Gibraltar. And it was Bonaparte who was mainly responsible, through his professional skill, for bringing the British occupation to an end. It was his views that the French command finally followed, his tactics that prevailed, his energy and organising ability that secured more guns, more powder, more ammunition. He, more than any other man, organised the French victory.

Within two days of his arrival, Captain Bonaparte had set up his first guns within range of the British ships. The cannonade began on September 18 from three batteries on the western side of the inner harbour, near the village of Brégaillon. Several British naval vessels were hit, one gunboat was sunk and several British sailors killed before the superior numbers and weight of metal of the Allies obliged the French army gunners to move to a safer spot.

Hood had at last become aware that, with the Le Caire peninsula unsecured, his fleet could be destroyed or driven out of the harbour. So, on September 21, a detachment of five hundred troops was rowed across the harbour, occupied the outposts of Balaguier and Eguilette and built a redoubt commanding the narrow neck of land to which they gave the name of Fort Mulgrave. The whole defensive system, with its many connecting trenches and barricades, was named Little Gibraltar.

It was during one of the artillery duels that Bonaparte met the future General Junot. Bonaparte would calmly write his reports during the shelling, and one day he called for a soldier with a good handwriting who could take dictation. A Sergeant Junot stepped forward. While Napoleon was dictating a letter to him, a cannonball from one of the British warships fell near Junot and sprayed the sheet of paper with sand. The sergeant, unperturbed, blew the ink-soaked sand away. 'Good,' he said, 'we won't need to blot this page.' Bonaparte admired coolness under fire and from that day Junot was attached to his personal staff.

It was at Toulon that Bonaparte also became acquainted with former aristocrat and future general Géraud-Christophe Duroc. Duroc had discreetly gone abroad when the Revolution began, but then chose to return home to fight, if not for his king at least for his country. Along with Junot he became part of Napoleon's little coterie of aides and

friends. A later arrival was Victor-Emmanuel Leclerc, a blond, pretentious young officer who was thoroughly disliked by the rank and
file because, to ingratiate himself with Bonaparte, he imitated, perhaps
unconsciously, all his mannerisms. He assiduously courted
Napoleon's sister, Pauline, when she was only fourteen. One day, so
the story goes, Bonaparte caught Leclerc and Pauline behind a screen,
in what is generally called a compromising position. After the required
Mediterranean shouts, screams, imprecations, admonitions and explanations, marriage followed and Leclerc's promotion to general.

Death and gore were, as often as romance, the partners of war and
glory and Napoleon's companions at Toulon were to know them in
abundance. Duroc, who fought in Egypt and all over Europe, died in
battle, perhaps gloriously but certainly messily. In a skirmish against
the Russians in 1813, a cannonball ricocheted off the trunk of a tree, hit
him in the stomach, tore open his belly and sent his intestines cascading
down his trousers and all over his saddle and his horse. Duroc apol-
ogised to Napoleon for his inability to serve him any longer, asked him
to be a father to his daughter and bade him leave the tent where he was
dying, as he felt the sight was upsetting his Emperor too much.

But all this gory glory still lay ahead. At Toulon Bonaparte and his
comrades were simply concerned with defeating the British. To which
end the next preoccupation of Bonaparte was how to get rid of his
commanding officer, General Carteaux.

Carteaux, a do-or-die type of soldier, could not understand Bonaparte's obsession with artillery. Carteaux believed in the bayonet, in
the deterrent effect upon the enemy of ardent young French infantrymen singing 'La Marseillaise' and charging. He wanted to take Toulon
by storm, while Bonaparte wanted to take it in a series of hops, gradually moving his guns into the Le Caire peninsula, thus acquiring control over the enemy fleet anchored within range of the French artillery.

Already the shelling of the British fleet had obliged Hood to move
his vessels to a less exposed position and to occupy Le Caire. Now, at
Bonaparte's insistence, General Carteaux grudgingly sent an infantry
detachment to attack the newly-built British bastion of Fort Mulgrave
on the little peninsula jutting out into the harbour. But he only
assigned three or four hundred men to the assault. This small force was
unable to break through the ramparts of 'Little Gibraltar'.

Fortunately for Bonaparte, he and General de la Poype, who was in
command of the eastern sector, were more in tune with each other. Ten
days after the unsuccessful French assault on Fort Mulgrave, de la
Poype sent in a substantial detachment under cover of night to occupy
Mont Faron, the mountain which overlooked Toulon from the north.
The successful attackers were led by a thirty-two-year-old major,
Victor Perrin, a lawyer's son who has come down in history as Marshal
Victor.

But Victor's occupation of Mont Faron was short-lived. Mulgrave immediately realised the immense and immediate peril that was now facing him. A hurried Allied council of war was held at seven that morning and within an hour fifteen hundred Spanish and British soldiers, led by Elphinstone and Gravina, were making their way up the hillside. By the afternoon the Allies had chased the French back down their own side of the hill.

There were more skirmishes to come in the next few weeks, surprise raids, desperate hand-to-hand encounters in scattered fruit orchards, olive groves and pine forests when enemy patrols accidentally met. The war then took on a fresh impetus with the appointment of new commanders on each side: General O'Hara succeeded Mulgrave and General Doppet took over from Carteaux. Doppet was a nonentity. O'Hara was not.

General Charles O'Hara arrived in Toulon from Gibraltar on October 27 with seven hundred and fifty infantrymen and a detachment of Royal Artillery gunners, to supplant Mulgrave. He had already played a significant but unfortunate role in his country's history. It was he who, as second-in-command to the British commander in chief, Lord Cornwallis, had heralded the end of British rule in what was to become the United States of America when he surrendered Yorktown twelve years earlier to General George Washington.

It is worth noting, at this point, the names of some of the men who accompanied O'Hara from Gibraltar, for they will make appearances again in this book. One of them was O'Hara's Scottish ADC, Captain James Leith. Also included in O'Hara's party was the German-born gunner, Colonel George Koehler, an international military adventurer and one of the more mysterious army figures of his day. A mathematician by training, he had invented a gun carriage which, by lowering its axis to an angle of seventy degrees, had greatly increased artillery accuracy. But a less reputable specimen of humanity in O'Hara's Gibraltar retinue was Captain Hudson Lowe of the 50th Foot, a snarling, mean-mouthed and even meaner-minded creature, marked by pettiness, an eye for finicky detail, subservience to superiors and an inability to make an even mildly generous gesture. This was the man the British government years later appointed Napoleon's gaoler in St Helena.

The noble Lord Mulgrave was most peeved at finding himself deprived of his command and seconded to General O'Hara. Unwilling to serve as deputy to a commoner (O'Hara was the bastard son of the Irish peer Lord Tyrawley), Mulgrave resigned his temporary commission and left as soon as possible for London, tea and crumpets with Prime Minister Pitt, and a chat with King George III. He was hardly missed, for the post of second-in-command went to General Sir David Dundas, writer of military textbooks and one of the intellectuals of the British army.

Dundas, who at fifty-eight was five years older than his chief, was a Scotsman from Edinburgh. He had heard of the Toulon expedition while journeying abroad and, like Mulgrave, had immediately rushed to the south of France to join in the fighting.

Events and people were also moving in the French camp. General Doppet, a doctor from Savoy who had exchanged his scalpels for the sword, arrived at Ollioules on November 12. He proved even more incompetent than his predecessor. Carteaux, perhaps because of his wife's influence, had managed to remain in command of the Toulon front for a couple of months. Doppet only survived five days.

He disgraced himself three days after his arrival by his failure to follow up a French attack on Fort Mulgrave which broke through the Spanish and British defenders and could easily have led to the capture of the Allied strongpoint. After his ADC was killed, Doppet ordered the retreat to sound and trotted nonchalantly away. A furious Bonaparte cantered up on his sweating, foaming horse and shouted at the general: 'The idiot who's ordering us to retreat is stopping us from taking Toulon today!' Two days later Doppet was sacked and posted to a quiet sector in the Pyrenees where he lapsed into well-deserved obscurity.

His replacement at Toulon, General Dugommier, is remembered as one of the great soldiers of the Revolution. Aged fifty-five, a former sugar planter from Guadeloupe, he had fought against the British in both the Seven Years War (in which France lost Canada) and the American War of Independence (in which Britain lost America), and, more recently, against the Austrians and Sardinians in Italy. He knew what soldiering was all about and he immediately understood and approved Major Bonaparte's plans. Under this able and dynamic general, victory for the French became inevitable.

O'Hara viewed the situation with realism. The British and their allies were in a cul-de-sac and as an experienced soldier he realised fully the immense danger in which his surrounded command stood. He sent warnings to London, informing the British government of the situation. But, lulled by Hood's early optimism, Pitt was not perturbed. Many in London believed Toulon was already for practical purposes within King George's realms. So Pitt and his advisers, on receipt of O'Hara's messages from Toulon, sipped their tea and unworriedly continued to spread their forces across the world, without giving any priority to Toulon, right on the doorstep of the enemy. They hoped to add a few more colonies to the growing British collection. They did too. But they lost Toulon.

The first major setback for the British after General O'Hara's arrival occurred a month later when O'Hara himself was captured during a minor operation in which such a senior officer should never have been personally involved. On November 29 he led a force of some 2,300 men against a French battery of eight newly-arrived 24-pounders harassing the British-held Fort Malbousquet, which Napoleon Bonaparte, creeping ever closer to the British positions, had set up in the foothills of Mont Faron, in an olive grove just northwest of Toulon.

The Allied sortie ended in disaster. Bonaparte claimed to have personally captured O'Hara. As the Emperor reminisced years later in St Helena, 'he was wounded in the arm by the fire of a sergeant and I seized him by the coat and threw him back amongst my own men, thinking he was a colonel as he had two epaulettes. While they were taking him to the rear, he cried out that he was the commander in chief of the English.'

Poor General O'Hara. This was his second stint as a prisoner of war. But at least, on each occasion, his captors were particularly eminent men. He had surrendered each time to a future head of state: at Yorktown to General Washington, the future President of the United States, at Toulon to Major Bonaparte, the future Emperor of the French.

O'Hara, who was in his mid-fifties when captured at Toulon, was held a prisoner for two years before he could be sent home as the British at that time held no French captives of equivalent rank. He was then exchanged for young General Donatien Rochambeau, recently captured in Martinique.

After O'Hara's capture, his deputy, General David Dundas, took over command of the British troops. But he was no more optimistic than his former chief over the outcome of the Toulon campaign. 'The fabric totters but we will prop it if we can,' he wrote to Henry Dundas, who was no relative but his minister in London, in charge of the navy and of colonies. Reinforcements were on their way from Gibraltar to Toulon, under the command of Colonel John Moore – destined to become one of the most heroic figures in British military history – to help in the propping, but it was obvious to the men on the spot that the end was near for Britain and her allies in Toulon.

On December 17 Dugommier and de la Poype launched a two-pronged night attack: one in Le Caire peninsula, the other on Mont Faron. The first assault took place at 2.00 am against Little Gibraltar, and was led by General Dugommier in person, with Victor Perrin, now a colonel, alongside. Close behind, Major Bonaparte was bringing up a battery of six guns to fire point blank into the British and Spanish ranks. Seven thousand French soldiers shouting 'Vive la République' came swarming up against the Allied ramparts. Bonaparte, now in the thick of the mêlée, had his horse killed under him and was stabbed in the leg by a British soldier with a bayonet. Nearby, Victor received a whiff of grapeshot in the stomach but survived.

Two hours later the fight was over and the French were in full control of Fort Mulgrave, later to be rebuilt and rechristened Fort Napoleon.

Over on Mont Faron, where de la Poype launched an attack with four thousand men immediately after the fall of the Little Gibraltar bastion, the French scrambled up the cliffs and also routed the Allies – British, Spanish and Neapolitan – from their positions.

Hood and Dundas were now faced by two simple but unsavoury facts: one, a French army was now up on Mont Faron looking down on Toulon, and two, across the bay, a second French army was setting up its guns, under the able and tireless Bonaparte, to fire into the massed British and Spanish warships. A few well-placed red hot shots and Hood's entire fleet might soon be blazing like a bonfire.

There are moments in life when discretion is the better part of valour. This was one of them. Hood gave the order to evacuate Toulon right away. The dream of a second Gibraltar was over.

To say that Hood's order to evacuate the city that day, given after a hastily summoned Allied council of war, provoked panic in Toulon would be a gross understatement. The royalist civilian population of Toulon knew that the first act of the victorious and vengeful Republicans would be to set up the guillotine in the main square. Sheer terror took over.

Hood gave the order to sink all the French navy ships, unmanned since the British took over the town. Captain (RN) Sir Sidney Smith, who had sailed from Smyrna, where he was on holiday, to join the fight, volunteered to lead the British demolition parties. He began early in the afternoon, helped by a number of volunteers including a young American loyalist lieutenant from New England, Ralph Willett Miller. But the demolition parties, now the target of French gunners, in their hurry to finish their task, bungled badly.

Of the thirty-one French ships-of-the-line in Toulon, only nine were destroyed. Another four were towed away by the British, one of which, the *Pompée*, went on to have a great fighting career under the Royal Navy's white ensign. The rest escaped destruction, even though fires burned throughout the night and explosions shook the city. Ashore across the bay, Bonaparte watched: 'For leagues around, the horizon was on fire. It was as bright as daylight. The spectacle was heartbreaking but magnificent,' he wrote. He would have found it even more heartbreaking had he known that Captain Hudson Lowe, the man who would one day be his gaoler in St Helena, was at that instant escaping from the inferno.

Nearly fifteen thousand citizens of Toulon were reportedly evacuated by the Allies. But thousands remained and for many of these life was tragically short. Barras and the abominable Stanislas Fréron, a syphilitic sadist madly in love with Pauline Bonaparte, who were in charge of the repression, took pride in the number of executions carried out. 'Every day since our arrival we have cut off two hundred heads,' Fréron wrote jubilantly to the Committee of Public Safety in Paris.

As well as executions for the defeated Royalists (eight hundred people were shot without trial between December 20 and December 23) came promotions and rewards for the victorious Republicans. Sergeant Junot became a lieutenant. Victor was promoted general on his hospital bed, and just two days before Christmas Bonaparte, a captain until only two months ago, also received his general's epaulette. He was then offered the command of the artillery in the French army in Italy.

General Dugommier, like O'Hara, now disappears from our story, but more tragically. He left Toulon in January, after pleading in vain for mercy for the misled citizenry of the city, and was posted to the Pyrenees to fight the Spaniards. He died a few months later when a cannonball hit him in the face and carried his head away. As for Carteaux, he managed to keep his head and continued his professional life as the highly paid director of the French National Lottery, presumably to the delight of Mme Carteaux.

Toulon's population, usually given as around twenty thousand before the siege, fell to seven thousand after the departure of the Allies. But at least, unlike Gibraltar, Toulon was never turned into a British colony.

That fate was being planned now by London for the island of Corsica where, after a short stay at Hyères, the evacuated British expedition was now destined. It had been joined off Hyères by Colonel Moore, and the latest reinforcements from Gibraltar which arrived off Toulon just as the British were precipitously leaving.

Moore, like Dugommier, was a soldier of heroic mould. The Corsican expedition, with which he was so closely connected, was to be a strictly British-only enterprise. No more Sardinians, Spaniards and Neapolitans to clutter up the scene with their foreign ways.

On arrival in Corsica, Moore's first role was as a diplomat rather than a warrior. As soon as the British fleet laid anchor off the coast, Hood sent him, with Elliot and Koehler, on a secret mission ashore to contact Pasquale Paoli, the Corsican independence fighter, who had a mass following on the island. Paoli disliked the men in power in Paris. Even so, as was the custom in the French capital, he addressed his countrymen and, much to their annoyance, his future British allies, as 'citizen'.

The purpose of the British mission was to use Paoli's antipathy to the Paris regime to establish British rule on the island, disguised as a sort of protectorate – an Anglo-Corsican kingdom, with George III as sovereign and Sir George Elliot as viceroy. And, of course, to turn the island into a valuable British base.

ISLAND CHIMERAS
Corsica and Corfu 1794-1797

Corsica, when the British three-man delegation arrived, was largely in the hands of Corsicans in rebellion against France. The French held Bastia, Calvi and the bay of San Fiorenzo, or St Florent to give it its French name. General Pasquale Paoli held the rest and governed it in the name of the Corsican people.

Paoli, whose only concern was to lead the Corsicans to independence, or at least to self-government, would have allied himself to the Devil if necessary. Instead he allied himself to the British.

He was a republican by reasoning, but he had no use for the creatures in Paris conducting their hideous bloody rigmaroles. He had lived in England, had many British friends and had been impressed by the British system of constitutional government, not as constitutional then as the British like to think but certainly far more liberal than the autocratic French monarchical system.

In a letter to Admiral Hood on January 4, 1794, he had offered to place his island under British protection. The British delegation sent a few days later by Hood and headed by Sir Gilbert Elliot, assisted by Colonel John Moore and Major Koehler, was quick to remind him of the fact. Britain's main interest, after the Toulon failure, was to turn Corsica into a British mid-Mediterranean base but presumably any reference to this purpose was tactfully omitted from the conversation.

Elliot, we learn, was almost as fascinated (at first) with Paoli as James Boswell had been – the publication of his *An Account of Corsica*, one of the best sellers of its day, in 1768 had won him the sobriquet, in which he revelled, of 'Boswell the Corsican'. That had been more than twenty-five years before when Paoli, fighting against the Genoese overlords of his island, had been only forty-three. Corsica was then British society's darling, a sort of Biafra before its time, in the support of which everybody who counted gave lip service and tea parties. But since the Boswell days Corsica had become French by deed of sale, General Paoli was now an almost forgotten old man, and there was another Corsican around, Napoleon Bonaparte, a rather disquieting individual who, the British sensed, would give them trouble in the years ahead.

Just the same, Elliot was enchanted with Paoli and so was Colonel Moore, only half the age of the old Corsican. There and then he established a solid relationship with the general, based as much on his respect for the older man's years as for his courage and experience.

Although Moore was much criticised by his peers, it is in fact difficult to overpraise him, there was so much nobility about the man. Not the nobility of a debilitated aristocracy but the nobility of character, of strength coupled to kindness, of professional ability and of courage. In short, he was a virtuous man, a man of virtue – not in the mealy-mouthed Victorian sense, but in the hardy, old Roman meaning of the word. 'Moore was a brave soldier, an excellent officer and a man of talent,' said Napoleon Bonaparte, not once but many times, and Napoleon was a man who could judge soldiers, courage and ability.

So, on February 7, Admiral Lord Hood's fleet sailed into the Gulf of San Fiorenzo to extend His Britannic Majesty's protection over a new lot of benighted foreigners; this time a bunch of Corsicans whose charisma might then have been fading in British eyes but whose romantic appeal as honourable brigands has managed to survive right down to modern times. There followed several days of local fighting against the French occupying forces, principally to capture a strange, circular defensive fort on Mortella Point, on the western shore of the bay. This required four days' pounding by Koehler's gunners before it surrendered. The hero of the attack was the young, one-eyed, brawling, bastard son of the Earl of Tyrone, Captain William Beresford, who led the storming party that captured the battered tower. He was promoted to major as a reward.

The Mortella tower having proved its value, the model was promptly exported to Britain and forts similar to it were built all along the south coast during the Napoleonic invasion scare. But the name changed a little. Two of its letters somehow became transposed and in England these strongpoints, which still stand to remind us of invaders that never came, are known as Martello Towers.

The fall of San Fiorenzo followed during the next few days, the French casualties amounting to around one hundred and fifty to Britain's fifty-two. Some three hundred survivors of the French garrison managed to break out and make their way to Bastia. One cannot say 'fight their way' through because Britain's Corsican allies, who were supposed to cut off the escaping French, were too busy going through the pockets of the dead and wounded, British and French with equal impartiality, to interfere with the French fugitives. Fighting may sometimes be an urgent duty of the military. Looting always is.

The French navy lost two of its frigates during a brief action around San Fiorenzo. One was burnt and sunk, the other, the 36-gun *Minerve*, partly scuttled in shallow water, was refloated by Admiral Hood's men and within a few days was fit for sea duty again. The new addition to the Royal Navy was rechristened HMS *San Fiorenzo*. She was to make her name in the East Indies as one of the top British fighting frigates. Nelson was also involved in this Corsican naval occasion when, to the anguish of his thirsty crew, he sank four coastal vessels loaded with casks of wine.

What marked the next phase of the Corsican operation was not the animosity between the British and the French but the enmity between the British army and the British navy. The insufferable Admiral Lord Hood, as commander in chief of the Corsican expedition, set the standard by his continuous rudeness and arrogance towards his army colleagues. General Sir David Dundas, who also had come over from Toulon, was his nearest and most obvious target. The dislike that existed between the two men filtered right down the two services, which behaved more like jealous rivals than joint forces united in spreading George III's dominion in the Mediterranean.

Hood, who had learnt nothing from his Toulon defeat, still thought of himself as a master tactician on land and he wanted Bastia, surrounded by mountains and the sea, to be taken by direct assault. Dundas wanted to blockade the town until hunger forced it to surrender. But Hood couldn't stand being opposed. The weary Dundas, anxious not to remain with the irascible and overbearing admiral any longer, requested and quickly received permission to return home on sick leave. He left by the first available boat, labelled 'an old woman in a red ribbon' by Hood's scoffing bluejackets.

Meanwhile the mischief-making Captain Horatio Nelson, anxious to get into battle, buzzed around waspishly, worsening by his comments the tense situation between the two services. The navy should take over the job the army wasn't doing, he suggested. To discredit the army more thoroughly, he wrote a petulant letter to Sir William Hamilton in Naples, accusing the army of refusing to attack Bastia – even though, he added, it was defended by only eight hundred soldiers. He knew the real figure was around four thousand but Nelson was never a man to let the truth stand in the way of his arguments.

Inside Bastia, the general commanding the French troops, Jean-Pierre Lacombe-Saint-Michel, also did his warrior act, issuing bombastic statements and generally behaving like the politician he was rather than as the soldier he wanted to be. To his credit he was a brave man, had volunteered for battle and been recently wounded, but posturing came more naturally to him than fighting.

Since the army would not attack, the navy did. Hood took his ships over to the east side of the long narrow peninsula on which Bastia is located, and an April 4, 1794 landed some thirteen hundred of his men with orders to take the town. Nelson was given the command of this contingent. 'My seamen are now what British seamen ought to be: almost invincible,' he exulted. Admiral Hood wrote to the Secretary of War in London that Bastia would be his in ten days.

But by the end of April, more than three weeks later, Bastia was still holding out and a now angry Hood was blaming army lack of support for the British failure to take the town. Sir Gilbert Elliot, weary of the army-navy quarrel, and even more weary of the Corsicans who were showing themselves very un-British in their ways, departed across the sea and went to admire Italy in the spring.

On May 21, seven weeks after Hood's pledge to take Bastia in ten days, its 3,500 surviving defenders, out of food and supplies, surrendered. Elliot hurried back to Corsica, Paoli summoned the Corsican consultative assembly to meet the following month in Corte, and Hood sailed off to capture the fort at Calvi, the last French stronghold in the island.

This mopping-up operation took nearly three months. The siege itself didn't begin seriously until mid-June as supplies and troops had to be brought over from the other side of the island, guns hauled up the hillsides, and reinforcements awaited from Britain.

Arrogant as ever, Admiral Hood continued to abuse and harass his army subordinates until he came up against a soldier just as strong-willed as he was, General Sir Charles Stuart. Sir Charles arrived on May 25 to take over the army command. He hadn't seen any fighting since the American War of Independence, nearly fifteen years before, but he was the fourth son of the Earl of Bute and that counted for something in England in those days. His aristocratic mien and his peremptory manner temporarily subdued the old bully.

The siege of Calvi, a forgotten and strategically minor episode of the war, was actually one of those occasional instances when man, whatever his nationality, whether it be in enterprises of war or peace, reveals the indomitable strength of the human spirit – and of the human frame. The summer heat made conditions intolerable for both the besieged and the besiegers. Inside the citadel the French troops, commanded by the Corsican General Raphael de Casabianca, suffered not only from the heat, but also from thirst, hunger, dirt, disease and nearly two months of heavy British bombardment. Around the citadel British soldiers, sailors and marines, straining and sweating, dragged heavy guns up the hillsides to shell the French, while malaria, spawned in the local marshes, debilitated the entire army. 'We have upwards of a thousand sick out of two thousand,' Nelson wrote. By the time the siege was over, the proportion had risen from half to two-thirds.

British battle casualties, however, were low: about one hundred. They included Nelson, who lost an eye when a French cannonball hit the ground and drove a blast of sand and gravel into his face; Moore, wounded in the head; and a young infantry officer, Lieutenant William Byron, the heir to a peerage, killed by a French shot. His six-year-old cousin in England, George, the future poet and fighter for Greek independence, inherited the title and became Lord Byron.

General Casabianca surrendered the citadel on August 10, 1794. Corsica was now entirely in British hands. General Stuart, exhausted, returned to Britain. So did crotchety old Lord Hood who, two weeks later, received the lucrative appointment of governor of Greenwich Hospital which he held for the next twenty years until he died, more cantankerous and bad-tempered than ever, at the age of ninety-two

He was replaced in the Mediterranean by Admiral William Hotham.

Two months before the fall of Calvi, the Corsican Assembly had voted the island out of the French Republic and into the British Empire, and acclaimed George III as its king. Corsica was now, officially, the Anglo-Corsican Kingdom, with Sir Gilbert Elliot as viceroy, his scheming Corsican henchman Charles Pozzo di Borgo as president of the State Council, and Paoli, third down the list, as president of the Assembly.

Corsicans might still be British today if, during the next two years, they had not come to the conclusion that the British were worse masters than the French. There was also in the French camp that Corsican general, Napoleon Bonaparte, defeating the Austrian Empire and showing his countrymen what a Corsican could achieve. Relations between native islanders and British outsiders grew strained. The two had very little in common.

Differences were not only political. They were also of a personal and social nature. Sir Gilbert believed fervently in the superiority of English order and attitudes, while Corsicans were rough mountaineers who lived, if not in an egalitarian society, at least in one in which there was no lord and no master. Every man's dignity was important. They would come and talk to Paoli as man to man, request or proffer advice, and Elliot considered this dialogue too democratic and contrary to the required deportment of political office. In Sir Gilbert's view, says writer Peter Thrasher, 'all forms of democracy led to anarchy and misery'.

With this outlook, blunders were inevitable, and perhaps Sir Gilbert's worst error was his transfer of the Corsican capital from its mountain fastness of Corte, in the interior of the island, to Bastia, on the coast. Here, brighter and more international, there were French émigrés, Italian visitors, British naval and army officers, a few stranded aristocrats, a little cosmopolitan society in what was essentially a sombre, provincial backwater. Life for his wife in particular was more agreeable there than among hill people wearing goatskins, eating chestnut porridge and speaking an Italian patois. For Lady Elliot found Corsicans tiresome. Her appreciation of the beauty of the island did not include its inhabitants nor their ways. 'All that nature has done for the island is lovely and all that man has added filthy . . . If the people were in a state of civilisation, it would be Elysium,' she wrote. As for her husband, after failing in Toulon, he hoped to turn Corsica into another little England.

To the Corsicans from the interior, on the other hand, Bastia was almost a foreign city, full of continentals, alien gaiety and mirth. Whatever their virtues, Corsicans were not a jolly lot. But they were undoubtedly, in the words of that tireless critic Fortescue, 'one of the most ungovernable peoples in Europe.'

The strain between Sir Gilbert and the Corsicans grew and the islanders turned more and more towards Paoli. Their resentment, at first strictly anti-Elliot, took on an increasingly anti-British tinge.

Corsica's scented air is heady brew which can make passion or distaste assume the outrageous proportions of the vendetta. Sir Gilbert, inevitably, began to regard Paoli as his rival for power and the Corsican's British friends as in league against him. The brew also went to the heads of the little circle of Sir Gilbert's supporters. Intrigue and back-stabbing became the norm at the viceroy's court. Nelson was a member of Sir Gilbert's coterie and did little to ease the already highly strained army-navy-viceroy-Paoli-Corsicans relationships. Nelson, anyway, was always at his best as a sailor and at his worst as a courtier. He was cut out for fighting, and we know, moreover, what he thought of foreigners and he must have considered Corsicans among the most obnoxious of that species. Nelson, in addition, disliked Moore.

The year 1795 in Corsica was one when nothing much happened, but when everything began to fall to pieces. By June the whole island was becoming unsafe for travel by the British unless moving in groups, and armed. In July, the viceroy's Corsican aide-de-camp, Captain Colonna, caused a scandal by deliberately smashing a plaster bust of the respected Paoli at a ball in Ajaccio. Elliot failed to reprimand him. News travelled fast on the torturous mountain trails and posters went up all over the island denouncing the viceroy, the anglophile President of the State Council, Pozzo de Borgo and Captain Colonna.

Colonel Moore, anxious over the security of his troops, set out to see Paoli in his village at Morosaglia, accompanied by the quartermaster-general, Colonel Sir Hilbebrand Oakes (another veteran of Yorktown – nearly every other senior British army officer seemed to have served in the North American campaign), and noted along the way that many of the peasants were armed. He was perhaps more alarmed than he need have been, for carrying a weapon, preferably a pistol, is a traditional necessity for the well-dressed man in Corsica, rather like wearing a tie.

Paoli was, as usual, courteous and affable. But he criticised the viceroy for his lack of judgment. Moore rode back to Bastia. 'Had the Corsicans been as intemperate [as Sir Gilbert], and one shot been fired, we must have been driven out of the country,' he observed.

Elliot's next blunder was his decision to dispense with the Corsican parliament. It was due to meet in September but he announced that its sessions would be delayed indefinitely. The news led to several minor uprisings in the island. The viceroy then asked London to recall Colonel Moore and to summon Paoli to England. Moore left on October 2, 1795, Paoli three days later. As the frigate taking Paoli to England sailed out of San Fiorenzo, thousands lined the shore weeping. His journey was both fruitless and tragic. King George III refused

Admiral Lord Samuel Hood   General Sir Charles Grey

to receive the Corsican leader, who died without ever seeing his island again. He is today still revered as Corsica's national hero.

The next month another admiral, Sir John Jervis, back in Europe from the West Indies where he and General Grey had just been tussling unsuccessfully with Victor Hugues in Guadeloupe, arrived in Corsican waters to succeed Admiral Hotham. Nelson and Jervis met early in 1796 and on April 4 that year, Jervis ordered Nelson to hoist a broad pennant as commodore and take command of a squadron in the Gulf of Genoa to cooperate with the Austrians. The latter were now facing an attack in northern Italy by the redoubtable French general, Bonaparte.

At the same time that Bonaparte was descending on the plains of Italy, in what was to become one of the most famous campaigns in military history, Commodore Nelson was assembling around him the Royal Navy officers who were to become the first of his 'band of brothers', as he later called them. They included Fremantle, Barry, Foley, the Canadian Hallowell, Troubridge, Hardy, Collingwood, and the New Englander Miller whom we have already met in Toulon.

Corsica was no longer an isolated little island that the war had passed by. It was now closely involved in the Italian campaign, for General Bonaparte, ranging over the northern part of the peninsula, was determined to liberate his nearby island home from the British intruders, and to bring it back into the fold of Republican France, the country which he had now adopted as his own.

A French army, under General Vaubois, captured Leghorn – Livorno to give it its more liquid-sounding Italian name. General

Bonaparte organised an army of Corsican exiles, five thousand men, there on the mainland, and sent French agents, most of them Corsicans, into the island's valleys and mountains to call its people to arms against the British.

Doubtful of the loyalty of the native officers of his Corsican battalions, Elliot sacked the lot and replaced them with British officers. Paoli's moderating influence had gone and nothing now stood between the confused British and the coming French invasion except a rebellious Corsican population. Old bandits who had taken to the maquis years ago came down from the mountains. The sons of one brigand, Zampaglino, joined Bonaparte's army in Leghorn. One of them returned to Corsica as a French agent. 'I congratulate you on your arrival in Corsica. I have ordered all the refugees to make ready to lead the brave Corsicans, to break the English yoke, and to reconquer liberty,' General Bonaparte wrote to him.

In Corsica, partisans attacked the British-held bridges between Corte and Bastia. A British regiment was cooped up in Ajaccio and couldn't break out of the town. Another regiment, two thousand strong, was marching inland from Bastia to attack the insurgent village of Bocognano, when news arrived that in another village, Bistuglio, near Corte, eight hundred armed Corsican rebels had assembled to fight the British. Elliot met their leaders and in desperation agreed to pardon everybody rather than fight; Corsica, torn apart in a war, he reasoned, would be useless as a British bastion in the Mediterranean.

But his peace gestures failed to appease the Corsicans. In church sermons the priests began to storm against the British heretics. In a massive riot on the quayside in Ajaccio, British soldiers and Corsican fishermen fought with knives, fists and broken bottles. More ominously, Bonaparte's army in Leghorn was preparing to attack the island.

In Bastia, a very depressed Sir Gilbert still did not grasp the full implications of these events. But in London, to Pitt and Henry Dundas, less emotionally involved in the Corsican enterprise, the meaning was clear: the jig was up. Pitt sent instruction to Elliot to pack up and go. The naval-base project was now so low on the list of British priorities that the government also ordered Jervis and his squadron to sail away to Gibraltar, leaving the whole Mediterranean to the French.

From Leghorn, two French army groups, one under General Darius Casalta, the other under General Antoine Gentili, both Corsicans, sailed across and invaded the island. Gentili had been wounded in San Fiorenzo, his home town, and had held Bastia after Lacombe-Saint-Michel's departure. Casalta, of an old, aristocratic Corsican family, had been wounded ten times in some obscure affray in 1793, seven shots in the thigh, two in the arm and one in the lower abdomen. But he did not seem the worse for wear; only three years later, on October 19,

1796, he and his men landed near Bastia and marched on the town, which they reached two days later.

Hard fighting had been expected. But the British troops were already packed and leaving, and there were only minor scuffles between the two enemies. The British rearguard left town during the evening. Nelson was in the last boat. History does not record whether Commodore Nelson and General Casalta met and saluted each other as the bluejackets rowed away from the quay in the fading daylight and the Anglo-Corsican Kingdom ceased to exist. But the moment was a solemn one and deserved a gesture of recognition.

After Corsica, the Italian campaign had what we could call another colonial extension in Corfu and the other Ionian Islands.

The Ionian Islands, off the coast of Greece, cluster down from the south of Albania in the Adriatic to the southernmost tip of mainland Greece in the Mediterranean. There are five main islands: Corfu at the top then, going down, Leucas (St Maure), Cephalonia, Zante and, at the bottom, Cerigo, the famous Cythera of Watteau's painting, site of the cult of Aphrodite, the goddess of love. Ulysses was once king of one of the minor islands in the group, Ithaca, and the whole archipelago reeks of mythology and classical remembrances. In 1797 the islands had been in the hands of Venice for four hundred years. They could not fail to impress a man like General Bonaparte, imbued with a romantic admiration for the ancient classics. Doubly so, as they were of great tactical importance, right on the threshold of the East, of which he was also so enamoured.

In 1796-97 he was defeating the Austrians and their allies in northern Italy. A month after seizing Corsica, he won a great victory at Arcola, two months later it was Rivoli. Mantua surrendered. The Pope signed the Treaty of Tolentino. In April 1797 Bonaparte signed the Peace of Loeben with Austria and the following month he declared war on the Venetian Republic, using an uprising in Verona as pretext for the new conflict. Venice immediately sued for peace and the Treaty of Campo Formio, signed on October 17, 1797, recognised French sovereignty over Corfu and the other Ionian isles.

General Gentili was bundled out of his new quiet post in Corsica, ordered to Venice, and from there dispatched at the head of a force of two thousand men to occupy the islands. There was no fighting, at least not yet. The Venetian garrison consisted of a handful of Italian troops and soldiers from Dalmatia, in what is today Yugoslavia. Gentili immediately shipped home the Dalmatians, who looked ready to give trouble. Shortly afterwards he fell ill and returned to Corsica where he died four months later in San Fiorenzo.

He was replaced in November 1797 by General Louis Chabot who, back from the fighting, was on garrison duty in Italy. It was a quiet posting at first. The fighting in the Ionians was to follow the next year, as an outgrowth of the Egyptian campaign. It was a three-sided conflict: against the British, against the Turks and against the Russians.

PRINCES AND PARTISANS
India 1793-1798

In their day, Napoleon's ambitious Indian projects seemed not only feasible to him but also to his apprehensive British enemies. They had every reason to be wary of the French. The two countries were still rivals in India, although France could only claim sovereignty over Pondicherry and a handful of small coastal settlements nearly all undefended and virtually indefensible. France had, however, strong friends among several of the anti-British ruling princes, notably Tipoo Sahib, Sultan of Mysore; the Nizam Ali of Hyderabad; and the Mahratta prince, Sindhia. Their realms covered more than half of India and hundreds of French soldiers were serving in their armies, several with the rank of general.

When war broke out between France and England in 1793, the British governor-general in India, Lord Cornwallis (of Yorktown fame) had ordered the British army to seize all French establishments in the subcontinent. The only major French garrison, at Pondicherry, made up of six hundred European soldiers and nine hundred Indian sepoys, held out for two months and then surrendered to the besieging army, over twenty times larger, commanded by General Braithwaite and a towering, blustering Scotsman, about six foot six, Colonel David Baird, who will come into this story many more times.

The other isolated French settlements, Mahé, Karikal, Yanaon and Chanderganor, never even had the chance of offering resistance. Cornwallis, who had been in India since 1786, then went home.

The war between France and Britain did not involve India again for another five years. In May 1798 – the month that General Napoleon Bonaparte sailed from Toulon for Egypt – Richard Lord Wellesley (also known, later, as Lord Mornington) arrived in Calcutta to become governor-general of India. Waiting to greet him at the quayside was his brother, Colonel Arthur Wellesley, the future Duke of Wellington, who had already been serving in India for several years.

Its toeholds on the Indian coast all occupied by the British, France was no longer officially present in the subcontinent. But the French were still there. French mercenaries, or 'partisans' as they were called, held most of the vital posts of command and training in the ponderous armies of the Indian princes. Many of the gunners were also French.

The largest of these princely armies was that of Tipoo Sahib, of Mysore, in southern India. It numbered 75,000 infantry and cavalry and his troops included a 'French Force' of 550 soldiers. Just north of

Mysore, in Hyderabad, General Joachim Raymond, a deserter from the French navy, commanded the Nizam's 14,000-man army. A strong supporter of the French Revolution, Raymond regarded his men as 'a French body of troops, employed and subsidised by the Nizam' and his regiments carried the French Tricolour flag on parade and in battle.

Last but certainly not least among France's native allies was the confederacy of the Mahrattas which straddled India from east to west, the greatest single power in the subcontinent, with its capital in Poona. Sindhia, the most powerful leader among the continually plundering and mutual warring chiefs of this martial empire, was one of France's best hopes in India. Sindhia maintained an army of some forty thousand men trained in modern methods of warfare by European officers, most of them French.

When the French Revolution broke out, Charles-Benoit Le Borgne, a professional soldier and adventurer from Savoy, was in command of Sindhia's army. He retired with his treasure to France a few years later, and became Napoleon's adviser on Indian affairs. He was replaced in India by General Pierre Perron, a former handkerchief salesman from Brittany who had found his true calling in the East after he deserted from the French navy.

At one time Perron had had three hundred European officers under him, most of them Frenchmen, but with a sprinkling of Germans, Italians and the inevitable Irish among them, and he was the key man in Napoleon's dreams of Indian conquest. Perron, as the governor of a vast territory which included Agra (and the Taj Mahal), Jaipur and the old imperial capital of Delhi, was the most powerful European in India. In Delhi the old, blind and decrepit Mogul emperor, Shah Alem, lingered on as nominal ruler of all India, but he was Sindhia's protégé, and under Perron's direct supervision. 'There is every reason to believe that the Government of France intended to make the unfortunate Emperor of Hindustan [Shah Alem] the main instrument of their designs in India, and to avail themselves of the authority of His Majesty's name to re-establish their influence and power,' commented the suspicious Lord Wellesley, for whom Perron and his troops were always 'the French Army' in India.

Lord Wellesley may have been exaggerating somewhat for he had an absolute obsession about the French and saw their malign influence at work everywhere in India. But in his personal life he had no aversion to them. He married a high-class French prostitute who gave him five children.

Wellesley knew that although the first loyalty of these French 'partisans' was to themselves, they were also loyal to their mother country. When news that an official army of the French Republic led by General Bonaparte had arrived in Egypt and that some of its warriors had reached the Red Sea, a whiff of panic swept through the command of the British army in India. But Wellesley saw the immediate threat coming not from Bonaparte, nor from General Perron and his Mahratta warriors, but from a newly invigorated alliance between Tipoo Sahib and the French.

The latter had recently sent Tipoo reinforcements from Mauritius. Tipoo, however, was disappointed. He had requested thirty thousand soldiers and all he received were two generals, thirty-five officers and senior NCOs, four shipwrights, one watchmaker and twenty-two mulatto and thirty-six French troopers. In Mauritius, however, the imprudent General Malartic issued a pompous proclamation announcing that Tipoo Sahib would drive the British troops from India as soon as he had enough French troops. Copies of Malartic's message were sent to London and Calcutta. The days of Tipoo Sahib were immediately numbered.

On reading Malartic's indiscreet message, Lord Wellesley ordered his army commander, General Harris, a veteran of the Battle of Bunker Hill in the American War of Independence, to assemble his troops and march on Mysore.

Wellesley also acted with speed to disarm the French-led troops in Hyderabad where the Nizam's army also included six British sepoy battalions, complete with artillery. The news of the arrival of General Bonaparte's French army in Egypt had reached India on October 11, 1798. Eleven days later the fourteen thousand sepoys of the French force and their officers in Hyderabad woke up to find themselves surrounded by their British comrades, with guns pointing down at them from the surrounding hills. General Raymond's splendid soldiery – he himself had died a few months earlier, from poisoning – were disarmed, dismissed and dispersed without fuss and without bloodshed.

The 'weak and foolish' (Fortescue) Nizam agreed to join the British in their attack on Tipoo Sahib. The command of the Nizam's army was given to Lord Wellesley's up-and-coming brother Arthur, the future Duke of Wellington. Sindhia for the moment was untouchable. He agreed to remain neutral in the coming war and the British had to be satisfied with this undertaking.

CHAPTER THREE

O My Island in the Sun

ISLAND MEDLEY

The West Indies 1793

Three years and nine months after the mutiny on HMS *Bounty*, in January 1793, Captain William Bligh arrived in Jamaica in his new ship, HMS *Providence*, with a cargo of Tahitian breadfruit plants to replace those thrown overboard by Christian Fletcher and the mutineers. Two hundred and forty-nine shoots were planted in Jamaica, to grow as cheap and nourishing food for the slaves; another three hundred were planted in the island of St Vincent.

A few days later, on January 30, General Donatien Rochambeau, son of the man who had commanded the French troops at the siege of Yorktown, arrived in Martinique from Haiti to become governor-general of the French Windward Islands. Two days afterwards, on February 1, Britain and France were at war.

The British immediately made preparations to attack, and during the next few months struck in four widely dispersed spots in the Americas: Tobago, Martinique, St Pierre and Miquelon, and Haiti. St Pierre and Miquelon were just a little sideshow up in the cold waters off Newfoundland. The tropical Caribbean islands were the main target and the attacks were two-pronged: from Barbados against Martinique and Tobago, and later Guadeloupe and St Lucia; and from Jamaica against Haiti.

Tobago was the first objective.

In April, a small squadron commanded by Admiral Sir John Laforey (whose Huguenot grandfather, Monsieur La Forêt, had found refuge in England from religious persecution in his own country about a

century earlier) sailed from the Barbados capital, Bridgetown, on the
12th and reached Tobago on the 14th. The British force, five hundred
strong, stormed the local fort and took the island in twenty-four hours
for the loss of three men killed and twenty-five wounded.

In May, in a completely unrelated operation, a small, British military
force operating out of Halifax in Canada, seized the fishing islands of
St Pierre and Miquelon. The sixty-man French garrison capitulated
and the fifteen hundred inhabitants were all deported to the Canadian
maritime provinces.

In June, General Bruce sailed from Barbados on the 10th with an
army of eleven hundred British and eight hundred French Royalist
troops for Martinique. He landed his men on the 16th. Five days later,
thwarted in his invasion endeavour, he re-embarked his troops for Barbados, blaming panic among his Royalist troops for the setback.

On September 9, Colonel John Whitelocke, commanding a detachment of seven hundred men, sailed from Kingston, Jamaica, and landed
ten days later at Jérémie, in the southern peninsula of Haiti, St Domingue or San Domingo – as the British then indiscriminately called it.
He received a huge welcome from the French planters, Royalists to a
man.

It was the start of a five-year campaign which wrecked the British
army. 'The secret of England's impotence for the first six years of the
war may be said to lie in two fatal words: St Domingo,' succinctly
wrote John Fortescue. Yellow fever was a far more fatal enemy than
the muskets and the cannon of the French.

The yellow fever – so called because it turns the skin of its victims
yellow – raged in the late spring and summer, not only in Haiti but in
nearly all the Caribbean islands and on the nearby American mainland.
There were other unpleasant local diseases, less easy to diagnose for
posterity—and also the region's almost equally lethal raw, cheap rum.
Counting up the casualties for his countrymen, Fortescue gloomily
reached 'the total of eighty thousand soldiers lost to the service,
including forty thousand actually dead, the latter number exceeding
the total losses of Wellington's army from death, discharges, desertion
and all causes in the Peninsular War.'

But the Yellow Jack, as the British troops called it, was no one's ally.
The French suffered equally. 'Epidemics could ravage a whole army
out of existence,' John Keegan reminds us in *The Nature of War*, quot-
ing figures for a later Haitian campaign. 'The best known example of
their fate is the one which overtook the army of General Leclerc in
Haiti in 1801. Sent to put down the rebellion of Toussaint L'Ouverture,
it had been reduced by yellow fever in 1803 from twenty-five thousand
to three thousand men.'

FATAL HAITI
Hispaniola 1793-1796

Writing about the 1793 war in Haiti is a daunting task. So many hostile and contrary forces were all struggling against each other at the same time that sometimes the campaign between France and Britain is lost among all the other conflicts: whites against blacks, blacks against mulattos, mulattos against whites, slaves against their masters, Republicans against Royalists, Spaniards against Frenchmen, then against British, then against Frenchmen again.

We shall try, therefore, in this account of the war, to focus attention on the main event – the war between France and England, the struggle between two imperialisms. We shall disregard, whenever possible, the ferocious civil and racial war being fought right alongside the international conflict, and sometimes part of it.

In the midst of all the turmoil, the British chose as their main allies in Haiti the French planters. The Pitt government in London negotiated in advance with a French émigré from the Jérémie region, Vernault de Charmilly. De Charmilly and his friends in southern Haiti offered their allegiance to George III, and the governor of nearby Jamaica, General Sir Adam Williamson, was instructed to send troops to Haiti to aid them.

Sir Adam was even more of an optimist than Lord Hood had been in Toulon. The governor of Jamaica had only eight hundred and seventy-seven troops available for service in Haiti but they would be enough to defeat the French Republicans, he assured his superiors in London.

Haiti was then at war against the neighbouring Spanish colony of Santo Domingo and already in the throes of its civil war as well, or rather several civil wars, between blacks, whites and mulattos, in an haphazard three-cornered contest of continually shifting alliances.

There were two main mulatto armies: one in the southern peninsula, where the British under Colonel Whitelocke had just landed, was led by the capable General Rigaud, who had fought in the French army at Savannah during the American Revolution and was resolutely anti-British. The other mulatto army, commanded by Vilatte in the north, was of dubious loyalty to France.

The French presence in the colony had been considerably weakened since a hideous massacre of whites in 1791 when slaves throughout the country revolted, tortured and murdered many owners and their families. The French had reacted ferociously, and thousands of blacks had been killed. Now Negro armies, under the command of various black self-styled generals had sprung up and were roaming over the countryside. The most famous was to be that of Toussaint L'Ouverture. The former coachman had loyally saved his master and his family first, had driven them in his coach to safety in Cap François and then joined the rebels and gone over to the Spaniards in adjoining Santo Domingo. He would soon be returning to Haiti at the head of a black, Spanish-paid army.

More than a thousand French regular troops and National Guards of royalist sympathies had also deserted to the Spanish.

To add to the general confusion, over on the French Republican side, ruling commissioners in the districts of Cap François, Sonthonax and Polverel, had just proclaimed the end of slavery and some one hundred and fifty survivors of an Irish regiment raised to serve the King of France went over to the British after Whitelocke's arrival, and asked to be sent to the United States. These men had not been the only defectors to the United States. The French naval squadron, largely Royalist in sentiment, had also made for a US port. Even so, a competent and honest French officer, General Lavaux, promoted governor after Sonthonax and Polverel had been summoned home for explanations (they, too, wisely chose to go to the United States instead) was trying desperately to keep Haiti together, and for a while succeeded.

During the next few months, Colonel Whitelocke occupied several localities in the country, but to little effect. First to fall was Mole Saint-Nicolas, at the western tip of the northern peninsula, the so-called Gibraltar of the West Indies. Almost without a fight, the British then occupied in turn a number of western and southern coastal towns, notably St Marc, Les Gonaives, Petite Rivière, Mirebalais, Jacmel and Léogane, places that were all controlled or under the influence of de Charmilly and his planter friends. At St Marc, a Spanish company from the other side of the island came to join the British occupants. In general the British found support among both whites and blacks. The French planters, all Royalists, fought for their estates, gun in hand, and raised irregular battalions of Negroes in support of Whitelocke. But the mulattos generally held aloof. They did not like the terms under which the British had entered Haiti which, under the prevailing British laws, made them second-class citizens.

Some places did resist British encroachment, notably Tiburon, some fifty kilometres south of Jérémie. It is at Tiburon that Rollo Gillespie, 'the bravest man who ever wore the King's uniform', as Fortescue has described him, received his baptism of fire.

Gillespie was an Ulsterman. Eight years previously, at the age of twenty, a cornet in the army, he had married a pretty Dublin girl called Annabel. His adventurous life then began. He shot and killed a titled man in a duel, escaped to Scotland, returned to face trial for wilful murder and was acquitted. Sent to the West Indies on garrison duty, his ship sank in a storm off Madeira, he escaped in an open boat, then survived a bout of yellow fever in Jamaica and, now immune to the disease, volunteered for more active service in Haiti.

The fight for Tiburon was short and sharp. A few hundred men, commanded by Major Brent Spencer, landed from three frigates and routed some eight hundred French troops, capturing a hundred and fifty of the enemy and twenty-five guns.

Colonel Whitelocke believed as much in the power of money as in the power of arms. He now offered Governor Lavaux a large bribe and a commission in the British army if he came over to them. Lavaux not only refused but challenged Whitelocke to a duel. The insensitive Whitelocke did not reply. Instead, he tried to bribe General Rigaud. But since Rigaud was a coloured man, the bribe was five times smaller than the one offered to Lavaux. And equally unsuccessful.

The freeing of the slaves had provoked a quiver of expectation among the Republican French and among the Negroes in those early months of 1794. The high hopes it provoked reached the Spanish camp in Santo Domingo, when Toussaint L'Ouverture heard that the slaves in Haiti were now free. Liberty-Equality-Fraternity was no longer a slogan but a reality. Toussaint decided the time had come for him to return to Haiti. He went to Mass at the cathedral, prayed ostentatiously and devoutly, marched out of the building when the service was over, courteously saluted the ladies, jumped on his horse and, with his entire army, rode furiously back west over the Haitian border and into French service.

Encouraged, the mulatto Rigaud attacked British-occupied Tiburon in the south of Haiti, killed twenty-eight of its defenders and wounded a hundred. In the west, at St Marc, British and Spanish protection failed to save the French Royalist inhabitants from massacre by a large band of armed Negro 'brigands'. In the north, an attack by the British officer, Major Brent Spencer, at the head of two hundred men, on the small French-held redoubt of Bombarde near Mole Saint-Nicolas, was beaten back with the loss of forty men. It was May now, furthermore, and the four-months rainy season was approaching with its deadly accompaniment of yellow fever.

'The British campaign in the West Indies cost England ... a little fewer than a hundred thousand men, half of them dead and half permanently unfit for service,' Fortescue reminds us in his *History of the British Army*. Every man in the 96th Regiment became a corpse. Only two hundred and fifty men landed alive in Haiti from four hundred and twenty sent by General Grey on the short voyage from Guadeloupe. By the end of June only about half of the four thousand British troops now on the island were fit for duty. All the others, seventeen hundred men in all, were either dying or seriously ill. Out of the sixty-four officers who arrived in July thirty-four were dead within a few days, writhing in great pain and vomiting black bile.

A small army commanded by General Whyte and made up of a few hundred British regulars and French Royalists arrived meanwhile from

England and, backed by local Negro levies, attacked, captured and occupied the capital of Haiti, Port-au-Prince. Two months later forty of the British officers and six hundred of their men were dead of yellow fever. But the British were now masters of nearly all the towns and ports in northern, western and southern Haiti. Only Jacmel and Les Cayes were still in French hands.

By now General Toussaint L'Ouverture was fighting for the French. He had switched sides, not out of any particular love for the French, but because he had become convinced that if the British became masters of Haiti, they would join the Spaniards to drive the blacks back into slavery. Toussaint's cause was not the French Republic, but the blacks, his people. He believed in the French Republic's abolition of slavery. In fact the slaves were now free. But in the end the French Republic under First Consul Bonaparte would betray him, and them.

Two future sovereigns of Haiti, both black, both ex-slaves, were serving directly under Toussaint's orders. One, General Christophe, was a future king: Henry I. The other, General Dessalines, was a future emperor: Jacques I. Christophe, formerly a cook born in the British West Indies, probably Grenada, had already served in the French army against the British at Savannah, during the American War of Independence. Dessalines loathed all whites and had formerly been the lowest class of slave in the colony: the slave of a black man. He was ferocious, cruel, looked like a toad and could neither read nor write.

Toussaint, who now bore the title of lieutenant-governor, also had a number of European officers under him, including General Edmé Desfourneaux, a fire-eating ex-private from the army of Louis XVI. He had been in Haiti three years, been wounded five times and seems to have had an unfortunate tendency to get on everyone's nerves and be unwanted everywhere he went.

In 1795, the British in Haiti suffered a major setback when the Spaniards, under the terms of the Treaty of Basle, handed over their colony of Santo Domingo to the French. The whole island of Hispaniola was now united under French rule. General François Kerverseau took over the former Spanish territory for the French Republic and General Lavaux, worn out after years in the tropics, returned in 1796 to Europe. In Haiti Toussaint L'Ouverture now bore the title of commander-in-chief of the French forces. Anxious to show his loyalty to distant France, he sent his two sons, Placide and Isaac, to study in Paris.

Meanwhile however, with their habit of clinging to the last shred of territory, the British still retained two footholds at the western extremities of the island, at Jérémie in the south and Mole Saint-Nicolas in the north. At best they could become future Gibraltars in the West Indies, at worst bargaining chips in the game of power politics.

THE JERVIS-GREY DUET
The West Indies 1794

At this time, back among the Lesser Antilles to the east, in Barbados and the French islands of Martinique, Guadeloupe and St Lucia, both sides were nursing their wounds after the first clash and readying themselves for the next.

It came on February 5, 1794, in Martinique. On one side were two old British stalwarts: sixty-year-old Admiral John Jervis, future Earl of St Vincent, who had been in the Royal Navy since he was fifteen, and sixty-five-year-old General Charles Grey, first wounded at the Battle of Minden in 1759. On the French side were also a scattering of experienced generals, many of them lukewarm revolutionaries, cut off from France by the British blockade, short on funds, men and health, and all worried by the guillotine which awaited defeated generals at home in France.

Among these was General Rochambeau, the man in charge of Martinique, already a colonel at the time of the American Revolution, who had accompanied his general father to Yorktown. Young Rochambeau, as the veterans in the French camp at Newport, Rhode Island, used to call him, was now forty. He had been serving in the West Indian islands for the past two years. His fellow commander in Guadeloupe, General Georges Collot, forty-four, also a veteran of the American War of Independence, had been captured by the British during that war and had remained in North America until repatriated to France in 1783. The third of this trio of French generals was Nicolas Ricard, in command in St Lucia. At sixty-eight, he was old, loyal but tired, unable to understand or cope with all these calls for liberty, equality and fraternity, and longing for a little peace and quiet.

Grey and Jervis provided an admirable example of close army-navy cooperation, most unusual in that era when the two services so often hated each other. A month after their arrival in the Caribbean, the seven thousand-man British expeditionary force sailed for Martinique in a quasi-invincible squadron of five ships-of-the-line, seventeen frigates and nine sloops and corvettes. On arrival off the coast, the troops split into three divisions, one under General Prescott, another commanded by General Thomas Dundas, a third led by Colonel Gordon, and landed on three different spots on the island. The Martinique campaign lasted six weeks. Rochambeau, outnumbered, shut himself up with a few hundred men (six hundred according to the French, twelve hundred the British say) in the main fortress, the island capital, Fort Royal, and prepared for a siege and bombardment. It started on February 28. The fire was so intense that, according to Fortescue, 'hardly an inch of the fortress was untouched by shot'. Within two weeks, a third of Rochambeau's men were out of action, either victims of dysentery or of the British fire, both equally devastating to morale. But Rochambeau held on. 'I am working for history,' he wrote in his diary. History, however, has long forgotten the siege.

On March 20, Rochambeau surrendered. The survivors marched out with flags flying. Rochambeau, unwilling to test the guillotine in Paris, was allowed to return to Newport in the United States on parole.

Perhaps the outstanding feature of this campaign was the august presence among the British troops of His Royal Highness Prince Edward, Duke of Kent, son of George III, who had managed to tear himself away from the arms of his French-Canadian mistress in London, Madame St Laurent. The royal prince's main contribution to British history did not occur during this campaign, however, but twenty-five years later. Abandoning the amiable Madame St Laurent, whose life and charms he had been sharing for twenty-seven years, he married a German royal widow, Marie Louisa of Leiningen, and fathered the girl who became Queen Victoria. Prince Edward was still a pleasant young man in these eventful West Indian days. He had not yet begun to show himself the fussy general he ultimately became – so much so that years later he provoked a mutiny in Gibraltar, was recalled to London and never allowed to set foot again in the British Mediterranean fortress.

One of the more active British heroes of the Fort Royal fighting was Lieutenant Robert Faulknor, captain of the sloop HMS *Zebra*. Faulknor, in the words of Admiral Jervis's dispatch, 'ran the *Zebra* close to the wall of the fort, and leaping overboard at the head of the sloop's company, he assailed and took this important post before the boats [of the landing party] could get on shore.'

The admiral afterwards greeted Faulknor on the quarter-deck of the flagship, publicly embraced him, directed the ship's band to play 'See the conquering hero comes', promoted him captain on the spot and gave him the command of the 32-gun frigate HMS *Blanche*.

Having taken Martinique, General Grey and Admiral Jervis left old General Prescott – he was sixty-nine – behind as governor of the island and sailed off for the next round of fighting at St Lucia. This island was defended by General Ricard who only had a garrison of a hundred and twenty regulars and a few hundred local levies. The campaign lasted two days. Prince Edward led one of the landing parties, but the hero was the eccentric ex-Etonian, Colonel Sir Eyre Coote, who seventeen years before had carried the colours of his regiment at the Battle of Brooklyn against Washington during the American War of Independence. At the head of his regiment once again, he stormed the redoubt of Morne Fortuné, killing thirty enemy soldiers without losing any of his men.

General Ricard, summoned to surrender, asked what terms 'an old man who had served his King faithfully for forty years' could expect.

Offered parole and a passage to France, he thought of Paris in spring-time, the Seine, and the lovely Place de la Concorde. He also thought of the guillotine standing there, with its sharp blade silhouetted against the skyline, a blood-soaked basket under it. He decided he would go to the United States instead and join General Rochambeau in Newport.

The bulk of the British naval and land forces then moved on to Guadeloupe, governed by General Collot and the second island north of Martinique, for another quick victory.

Guadeloupe is made up of two more or less equal-sized parts separated by a narrow strip of water, the Rivière Salé, where, at the southern end, the capital, Pointe-à-Pitre stands, on the eastern part of the island. This is called Grande-Terre, while the other half of the island is Basse-Terre, with the main town of the same name located near its southern tip. So the campaign to capture Guadeloupe was divided into two parts. Both were carried out with the smoothness which characterised the Jervis-Grey partnership, described by Fortescue as 'an extra-ordinary example of a small but efficient army working in perfect harmony with a small and efficient squadron upon a fortified coast.'

The first strike was against Grande-Terre, near Pointe-à-Pitre. Prince Edward's detachment was ordered to take the hill of Morne Mascotte. General Thomas Dundas was sent to attack the more re-doubtable nearby fort of Fleur l'Epée and a third senior officer, Colonel Symes, marched off along the coast road. The attack against the fort was carried out by a combined force of British soldiers, sailors and marines, in the early dawn light, on April 12. The brave Captain Faulknor led the bluejackets and was nearly killed twice. One French soldier stabbed him with a bayonet which missed his body and cut harmlessly through his sleeve. Another French soldier tackled him round the neck, forced him down to the ground by sheer brute strength, wrenched the sword out of his hand and had his arm raised to stab him when two 'of my seamen flew to my relief and saved my life', Faulknor wrote to his mother. By the evening, Grande-Terre was in British hands.

Two days later it was Basse-Terre's turn to endure the British assault. After a week of combat and skirmishes General Collot surrendered and asked to join his colleagues from Martinique and St Lucia in the United States. The guillotine in Paris clearly had a discouraging effect on defeated French generals. None of them wanted to go back to France.

His glory won, Prince Edward sailed away in Faulknor's ship to Halifax on the first lap of his voyage home to Madame St Laurent. 'His Royal Highness was a pleasant, kind companion,' Faulknor wrote to his mother, who must have been very impressed by her son's social standing.

When Collot too sailed away, General Dundas, with the courtesy

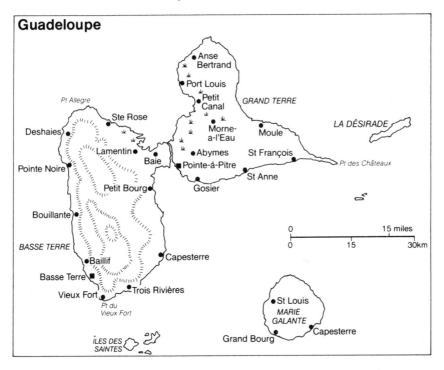

Guadeloupe

Anse Bertrand
Port Louis
Petit Canal
GRAND TERRE
Pt Allegre
Ste Rose
LA DÉSIRADE
Deshaies
Morne-a-l'Eau
Moule
Lamentin
Baie
Abymes
St François
Pointe Noire
Pointe-á-Pitre
Pt des Châteaux
St Anne
Petit Bourg
Gosier
Bouillante
0   15 miles
0   15   30km
BASSE TERRE
Baillif
Capesterre
Basse Terre
Vieux Fort
Trois Rivières
St Louis
Pt du Vieux Fort
MARIE GALANTE
Capesterre
ÎLES DES SAINTES
Grand Bourg

that often marked the conduct of gentlemanly enemies towards each other, came to the quayside to bid him farewell and Godspeed to the United States. He then took over the governorship of the island.

These quick victories over the French must have been sweet moments for the British officers, many of whom had fought against the Americans during the War of Independence and who felt that France's entry on the Yankee side had been responsible for the British defeat. Which, of course, it had.

GUILLOTINE IN GUADELOUPE
The West Indies 1794-1796

Six weeks after taking over Guadeloupe Dundas was a dead man. On the last day of May he got up from a meal, said he didn't feel well and was going to lie down. He had yellow fever and was never to leave his bed again.

Two days later, Victor Hugues, the former public prosecutor at Rochefort and Brest, arrived off Guadeloupe with two frigates, a brig, six transports, 1,153 French Republican soldiers, a guillotine and a copy of the decree emancipating the slaves. For he was the new governor, sent out by Robespierre to Guadeloupe to defend the island after news of the capture of Martinique had reached Paris. Now his island too was occupied by the British, but he intended to take over his post whoever and whatever stood in his way.

Who stood in his way was the dying General Dundas and eight thousand British soldiers in the islands. What stood in his way was Admiral Jervis's squadron of fourteen ships-of-the-line and frigates in nearby Barbados.

Yet Hugues triumphed. In his own way, he was a military genius, possessed of unflagging courage and motivated by a refusal ever to admit defeat or the superiority of the enemy. Had he not been such a loathsome specimen of humanity he would deserve a revered place in French history. For he recaptured Guadeloupe after a six-months campaign, temporarily retook St Lucia, and organised and encouraged revolts in all the British West Indian islands, notably by the Carib Indians in St Vincent and by the Negroes in Grenada. For five years he set the West Indies ablaze.

However much we would like to ignore this unpleasant man, we cannot do so. He influenced events too much. And he wasted no time. Within a few hours of his arrival he had landed his troops and, brushing aside unexpectedly weak British resistance, he retook the Fleur l'Épée fort, the capture of which had earned Captain Faulknor such distinction. The British evacuated Pointe-à-Pitre and the French seized the town, the port and eighty-seven merchant vessels, mostly schooners, in the harbour. The reconquest of Guadeloupe was about to begin.

For the French, the timing of Hugues's arrival had been ideal. Jervis and his fleet were absent and the British command on the island was completely distraught and disorganised by Dundas's approaching death.

Hugues's first action after occupying Pointe-à-Pitre was to unload the guillotine and set it up in the public square. That gesture, in itself, symbolises the man's character. At the same time he waved the copy of the recent (February 4) decree granting freedom to the slaves. The result was as could be expected: the blacks, elated by their freedom, flocked to his side, and Royalist sympathisers flocked in the opposite direction, out of Pointe-à-Pitre to join the British troops in the island.

An Anglo-American (for want of a better word to describe his quality) visitor, who was in Pointe-à-Pitre at the time, was captured but managed to escape before Hugues's men could discover who he was. He called himself Anderson but his real name was Benedict Arnold. At one time a major-general in the American army, he had betrayed his country and was on a business trip in the island – although one wonders in what business the old traitor could be engaged in this French West Indian island. He was taken to a converted prison ship but escaped the same day on a raft and reached the British lines where he demanded, as a British officer of considerable seniority, to take over the British troops. But somehow General

Grey managed to retain command.

Fighting in Guadeloupe spread rapidly. Each side was eager to eject the other from the island, and each thought it had the advantage: the British had the numbers, the French had the enthusiasm.

The British were in Guadeloupe in force. Grey had learnt on June 5 in Barbados the news of Hugues's landing. By the 7th he was back in Guadeloupe with substantial reinforcements. The British were determined to throw the French out before they could secure a strong footing on the island. They tried several times to recapture Fort Fleur l'Epée. Continual fighting went on around Pointe-à-Pitre. Finally, checked all along the line, Grey took all his troops out of Grande-Terre and removed himself, his British and his French Royalist troops over to Basse-Terre, there to consider what to do next.

The ball was no longer in the British camp. At least if it was they didn't know what to do with it – and that even though they had numerical superiority in both men and ships. Jervis lay off Pointe-à-Pitre with six ships-of-the-line, a dozen frigates and corvettes, five gunboats and sixteen transports.

Eventually Grey came ashore again with some troops. He tried again, but half-heartedly, to recapture Fort Fleur l'Epée, began a heavy shelling of Pointe-à-Pitre and launched a grand assault on the French positions. It was a total fiasco. Some of the British attacking columns were lost during the night attack, blundered into the streets of the town, fired into each other, blew themselves up when they set fire to a house in which explosives were stored and finally withdrew with their commander, Colonel Symes, mortally wounded.

The time had come for General Grey to do some serious strategic thinking. He left Grande-Terre in the hands of Hugues, ordered hefty contingents to remain and defend Basse-Terre and sailed away to Martinique, safely in British hands.

A British army of eighteen hundred men under General Colin Graham was left at Camp Berville just over the Rivière Salè that separated the two portions of Guadeloupe. Graham's command also included an additional battalion of about nine hundred local French royalists and three hundred blacks and men-of-colour. Their orders were to prevent Hugues from breaking out from Grande-Terre and across into adjoining Basse-Terre where, near the town of the same name, the main British occupation force was entrenched at Fort St Charles under old General Prescott, an irascible but clean fighter, always respected by his enemies.

The siege of Berville that followed ended in a French Republican victory, but it was a disgrace to both French victor and British vanquished. Hugues conducted himself afterwards like the sadistic mass-murderer he was. General Graham's surrender was understandable, for his troops were decimated by fever and rum. Three hundred and fifty of his soldiers had died in August and on September 1st, fifteen hundred of his men were on the sick list. But he dishonoured himself by accepting Hugues's capitulation terms.

With its dead, sick and wounded, Camp Berville was a stinking charnel house. Graham asked for terms and surrendered on October 7 on the sole condition that his British troops should march out with the honours of war and be shipped home by the first available vessels.

'One hundred and twenty-five ghastly figures staggered out of the lines,' says Fortescue. A French account says fourteen hundred British troops surrendered on that day.

Whichever figure is correct – and they are probably both wrong – is irrelevant. What is indisputable is that the French Royalists, perhaps more used to the tropical climate, seemed to be nearly all quite fit and, before the capitulation, their commander, Count de Richebois, had requested permission from General Graham for him and his men to cut their way out and make their way down to Basse-Terre, to join General Prescott. Permission was refused.

When Graham surrendered, he cravenly abandoned eight hundred and sixty-five white French Royalists and some three hundred Negroes and mulattos to the mercy of Hugues, only obtaining authorisation for a boatload, twenty-two men in all (including de Richebois), to row to HMS *Boyne*, one of the British warships lying offshore.

Immediately after the surrender Hugues ordered the executions to begin. Three hundred and sixty-five French Royalists were shot in batches. Hugues then ordered up the guillotine. But it was too slow. After twenty-seven Royalists had been decapitated, the remaining four hundred and seventy-three, tied together, were shot on the camp parapets and kicked over the side, whether dead or only wounded, into the sea. Whitened bones, picked clean by fish and sea birds could still be found scattered in the sand a few years ago.

Hugues spared the coloured men and the slaves, on the grounds either that they had been forced to follow their masters or that they did not understand what they were doing. Even this little sign of mercy soon vanished. In the months that followed, to deal with those emancipated slaves who could not always discriminate between slavery and forced labour for a nominal wage – daily long hours of toil in a plantation under a tropical sun were not part of the old West African tradition – Hugues reintroduced the guillotine.

Four days after the capture of Camp Berville, the French Republicans were on the move again, this time to attack the town of Basse-Terre, defended by General Prescott. The recently promoted General Pelardy was given the command of the new operation and Hugues added a second new general to his military establishment: his brother-in-law, Marie-Auguste Paris. Paris, who in spite of his name was from the Pyrenees region, had accompanied Hugues to Guadeloupe as a lieutenant. His promotion to general was even more rapid than Bonaparte's at Toulon but, one feels, with less reason.

Within a few days the town of Basse-Terre was in French Republican hands while General Prescott's forces, holed up in Fort St Charles (or Fort Matilda as the British called it) prepared to withstand another siege. As soon as he had taken the town, the psychopathic Hugues once again went on the rampage. He ordered the corpse of General Dundas, who now had been dead for four months, to be dug out of its grave, taken to the main square, placed on the guillotine and beheaded. Bits of rotting corpse were then scattered over the public highways to be eaten by vultures. On Hugues's orders, a monument was then erected on the site of the former grave: 'This ground,' said an inscription, 'restored to liberty by the valour of the Republicans, was polluted by the body of Thomas Dundas, major general and governor of Guadeloupe for the bloody King George the Third.'

With the best will in the world, one can only abominate Victor Hugues, whatever the success of his enterprises.

Strangely enough, very little is known about the origins of this vile creature. He is said to have been born in Marseille on July 21, 1762 and to have been a baker in his early life. He went to Haiti with his brother as a young man and they opened a bread shop. Victor Hugues's brother was killed in the slave uprising of 1791, and the shop burnt down in the riots. Hugues returned to France soon after the death of his brother and became, so to speak, a professional revolutionary. During some period of his life, Hugues also served as mate on a merchant ship and became friends with a sailor called Conseil, as ruffianly as himself, who later accompanied him to Guadeloupe.

In his book *The Loss of Eldorado*, Trinidad-born writer V.S. Naipaul describes Hugues before his arrival in Guadeloupe as 'a failed hairdresser, failed innkeeper, failed ship's master, later a lieutenant in the French army'. Naipaul says he was a West Indian mulatto, and Fortescue also describes him so. But for Sainte-Croix de la Roncière, a French writer from Guadeloupe who wrote a book on him in 1932, Hugues was a typical citizen of the noisy Mediterranean city of Marseille, with a strong local accent, vain and voluble, with grey eyes and fair, sparse hair. Nothing very mulatto-sounding there. Another clue, dating from 1800, gives a very different impression. Royal Navy Lieutenant Paul, of the frigate HMS *Nereide*, wrote to his father that year from the West Indies, after Hugues was captured at sea. 'I am now keeping guard over the famous black captain, Victor Hugues, who has done so much mischief to our country this war, and who has been so long commander of Guadeloupe.' Presumably Lieutenant Paul had plenty of time to watch his prisoner and see what he looked like. But whether black, mulatto or white, Victor Hugues was the nearest human equivalent to a monster.

While his troops laid siege to Prescott's army in the old fort, Hugues set up an itinerant military tribunal headed at first by his old friend Conseil, which travelled from village to village in the island, taking its portable guillotine everywhere it went. To be tried meant virtually to be found guilty. To be found guilty meant to lose one's head. Conseil carried out his duties so efficiently that Hugues promoted him and gave him the command of the frigate *La Pique*.

General Prescott, meanwhile, was hanging on desperately in Fort St Charles with his diseased and dying garrison. Isolated and without re-inforcements, he received orders from Martinique to evacuate the fort. During the night of December 10, the 32-gun frigate HMS *Terpsichore* came in quietly offshore; the British survivors climbed silently down the cliffside and sailed away.

Jervis and Grey had left Martinique for home a fortnight earlier, under suspicion of dubious real estate deals, a favourite and very lucra-tive pastime of British (and French) officers in the islands, and had been replaced by Admiral Caldwell and Sir John Vaughan.

The Guadeloupe campaign was now over and, for the next eighteen months or so, it was the French who were now on the offensive and the British on the defensive. The two sides could, in the meantime, begin to add up their losses. These were extensive. The tropics were the white man's grave. Not even the bloodiest battles in Europe could rival them, proportionally, in terms of dead bodies.

French and British suffered equally. The yellow-fever bearing mos-quitoes bit the soldiers of both sides impartially. Of the seven thousand soldiers who had originally sailed with Grey from Britain, at least five thousand were now corpses. The officer casualties in the island of Mar-tinique highlighted the deadly nature of the disease: twenty-seven of General Grey's officers were killed in the fight for the island, or died of wounds, a hundred and seventy died of yellow fever. On the French side, some four-fifths of Hugues's original force were dead: some had been killed outright in the fighting, some died of wounds, but most were victims of yellow fever.

Until reinforcements could come from France through the British blockade, Hugues had to depend on local recruits, mainly black and mulatto. Providentially, troop reinforcements did arrive in January 1795, bringing fifteen hundred soldiers according to the historian Sainte Croix de la Roncière, six thousand according to Fortescue.

The arrival of these ships led to a spirited duel between the French ship *La Pique*, commanded by the villainous Conseil, and HMS *Blanche*, commanded by the gallant Faulknor, back recently from Halifax. Conseil had gone out to protect the convoy, Faulknor to attack it. It was a hard fought, ship-to-ship contest that lasted nearly twenty-four hours in which Conseil who, whatever his faults, did not lack guts, tried repeatedly to lay his ship alongside the *Blanche* and board, the favourite French and privateer method of conducting naval warfare. Finally, the French captain tried to ram his enemy on the port quarter, only to be blasted out of the water by the British guns as his bowsprit smashed into the British frigate's capstan.

Faulknor, always in the middle of every fight, was lashing the *Pique*'s bowsprit to his shattered capstan when he fell dead, shot through the heart. Britain that day lost another Nelson. But his crewmen secured the French ship, which could no longer aim its guns, and the *Blanche* began to pour raking shots into the now defenceless *Pique* until she surrendered. Casualties were heavy on both sides. *La Pique* had a hundred and one men killed (including, one hopes, the unsavoury Conseil) and ninety-six wounded. On HMS *Blanche*, eighty-three officers and men were killed, and ninety wounded.

The battle between *La Pique* and HMS *Blanche* became one of the patriotic inspirations of the time. An engraving of 'The Death of Captain Faulknor', by Stothard, hung on the wall in many patriotic English homes, and a monument was erected for the brave captain in St Paul's Cathedral. Now he is just one of the forgotten naval heroes of Britain, one of many, overshadowed, as all sailors were, by the towering historical figure of Nelson.

Hugues, for his part, was the most active of French patriots. Long after the Terror had ceased in France, it continued in Guadeloupe. Three guillotines were functioning on the island: one in Basse-Terre, one in Pointe-à-Pitre and one in the countryside. About twelve hundred supposed Royalists were executed. It is said that the population in Guadeloupe is darker in colour today than that of Martinique because so many white men were sent to the guillotine by Victor Hugues.

There was no limit to Hugues's baseness. He was as depraved sexually as he was mentally. To seduce a young, well-bred, married lady of Guadeloupe, Mme de Lacroix, he had one of her friends arrested. When Mme de Lacroix agitatedly came to plead for her friend's life, he listened to her without saying a word, then pushed her onto the couch and raped her. 'Madam, your friend's life is now saved,' he told her as he buttoned up his pants afterwards. Mme de Lacroix, who was married to a ship's captain, died, so the story says, of shame.

In spite of his criminal instincts and his depravity, Hugues believed in bourgeois values, notably in private enterprise, which he practised assiduously. By organising and fitting out in Guadeloupe dozens of privateers, often more pirate than patriots, he amassed a vast fortune. The British seemed powerless to hinder him. Against an immensely more powerful enemy with a large fleet and several ships-of-the-line, he seemed to be all over the Caribbean.

More than any man of his time, he was responsible for the only armed conflict that has ever been fought between the United States and

France, which he provoked by his unrelenting attacks on American shipping.

Between October 1795 and October 1797, a period of exactly two years, Guadeloupe corsairs acting under his direction captured no less than eight hundred and eighty ships of which the great majority flew the Stars and Stripes. Not surprisingly the United States decided to attack all French ships on sight in retaliation.

His island campaigns on land, against the British, however, were the most spectacular. Hugues began by attacking, one by one, the islands of the Lesser Antilles, starting in March 1795 with the most distant, Grenada.

In a few months, helped by a black uprising in the island led by the mulatto Fédon, all of Grenada with the exception of the capital, St Georges, was his. So was St Lucia. Although British technically, the two islands had once been French and their loyalty to Britain had always been rather unsteady. The blacks also knew that a return to French rule meant the end of slavery. They were ready and willing for a change.

The British hold on Martinique, however, was too strong for Hugues. A French detachment of some one hundred and twenty men landed there from St Lucia, hoping their arrival would provoke a mass uprising. When nothing happened they tiptoed back to their boats and returned to St Lucia, glad to be alive – for the British had announced they would execute as spies any French interlopers on the island.

In Dominica, also once French, the local Negroes proved loyal to Britain, much to the disgust of Hugues. There was a French raid on Anguilla, and his soldiers also landed to rather better effect on some of the minor specks in the Caribbean sea, such as St Eustasius and St Martin, belonging to the Dutch, which was split in two and remains to this day half French and half Dutch.

The hardest fighting was in the green, mountainous island of St Vincent with its razor-sharp ridges and deep precipices, where the Caribs, the last original Indian survivors of the original Caribbean population, rose up against their British masters. They were often officered by Frenchmen and at first the fighting against this Carib-French army was led by General Sir Paulus Aemilius Irving, son of Colonel Paulus Aemilius Irving, a family with obvious classical interests as well as military ones.

But nemesis for the French in the West Indies, and for the unfortunate Caribs also, came in the person of another soldier, one of the most humane, courtly and chivalrous officers of the British army, doughty, brave, ageing (he was sixty-one) General Sir Ralph Abercromby, of Scotland. One of the great soldiers of his times, he had been dispatched to the Caribbean by a British government anxious to see an end to the confusion in the Antilles. Soon afterwards, as one of his chief aides, came young Brigadier-General John Moore, a Lowlander from Glasgow whom, just over two years ago, we left a colonel, in a boat off Corsica, on his way back to England, in semi-disgrace after his tussles with Sir Gilbert Elliot and Captain Horatio Nelson.

GENOCIDE AND THE YELLOW JACK
The West Indies 1796-1797

From the moment that Abercromby arrived in the West Indies in March 1796 the blitz, to use a modern word, was on.

But the journey out had been a near disaster. After serving against the French general, Pichegru, in the Flanders campaign, the general had been ordered to the West Indies in November 1795 as commander-in-chief of an army of twelve thousand. Abercromby sailed from Chatham on December 3 in a large convoy commanded by Admiral Sir Hugh Cloberry Christian (a relative of the better known HMS *Bounty* mutineer Fletcher Christian). He ran immediately into a horrendous winter gale which scattered the British expeditionary force all over the ocean. After seven weeks at sea, Abercromby had sailed only a few dozen miles. On January 29, 1796, the expedition put into Portsmouth for repairs and rest.

Abercromby counted his ships and found that a hundred out of a hundred and thirty were missing. Some had been forced onto the French coast and captured, one was blown straight through the Straits of Gibraltar into the Mediterranean, many had sunk to the bottom and the bodies of British soldiers and sailors fed the seagulls on the English south coast for weeks afterwards.

Most of the vessels, however, had in fact survived the storm and in dribs and drabs they reached Barbados before their general, who arrived on March 17.

General Abercromby was accompanied by his son John, a twenty-five-year-old lieutenant-colonel, who served on his staff as personal secretary, and whose job consisted largely of reading maps for his father and, during the fighting, of describing to him was was happening and where and who was doing what, for General Abercromby was exceedingly short-sighted. But as soon as he reached a battlefield, he knew how to strike, and strike fast. His prey now were the French-occupied West Indian islands: St Lucia, Grenada, St Vincent. But not Guadeloupe itself, the heart and core of Republican France in the Caribbean. Victor Hugues's reputation was his best protection.

The first target was Grenada. Once in Barbados, Abercromby took just the time required – one week – to assemble a few detachments to add to the six hundred British soldiers holding Grenada's capital, St Georges, under General Nicolls's command. The rest of the island was occupied by French-led rebels. Within a few days Abercromby had re-occupied most of the island and, promising General Nicolls he would soon be back, he then sailed north to attack St Lucia. For this new expedition he relied mainly on General John Moore who arrived in Barbados on April 13.

On the same day that this expedition sailed for St Lucia, another, under General John Whyte, sailed from Barbados to attack the Dutch – who had just switched sides from the British to the French – in their colony of Demerara (Dutch Guyana) on the South American mainland.

Eight thousand British troops landed on St Lucia on April 27. Three separate landings were made – this was the usual British tactic in these island attacks – so as to disperse the enemy force. Fighting went on for a month until the French defender, General Goyrand, holding out in the fortress of Morne Fortuné, capitulated on May 24. Its two thousand defenders, only ninety of whom were white, marched out and laid down their arms, many to become slaves again, this time with British masters.

After the capture of St Lucia, Abercromby didn't waste any time but sailed back south, to finish the Grenada campaign and then to go on to St Vincent and capture that island. He left General Moore, as his deputy, in command at St Lucia. 'Everything is to be expected from his spirit and good sense,' Abercromby wrote to his superiors in London.

Hundreds of armed Negroes were still hiding in the St Lucia jungle. They were officially called 'brigands' but they were probably only ordinary men determined never to be slaves again. It was Moore's unenviable task to round them up. He must have hated the operation. Stern and just, he shared his soldiers' hardships and lived, we are told, on salt pork and biscuits, which sounds dreadfully British. Surely he must have eaten an occasional banana or two, or a mango, or a pineapple, as tropical fruits grow plentifully in this lush island?

Yellow fever, as usual, decimated the troops on the island. Moore fell ill but survived. Total British casualties during the month of fighting had amounted to six hundred in killed and wounded, but in one regiment alone, eight hundred and sixty-three officers and men died from the disease. Moore had been left in the island with a garrison of four thousand when the fighting ended in May. By November, fifteen hundred were dead, nearly all of the Yellow Jack.

Further south the Abercromby offensive was under-way on Grenada and St Vincent. In June, the general ordered Generals Nicolls and Campbell to go to the attack in Grenada and recapture all the island, and to General Knox and Colonel Dickens to do the same in St Vincent. He managed to supervise personally both operations.

The fighting in Grenada took ten days. Fédon, the French leader, a mulatto, managed to escape but although the island had been British only for the past ten years, fourteen of the French colonists who had joined Fédon were hanged as traitors to the British Crown, and another sixty-six were sent to prison in England.

The fighting in St Vincent was tougher and went on longer. Many of the men fighting against the British were Carib Indians, survivors of the original Spanish holocaust of the seventeenth century, and temperamentally more sympathetic towards the light-hearted French than the stolid British. The Caribs were tough and determined fighters and it took Abercromby four months and four thousand soldiers to beat them. When the first large body of Caribs offered to surrender in July on condition they could keep their land, Abercromby offered them their lives only. The Indians then went back to their guns.

Martin Padre, the French commander in the island (he was a Negro from St Lucia), finally surrendered on October 2. The British found they held 5,080 Carib Indian prisoners, men, women and children. Their land was sold or given away to officers; this type of real-estate transaction, although it led to gross abuses, was considered normal. Even Abercromby received his share.

In March 1797, the Carib survivors were shipped to the island of Rattan, off Honduras, where half of them died of the plague in the next five months. The survivors were largely absorbed by the Hondurans. So this people vanished from our planet.

It is unfortunate that a man of General Abercromby's moral stature should have been associated with what we would call today an act of genocide. But genocide, as a criminal concept, did not come into being until the mid-twentieth century, and we prefer to remember Sir Ralph Abercromby for other achievements. He was open-minded, outspoken, a liberal in politics and, when he was elected to Parliament, he refused to defend the personal interests of some of his wealthy constituents. He had also refused, at considerable sacrifice to himself, to fight against the American colonists, judging their cause to be just, a stand unlikely to make him popular with King George III or with the British military establishment. Unlike many officers of his day, he was most attentive to his men's welfare. During the West Indian campaign, he forbade the holding of parades in the heat of the sun, sent the sick to mountain resorts and had uniforms changed to suit the climate. When back in Britain, he tried to find jobs for the soldiers who had served under him. He was probably, before the emergence of Wellington, the finest soldier in the British army.

After the capture of French St Vincent, Abercromby quickly and methodically set about attacking the territories of France's allies in the region. That meant Spain as well as Holland. The Dutch territories of Demerara, Essequibo and Berbice, on the mainland, all fell rapidly. In February 1797, in a one-day operation, he occupied Spanish Trinidad at the cost of one British casualty. He then moved on to tackle Puerto Rico, leaving as governor of Trinidad Colonel Thomas Picton, who later made his name in the Spanish campaign and lost his life at the Battle of Waterloo. Puerto Rico proved too strong for British arms and thus failed to join the British Empire, but a hundred and one years later it was acquired by the United States.

During the course of the next two or three years, after Abercromby's departure and before the Treaty of Amiens came into force in 1801, the British occupied the Dutch colonies of Curaçao, St Eustatius, Saba and St Martin (some of which the Republican French had taken over). When Denmark and Sweden became involved in the conflict, Britain promptly occupied the Swedish West Indian island of St Bartholomew and the Danish islands of St Thomas, St John and St Croix. But the British continued to abstain prudently from any raids on Victor Hugues's Guadeloupe and even more prudently withdrew from the disease-ridden mortuary that was Haiti, filled with so many British dead.

The survivors from that island had one man to thank: General Thomas Maitland.

THE BLACK STANDARD OF REVOLT
Haiti 1796-1798

Maitland, who had served briefly in Haiti before, had sailed from England in the same convoy as General Moore. He replaced General John Simcoe who was commanding the operations in Haiti, after having founded the town of London in the Canadian province of Ontario (it was then called Upper Canada).

General Maitland was the exception among successive British generals in Haiti. He knew exactly what he had to do: to get himself and his army out.

Disentanglement had long been the only sensible policy, but it was Sir Thomas Maitland who made it possible. His aim, at the same time, was to secure the best conditions for future British trade and to make the situation as unbearable as he could for the French, once the British had evacuated the island. It was a simple plan, not particularly honourable, but far less dishonourable than the policy the French would soon be practising: brutal repression.

But before the British could leave, careful negotiations had to be undertaken between His Britannic Majesty's representatives and the black commander in chief of the French Republic, 'the monkey' as some of the French in the island, jealous of his fame and importance, called Toussaint. The new French government commissioner, General Gabriel d'Hedouville, to his intense fury, was carefully bypassed during negotiations between blacks and Britons.

Confident of his own strength, Toussaint bluntly told General Maitland that unless the British left their two bases on the western edge of this island, Jérémie and Mole Saint-Nicolas, he would attack them with twenty thousand men. He and General Maitland met near Mole Saint-Nicolas. In the name of the British government Maitland offered recognition of Toussaint as king, protection against the French, a trade pact between the two countries, and British assistance in securing a trade agreement between Haiti and the United States. Toussaint showed no interest in becoming king and refused to be protected against the French. But he was all in favour of more trade and he also accepted as a gift from George III the silver table service used at the banquet in his honour.

On October 2, 1798, the survivors of the British army marched away to their waiting ships and sailed out of Haiti's tortured history.

General Maitland went back to London to present the treaty to Pitt's government and, with their genius for snatching victory out of defeat, the British presented their army's departure from Haiti as a moral triumph in which Britain had managed to obtain independence for Haiti.

D'Hedouville, who had been fuming and fulminating in the wings ever since his arrival, took ship back to France, and three days later, on October 25, Toussaint L'Ouverture became the governor of Haiti in the name of the French Republic.

Before his departure, however, Hedouville made sure the hatred which existed between blacks and mulattos in the island would intensify. He promoted the mulatto Rigaud to the same military rank as the black Toussaint, declared Rigaud's command in the south independent from that of Toussaint and ordered Rigaud to act independently from Toussaint. The stage was set for a racial war.

Toussaint acted more and more as chief of an independent state. In particular he negotiated a trade and shipping agreement with President John Adams of the United States at a time when the USA and France were engaged in their semi-war. In his man-to-man letter to the United States president, Toussaint referred to himself as 'Général-en-chef de l'Armée de Saint-Domingue' and to Haiti as 'la République de St Domingue'. Accounts of his agreement with Britain began to appear in the London press in which the blacks, previously 'so shamefully stained by their creator', at last seemed accepted as human beings.

'All men of virtue [presumably that was a reference to the English] will rejoice at the sight of the standard of the black people, which now flies proudly high,' ended a *London Gazette* article unctuously. Still, the British in Haiti had been no worse than the French; but if not quite as brutal, not quite as cynical, they had been considerably more hypocritical. That is the price for having a good conscience. Or pretending to have.

PLUCK THE GILLS OF THE GALLIC COCK
The US/French confrontation 1794-1799

When the French Revolution broke out, the Americans cheered. It is flattering to be imitated and the influence of the American Revolution was discernible in this major upheaval of French society. At first the American Republic welcomed Republican France. But the cheering declined as the more virulent French revolutionaries took over, and it stopped completely when they cut off the head of the king.

Citizen Genet, the tactless and bullying French envoy to the United States, antagonised even more Americans when, invoking the terms of the 1778 alliance between France and the United States, he tried to raise an army in the United States to invade Spanish Florida, and to commission and man in American ports privateers flying the Tricolour.

Most Americans resented the French argument that American support for France was an unalienable right that the French had won at Yorktown. Gratitude rarely influences politics and the majority of Americans were not interested in helping their old ally. They considered the war overseas none of their business.

Their business was to do business – with everybody, French and British – and the war provided them with vast opportunities. Neutral ships were greatly advantaged by the rules of war. According to the maritime laws of the time belligerents did not interfere with neutrals' trading activities, and since the British navy dominated the seas and intercepted many French ships the moment they left harbour, the French were happy to give American vessels the right to trade between North America and the French West Indian islands, as well as with France itself.

But then Britain changed the rules, announcing a new policy of 'visit and search' for neutral ships, under which those discovered to be bound for French ports could be seized and their cargoes confiscated. Anxious not to antagonise Britain, whose powerful navy hovered off its shores, the United States then signed an agreement, Jay's Treaty, in London on November 19, 1794. Under this treaty, in return for wide British concessions, trade between the United States and Britain was now organised on the supposed basis of 'reciprocal and perfect liberty' but many of its terms were vague. Some of the clauses, however, were painfully clear, notably those imposing severe restrictions on American trade in the West Indies. From now on American shipping would accept British law on the high seas. France and the French islands would therefore be out of bounds to American ships.

The French were furious. They had a point. They maintained that since the United States was not defending its rights as a neutral nation against Britain, it was, in fact, helping France's enemy. And therefore, seeing that the Royal Navy, with official US approval, could now seize an American vessel and its cargo if it was considered to be carrying war contraband to the French, the French navy would do the same: any American ship carrying supplies to the British would now be considered a legitimate prize.

In Guadeloupe, Victor Hugues gleefully rubbed his hands, told his corsairs to go ahead and attack, and to make no difference between British and American vessels – all cargo the neutral Americans carried would be considered contraband. He sent his ruffianly sailors in their hundreds scouring the nearby seas. One of them was Jean Laffite, to become in a few years one of the great heroes of the Battle of New Orleans. Privateers and French naval vessels were active off Europe also.

Guadeloupe became the emporium of the West Indies as hundreds of American and other neutral or enemy ships and their cargoes were confiscated by the corsairs. The Americans estimated their overall losses from 1794 to 1797 at $25 million, a huge sum in those days. A State Department official, Somerville P. Tuck came up in his report 'French Spoliations' with the figure of 1,571 vessels taken by the French. Hugues's corsairs were responsible for between one third and one half of these losses. According to Hugues's own claims, 563 of the 880 vessels captured by Guadeloupe privateers from October 1795 to October 1797 were American.

In spite of the British blockade (which was rather ineffective in the islands), Guadeloupe was booming. Rum flowed in vast quantities and 'La Marseillaise' was the hit song of all the taverns. The bars, brothels and gambling dens of Pointe-à-Pitre and Basse-Terre were busy twenty-four hours a day. The favourite meeting place of the corsairs was the café 'Le Rendez-vous des Sans-Culottes' where the sailors liked to carouse all night, smash the crockery, send the empty bottles flying across the room and gamble away their money. Hugues, it is said, often joined the corsairs in their fun and games ashore.

The guillotine was busy, also. Because the smell of blood under the guillotine inconvenienced passersby and encouraged flies, an improved gutter system was installed. During the first two years of Hugues's reign six thousand whites were executed or forced to flee.

When Spain and the Netherlands joined the French, the corsairs began operating out of their territories too. Goods filled the warehouses, and while Hugues and his two brothers-in-law, General Boudet and General Paris, were amassing fortunes, stranded American skippers and seamen, whose ships had been taken at cutlass or gun point, wondered desperately how they could get back home. Fletcher Pratt, in his history of the United States navy, gives the text of an appeal sent to State Secretary Thomas Pickering and signed on June 12, 1797 by the masters of twenty-seven American vessels brought into the

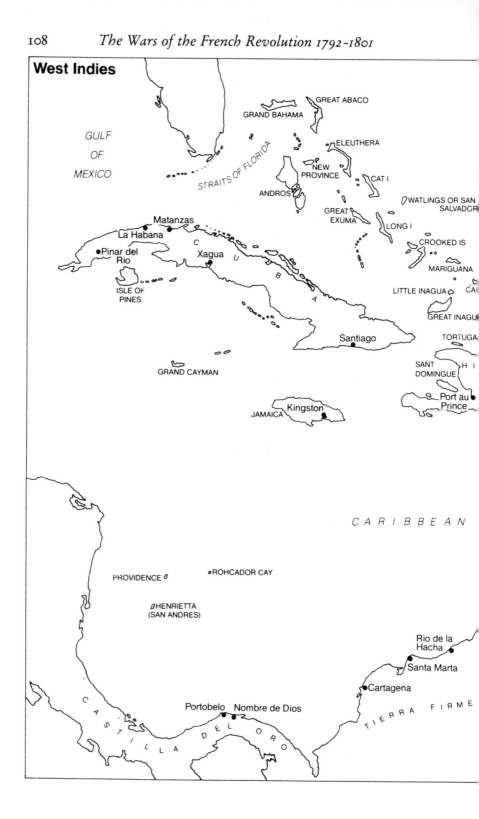

West Indies

GULF
OF
MEXICO

GREAT ABACO

GRAND BAHAMA

ELEUTHERA

STRAITS OF FLORIDA

NEW
PROVINCE

CAT I

ANDROS

WATLINGS OR SAN
SALVADOR

Matanzas

GREAT
EXUMA

LONG I

La Habana

Pinar del
Rio

Xagua

C
U
B
A

CROOKED IS

MARIGUANA

ISLE OF
PINES

LITTLE INAGUA

CA

GREAT INAGU

Santiago

TORTUGA

GRAND CAYMAN

SANT
DOMINGUE

H I

Port au
Prince

Kingston

JAMAICA

CARIBBEAN

PROVIDENCE

ROHCADOR CAY

HENRIETTA
(SAN ANDRES)

Rio de la
Hacha

Santa Marta

Cartagena

Portobelo Nombre de Dios

TIERRA FIRME

CASTILLA DEL ORO

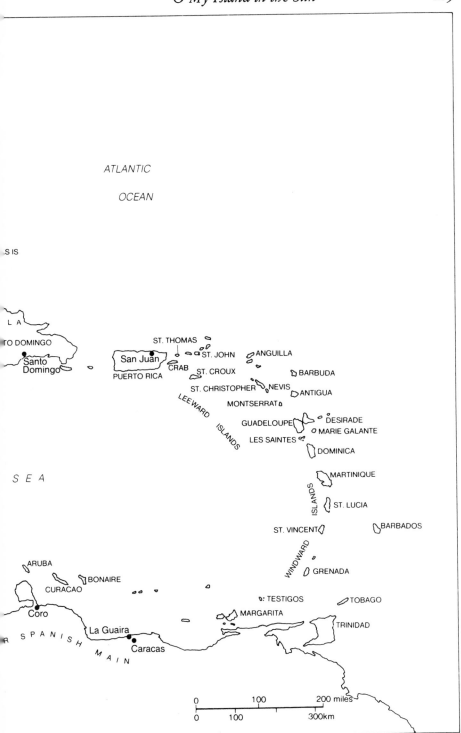

ATLANTIC

OCEAN

S IS

L A

TO DOMINGO

Santo
Domingo

San Juan

ST. THOMAS
ST. JOHN   ANGUILLA
CRAB
PUERTO RICA   ST. CROUX   BARBUDA
ST. CHRISTOPHER   NEVIS
                          ANTIGUA
LEEWARD   MONTSERRAT
                 GUADELOUPE   DESIRADE
        ISLANDS   MARIE GALANTE
              LES SAINTES
                          DOMINICA

S E A   MARTINIQUE

                    ISLANDS   ST. LUCIA

              ST. VINCENT   BARBADOS

ARUBA   WINDWARD
      BONAIRE   GRENADA
CURACAO
                          TESTIGOS   TOBAGO
Coro   MARGARITA
      La Guaira   TRINIDAD
R S P A N I S H
      M A I N   Caracas

0   100   200 miles
0   100   300km

Cuban port of Santiago by French corsairs. 'The Captains, Masters and people are put on Shore, deprived of their money & means of getting their bread,' the marooned signatories ended their letter bitterly.

The United States could not continue to accept the attacks on its shipping. But during these first two years it simply lacked the force to fight back. It had no navy. It had an army, but only of 3,500 men, not enough to impress anybody.

Back in 1794, admittedly, Congress had authorised the construction of six frigates to protect American shipping from the depredations of another set of even fiercer corsairs, the pirates of the Barbary Coast of North Africa, but their construction had been interrupted for various reasons. Three of the frigates were, at last, launched in 1797: the USS *United States*, in May; the USS *Constellation*, in September; and the USS *Constitution*, to be affectionately known thereafter as *Old Ironsides*, in October. The United States now had at least the nucleus of a navy.

Over the next few months, work was speeded up on the remaining three frigates, the *Congress, Chesapeake* and *President*. The United States Congress authorised the construction also of a dozen quite substantial vessels and ten smaller ships and in imitation of the French, gave letters-of-marque to dozens of merchant vessels, turning them into potential, if rarely active, privateers.

It was also in October 1797 that an American delegation made up of three commissioners, Charles Pinckney, John Marshall and Elbridge Gerry, arrived in Paris to discuss the state of Franco-American relations with the French Foreign Minister, Monsieur Talleyrand. They never met. According to the American delegates, they were first asked for a large bribe ($250,000) by a secretive three-man group who were to arrange their meeting with Talleyrand. This was the famous XYZ Affair. The identity of the three rogues is now well known. X was Mr Hottinger, a Swiss banker. Y was Mr Bellamy, an American financier. Z was another Swiss banker, Mr Hauteval.

In those days the Puritan code motivated American public men and bribery and corruption were abhorred. The outraged US officials refused to pay, packed their bags and returned home, not only to make their report to Congress but also to have ten thousand copies of it published and distributed across the nation. The report roused their countrymen to fury against the devious French. The slogan 'Millions for defense, but not one cent for tribute' which Pinckney supposedly shouted at his three banking interlocutors in Paris, summed up the nation's feeling. Mr Pinckney had actually said: 'No, no, not sixpence' when asked for the bribe.

Meetings were held all over the country demanding retaliation against the French. Boston subscribed $125,000 to build two frigates. New York collected $30,000 in an hour for the Navy Department.

'May the American eagle pluck the gills of the Gallic cock' became a favourite banquet toast. A Philadelphia audience stood up and cheered for several minutes when it heard for the first time a new, stirring song called 'Hail Columbia'. Harvard students added a new verse to the tune of 'Yankee Doodle': 'If the Frenchmen come, we'll spank 'em hard and handy'. France was no longer the ally to whom the United States largely owed its independence, and on July 7, 1798 Congress annulled the old treaty of alliance. Even so, war was not officially declared. Four years after Hugues's depredations had begun President John Adams signed and sent to the commanders of all United States armed vessels a precise little note. 'You are hereby authorized, instructed and directed to subdue, seize and take any armed vessels of the French Republic.' It was short and to the point and could not be misconstrued. But it wasn't quite war. To Americans it became the Quasi-War with France.

Just about that time, the weary Directory government in Paris decided to bring Hugues home. Hugues's corruption and his sanguinary abuses should long ago have brought his rule in Guadeloupe to an end. The Directory, moreover, was particularly concerned with Hugues's incredible threats against Americans. His latest decree, announcing that Americans serving on ships bound for British-occupied French ports in the West Indies would be considered pirates and treated as such, was immediately countermanded in Paris. Officials and ministers in the French capital feared that Hugues might, on his own, succeed in bringing the United States to open war against France, and now was not the time to seek new enemies: Nelson had just sunk a large part of the French fleet in Egypt, and Russia and Turkey had just declared war against France.

The Directory chose General Desfourneaux to replace Hugues in Martinique. It was a strange choice for such a delicate and dangerous task. Desfourneaux, who entered our story earlier fighting in Haiti under General Toussaint L'Ouverture, was a brawling, fighting man. There was nothing of the diplomat in his make-up. Brave, quick-tempered, irritating and irritable, Desfourneaux was not the man for sensitive situations and his appointment was in line with the poor judgment that the Directory never failed to display.

Desfourneaux and his staff sailed aboard the frigates *L'Insurgente* and *Le Volontaire* on September 28, 1798 and arrived at Guadeloupe two months later, not knowing quite what to expect from Hugues. Paris had warned Desfourneaux he might require 'force or great skill to get rid of the Guadeloupe tyrant.' But the tyrant proved remarkably meek. When Desfourneaux arrested him as he came on board to greet the new arrivals, he did not protest and only asked that his wife and his brother-in-law, General Boudet, be allowed to join him. The trio were sent back to France on the frigate *La Pensée*.

Desfourneaux had of course arrived too late to prevent the outbreak of the Quasi-War with the Americans, but to placate President Adams and help to lessen the tension he did send back to its home port a recently captured American schooner with a friendly note for the White House suggesting Guadeloupe and the United States start trading again, as in the old days. President Adams didn't reply.

The President didn't believe in these French expressions of friendship. He had just lost one of his best captains, William Bainbridge, captured with his ship, the 18-gun *Retaliation*, by Captain Barrault's *L'Insurgente*, one of the frigates that had recently brought over Desfourneaux and his party from France!

Three months later it was *L'Insurgente*'s turn to meet defeat. Cruising off the British West Indian island of Nevis, she ran against the new 38-gun United States frigate *Constellation*, commanded by Captain Truxtun. Barrault fired high, in the traditional French fashion, trying to bring down masts, yards and rigging. He nearly shot down the American ship's fore-topmast which was saved by Midshipman David Porter, who ran up the rigging and cut the loose yards. Truxtun fired five broadsides and, after losing seventy men, Barrault surrendered. The *Constellation* had three casualties.

Away in Paris, Hugues, his crimes forgotten (or at least forgiven) was promised the governorship of French Guyana. Never a man to remain on the defensive, he demanded and obtained the dismissal of General Desfourneaux for abusing his authority when he took over Guadeloupe! The Directory sent a three-man governing board, which included Lavaux, Toussaint L'Ouverture's old friend from Haiti, to replace Desfourneaux. When they arrived in Guadeloupe, on December 11, 1799, they found to their great surprise that Desfourneaux was no longer there. The people of Guadeloupe, tiring of the irascible general, had placed him on board a Europe-bound ship and sent him back to France!

A stickler for order and military discipline, the spit-and-polish general had managed to antagonise the whole island. Appalled by the freebooting atmosphere he had found in the colony, which was more like a pirate den than a republican paradise, he had infuriated the whites by cutting down on their roistering, and had alienated the blacks by forcing them back to work in the plantations, flogging them if they protested.

The garrison, which was mostly black, joined in a spontaneous rebellion against Desfourneaux, marched him to the quayside under escort and sent him back to France.

The new ruling trio, bewildered but willing, took over the island, while at sea the French and Americans went on quasi-warring.

CHAPTER FOUR

The French Cock Crows

Napoleon Bonaparte, meanwhile, had not been idle. Now a general, he had been sent in 1796 to Italy as commander-in-chief of the French army. In one year, he won a succession of dazzling victories – the number was officially given as sixty-three. He defeated the Austrian Empire and the Sardinian Kingdom, recovered Corsica from the British, humbled the Papacy, secured Nice and Savoy for France, looted Italy and sent the spoils, the gold and the specie, the works of art, the captured flags and trophies to a Paris delirious with pride and happiness. He destroyed the Venetian Republic and, enthusiastically as we saw, seized their Ionian Islands which he considered more important than the whole of Italy. And, during the campaign, he assiduously read *Memoirs on Turkey, the Tartars and Modern Egypt*, written twenty years previously by the Baron du Tott, a military expert and diplomat.

Indeed, General Bonaparte first conceived of his Egyptian expedition during the Italian campaign. It all tied in with his old Oriental dream, his fascination with the East that had never wavered since late childhood. At sixteen, his mind already wandering in the desert sands, he had written a story: *The Prophetic Mask*. In spite of his youth, there was nothing childish about it. It was about an Arab prophet who, defeated after a long run of victories, commits suicide along with all his followers.

It is important to remember that in a choice between Europe, as symbolised by Italy, and the East, as symbolised by Corfu, Bonaparte opted for the East. His later European wars were, in a way, a substitute for eastern conquest, forced upon him by rival and fearful sovereigns funded and armed by a Britain that instinctively recognised in the 'Corsican ogre' the only serious threat to her own imperial ambitions.

While General Napoleon Bonaparte was rampaging through Italy, his next campaign was being largely prepared in Paris by the conniving Foreign Minister, Talleyrand, recently returned from exile in London and the United States. In July 1797 Talleyrand, not yet minister, gave a lecture before the Paris Institute of Sciences and Arts on 'The Advantages of Acquiring New Colonies'. In his talk Talleyrand proposed that France obtain new colonies on the nearby Mediterranean shores, as had been suggested years before by Choiseul. Choiseul, who had bought Corsica from Genoa, had also been in favour of buying Egypt from Turkey. Now Talleyrand was suggesting that Egypt, being nearer France and less vulnerable than Haiti and the other French West Indian colonies, could advantageously replace them.

Talleyrand's lecture was a sensation in Parisian political and intellectual circles. Fifteen days later he was appointed Foreign Minister, replacing Citizen Charles Delacroix, whose wife, for good measure, he then seduced, fathering the painter Eugene Delacroix, one of the great names of nineteenth-century French romantic painting. Politics, sex and the arts have always nicely blended on the Parisian scene.

The Directory, the ruling five-man government of France, was in a state of advanced decomposition. Corrupt and inefficient, it was despised by the population at large. Bonaparte described it as 'fit only to piss on' and France seemed to be moving towards a new upheaval, perhaps civil war. Talleyrand, a man of high ambitions, began to prepare the ground for the days ahead. He courted the victorious General Bonaparte in Italy, writing him a fulsome letter of praise within a week of his appointment as minister. It was the beginning of a subtle complicity between the two men, carried on by correspondence and based on their mutual dislike of the Directory and their shared appreciation of conditions in France and what should be done to change them.

In October 1797, after signing the Treaty of Campo Formio, one clause of which gave the Ionian Islands to France, General Bonaparte returned to Paris. He arrived at 5.00 pm on December 5, 1797. Whatever his pleasure at seeing his wife Josephine again – he had married her the previous year, shortly before taking over the Italian command – Napoleon gave priority to his official duties, and that same evening he sent a note to Foreign Minister Talleyrand suggesting they meet the next day.

Several guests were at Talleyrand's house. Bonaparte ignored all of them – even the enterprising bluestocking Mme de Stael who liked to collect famous men for her bed, her boudoir and her salon – except the famous Pacific navigator and explorer Bougainville, then an old man.

Bonaparte asked him many questions about Tahiti and the South Seas. He could never resist the lure of distant places.

The main purpose of Bonaparte's visit to Paris was to propose to the Directory an early invasion of Egypt. 'With Malta and Corfu in our hands, we should be masters of the Mediterranean. If we cannot dislodge England from the Cape [of Good Hope], we must take Egypt,' Napoleon had told Talleyrand, who agreed. The two men had a global concept of the war, not just a European one.

Instead of sending him south, however, the Directory gave Bonaparte the command of 'the Army of England' and sent him north to prepare the invasion of the British Isles. But he did not appear unduly frustrated: 'I shall make a tour of the northern coast to see for myself what may be attempted,' he told his friend Bourrienne. 'If the success of a descent upon England appears doubtful, as I suspect it will, the Army of England will become the Army of the Orient and I shall go to Egypt.'

On February 11, 1798, he visited several ports in Flanders and northern France from where the invasion of England might be launched. Tireless, he ranged up and down the coast. But all this activity was a sham. Britain had no place in his immediate military projects except as a country to avoid. His victories in Italy had made him the hero and saviour of France. His ambitions to become a figure of history were crystallising. Bonaparte had no intention of trying to invade the British Isles. To nourish his budding heroic image, he needed new victories and with the British navy standing guard between France and the English coastal counties of Kent, Sussex and Hampshire, his annihilation seemed more probable than his triumph. His model in 1798 was not William the Conqueror but still Alexander the Great.

On February 23 he wrote his report to the Directory. In view of the Royal Navy's supremacy at sea, he said, a direct assault on England was out of the question. Instead, England should be attacked indirectly, either in Hanover or through 'an eastern expedition which would menace her trade with the Indies.' The stress was on the latter suggestion.

In spite of the vast wealth he had sent to Paris from Italy, Bonaparte was not a favourite with the Directory. They feared his ambition, his popularity and his military ability and prestige. Suspicious of his objectives, anxious to avoid a military coup and fearful for its very existence, the Directory was happy, this time, to agree to the general's request – backed by Talleyrand – for the formation of an Army of Egypt, with Bonaparte as its commander-in-chief. It would be officially named (to confuse the British) the Left Wing of the Army of England, and would take him safely out of France, with any luck for several years. At least for a while there would be no threat from him of a *coup*.

Thanks to his organising genius, his meticulous attention to detail and his personal supervision of all the arrangements, General Bonaparte was able to complete the preparations for the expedition – some four hundred ships and fifty thousand soldiers and sailors – in only two and a half months. There were convoys to be readied and assembled in Toulon, Ajaccio in Corsica, and Genoa and Civitavecchia in Italy. The bulk of the expedition – thirteen battleships, forty-two frigates, sundry smaller warships, and a hundred and thirty transports – were assembled in Toulon. Large quantities of food, supplies and ammunition had to be ordered, checked and loaded. Plans had to be made for all the naval forces to meet at sea and voyage on to Egypt together. Malta was to be captured on the way.

Inspired by Alexander the Great who had marched on his expedition to the East accompanied by men of science and philosophy, Bonaparte also recruited a force of scientists, men of letters and of various cultural attainments (including a musicologist and a poet).

General Bonaparte was particularly anxious to recruit the mathematician Gaspard Monge for the expedition's Scientific and Artistic Commission, as it was called. Knowing that Madame Monge wanted her husband to stay at home, Bonaparte simply went to her house, knocked at the door and pleaded with her to allow her husband to go. She finally gave her consent, saying that if Gaspard wanted to go and make a fool of himself in military campaigns, under a general only half his age, then let him!

Another of Bonaparte's outstanding recruits was the chemist, Nicolas Jacques Conté who, unlike most scientists, managed to leave a fortune to his progeny. During the British blockade, when lead was in short supply in France, he invented a mixture of graphite and clay to replace the mineral in pencils. It is still used today in the falsely named 'lead pencils'. Along with sugar made from beet, it is one of the substitutes forced on the French by the British blockade which have lasted from the Napoleonic era right down to our present day.

We must not forget to mention Mathieu de Lesseps, a civilian administrator who accompanied the expedition. A few years later, when back in France, he had a son, Ferdinand, and he used to tell the boy about a project that was often discussed by General Bonaparte and his engineers, a canal that should link the Mediterranean to the Red Sea. Half a century later Ferdinand de Lesseps built the Suez Canal.

The bulk of Bonaparte's military force was made up of soldiers from the Army of Italy, men he had already led to numerous victories and whom he could trust. He rounded up twenty-seven generals, nearly twenty of whom had already served with him in Toulon and Italy. Several of them became in due course Marshals of France. Generals, by the way, were not in short supply in the French army during these wars. Close to 2,400 officers attained that rank during the years of the

French Revolution and Empire, but attrition made the actual increase really quite modest.

One of the most famous French soldiers of the Egyptian expedition was the dashing cavalryman, Joachim Murat. He loved gorgeous uniforms which he designed himself – pink trousers, plumes, ruffles, yellow jackets, there was no limit to his brilliance on the battlefield. Murat was in love with Bonaparte's sister, Caroline, but he had not been able to resist the call of the desert and had accompanied Bonaparte to Egypt.

The one-legged General Louis Caffarelli was Bonaparte's chief of engineers. Bonaparte always enjoyed his witty and piercing conversation. As the campaign dragged on Caffarelli retained his cheerful disposition. The troops, who hated being in Egypt, said it was because he still had one foot in France!

The novelist Alexandre Dumas's father, also called Alexandre, a mulatto from Haiti, was in command of the cavalry. Also in the party was General Vaubois, who had captured Leghorn and was now destined for the command in Malta, which Bonaparte planned to attack and occupy on the way to Egypt.

The Corsican had also succeeded in persuading two of his most brilliant military contemporaries to accompany him. Both had originally been his superiors: Generals Desaix and Kléber. Desaix was an aristocrat who had refused to emigrate with his family at the time of the Revolution. Kléber, an Alsatian and former architect, had done most of his fighting against the Germans and Austrians in Germany.

Bonaparte's chief of staff, General Louis Berthier, had served with the French army in the United States during the American War of Independence. He was madly infatuated with an Italian woman, Madame Visconti, who had been left behind in Italy, and carried around a little shrine with candles and her picture. In spite of Bonaparte's mocking comments, he would put up the shrine in his tent and kneel before it in silent adoration.

There were a few women who accompanied the expedition. One, also an Italian, was the wife of General Verdier. She was very popular among the officers for her liveliness, courage and sense of fun. She was no prude, a real soldier's wife. The gossip was that she was a little fonder of General Kléber than she should have been. The officers – Bonaparte included – found her very useful when they were later in Cairo as she used to go around the harems rounding up girl friends for them. Some of the lower-ranking officers also were accompanied by their wives or mistresses. Lieutenant Fourès, of the Chasseurs, brought his wife Pauline along, and he lived to regret it. A blue-eyed, long-legged blonde, with a pert, mischievous look, she soon caught the wandering eye of General Bonaparte, and against a general, what can a lieutenant's wife do?

The British were puzzled by all these preparations under way in Toulon and the other ports. Something was afoot. But what? The British fleet had kept out of the Mediterranean since the Corsican fiasco of 1796 but now the Lords of the Admiralty ordered Admiral Jervis, who was blockading the Spanish port of Cadiz, to detach one of his squadrons and send it to guard the approaches to Toulon. Their Lordships went on to suggest that Admiral Nelson would be the right man for this new assignment. Jervis agreed. For, since we were last with him in Corsica, Nelson had acquired new glory for his share in Jervis's victory over the Spaniards at the battle of Cape St Vincent.

After the battle, Jervis had been raised to the peerage as Earl of St Vincent, and Nelson had been knighted and promoted. He was now Rear-Admiral Sir Horatio Nelson. But he was also more battered looking than ever. Since losing an eye in Corsica, he had also lost his right arm in another encounter against the Spaniards during a raid on Santa Cruz, in the Canary islands.

So, on May 2 Sir Horatio, with his flag on HMS *Vanguard*, left Jervis's fleet off Cadiz and headed east through the Straits of Gibraltar into the old familiar blue waters of the Mediterranean. Nelson's flotilla was made up of several battleships, two frigates and one sloop. Their orders were to patrol off Toulon and prevent the French fleet from sailing out.

Thirty-seven thousand soldiers aboard two hundred and thirty-two transports, the bulk of the expedition, sailed from Toulon on May 19, 1798, commanded by Admiral Brueys. Fortunately for Bonaparte, a strong gale had been blowing for the past twenty-four hours and Nelson's command – he had fourteen ships-of-the-line under his command by this time – had been scattered. The flagship, HMS *Vanguard*, had been dismasted and nearly wrecked but under a spritsail had been able to find refuge in a Sardinian harbour. The message for Nelson was clear: God, by saving his ships and his life, had once again shown his preference for the British cause. On reaching safety he ordered a special religious service of thanks to be held. There was a tedious servility to Nelson's rapport with God. But we must remember he was always somewhat obsequious towards those he considered his social betters.

When a few days later the scattered ships all reassembled off Toulon, the French fleet was gone. But where? Nelson was in despair, and on a hunch he set off east. His hunch was correct, but nevertheless he missed the French and uselessly crisscrossed the Mediterranean for more than six weeks. And in the meantime the French had occupied Alexandria and Cairo, won the Battle of the Pyramids and, on his way to Egypt, Napoleon had captured Malta.

THE AMIABLE KNIGHTS OF ST JOHN
Malta 1798

Malta was a sideshow to the main Egyptian campaign, rather as Corsica had been to the Italian campaign a couple of years before. Its importance was solely strategic. Lying between Sicily and Tunisia, the island controlled the vital sea lane between the western and eastern Mediterranean and none of the great powers wanted any of the others to possess it. Since 1530 it had been owned and governed by the crusading Knights of St John, to whom it had been given by the Hapsburg Emperor, Charles V, in his capacity as King of Sicily, as a base for them to wage war against the Muslims.

General Bonaparte's capture of the island should have been a formidable undertaking. In fact he took it in one day and with only three casualties, which were caused only through a misunderstanding.

The French fleet arrived off Malta on June 9, 1798 and General Bonaparte immediately called for its surrender. Complicated negotiations began at once. The Knights went into conference, Bonaparte sat down to wait, the faithful ashore went to pray, and the officers of the Maltese garrison announced they would not fight against the French Republicans who, according to their priests, were the incarnation of the Devil. And what mortals can fight against demons? they very sensibly asked. Besides, two hundred of the three hundred and thirty-two Knights were French and unwilling to fight against their compatriots.

So Bonaparte conquered Malta in twenty-four hours and spent the next week organising island life and placing it on a war-footing. He declared Malta part of France, left a French garrison of 3,500 men under the command of General Vaubois and sailed away on June 18, destination Alexandria.

In strategic terms, it had been necessary for the French to occupy Malta before invading Egypt. If they hadn't, another country would have done so and very soon, for Malta had lost its martial, unassailable reputation. The local women were famed for their beauty and their ardour, and fornicating instead of fighting had become the main activity of the Knights of St John.

Tsar Paul I of Russia for one, eager to obtain a warm sea base in the Mediterranean from where to operate initially against the traditional Turkish enemy, had already offered the Knights his protection. Then again, Britain's ally, the King of the Two Sicilies, had asked Nelson to help him reoccupy it, but curiously, in spite of Britain's powerful imperial instincts, the British were not interest in the island. Sir Horatio did not consider it of much use to Britain. It was only later that he realised its importance as a bastion on the route to the East.

THE VIEW FROM THE PYRAMIDS
Egypt 1798

The French fleet under Admiral Brueys reached Egypt on July 2. The voyage from Toulon had taken over six weeks. The troops started to come ashore in the middle of the night, on the beaches a few miles west of Alexandria. Heavy seas were running and nineteen soldiers were drowned. Everyone, including the commander-in-chief, slept on the beach, wet, hungry and miserable. Then, at three o'clock in the morning, three thousand men were awakened and ordered to march to Alexandria and take the city.

The attackers were led by three generals, as well as by Bonaparte himself: Bon, a veteran of Toulon and Italy, five times wounded; Menou, of aristocratic lineage but who looked like the seedy waiter of a third-class restaurant; and Kléber, who did not really like Bonaparte and was in a towering rage at the makeshift arrangements over the coming battle. 'Bonaparte always does things by fits and starts,' he stormed. 'He never has a fixed plan.' Without knowing, Kléber had just described Bonaparte's genius: his adaptability, his talent for making plans, or changing them if they were already made, at any time of the day or night and whatever the circumstances.

The French marched five hours without water, Bonaparte sucking on an orange for refreshment. They reached the outer walls at eight o'clock that morning and immediately stormed the city. About a hundred Frenchmen were killed, two hundred wounded, but after three hours of fighting Alexandria was theirs. Between seven and eight hundred of the defenders were killed and wounded. But the French were disappointed in their capture. They found Alexandria a broken-down, dirty, ramshackle town of about ten thousand people, very different from the city which had been one of the wonders of the civilised world in ancient times.

At this point, it is necessary to consider the eighteenth-century Egyptian political scene. Egypt was, nominally, part of the Ottoman Empire and its ruler was, nominally, the sultan in Constantinople. The sultan's representative in Egypt was a viceroy in Cairo who was in fact virtually powerless. The real power lay, and had lain for the past five hundred years, in the hands of a hereditary caste called the Mamelukes who originally came from the Caucasus region, numbering with their families around a hundred thousand. Some ten thousand of them were serving in the famous Mameluke cavalry – considered, quite wrongly, the best in the world.

The Mamelukes were one of the contemporary plagues of Egypt. Robbers and plunderers by vocation, they taxed the local people outrageously, imposed exorbitant customs dues on all goods entering or leaving Egypt whether by ship or caravan, and lived like potentates in palaces and fine mansions, served by dozens, sometimes hundreds, of slaves. They often defied the sultan in Constantinople who now and again sent Turkish janissaries (an elite corps in the Ottoman army) in hopeless campaigns against them. As for the local Egyptians, they never dared to protest against the vile exploitation to which they were subjected.

Napoleon picked on the excesses of the Mamelukes as his official reason for invasion, claiming that they had recently subjected French merchants trading in the country to a number of unacceptable vexations. In addition, not wishing to antagonise the sultan in Constantinople whose faraway dominion he was violating, he insisted he was in Egypt as the sultan's ally, to subjugate the Mamelukes on his behalf.

Having made his political pitch, General Bonaparte planned his military strategy. After Alexandria, Cairo, about a hundred miles across the desert to the south, was the next objective. The van of the French army left the next day, on July 3, under General Desaix. A soldier of tremendous skill and fighting ability, Desaix feared nothing. He was an aristocrat, but a very ugly one, with a sabre slash across the side of his face seldom shown in contemporary sketches. His family had been divided by the Revolution: several of his brothers fought in the French Royalist emigré armies but Desaix himself never for a moment considered joining the enemies of Republican France.

If he had any political opinions he kept them to himself. The army was his life and glory was his god. His soldiers worshipped him because, himself always in the van of the fighting, he was sparing of their lives. 'He was intended by nature to be a great general,' Napoleon said. He was totally indifferent to comfort, an untidy dresser, careless of his appearance, and very fond of women. He later kept in Egypt a collection of girl friends of all races and colours, a sort of miniature, friendly harem: Astiza, a Georgian girl of fourteen, 'blonde and gentle'; Sarah, an Ethiopian girl of fifteen; Mara, from the Tigris River; Fatima, by her name probably a girl from the Arabian peninsula; and three Negro girls. He listed them all in a letter to a friend in France, quoted by J.Christopher Herold in his book on the Egyptian expedition.

After landing the remainder of the troops and standing by while Desaix and his men began to march south, Admiral Bruey's fleet moved to anchor in nearby Aboukir Bay. The transports anchored in Alexandria harbour. In nearby Rosetta, on the Nile, General Bonaparte organised a flotilla of fifteen river boats manned by six hundred French sailors to go upriver to Cairo. Numerous civilians and army wives were thus spared the ordeal of marching more than a hundred miles over the desert. The command of the flotilla was given to navy Captain Jean-Baptiste Perrée, and the command of the troops in them to General Andréossy, a competent but colourless military gentleman who was one day to be the French ambassador in London.

About a quarter of the expeditionary corps was left in garrison at Alexandria, Aboukir and Rosetta but the remainder, twenty-five thousand men, followed General Desaix's vanguard in the march south to attack Cairo. The first two days' march across the desert was a merciless ordeal. After reaching the Nile, there was no longer a shortage of water but the supply of food remained a problem, and dry biscuits, lentils and watermelons formed the men's main diet. The whole army suffered from diarrhoea.

The invaders were also harassed on the march by bands of thieving Bedouins who killed stragglers and slaughtered even a general, the cavalryman Mireur. The Mamelukes also launched a couple of whirlwind cavalry attacks. One of them was led by Murad Bey, one of the two most important chiefs in Cairo. The attacks were beaten off and the Muslim horsemen galloped back to Cairo and spread the rumour that the French were invincible. Panic swept the capital and the best families prepared for the worst by packing their bags and fleeing east.

On July 21, in the scrubby countryside a few miles west of Cairo, in a huge field of watermelons, came the big clash between the Mamelukes and the French. It has come down in history as the Battle of the Pyramids, but it was actually fought about eight miles from these ancient monuments.

The French were thirsty, hungry and tired, but on reaching what was to become one of the most famous battlefields in history they were able to gorge themselves on watermelons which, if they didn't help the dysentery, at least quelled their thirst and, in part, their hunger.

Bonaparte had twenty-five thousand men under him, most of them infantry but with some thirty guns and a sprinkling of cavalry led by the dashing General Murat. The Mameluke army was divided in two, each part under one of the two Cairo Beys, Ibrahim and Murad. Ibrahim had eighteen thousand infantrymen, made up largely of untrained peasants, massed uselessly on the opposite bank of the Nile about twenty miles from Cairo, just south of the Delta. The other Mameluke leader, Murad Bey, had forty guns and fifteen thousand infantry, also untrained, centred around the strong point of Embaba, on the Nile, just north of Gizeh, where the Pyramids are. But at least his army stood on the same side of the river as the French and, for a quick victory, he was relying on his elite troops, some six thousand Mameluke cavalry.

On their prancing Arab mounts, these warriors greatly impressed the French. Each horseman, accoutred in gorgeous coloured robes and wearing an enormous plumed turban, held a razor-sharp, curved, bejewelled sword in his right hand with which he could slice off an infidel's head with one dexterous blow. All the time, as they prepared to charge, the Mamelukes shouted and screamed at the invaders and invoked in their harsh tongue the sacred name of Allah while drums resounded, trumpets blared and their imams, summoning their god's aid, promised them the joys of eternal life if they died fighting the Infidel. Islam, since the Crusades, hadn't changed.

The battle started at about two in the afternoon, in the worst heat of a North African midsummer day. The French fought bravely and skilfully, the Mamelukes, charging as in the days of the Crusades, fought bravely and ineptly.

Ignoring all the noise from the enemy camp, General Desaix, followed by General Reynier, marched quietly with his men to cut off the Mameluke infantry from its cavalry. Murad Bey, seeing that the French were trying to divide his forces, gave the order to his horsemen to charge the advancing French columns. The French officers coolly formed their men into squares, six deep, told them to wait until the enemy were only fifty paces away and then fire. The frantic Mamelukes, calling on Allah, attacked the hedgehog formations of the French for an hour.

The French infantry never wavered. Their fire was so intense that bullets often set fire to the Mamelukes' lavish, flowing robes and the wounded horsemen, writhing on the ground, would burn to death a few yards from the unharmed squares. Every attack was beaten off although their sheer ferocity and force sometimes drove the horses into the middle of the squares, where their riders were clubbed or bayoneted to death.

Two other French divisions, commanded by Generals Bon and Vial, moved up to attack the Mameluke infantry and the fortifications where the guns, manned by tough Albanian soldiery, were located. Again it was slaughter. The untrained Muslim infantry fled.

Within two hours, the Battle of the Pyramids was over. Murad Bey and his cavalry were fleeing south. Ibrahim and his hordes, untouched on the other side of the Nile, were fleeing east. Murad's infantry, pursued by Desaix, were also heading east in headlong flight, but many got no further than the river. There were no boats to carry them over, so many plunged in and tried to swim to the other side. Most drowned. Mameluke dead from battle or drowning amounted to five thousand. Total French casualties were two hundred which included forty dead. The next day Cairo surrendered. Led by a band playing martial music, the French entered the city.

Nelson, meanwhile, was still looking for the French at sea.

SLAUGHTER IN ABOUKIR BAY
Egypt 1798

On that same July 21, while Bonaparte was winning the Battle of the

Pyramids, Sir Horatio and his despondent and exhausted squadron were resting in the Sicilian port of Syracuse. 'We have gone a round of six hundred leagues [1,800 miles] . . . and I am as yet ignorant of the enemy as I was twenty-seven days ago,' he wrote to his wife Fanny.

The trans-Mediterranean chase had begun on June 7 when, after repairing his ships' storm damage and returning from Sardinia to his watch station off Toulon, Nelson discovered the French were gone. On a hunch he had set off east in pursuit. On June 22 a passing ship had informed him the French fleet had sailed from Valletta three days before. He then guessed their destination might be Egypt. 'They are going on their scheme of possessing Alexandria and getting troops to India,' he wrote to the Admiralty in London. Acting as scout for Nelson, Captain John Masterman Hardy, in command of HMS *Mutine*, a former French brig he himself had boarded and captured in the Canaries while her captain was ashore carousing, hurried to Alexandria. But he found no French there (they hadn't arrived yet!). The French might have gone instead to Corfu, Nelson now decided. Or they might have sailed to Turkey.

'The devil's children have the devil's luck,' he wrote dispiritedly to the British ambassador in Naples, Sir William Hamilton. God had been on Nelson's side in the past but now the Devil himself had joined in the fray – on the French side. Nelson's theology was straightforward, practical and patriotic: God was pro-British and Satan pro-French.

After all, Nelson was an English parson's son, so God could only be an Englishman or someone very close to it, on the side of England in every battle, the happy witness to her victories – and also personal friend and ally who watched over Nelson's shoulder every time he went into battle but who, presumably, looked the other way every time he climbed into bed with Lady Hamilton.

God appears time and time again with awesome tediousness in his reports, letters and dispatches. 'Almighty God has blessed His Majesty's arms in the late battle by a great victory over the fleet of the enemy,' he wrote to his commander, Admiral Jervis, after the Battle of the Nile. A storm on the French coast was a personal warning from God to Nelson to be a little less cocky in the future. 'I believe it was the Almighty's goodness to check my consummate vanity,' he wrote with unexpected humility to Lady Nelson. God was always around him, even when he slumbered. 'When I lay me down to sleep, I recommend myself to the care of Almighty God, when I awake I give myself to his direction.'

Nelson was a hypocrite. His wife appears to have been an incredibly dull woman, but even so he behaved to her abominably. He sullied his record by having the Neapolitan (only another foreigner, of course) Admiral Caracciolo hanged from the yardarm of his own ship for rebellion against the royal House of the Two Sicilies. He was vain and conceited, and personally coined the expression 'The Nelson Touch' to describe his own brilliance. The British loved and admired him, but no one loved and admired him more than he loved and admired himself.

Even the doughty Wellington would have to endure his boasting and bombast. It was on September 12, 1805. Wellington had only just arrived back the day before from India where he had spent the last eight years. Nelson was sailing the next day on the cruise which was to end the following month with his victory and death at Trafalgar. Nelson and Wellington met in Lord Castlereagh's antechamber while waiting to see the colonial secretary. It was their first and last meeting. Nelson did not recognise the young major-general, still relatively unknown. But Wellington knew immediately his interlocutor was the famous Lord Nelson by his one eye and one arm, and also by his notorious vanity.

'He [Nelson] entered at once into conversation with me, if I can call it conversation, for it was almost all on his side, and all about himself, and really, in a style so vain and silly as to surprise and almost disgust me,' Wellington reminisced years later.

Four days after the Pyramids slaughter, on July 25, Nelson sailed from Syracuse in search of the elusive French fleet. He was in a desperate and particularly anti-French mood. 'Nelson had such a horror of Frenchmen,' one of his officers recalled, 'that I believe he thought them at all times as corrupt in body as in mind.' Three days later a merchant vessel at sea informed one of Nelson's captains, Thomas Troubridge, that he had sighted the French ships a few weeks ago headed for Alexandria. Once again all sails were set for the Egyptian coast and this time Nelson was lucky. In the afternoon of August 1, on watch on a crossyard high up in the rigging of HMS *Goliath*, Midshipman George Elliot, the son of the former viceroy of Corsica, sighted the masts of the French fleet in Aboukir Bay. The long pursuit was over. Nelson was about to fight the Battle of the Nile.

This is the right moment to have a look at some of the unfortunate men who had to fight Nelson, people for whom he felt an almost insane hatred. His feelings against them were so virulent that perhaps they can only be ascribed to straight, undiluted, insular arrogance, an attitude which sometimes metamorphoses the English when faced with the necessity of recognising that, unfortunately, foreigners do exist.

The French fleet was in command of Vice-Admiral Brueys d'Aigailliers, a forty-three-year-old southerner from the Provençal town of Uzès, who had served on the *Zélé* at the battle of the Chesapeake, off Yorktown, in 1781. He was flying his flag on the *L'Orient*, a gigantic 120-gun battleship, which had carried Bonaparte and his personal staff. Brueys's flag captain, Luc de Casabianca, a Corsican and cousin of the defender of Calvi, had also served on the *Zélé* at the Chesapeake. Casabianca, unwisely, had signed on his ten-year-old son as a midshipman so that the boy could learn on the voyage to Egypt the rudiments of seamanship. Bruey's chief of staff, Admiral Honoré Ganteaume, another southerner, from La Ciotat, near Marseille, and veteran too of the American War of Independence – he had fought at Savannah – had become a personal friend of Bonaparte during the voyage.

A few other names among these French sailors should be mentioned. The Provençal Admiral Pierre de Villeneuve, yet another Chesapeake veteran, who a few years later led the French fleet to disastrous defeat at Trafalgar, was in command of one of the squadrons of the Egyptian expedition. Admiral Decrès (also an ex-Chesapeakian), Napoleon's future weasely minister of marine and colonies, commanded the frigates. The Norman, François Motard, who was to distinguish himself in the Far East in later years, was a young commander in Egypt, and was serving on Brueys's personal staff on *L'Orient*. He, like Elphinstone in the Royal Navy, was considered an expert on army-navy joint operations and was in charge of the landing operations when the French fleet reached the Egyptian coast.

One of the future heroes of the Battle of the Nile was the man who commanded the 90-gun battleship *Tonnant*, Captain Aristide du Petit-Thouars. He too had served in North America during the War of Independence, first with Admiral D'Estaing at Savannah, and later in Admiral de Grasse's squadron.

Du Petit-Thouars had been a refugee in the United States in the early years of the Revolution and was, at one time, the partner of Robert Morris, banker and signer of the Declaration of Independence, in a real-estate project on the banks of the Susquehanna. The aim was to found a settlement for French Royalist exiles in Pennsylvania to be called Azylum. The deal fell through when most of the French – including du Petit-Thouars – went home. All that remains of the settlement today is the little aptly-called locality of Frenchtown.

These men were all good, brave sailors. Professionally-speaking, however, most of them were second-raters when compared to Nelson's invincible 'band of brothers', honed to perfection through years of sea service.

As the two fleets prepared for battle the odds, theoretically, were about even. Brueys had dysentery, Nelson had toothache. Nelson had fourteen ships-of-the-line, all 74-gun ships but one, the 50-gun HMS *Leander*; Brueys had thirteen battleships under his command. His flagship, the giant *L'Orient*, carried a hundred and twenty guns; two others, the *Franklin* and the *Guillaume Tell*, were both 80-gun ships. Du Petit-Thouars's *Tonnant* had ninety guns. The nine others were seventy-fours. It was a battle of giants. But one of the giants had feet of clay.

The French ships, under the rickety discipline of the Revolution, were in shambles. More than a quarter of the crews were ashore on errands, some had gone as far as Alexandria for food and supplies. Some of the installations, put up to shelter the passengers during the crossing from Toulon to Egypt a month earlier, still littered the decks. The crews were young and untrained, half of them were under eighteen. One of the youngest was ten-year-old Jacques Casabianca, son of the *Orient*'s flag captain. He was destined to become a hero of English poetry as the boy who 'stood on the burning deck'.

Admiral Brueys had anchored his ships, bows facing the open sea, at the western end of the Bay of Aboukir, each ship about a hundred and fifty feet from the next, in a long line parallel to the coast. The ships were all lined up one and a half miles offshore, and since there is no more distressing situation for a man o' war than to be attacked simultaneously on both sides, this was near enough to the land, he thought, to prevent any attacking ships from coming between his vessels and the coast.

The way he had disposed his ships, Brueys reasoned, would oblige Nelson, when and if he turned up, to fight the French fleet only from the east, from the side open to the sea, against an impenetrable wall of fire, almost a mile long, belching from the four hundred and seventy-three starboard guns of thirteen firmly anchored and powerful battle-ships. The British ships, he believed, would be devastated. Alas, Brueys did not know his opponent. He was about to become acquainted with 'the Nelson Touch'. It was an experience he did not survive.

Shortly after 4.00 pm, the British fleet was in full, untidy sight, coming in higgledy-piggledy to attack – 'in dispersed order', to use a more naval term. Brueys had expected the British to lay to for the night, and go into battle in the morning. Instead, to his great surprise, he realised they were planning to fight right away, each ship entering the fray as it arrived.

In the British fleet, Nelson summoned the officers of HMS *Vanguard* to his great quarters in the ship's stern and they all toasted his coming victory. 'I shall soon be either seated in the House of Lords or buried in Westminster Abbey,' Sir Horatio quipped cheerfully.

His sharp, and only, eye had noted that in their anxiety to avoid the shallows, the French ships had anchored too far from shore. Part of the British squadron, led by HMS *Goliath* (Captain Foley) and HMS *Zealous*, commanded by Lord Hood's young cousin, Captain Samuel Hood, slipped into this gap with the superb seamanship one expects from British sailors, and began to pound the immobilised French ships on their port side. Firing began shortly after 6.00 pm. It was most effective. The French had not expected an attack from that side, their gun ports facing the land were often blocked, and that side of the decks was cluttered with rubbish.

But Nelson's ships did have some navigational problems. Troubridge's ship, HMS *Culloden*, cut it too fine, struck a sand bank, and to the chagrin of captain and crew, was unable to join the battle.

Four other British ships joined Foley and Hood on the inland side: HMS *Audacious*, HMS *Orion*, HMS *Alexander* and HMS *Theseus*, this last vessel commanded by the American Ralph Willett Miller. HMS *Leander* joined them at about 10.00 pm when she slipped through the French line between the *Franklin* and the *Aquilon*, whose captain had just had both his legs shot off.

The British tactic was now simple: they worked their way slowly down both sides of the moored French line and thoroughly pounded each ship in the van and centre of the fleet. At the far end of the line Rear-Admiral Villeneuve's two battleships, the *Guillaume Tell* and the *Généreux* were, for all practical purposes, out of the battle until the early hours of the morning when, in the company of two frigates, they worked their way upwind and bore away, hardly firing a shot.

Admiral Brueys, the French commander-in-chief, on *L'Orient*, was wounded in the head early in the fighting and was killed about half an hour later, shortly before 8.00 pm, when a shot carried off his left leg and thigh. He refused to go below to the surgeon's work place where the wounded were treated. 'A French Admiral should die on his quarter-deck,' he said, and he died as he wished, a brave, fighting sailor to the last.

Nelson too was struck on the head. A flap of skin fell over his good eye and temporarily blinded him. 'I am killed. Remember me to my wife,' he said, and fell to the deck. But after the wound was cleaned by the surgeon he recovered quickly enough to continue blasting the French ships.

HMS *Bellerophon* (the English sailors called her the 'Billy Ruffian'), badly damaged, dismasted and with many casualties, moved out of the action where she had been tussling with *L'Orient*. The Canadian Hallowell, on HMS *Swiftsure*, from the outside, and Captain Ball's HMS *Alexander*, from the inside, sailed in to replace her and continued hitting the French flagship. *L'Orient* began to burn at about 9.30 pm and the two British ships then concentrated their fire on the area in flames, the most vulnerable part of the ship.

What was the boy who stood on the burning deck doing all this time? One story is that Captain Casabianca had told his son he must show his courage and remain on board until told to leave the ship. Captain Casabianca was killed and the child, having no orders from his father, refused to abandon the flaming ship. One of the survivors from *L'Orient*, Blanquet, tells of a different drama, heart-rending in its simplicity. Father and son, 'neither able to swim, were in the water, seeking each other until three quarters past ten, when the ship blew up,

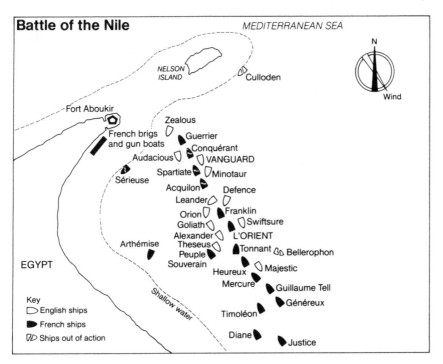

Battle of the Nile — MEDITERRANEAN SEA

NELSON ISLAND
Culloden
N
Wind
Fort Aboukir
Zealous
French brigs and gun boats
Guerrier
Conquérant
Audacious
VANGUARD
Spartiate
Minotaur
Sérieuse
Acquilon
Defence
Leander
Orion
Franklin
Goliath
Swiftsure
Alexander
L'ORIENT
Arthémise
Theseus
Peuple
Tonnant
Bellerophon
EGYPT
Souverain
Heureux
Majestic
Mercure
Guillaume Tell
Généreux
Shallow water
Timoléon
Key
English ships
Diane
French ships
Justice
Ships out of action

and put an end to their hopes and fears.'

Captain Motard, wounded, had jumped into the water shortly before and been picked up by a British ship. The explosion stunned the combatants. For a few minutes afterwards there was almost a total silence. Then the French ship *Franklin*, with two-thirds of her crew dead and wounded, her deck set on fire by falling, burning debris from *L'Orient*, began firing again. She was surrounded by five of Nelson's ships, including Hardy's little *Mutine* which had edged into the battle. The *Franklin* fought for one more hour and then struck her colours. One by one, except for the four that managed to escape, the battered French ships surrendered. On the *Tonnant*, when Captain du Petit-Thouars had his two legs shot off, he ordered his men to lift him into a barrel of sawdust to absorb the blood gushing out of his body and continued to give orders until he died. At 3.30 in the morning the *Tonnant* stopped fighting, the last ship to surrender. She had lost three hundred and fifty of her men. Her decks were covered in blood and with survivors from the other French ships, no less than sixteen hundred of them.

The British repaired and refitted the *Franklin* and the *Tonnant* and both – the *Franklin* rechristened HMS *Canopus* – became flagships in the Royal Navy, HMS *Tonnant* fought at Trafalgar, in 1814 was the flagship of Admiral Cochrane at the Battle of New Orleans, and remained a fighting ship to the end.

The Bay of Aboukir on the morning of the battle was dotted with wreckage and with the bodies of French sailors 'mangled, wounded and scorched, not a bit of clothing on them except their trousers', recalled a British tar. In that one night, seventeen hundred Frenchmen were killed. In a special religious service held on HMS *Vanguard* the next day, Nelson thanked Almighty God for his help in the battle, and Lady Spencer, the wife of the First Sea Lord, wrote him an ecstatic letter of happiness when the news of his victory reached London. 'May the great God, whose cause you so valiantly support, protect and bless you to the end of your brilliant career.'

'Blessed be God for His goodness to me,' Nelson wrote, more humbly, to his wife.

A few days earlier the Nile had carried hundreds of bodies down to the sea, those of the Mamelukes and Egyptians who had died in the Battle of the Pyramids. Great triumphs mean great slaughter, and the killings by the banks of the river had been as merciless as Nelson's. But at least, the French didn't thank God for their victory – perhaps because, as revolutionaries imbued with new ideas, they didn't believe in Him, or at least not too much. There must be moments when God is grateful to atheists. At least they don't kill in His name and thank Him for the corpses afterwards.

The French Mediterranean fleet, for all practical purposes, had ceased to exist. Of Brueys's thirteen ships-of-the-line, six had surrendered, four were beached and the shattered *L'Orient* lay in little pieces at the bottom of the Bay. Most of the British ships were dismasted, but not a single one had been lost. Nelson's triumph was complete. 'If I was King of England,' the enamoured Lady Hamilton wrote to him from the British Embassy in Naples, with that sense of fun which made everybody who knew her love her in spite of her vulgarity, 'I would make you most noble puissant Duke Nelson, Marquis Nile, Earl Alexandria, Viscount Pyramid, Baron Crocodile and Prince Victory.'

The actual King of England, less resoundingly, made him Lord Nelson of the Nile.

But there were other rewards. The East India Company, always quick to spot a good investment, presented him with £10,000, and Parliament voted him a pension of £2,000 a year for life. His captains gave him a sword of honour and one of them, Ben Hallowell, added as a sort of bonus a coffin made from the mainmast of *L'Orient*, which had been found floating in the water. Nelson lies in it today in St Paul's Cathedral in London.

In Cairo, Bonaparte must have blanched when he heard the news of the destruction of Brueys's fleet. His army – and himself – were now marooned in Egypt, with no means of returning to France. After the victorious Battle of the Pyramids, with its promise of easy conquests ahead, the naval defeat at Aboukir was a particularly hard blow. It was his second that week.

The first had been more personal. His friend, General Junot, had revealed to him that in Paris Josephine was having a love affair, and had been for several months, with a cavalry officer, the dapper Lieutenant Hyppolite Charles, hero of the Paris boudoirs. 'That she should have deceived me,' Bonaparte struck his head in anguish when told. 'Woe to them. I will exterminate the whole race of fops and puppies. As to her, divorce, yes divorce, a public and open divorce,' he raged.

The destruction of the French fleet, coupled with the return in force of the Royal Navy in the Mediterranean meant a basic reversal to French fortunes in the region. Malta and Corfu, which Napoleon had so recently acquired for France, could be invaded and occupied. Also the French defeat would encourage Russia, with her warm-seas ambitions, to enter the war against the Republic. Turkey, humiliated in Egypt, would be likely to get her revenge by allying herself with Britain. The prospects for the French were gloomy.

There was always the lure of India, of course. Even if the fleet was shattered, the road to the East still lay open for General Bonaparte and his army, either through Syria and Persia, or from the adjoining Red Sea ports of Suez and Kosseir.

In Paris too, the Directory was thinking offensively. Back in December 1796 General Hoche had been placed at the head of a massive (forty-five ships, including eighteen battleships, and fourteen thousand men) expedition supposed to land in Bantry Bay and invade Ireland. But the fleet had been scattered by violent winter gales, losing many ships and very many men, so now a second invasion of Ireland was getting under way – even though, at Bonaparte's urging, the befuddled Directory members had abandoned, as too dangerous, a planned invasion of England only a few months before.

THE ROAD TO DUBLIN
Ireland 1798

On August 6, 1798, five days after the Battle of the Nile, an almost unknown French general, Amable Humbert, sailed with one thousand and eighty men from Rochefort to invade Ireland.

Most of the soldiers of this little army were tough veterans who had fought under General Moreau in the Army of the Rhine, and under General Bonaparte in the Army of Italy. Facing them in Ireland, however, were a hundred thousand men: Irish militiamen, Scottish and English Fencible regiments, Dragoons, English Militia and a number of British Regiments of the Line.

Many of these troops had already been engaged that year in brutally putting down violent uprisings against English rule, notably in the northern counties of Ulster, in the midland counties of Kildare and

Meath and in the southern county of Wexford. Perhaps thirty thousand Irishmen had been killed in battle, massacred, or flogged to death for rebellion and disloyalty to the British Crown. Thousands more were impressed into the British army and navy, or transported to the convict settlements of New South Wales where they now made up a quarter of the colony's population.

The British army in Ireland was a collection of drunken, incompetent and corrupt ruffians who bullied, abused, plundered and slaughtered the peasant population with utter impunity. This accumulation of brigands received a new commander-in-chief in 1797: General Sir Ralph Abercromby, just back from the West Indies. He wasn't favourably impressed by his new command. In February 1798, in a strongly-worded order that caused a sensation not only in Ireland but also in the highest government and army circles in London, the forthright Scotsman publicly stigmatised the army in Ireland for being in a state of 'licentiousness that made it formidable to everyone but the enemy'. Even the newly-arrived viceroy, Lord Cornwallis, now doing a stint in Ireland after his years in India, could only shake his head sadly at the condition of the army in Ireland, 'totally without discipline . . . contemptible before the enemy . . . ferocious and cruel when any poor wretch, with or without arms, comes within their power', he wrote in a secret report to the Pitt government.

But, because of its public nature, it was Abercromby's report that provoked the strongest reactions. 'Abercromby must have lost his senses,' thundered the Irish Lord Chancellor, Lord Clare. Many prominent citizens called for his impeachment. 'Poor creature, I pity him. He is quite in his dotage,' sneered the unpleasant General Sir Gerard Lake, army commander in Ulster, who hoped to take over his commander-in-chief's post.

Abercromby was duly recalled to London in semi-disgrace and Lake became, as he had hoped, commander-in-chief of the British army in Ireland.

Poor Ireland! It was a land of misery, ruthless exploitation, repression and death, ruled from Dublin by a government representing solely the interests of the Protestant 'ascendancy', largely for the benefit of landlords, who were usually of English descent.

Yet many of these descendants of the English colonisers, the Anglo-Irish, became great Irish patriots. Among the leaders of the United Irishmen, the secret group dedicated to the liberation of Ireland, were a number of Protestant upper-class gentlemen. Their love of Ireland went beyond the narrow confines of their racial background, their class interests and their religious loyalties. They had become Irishmen. The greatest of these patriots was Wolfe Tone who had gone to France two years previously, via the United States, to win French support for Irish freedom.

For the French in 1798, notwithstanding Bonaparte's reservations on the possibility of invading the British Isles, Ireland seemed the country from where England could most easily be assailed, perhaps even invaded, so orders were given accordingly.

General Bonaparte had met Wolfe Tone in Paris and praised him as 'a brave man', but considered the Irish unreliable, and their cause obviously failed to arouse his enthusiasm, perhaps even his interest, since he chose to go to Egypt instead. The command of the Irish expedition was given to thirty-six-year-old General Jean Hardy, who had been a sergeant in the royal armies of Louis XVI.

The French expeditionary force was divided into two main parts: one, of three thousand men directly under Hardy and with General Wolfe Tone as his deputy, had instructions to sail from Brest in a convoy escorted by the 74-gun battleship, *Hoche*, and several frigates. The second part, under Humbert, with about a thousand men, was to sail from Rochefort in three frigates. Wolfe Tone's brother, Matthew, also with a commission in the French army, accompanied Humbert as interpreter and liaison officer. The ships were under the orders of Captain Daniel Savary.

The two sections of the expedition were supposed to sail at the same time and make for the northern county of Donegal. But by early August only Humbert's little flotilla was ready, so it sailed first. Humbert arrived off Killala, County Mayo (contrary winds prevented the French ships from reaching Donegal) on August 23 and the first French invasion of the British Isles since 1066 began at eight o'clock in the evening when General Humbert knocked at the door of the startled local Protestant bishop, Dr Joseph Stock, and announced he had arrived to liberate Ireland.

The rough and almost illiterate General Humbert will appear several times more in this narrative, notably in Haiti, in Pauline Bonaparte's bed in her mansion on Tortuga island, and with General Jackson in New Orleans.

By birth a peasant, by early profession a rabbit-skin salesman who supplied mainly glove manufacturers in Lyons, Amable Humbert had joined the army from his native Vosges mountains on April 1, 1792 and had been elected a colonel three months later. He had been a general since 1794 and, so far, had done most of his fighting in the Vendée, against French royalist armies made up largely of Catholic peasants very similar to those he was now coming to help in Ireland.

A tall, blond, goodlooking, impressive man, he knew how to sign his name, but not much more. He was uneducated but he had a way with the ladies, even high-born ones. His talent as a seducer was, finally, to prove his undoing.

This was Humbert's second Irish voyage. He had taken part in General Hoche's ill-fated 1796 expedition. General Humbert had then

been on the magnificently named *Les-Droits-de-l'Homme*, commanded by Captain Pierre Lacrosse, which was wrecked on its return
voyage on a sandbank on the Brittany coast while being attacked in a
gale by two frigates, HMS *Indefatigable*, commanded by Captain
Edward Pellew, and HMS *Amazon*.

It was one of the epic sea-fights of the war, a credit to the immense
fortitude of the sailors of the two nations who went on fighting in
heavy seas, high winds and pelting rain for sixteen hours. One thousand French sailors were drowned but Captain Lacrosse and General
Humbert hung on to the wreckage of the ship and reached safety
ashore when the weather cleared four days later.

Humbert had vowed to return to Ireland and now here he was with
his little army at Killala, ready to march across Ireland and free the
Irish.

His first gesture, as the liberator of Ireland, was to hoist the green
flag with the harp and the motto *'Erin go Brough'* (Ireland Forever),
and announce he was recruiting an army of Irishmen to be armed,
clothed, fed and supplied by the French. Over a thousand volunteers,
mainly peasants, demanded to be enrolled – all very enthusiastic, but
untrained and useless.

The only armed resistance to the French at Killala had come from
some yeomanry and a few dozen troopers from the Prince of Wales
Fencibles. Two French soldiers were wounded, four British were
killed and twenty-three were made prisoner and shipped off to intern-
ment in France.

Delighted with this early success, Humbert promoted to general his
adjutant, Colonel Jean Sarrazin, a dragoon and, as it proved several
years later, one of the biggest scoundrels in the French army.

There was no sign of General Hardy's three thousand troops yet,
but Humbert decided not to wait around Killala but to move on. Two
days after the landing, he marched out of Killala, leaving behind a few
dozen troops and three officers. Advancing south, Humbert brushed
aside the garrison of the small town of Ballina and, now with about
fourteen hundred men, several hundred of whom were Irish volunteers, and one solitary gun, marched another twenty-five miles over a
rough mountain path to Castlebar, the main town of County Mayo.

Advised of the French landing, General Cornwallis, in the viceregal
palace in Dublin, prepared to meet the invaders in person. He ordered,
meanwhile, the redoubtable General Lake to go to Mayo with all speed
to reinforce General John Hely-Hutchinson, who was in charge of the
defence of the west. Hely-Hutchinson had already moved north from
Galway with a force of four thousand men which included some fear-
some Highlanders, several squadrons of Militia, volunteer Carabineers,
Yeomen, Lord Roden's colourful Foxhunters and eleven guns, manned
by the elite Royal Irish Artillery. He planned to meet Humbert's ad-

vancing army at the market town of Castlebar, and smash it there.

General Lake arrived at Castlebar shortly after Hely-Hutchinson, took over the command and prepared to rout the heavily outnumbered French.

Humbert's weary little army, after marching all night, appeared outside Castlebar at eight o'clock in the morning of August 27. The French, who had hoped to take the town by surprise, saw with consternation the enemy British troops and guns lined up in formation waiting for them and outnumbering them by at least three to one. But, to Lake's disagreeable surprise, instead of taking to their heels in the face of this superior force, the invading troops shouted 'Vive la République', charged the British positions, and it was Lake's men who fled instead, throwing away their muskets, in a panic to escape from the French veterans and their inept but equally vigorous Irish volunteer comrades.

British losses amounted to fifty-three men killed, thirty-six wounded and two hundred and seventy-eight missing, most of them prisoners or deserters. The French also captured nine of the eleven British guns.

The defeated British ran away so fast that the Battle of Castlebar became maliciously known in local Irish lore as 'the Castlebar races'. The fleeing troops did not stop running, we are told, until they reached Tuam, thirty miles away, and some of the cavalry broke all records, hardly stopping until, twenty-seven hours later, they arrived in Athlone, sixty-three miles from their starting point.

Humbert had a problem after taking Castlebar. Where should he go next? He was still awaiting the arrival of General Hardy and his army, and his main purpose was to find allies among the Irish. Hearing that Ulster was restless, he decided to march north. On September 3, at the head of an army of eight hundred Frenchmen and fourteen hundred Irish volunteers, he left Castlebar and clashed two days later with the Sligo garrison, commanded by Colonel Charles Vereker, at the village of Collooney. It was a short, sharp, inconclusive affray which lasted about an hour, in which each side suffered about fifty casualties. The British, in addition, lost about another hundred men, taken as prisoners by the French, who released them all immediately on parole.

Then, suddenly, while Humbert and his men were resting in Dromahair on their way north, news reached them that thousands of Irishmen in the midlands, in the counties of Longford and Westmeath, had broken into rebellion again. Humbert immediately ordered his army to swing east to effect a junction with the rebels. By the evening of September 7 he was at Cloone, halfway to Dublin when the remnants of the rebel army, armed with the long pikes with which they went into battle, staggered, shattered, into the French camp. The rebels in the midlands had been defeated by the British and their rebellion was over.

Humbert now decided that he had only one course to pursue: to march to Dublin, in the hope that the presence of his army would lead to more revolts among the peasants of Longford, Kildare and Meath through which he would have to pass. It was the gamble of a desperate man. There was still no news of Hardy, whose departure from Brest had in fact been delayed first by contrary winds, then by supply problems, and Cornwallis's net was closing in. Some forty thousand British troops were now moving towards him, led by Lord Cornwallis and Sir Gerard Lake. Among the pursuers were two of Britain's greatest soldiers, Colonel Robert Craufurd and General Sir John Moore, and a young officer, Edward Pakenham, who would one day become Wellington's brother-in-law, a hero of the Peninsular campaign, and a corpse outside New Orleans.

The village of Ballynamuck in County Longford was the scene of the final clash between British and French. Humbert only had about nine hundred French soldiers, backed by his Irish recruits, maybe a thousand untrained levies. Opposing them was an army about twenty times larger. Even the hardiest of the French veterans gasped when they saw the numbers opposing them. They fought for half an hour, what the French call a *baroud d'honneur*, more as a matter of principle and honour than with the slightest hope of victory. 'I was obliged to submit to a superior force of thirty thousand men,' Humbert later wrote in his report.

In all, precisely 878 French soldiers were made prisoners at Ballynamuck. Before being sent back to France on parole, they were joined in detention by another eighty from Killala, Castlebar and Ballina. Humbert and the other captured French officers were taken to Dublin under a military escort where they were lodged in one of the best hotels while awaiting a ship for France. The officer in charge of the escort was Captain Denis Pack, a typical member of the English-descended 'ascendancy', and unlike the Tone brothers a loyal subject of King George III. We shall meet him again fighting the French and their allies in South Africa and South America, and later in the Peninsular and Waterloo campaigns.

Matthew Tone and another officer of Irish origin who had come over with the French from Rochefort, Bartholomew Keeling, were less hospitably received by the victorious British. In spite of their French naturalisation papers they were jailed, judged and hanged as traitors.

While immediately after Humbert's capture, the courteous and civilised Lord Cornwallis had been affably entertaining the French general to tea, General Lake's Dragoons, urged on by their sanguinary commander, had systematically and with great gusto started on the slaughter of the French general's bewildered Irish followers left abandoned on the battlefield. 'We had a most glorious day,' commented one of the victors, surveying the carnage. Ninety of the Irishmen who, somehow, had survived the massacre were led away and a number were selected by lot to be hanged. A detachment of British troops was sent to Killala to mop up the rebels, and a few more hundred were slaughtered there, at Ballina and at Castlebar.

A blockheaded, inarticulate, brutal and sadistic nitwit, who believed not so much in victory over the enemy as in his extermination, General Gorard Lake remains one of the most unpleasant of British military figures. In Ireland his troops deliberately set fire to a captured hospital, burning all the wounded inside. During the rebellion, he stopped at nothing, not even the most cruel tortures, in his efforts to stamp out the insurrection. One of his prisoners received five hundred lashes in an attempt to obtain information from him and then was found to be an innocent man, totally uninvolved in the revolt.

Like most stupid men, Lake had a great belief in the importance of appearances. Sent later to India, where he slaughtered Indians with the same enthusiasm as he had killed Irish peasants, he always turned up at meals unfashionably peruked and in full uniform, buttoned to the chin, and insisting on his glass of claret. All in all, he was a disgusting man. Humbert, a hard-drinking and hard-fighting roughneck, who could barely read, was a gentleman compared to Lake.

So, with Humbert's defeat, the Irish rebellion was over for the French. Or almost.

Three more French expeditions, including Hardy's long delayed sortie, set out for Ireland, in dribbles and uselessly, during the next month. On August 27, the day of the battle at Castlebar, another Irish independence leader, Napper Tandy, sailed from Dunkirk on the French corvette *Anacréon*, with a party of two hundred and seventy French grenadiers, and a shipment of arms enough for several thousand men. The corvette reached the Donegal harbour of Rutland on September 16, more than a week after Humbert's defeat at Ballynamuck. Tandy went ashore to enquire about the situation and was told by the postmaster, an old acquaintance, that Humbert had surrendered to Cornwallis. The two men sat up all night drinking. Napper Tandy was carried back dead drunk to his corvette early in the morning and the *Anacréon* sailed back to France with Napper Tandy, his French grenadiers and his shipment of arms.

General Hardy's three-thousand-man expedition finally sailed from Brest on September 16 aboard the *Hoche* and eight frigates, unaware that Humbert was already a prisoner. On October 11 the French squadron was intercepted off the coast of Ireland by a British squadron of five frigates and three battleships, under the orders of Commodore Sir John Borlase Warren. After a ten-hour fight, the *Hoche* and several of the frigates were taken. Aboard the *Hoche*, the British captured Wolfe Tone who, with his usual gallantry, had refused the French commander's offer to send him aboard one of the faster frigates, giving him a better chance to escape. The British sent Tone in chains to

Dublin and condemned him to death but he escaped the hangman's noose by cutting his throat in his prison cell.

The last of these useless Irish forays was made on October 12 by Captain Savary, again from Rochefort, although the news of Humbert's defeat and capture was already known in Paris. With the same ships as on his original voyage with Humbert, plus the band of the 70th Regiment of Infantry, trumpets, trombones and all, Savary sailed into Killala harbour a few weeks later, perhaps played a tune or two, and then sailed out again. The purpose of this last, strange enterprise must remain one of the minor mysteries of military buffoonery.

The French attempt to free Ireland was a failure, and has left virtually no trace in history. Castlebar is not listed among the one hundred and twenty-six victories inscribed on the Arc de Triomphe in Paris, nor does Humbert's name figure among the six hundred and fifty-eight fightingest marshals, generals and admirals also inscribed on the arch. The lapse can only be explained by the disgrace which fell upon Humbert on his return a few years later from a campaign in Haiti. Humbert's downfall was not upon a battlefield but in the sumptuous bed of Napoleon's sister, the ardent Pauline, in her mansion on Tortuga Island where she held court while her husband fought – and died – on the Haitian mainland. The affair became public and for the vindictive Bonaparte, Humbert ceased to exist.

Humbert, the only Frenchman to have ever defeated the British on their own soil since William the Conqueror, is an unknown figure in France. As a final disgrace, he was never awarded the Legion of Honour, perhaps the only French general ever to have been denied this coveted distiction.

'If instead of leading the Egyptian expedition, I had led that of Ireland, what might England be today?' Napoleon Bonaparte reflected years later on St Helena. The course of history might have been very different. But instead of the bogs of Ireland, he chose the sands of Egypt.

He probably made the wrong choice.

CHAPTER FIVE

The Vultures Gather

A HORRID SET OF ALLIES
Corfu 1798-1799

You shouldn't hit a man when he's down. It's not cricket, the English say. But it's exactly what they tried to do to the French after Nelson had blasted their fleet in Aboukir Bay. They called in the Turks and the Russians to help them, and also the Portuguese, who were already hovering on the scene.

To have obtained the joint aid of the Russians and the Turks was almost a miracle, for the two nations were traditional enemies. Britain had to use a little bribery. It offered Russia for its help a payment of £1,380,000, a huge sum in those days.

Encouraged by this subsidy, when he learnt that Bonaparte was now stranded without a fleet in Egypt, Tsar Paul I of Russia (being also Grand Master of the Knights of Malta) decided this was the right moment to come into the war in defence of the expelled Knights. At the same time Turkey became aware of the marooned Bonaparte's violations of its distant Egyptian province, and also declared war on France. So did the Kingdom of the Two Sicilies. So did the Austrian Empire. Britain and Portugal now had plenty of allies.

In early September 1798 the Russian Black Sea fleet, under Admiral Fedor Ushakov, sailed through the Dardanelles into the Mediterranean to join Nelson. Ushakov was in command of six ships-of-the-line and ten frigates and corvettes, an appreciable addition to the Allied fleet in the Mediterranean. The Russian admiral's orders were to capture Malta and Corfu (and the other Ionian islands) from the French, and to join in the British blockade off Alexandria.

On reaching the Mediterranean, Ushakov combined with a Turkish squadron under Kadir Bey of four battleships, six frigates, four corvettes and sundry gunboats. The bulk of the Ottoman-Russian fleet (twelve ships-of-the-line and eleven frigates) then sailed north to attack the Ionian Islands, and the remainder sailed south to join the blockading British squadron off the Egyptian coast, which was made up of battleships, a few frigates and several Portuguese vessels, all under the command of Captain Samuel Hood. The British commander of the blockading fleet did not appreciate the Turks, whose habitual standards of barbarity repelled him. 'As horrid a set of allies as I ever saw,' was Hood's comment to Nelson about his Turkish comrades. As for Nelson, as we shall see, he didn't like the Russians.

The Ionian islands, towards which the Russian-Turkish fleet was now sailing, were defended by about four thousand soldiers, many of them Italians, under the command of General Chabot. The Russo-Turks struck first at Cerrigo, the southernmost island. Outnumbered and outgunned, the French marines (today's *fusiliers marins*) defending the island soon had to capitulate and the Allied fleet then sailed ponderously north along the Greek coast, to attack the other major islands in turn. Zante fell on October 24, Cephalonia and St Maure followed. All had only been defended by a few dozen troops, and it wasn't until the Russians and the Turks came to Corfu, on November 4, that the serious slaughtering began.

Corfu, after Malta, was the strongest French island base in the eastern Mediterranean. Chabot had the bulk of his troops there, manning five thick-walled citadels, the main one of which was St Saviour. Admiral Ushakov was very surprised to spot in the harbour two substantial warships: the 74-gun *Généreux*, one of the two French battleships which had survived the Battle of the Nile, and the 50-gun HMS *Leander*, which had also fought at Aboukir and which had since been captured on the high seas by the French.

The siege went on for four months. The Allies hoped to starve the French out. The French, outnumbered as usual and short of ammunition – they could return only one shot for ten – fought desperately. The Russians fought with the stolid valour of their race, and the Turks fought with their usual savagery – time and time again the Russians had to intervene to save French prisoners from being massacred by St Petersburg's Ottoman allies.

The siege had been under way about three months when the British came on scene in the person of Lord William Stewart, captain of the 18-gun British brig, HMS *El Corso*, 'a young man of particularly bold and imperious disposition' as a nineteenth-century history of Corfu describes him. He arrived in February 1799 bringing a note from Nelson to the Russian and Turkish admirals requesting reinforcements in ships and men for the British in Sicily, where the distraught King

Ferdinand and his court (including Sir William and Lady Hamilton) had taken refuge after being forced out of Naples by the French.

Ushakov and Kadir Bey both said no to any reduction in their forces. Ushakov was highly suspicious of the British motive. 'They have always wanted to take Corfu for themselves and wished to send us away under various pretexts, or by splitting us up reduce us to incapacity,' he wrote to the Russian ambassador in Constantinople. A shrewd and, as later events proved, an accurate judgment.

If the Russians and the Turks did not want to help Nelson, the uppity British aristocrat Lord Stewart was more than happy to tell them what to do instead. The young lord 'caused the [Corfu] operations to proceed with more vigour' and helped in a simultaneous attack on three points, all strongly defended by the French: the two citadels of Fort Abraham and Fort St Saviour, and the nearby little island of Vido, which was defended by a small force under the command of General Piveron, a senior French officer who had stopped at Corfu on his way to India and, unable to proceed further, had placed himself under the orders of General Chabot.

The Allied fleet anchored off Vido on February 28, and eight hundred naval guns fired on this tiny piece of land for three hours. Two hundred of the six hundred and fifty French defenders were killed and all their artillery was destroyed in the intensive gunfire and in the hand-to-hand fighting which followed. One thousand Turks landed in the north of the island, and a thousand Russians to the west. A few of the French managed to get away by boat back to Corfu, but the remaining defenders, including General Piveron, were captured. The Russians, on landing, formed an immense human square in the centre of the island into which the French survivors crowded to escape the Turkish massacrers who, possibly anxious to kill a Christian in order to ensure their safe passage to paradise, gave no quarter.

The two Allied attacks on Corfu itself failed. Even so, exhausted after the four-months siege, short of food and supplies and demoralised by the loss of Vido, the French decided to ask for terms, which included their repatriation to Toulon on Allied ships at Allied expense. The warship *Généreux* had managed to slip through the Allied squadrons before the capitulation but the ex-HMS *Leander* now became a Russian prize and Ushakov returned it to the British six months later.

RUSSIANS, KEEP OUT
Malta 1798-1799

While General Chabot was fighting to preserve a French Corfu, General Vaubois was fighting for a French Malta. The main attackers there were not the Russians and the Turks but rather the British and the Portuguese.

The reader will recall that General Bonaparte, on his way to Egypt, had seized Malta and left a French garrison there under General Vaubois. The revolutionary French and the religious Maltese proved incompatible. The Maltese objected particularly to the billeting of French officers in their homes.

When news of the French defeat at Aboukir by Nelson reached Malta, the islanders prepared to rid themselves of their unwelcome Republican guests. The igniting spark for the revolt was provided early in September 1798 by the tactless order of a French civilian official requiring the silver from the cathedral of Citta Vecchia to be melted down for coinage. An outraged crowd attacked and killed the sixty-three men of the nearby French garrison. In a few hours the whole island had erupted into revolt and the French hurriedly retired behind the thick walls of Valletta, the capital.

From then on, the French remained untroubled until September 25, when a powerful British squadron of six of Nelson's ships-of-the-line, under the command of Commodore Sir James Saumarez, arrived off the island on its way from Alexandria to Britain, escorting six of the captured French prizes.

Saumarez found a recently-arrived Portuguese squadron under Admiral the Marquis de Niza, a French Royalist, on blockade duty outside Valletta and, inside Valletta harbour, a number of French Republican warships, including three survivors from the Aboukir Bay holocaust, the *Guillaume Tell* and the two frigates, the *Diane* and the *Solide*, and also the old French frigate *La Boudeuse*, in which Bougainville had sailed on his voyage of discovery to the South Seas and around the world thirty years before. *La Boudeuse* was to end her career ingloriously, during the two years of the Malta siege, as firewood for the French garrison.

In a peremptory note Saumarez summoned the French to immediate surrender. But General Vaubois was not easily intimidated. 'The future of [Malta] is a matter which does not concern you,' he wrote back pointedly.

Saumarez didn't insist. He sailed to Gibraltar and onward to Britain, after Captain Ball, in command of HMS *Alexander* and four other ships, had arrived from Naples in October to take over command of the blockade. He was joined a few days later by Nelson himself who had been urged by King Ferdinand in Naples to seize the island for the Kingdom of the Two Sicilies. Nelson, too, found the French unwilling to surrender, so he rushed back to Naples and Lady Hamilton. Their romance was still unconsummated. At least, so experts have regularly told us.

Captain Ball, always an optimist, wrote to Nelson that he expected the French to surrender very soon. A quarter of the garrison were sick, and rations for two vital ingredients of a Frenchman's diet, bread and wine, were down to only half a loaf a day and a quart of wine every ten days. Yet the siege lasted two years.

Meanwhile Nelson faced urgent problems in Italy. A French army under General Championnet overran southern Italy and forced the king, his court and even Nelson and his ships, to flee Naples and seek refuge in the port of Palermo, in Sicily, where amid the bric-à-brac and the noisy rumble of the Neapolitan collapse, the romance between Admiral Lord Nelson and the lovely Lady Hamilton came at last to fruition. With, we must add, the tolerant understanding of the ageing Sir William who managed, with considerable aplomb, to maintain his dignity throughout what became one of the great sex scandals of the epoch.

Captain Ball, meanwhile, was trying to interest Nelson in taking and keeping Malta for Britain. But Nelson, at first, was not very interested. 'The possession of Malta by England would be a useless and enormous expense,' he wrote to the Admiralty in London. But, he added, covering all the options, 'any expense should be incurred rather than let it remain in the hands of the French.'

France was holding Malta; the Kingdom of the Two Sicilies wished to take it; Austria was considering having designs on it; Britain was not interested but finally did take it; in addition there was a fifth country with plans for the island: Russia.

Nelson, at any rate, was determined to keep the Russians out of Malta. 'Should any Russian ship . . . arrive off Malta you will convince them of this very unhandsome manner of treating the legitimate sovereign [King Ferdinand of the Two Sicilies] by wishing to see the Russian flag fly in Malta,' he wrote ungrammatically but feelingly to Captain Ball. He ended his letter on a note that brooked no contradiction: 'The Russians shall never take the island.'

Lord Nelson met Admiral Ushakov, who had hoped to visit Malta, in August 1799, five months after the Russo-Turkish capture of Corfu. The two sailors did not take to each other.

'The Russian admiral has a polished outside, but the heart is close to the skin. He is jealous of our influence,' Nelson commented.

'I first made suggestions [to Nelson] about Malta,' Ushakov complained to the Russian ambassador in Palermo, 'but he had made up his mind in advance . . . and did not designate any common action with me.' Ushakov also objected to what he called Nelson's 'tricks and turns, under cover of politeness'.

Nelson, at this period, was finding it difficult to tear himself away from the charms of Lady Hamilton. His naval duties came second. He spent more time in bed than at sea. But he did keep the Russians out of Malta and Ushakov never obtained the opportunity to impress the islanders with the symbols of Russian power. As from September 1799, the command of the besieging troops on Malta – British, Portuguese and Maltese – devolved upon General Thomas Graham.

Graham had taken late to soldiering. He had joined the army only five years ago, at the age of forty-five, at the siege of Toulon. Son of a Scottish laird, Thomas Graham was on a European jaunt, trying to get over the recent death of his wife from tuberculosis, when the British occupied the French Mediterranean port. He offered his services to Lord Mulgrave, a fellow-aristocrat who engaged him as his aide-de-camp, and he proved to be a natural soldier.

Graham's decision to serve against the French was spurred by his hatred of the revolutionaries. His wife, the beautiful Catherine, Lady Cathcart, painted four times by Gainsborough, had died two years previously in the south of France. He shipped her body home but, to his distress and disgust, the French customs officials insisted on opening her coffin to make sure there was no contraband in it. Their gross and stupid gesture turned the French into his personal enemy.

The key man in Malta, however, was not Graham but Ball. Ball had only one idea on mind: to make Malta British. But it wasn't only Nelson's reluctance to take over Malta that he had to overcome; it was also Vaubois's determination to keep it French.

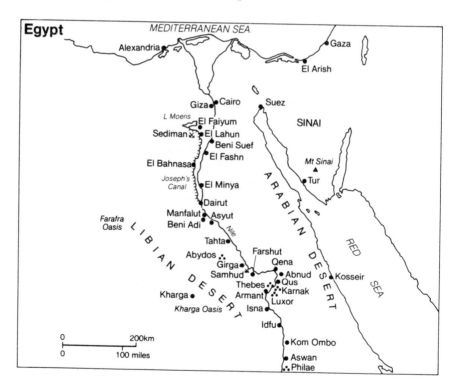

CHAPTER SIX

And There Was a Great Cry in Egypt

EXTERMINATION IN THE MOSQUE
Cairo 1798-1799

Meanwhile, in Egypt, General Bonaparte had no place to go. Deprived of his fleet, cut off from France, he had no alternative but to soldier on. The problem was against whom, and where.

Bonaparte, in his proclamations to the Egyptians, and in his letters to the Ottoman ruler in Constantinople, stressed ceaselessly that the Mamelukes were his sole foe – in addition to the British, of course. But there were no Mamelukes and no British at hand. The nearest Mamelukes were Murad's elusive horsemen up the Nile valley. There were no British soldiers – not yet, at least – in Egypt either. The nearest British armies of any consequence were in India.

In due course, in addition to the Mamelukes, the French would have plenty of Turks and Britons to fight against, even Indian regiments from the Asian subcontinent, but for the time being, because of the absence of the enemy, they faced a tactical void. Bonaparte had no great desire to fight the Turks. The enemy he wanted to fight were the English, and the country he wanted to invade was India.

After taking Cairo, he set about governing Egypt, following what we could call a wait-and-see policy. After receiving news of the destruction of the French fleet in Egypt, the Directory had given him permission to decide on his own future course of action. 'To return to France seems difficult at the moment, and it leaves us with three alternatives for you to choose among: to remain in Egypt and set up there an establishment which the Turks cannot attack; to go to India where, once you arrive there, you will undoubtedly find men ready to join

145

you to destroy British rule; finally, to anticipate the enemy who threatens you and march on Constantinople. The choice is up to you.'

It was the ideal recipe for a conqueror with Bonaparte's dreams. The government gave him the right to choose his own options. He tried all three. He set up an establishment in Egypt. He also tried to march on Constantinople, or India, or both.

The establishment he founded in Egypt dragged this backward country into the stream of modern life. There could be no question of a full military occupation. Egypt was too large, Bonaparte's ambitions were too diffuse and his army was too small. He occupied Cairo, and the ports on the Mediterranean. He sent General Desaix up the Nile valley to find the elusive Mamelukes and fight them. He collected taxes and he turned Egypt into a virtual, if rebellious, French colony.

He set up a council of Arab dignitaries, but no one was fooled. The real power lay in his hands. He paid lip service to Islam, but no one was fooled again. Cairo, just the same, took on a certain liveliness thanks to the presence of the French soldiers, with coffee shops and restaurants and music, organised tours to the Pyramids, singsongs in the taverns and other simple pleasures of the West.

There was even a certain careless jollity at times. 'The French soldiers love to ride donkeys,' wrote a local sheikh. 'Some spent their entire day riding a donkey. Others gathered in groups and went on excursions, singing and laughing. The donkey drivers joined in their fun.' Many Egyptian women, to the horror of their menfolk, went about unveiled and consorted freely with the invaders. (Hundreds of these women were executed after the French left, for desecrating Islam by their behaviour.)

It was Madame Verdier, so the story goes, who found an Egyptian girl friend for the unattached Bonaparte who had gone into a mood of deep melancholia after discovering Josephine's infidelities to him in Paris. She recruited her candidate for Bonaparte's bed in the harem of Sheikh El Bekri, one of Bonaparte's main local allies. The girl's name was Zenab, she was sixteen, the daughter of one of the sheikh's wives. She is one of the tragic little figures of history, for her brief affair with Bonaparte was, three years later, to cost her her life.

Sheikh El Bekri looked the other way when the girl's ambitious mother took her to meet Bonaparte. But the liaison did not last. Bonaparte probably found the childish Zenab boring and exchanged her for the more experienced and fun-loving Pauline Fourès, a Paris milliner who, in search of adventure, had dressed herself up as a soldier to accompany her lieutenant husband. After the general spotted her one day in Cairo, the lieutenant's place in her life vanished.

Two weeks after their first meeting, Bonaparte sent her husband back to France in order to have the exclusive enjoyment of her company. The affair smacks more of farce than romance, or even scandal.

Lieutenant Fourès, whose ship had been intercepted by a British warship, returned unexpectedly to Cairo and made a most unmilitary scene when he found his wife living with his general. Pauline obtained a divorce and became Bonaparte's official mistress while Lieutenant Fourès vanished into obscure military duties.

But Pauline Fourès, with her pouting lips and bedroom eyes, was only a minor interest in Bonaparte's life. The government of Egypt and the modernisation of the country were his major day-to-day concerns. During his first two months in Egypt, Bonaparte's functions were more those of a politician and governor – dictator would be the more appropriate term – than of a soldier. He had the power of life and death over the population. General Dugua, the French commandant in Cairo, was at times kept so busy by Bonaparte's demands for the execution of certain prisoners in the Citadel dungeons that he finally protested at the number of people he had to shoot. 'Since executions are becoming frequent in the Citadel,' he jocularly told Bonaparte one day, 'I intend to substitute a head-cutter for the firing squad. That will save us ammunition and make less noise.'

The executions were not only political. Aghast at the spread of venereal disease, the jovial-looking General Dugua suggested that all prostitutes caught in the barracks should be drowned. Turkish janissaries were given the job of rounding up these unfortunate females, a good many of whom were hospitalised and treated. But General Belliard, in his memoirs, said the janissaries beheaded four hundred girls, tied their bodies into bags and threw them into the Nile.

The French occupation of Egypt was perhaps abominable. But it was no worse than the rule of the Mamelukes and of the Turks, although less acceptable locally than theirs. For they had been part of the scene for hundreds of years, while the French were newcomers and their dominant presence was Christian and intolerable. The result was revolt.

It broke out on October 21 and the Middle East being what it is, religion took over. A messenger ran through the streets of Cairo shouting: 'Let those who believe that there is but one God take themselves to the Mosque El Azhar! For today we fight the Infidel!' One of the first victims was General Dupuy, at the time governor of Cairo, speared to death when he walked out into the street to find out what all the shouting was about.

The mob, led by their religious leaders, went on a rampage that lasted until the evening of the next day. They broke into all the warehouses and stole or destroyed all they could find. They massacred thirty-three French hospital patients caught in a convoy of ambulances, slaughtered General Bonaparte's aide-de-camp, the Polish patriot General Sulkowski, and gave his body to the dogs to eat. Bonaparte, in a fury, ordered his artillery to start shelling the mosque, where many of the rebels were grouped. 'Exterminate everybody in the mosque,' he roared to General Bon, who had replaced the slain Dupuy. Terrified at the noise and at the damage, the rebels surrendered. French cavalrymen, led by the Haitian, General Dumas, rode into the mosque, tied their horses to the pillars, drank wine, broke the bottles all over the floor and smashed everything they could find. The rebellion was over.

Some three hundred Frenchmen had been killed, and between two and three thousand rebels. Prisoners who had been caught carrying weapons were unobtrusively beheaded during the next few days and their heads and bodies flung into the Nile. Peace, however uneasy, fell upon Cairo again.

But in the countryside the unrest continued. It was never safe for the French to travel between Cairo and the coast except with an armed escort.

Several other revolts broke out. The most dangerous was stirred up by a dishevelled near-naked fanatic from Libya called Ahmed, who claimed to be the Mahdi, one of those angry envoys who periodically appear in Muslim lands and arouse the people to frenzy and violence.

Thousands of peasants and nomads in the Alexandria region rallied to his standard and went to war against the French, certain they were invulnerable since the Mahdi had assured them he could stop bullets and cannonballs in mid-air. The rebels massacred the small, sleeping French garrison at Damanhur but a French punitive expedition led by General Lanusse caught up with them soon afterwards.

This was the moment of truth. Lanusse's men fired into the charging mob who, on account of the Madhi's magic incantations, had expected to reach the French line unscathed. Instead, the bullets kept coming and hitting them. The rebels at first couldn't believe it. Then they turned around and fled, screaming. It is not known whether Ahmed was among the dead. Maybe his outraged followers slew him.

The French establishment in Egypt remained unshaken by these insurrections. The Egyptian expedition was a scientific and cultural enterprise as well as a military one, with its accompanying mission of botanists, zoologists, geologists, mathematicians, poets, engineers, musicians, philosophers and eggheads of all types. Let us not forget the great contribution to knowledge made by the thirty-eight-man Institute of Egypt, an offshoot of the expedition, recruited among the scientists, professors and medical men who had accompanied Bonaparte. The Institute looked into every aspect of Egypt, physical, geographical, archaeological and economical. It notably planned the construction of a canal across the isthmus of Suez and Bonaparte studied the site in person.

Three printing presses were set up by the French, in Arabic, Greek and French, which put out newspapers, grammars and dictionaries. The archaeologist Dominique Denon, in spite of the danger, accompanied General Desaix and his troops on their lengthy campaign up the

Nile valley to Aswan and Philae and discovered and sketched some impressive ancient monuments. Many army men turned to archaeology and exploration also, and Major Bouchard, while digging for the Institute, discovered the Rosetta stone, on which parallel texts revealed the secrets of the ancient Egyptian hieroglyphs.

The French army in Egypt was essentially an army of occupation, with the exception of General Desaix and his men fighting up and down the Nile valley. It was not until February 1799 that Bonaparte left Cairo and resumed his role as an active military man, leading soldiers to battle. The Ottoman Empire had by then been at war with France for several months and two Turkish armies were assembling, one on the island of Rhodes and the other in Syria, to attack the French in Egypt.

Djezzar, who although Bosnian, from Sarajevo, was the Turkish Pasha of Acre, had already sent a considerable number of troops to occupy an Egyptian town, El Arish, close to the Syrian border. Bonaparte expected the Turks to attack in May. So, following the full powers he had been given by the Directory, he decided to march into Syria, to take Constantinople. Or was India the ultimate target, also mentioned in the Directory message as a possible objective?

We cannot know for sure what was Bonaparte's ultimate purpose when he invaded Syria. Neither probably did he. Kléber grumbled that Bonaparte never had a fixed plan. Yet improvisation was the key to the Corsican's success. Bonaparte hoped to take Acre and then perhaps raise a mixed army of French, Arabs, Druses, Lebanese Christians, Mamelukes and Negroes, force the Sultan of Constantinople to acquiesce to their march across his territory and 'reach the Indus by March 1800 with forty thousand men', as he reminisced later. With genius and imagination, all was possible. Bonaparte always had half a dozen alternatives in mind and he was always ready to change his tactics, and even his strategy, at a moment's notice. He was, but in a much more exalted form than the word conveys, an opportunist.

He wrote, anyway, to the Shah of Persia, asking for the right of way for his troops whom he was shortly to lead into what might be the first phase of his planned invasion of India. The Indian invasion plan may have been an insane project, as many historians have claimed. Yet each of the two options, India and Constantinople, was possible. Boldness was always one of Bonaparte's qualities. He believed he should go forward and then, in the words of the historian C. de la Jonquière, author of a five-volume history of the Egyptian campaign, 'let circumstances determine the rest'. Those are the key words of his tactics and strategy.

Not knowing that his Indian dream had already been very much compromised in India itself by Lord Wellesley's measures against the Indian princes, Bonaparte also tried, in January 1799, to contact Tipoo Sahib, the Sultan of Mysore.

'You will already have heard of my arrival on the Red Sea with a huge and invincible army anxious to free you from the iron yoke of England,' he wrote Tipoo. He asked the Indian prince to send an ambassador to Cairo, not just any envoy, he specified, but 'an able man who has your confidence'. In other words, a man with whom the French general could work out future military cooperation.

The Sultan of Mysore never received his letter. It was intercepted by a British agent in Arabia. But meanwhile, a few days after sending the letter to Tipoo, Bonaparte set out at the head of an army of thirteen thousand men to conquer Syria.

WATER TO FLOAT A SHIP
Suez, the Red Sea and India 1798-1799

Distance, logistics, the slowness and unreliability of communications were all against Napoleon Bonaparte at this time. He was not too sure, either, whether he had enough soldiers at his command and was dispiritedly calculating the number of men he would require for the great Asian conquest, whether by ship from the Red Sea or overland through the territories of the Sultan and of the Shah. 'Only if fifteen thousand can be left here, and I have another thirty thousand at my disposal, shall I be able to venture a march upon India,' he wrote.

Meanwhile, as soon as news of the arrival of a French army in Egypt had reached London, the British government set in motion moves to counter any French plans to invade India. There are few people more thorough than the British when they wish to be, and Pitt's government, which considered that only the British had a right to dominate India, decided to extirpate once and for all the impudent French threat to that country. The Secretary of War, Henry Dundas, had written to Lord Wellesley back in June 1798, even before the full extent of the French menace was known, and ordered him to spread his defences well beyond the immediate perimeter of India itself, all the way to the Red Sea. For, from the African shore of that sea's hot, shark-infested waters, the French might one day sail in conquest of Hindustan, the Deccan and the Carnatic.

It was certainly a possibility in Bonaparte's mind. He had sent General Bon, in November 1798, with six hundred soldiers and a naval party to occupy Suez, report on the state of the port and its defences and advise whether 'some frigates which I am expecting could come within six hundred feet of the shore for protection by the coastal batteries', a reference, undoubtedly, to a squadron commanded by Admiral de Sercey, operating out of the Indian Ocean island of Mauritius, which in fact never arrived.

On receiving word from General Bon that Suez could be easily defended from an attack by the sea, Bonaparte the next month ordered a naval detachment of fifty sailors, several shipwrights and thirty-five engineers to join the general's group in Suez, and he himself visited the port a fortnight later, before leading his army's advance into Syria. It was plain, concludes the British writer C. Northcote Parkinson, in his *War in the Eastern Seas,* that Napoleon Bonaparte 'at this period was evidently considering the construction of a Red Sea squadron, and had even begun to draw up plans for naval operations in the near future.'

The British were not idle either. The British command in Bombay sent a small military force to Aden, on the Yemen coast at the southern entrance to the Red Sea. Colonel John Murray, a Scotsman, was in command of this isolated detachment. He was given an additional three hundred men a few months later, in May 1799, to garrison the nearby island of Perim and to intercept any French convoy that might heave into view.

Admiral Rainier, the commander in chief of the East Indies, detached two ships from his station to the Red Sea: one of them, the 50-gun *Centurion,* commanded by his nephew Captain John Sprat Rainier, the other the 18-gun HMS *Albatross.* The two Royal Navy vessels appeared off Suez on April 27, 1799, chased two bewildered French gunboats back to shore and remained off the coast for the next couple of months doing little damage but creating much alarm.

From Britain itself arrived, after a ten-month voyage, a small but powerful squadron led by Commodore John Blankett, described by the philosopher Jeremy Bentham, who met him at a party in London, as 'a coarse-mannered blockhead'. A biographer, however, says he was 'an accomplished and amiable gentleman, notwithstanding a certain irritability induced by gout'. The navy hoped he would establish valuable contacts with the local merchants and sheikhs. He did so and found them 'the most artful and deceitful scoundrels'.

Soon after his arrival, Blankett confronted in Kosseir a small French force that had been left there by General Desaix to hold the fort and the town to prevent the landing of fierce and fanatical Arabian warriors and equally warlike pilgrims from Mecca who had been arriving in their hundreds in dhows from Jeddah to attack the French. In August 1799, Blankett's squadron carried out a three-day bombardment of Kosseir and tried several times to land. French troops, holding the fortress under the recently promoted General Donzelot, repulsed the British attacks, and Commodore Blankett, after sinking a few dhows in Kosseir harbour, crossed the Red Sea to Jeddah.

During the next few months, the unfortunate Blankett, suffering terribly from the heat and the gout, sailed up and down the stifling Red Sea, helped to transform Egypt from a springboard to India into a useless French cul-de-sac and, sweating and swearing, wrote long and plaintive letters to his superiors in London and India.

While General Bonaparte was campaigning in Syria, while General

Desaix was marching up then down the Nile valley in pursuit of the slippery Murad Bey, and while Commodore Blankett was rummaging all over the Red Sea, Tipoo Sahib, friend of France and foe of Britain, had fought and died. He was killed, like a warrior, sword in hand, fighting the British, whom he hated, when they attacked his capital, Seringapatam, on May 4, 1799.

The hero of the assault was Colonel David Baird. He found the storming of Seringapatam a tougher operation than the capture of the undermanned defences of Pondicherry a few years earlier. Nine hundred British soldiers and six hundred Indian sepoys fighting under the Union Jack were killed or wounded in the attack. Significantly, ten French partisan officers were among the prisoners taken by the British.

Baird's pugnacity was largely motivated by a desire for sheer revenge: he had been captured by Tipoo Sahib and his father, Hyder Ali, eighteen years before and kept in chains for three years, attached to another British officer.

Colonel Wellesley – the future Wellington – also took part in the assault, but he came out of the battle with his reputation still unmade. He managed to lose first himself and then his troops on the battleground. Eight of his British soldiers, who had strayed from the main body of troops, were captured by Tipoo's soldiery who viciously executed their prisoners by hammering nails into their skulls. When the battle was won, however, it was Wellington who discovered Tipoo Sahib's body, 'short-necked, broad-shouldered and corpulent, with tiny hands and feet' under a pile of corpses. To Baird's fury, it was also the wealthy and well-connected Wellington (as we shall call him from now on) who received the lucrative appointment of governor of the captured city. The appointment led to Baird's lifelong feelings of resentment towards Wellington who, he believed (rightly), had benefited from his family relationship as brother to the governor-general.

The only potential native ally left to the French in India was now the Mahratta chieftain, Sindhia, formidable but unreliable, and his army, still led by General Perron, still powerful but weakened by internal rivalries among its French and Mahratta officers.

The course of these events in India was, of course, unknown for many months to Napoleon Bonaparte. But always a realist and always ready to adapt to changing conditions, he was becoming very aware of the immense difficulties that lay on the route from Cairo to Delhi.

Between the French and India, whether by seaway or even by an overland march, lay the Royal Navy, as Bonaparte and Desaix were to find out. For both Bonaparte's army in Syria and Desaix's army in the upper Nile valley, after their long marches over the desert, when they came to their final halts, one at Acre on the Mediterranean, the other at Kosseir on the Red Sea, found themselves facing the British navy: Sir Sidney Smith's squadron at Acre, Commodore Blankett's at Kosseir.

There was enough water just offshore to float a ship and so, true to its tradition, the Royal Navy was there.

EYELESS TO ASWAN
The Nile Valley 1798-1799

Two military expeditions set out from Cairo during the French occupation, one into Syria (which, in those days, as well as the Syria of today, included parts of what we now call Jordan, Iraq, Lebanon, Israel and Palestine), the other up the valley of the Nile.

The Syrian campaign is by far the best known, undoubtedly because it was led by General Bonaparte himself. The more stirring, however, and the one that achieved the most, was the long campaign that General Desaix waged upstream in the Nile valley, between El Lahun and Philae, sixty to six hundred miles south of Cairo, from August 1798 to October 1799.

Desaix, with nearly three thousand men, set out only a few weeks after the capture of Cairo to bring Murad Bey and his army to battle in the Nile valley, where he and his men had gone to regroup after their defeat at the Pyramids. In support were some artillery, a camel caravan and a small flotilla of river boats to bring up supplies. Desaix was accompanied by two generals: Donzelot, his chief of staff, and Friant, who commanded a brigade. Two more generals were later added to the force: Belliard, who came up with some reinforcements on November 8, and the cavalryman Davout, who joined Desaix with a thousand mounted dragoons and hussars on December 10.

General Louis Friant was the most colourful of these subordinates. A former farm labourer, he had joined the army as a private in 1781, at the age of twenty-three, and was already an old soldier when he went to Egypt. He never took on the fanciful language of the *nouveaux riches* or, later, of the new nobility of the Empire. At Austerlitz, when cannonballs were hurtling and whistling across the battlefield in such quantities that his soldiers lowered their heads, he shouted at them to look up. 'What are you scared about,' he roared at them, 'it's only cannonballs that are flying around, not pieces of shit!'

There is a certain blurred quality to the French pursuit of Murad Bey. For that is what the Nile campaign came essentially to be: bouts of shadow fighting across hundreds of miles, to the very edge of the Tropic of Cancer, against a phantom enemy. Throughout these long months of campaigning, Murad Bey and his few thousand Mamelukes came and went east and west and north and south, disappeared into the Nubian wastes and then, almost magically, reappeared. Then faded away again.

It was a gigantic game of hide-and-seek, the French, many of them suffering from trachoma and half-blind from the pus in their eyes, always doing the seeking, always in conditions of terrible want. 'We are practically naked, without shoes, without anything,' Desaix wrote to Bonaparte. 'The division lacks shoes,' General Donzelot reported to Cairo headquarters on another day. 'The troops are suffering excessive hardship, having to march barefoot on the burning sands.'

The army faced flash floods and desert storms, followed up all the clues that came its way but only rarely found the enemy. Their most unpleasant foe was not human but viral. Trachoma, unlike the elusive Mamelukes, was part of their daily life. Many of the soldiers could hardly see. 'More than three hundred men have the eye disease . . . all our ambulance surgeons, except the chief surgeon, have eye infections,' Donzelot reported only three weeks after the start of the expedition. Trachoma wasn't the only health problem. Dysentery, gonorrhea and syphilis, old and habitual companions of every campaigning army, flourished even more in Egypt than in Europe. 'Dysentery has reappeared. . . . Tomorrow we shall send back to Cairo all the men with acute venereal infections,' Donzelot reported.

The Nile valley campaign has been described as a guerrilla war. It wasn't, at least not quite. Murad Bey was not waging the classical guerrilla warfare which, for instance, the Spaniards later adopted against the French. The French met the Mamelukes and their allies several times in open battle, with artillery and battalions of infantry and squadrons of cavalry, thousands of men engaged in face-to-face, mortal combat. And on these occasions the blood flowed plentifully, particularly among the warriors of Islam, unversed in the ways of modern warfare and eager to die in battle against the unbelievers. But most of the time Murad Bey avoided direct encounters. He preferred to lead the French in an endless chase up and down the valley, wearing them down, exhausting them in pursuit of his armies that were never there when Desaix or one of his generals caught up with them.

Desaix's men were often harassed as well by roving bands of Arab and Bedouin marauders who robbed and murdered any army stragglers that might come their way, and by miserable villagers who hated the French as much as they feared the Mamelukes.

When the French were in the region of Qena and Thebes and Luxor, some eighty miles east of the Red Sea port of Kosseir, a new species of enemy appeared. The French called them Meccans, for they came across the Red Sea from Mecca. Most of them in fact were fierce and fanatical tribesmen from what we call today Saudi Arabia, and they were all devoured by one ambition, overwhelming in its intensity: to kill the Infidel in the name of Allah. 'Their ferocity is equalled only by the misery of their standard of life,' said Napoleon Bonaparte. They hadn't discovered oil under the hot sands yet.

There were also among these warriors equally fanatical pilgrims, returning home from Mecca to Morocco, Algeria, Turkey, Albania and

The French army discovered a forgotten civilisation during their three years in Egypt, 1798-1801

other Islamic parts. Inspired by their recent sight of the Kaaba, the sacred black stone of their religion, by the incantations of the mullahs and by the Holy War teachings of Islam, they were eager to die in battle against the Infidel as a sure way to reach Paradise.

Finally, off Kosseir itself, were to be found the prime enemy: Commodore Blankett's British tars and marines.

But it is not through its military achievements that Desaix's campaign has its place in history. It is as a great adventure story and through its impact in the field of human knowledge that the expedition has to be remembered. Egyptology was born out of it. Many of the thanks must go to Denon, the archaeologist – antiquary, he was called then – who accompanied the army and by his notes and drawings of great monuments half sunk in desert sands brought back to life the civilisation that the Greek historian Herodotus had portrayed more than two thousand years before.

Denon, who was then a man of already fifty-one, often lagged behind the main body of troops to finish his sketches. Because of lurking marauders, this was a dangerous practice. But a few soldiers, sometimes Desaix himself, were always willing to stay with him to protect him against thieves and hostile bands. The whole army shared in this tremendous archaeological adventure.

There was a particularly moving moment which has come down to us as a still-stirring tribute to the power of civilisation. One morning, on January 27, 1799, the soldiers marching along the river bank suddenly saw stretched out before them the ancient glories of Thebes, the splendid temples of Karnak and of Luxor, bathed in the early light of day. The whole army came to a halt, applauded and then, quite spontaneously, without orders, these hundreds of rough, weary and diseased warriors drew up in lines, stood to attention and presented arms, while the drums beat and the trumpets sounded their homage to the grandeur of man.

In his account of his travels in Egypt, Denon passed on to us the emotions he felt in the company of these often unlettered soldiers who tried, in every little way they could, to help him. Their 'refined sensibility made me rejoice in being a Frenchman,' he wrote. The elation which he shared with his military comrades is still poignant two centuries later.

The strictly military side of the campaign was less exhilarating. The first clash between Murad and Desaix occurred on October 7, 1798, six weeks after the start of the chase, in a little spot called Sediman, in the vicinity of El Faiyum, not very far from where the pursuit had started. Murad's tactics resembled the rotation of a merry-go-round. Desaix had chased him down the Nile to Beni Adi, about two hundred miles south of Cairo. When the Mameluke chief made a detour and turned north again, Desaix's tattered soldiery, often barefooted, followed as best they could. At Sediman, Desaix at last caught up with his adversaries, some four to five thousand Mameluke cavalrymen against whom the Frenchman could only oppose his worn, trachoma-afflicted infantry, inferior in numbers by at least one-third.

Murad Bey had obviously learnt nothing from his Pyramids thrashing. He threw in his baggy-pantalooned horsemen with their jewelled scimitars in mass attacks against the French squares, and once again the Mamelukes were slaughtered. The French waited steadily until the charging horsemen were only twenty paces away and then fired. The fighting was ferocious – in their hatred of each other, the wounded and the dying were killing each other on the ground. Final casualties were approximately four hundred Mamelukes and a hundred French. Defeated, but not dispirited, Murad withdrew and the merry-go-round pursuit continued.

The next clash, on November 8, was between some five hundred of Desaix's troopers, defending the general's temporary headquarters at El Faiyum, and several thousand rebellious peasants and villagers. Military professionalism once again won over disorderly rage. The French lost four men, the Arabs two hundred. Bruised and battered, the poor fellahin retired to their villages and pondered on the mysterious way of Allah who gave victory to the Christians and withheld it from the Faithful.

More marches and countermarches followed. Desaix had now been joined by General Belliard, with his infantry, and General Davout, with his cavalry. On Christmas Day, 1798, the French captured the

Mameluke flotilla moored at Asyut, and continued south, trying to catch up with the ever-fleeing Murad. Many of the sailors, who were Greeks, went over to the French side.

It was on January 22, 1799, at Samhud, near the central Nile capital of Garga, that Desaix's men, about four thousand in all, finally overtook the Mameluke horde. Murad lined up his fourteen thousand men, including about two thousand from the Arabian peninsula and two thousand Mameluke cavalry. Once again the Mameluke cavalry launched its whirlwind attacks against the French squares. Once again they were repulsed. Murad Bey then ordered his Meccan infantry to attack. They were also slaughtered in their hundreds. Total French casualties for the day: one dead.

After the Battle of Samhud the French army in the Nile valley split in two. One part under Desaix marched north, the other, under Belliard, moved south in pursuit of Murad. Ten days and two hundred and fifty miles later Belliard reached Aswan, but Murad was still ahead of him, somewhere in the forbidding desert that stretched away south into the Sudan.

Whatever his other qualities, leading an army to victory was not Murad Bey's forte. A big, brawny man, with a huge blond beard, Murad Bey was from Circassia, on the Black Sea (now within the borders of the Soviet Union). He was about fifty years old at the time and was said to be 'unjust, cruel and proud to excess' and extremely brave. But he never won a battle against the French.

Belliard now sent a detachment up to the island of Philae, site of some of the most glorious monuments of Egyptian antiquity. Many of the native women, terrified at the appearance of the French, drowned their daughters or sewed up their genital organs to save them from being raped. Bemused and shocked, the French turned around and marched back north. On hearing that Murad was trying to cut him off from Desaix, who had taken the rest of the army north towards Asyut, he, too, marched on to Asyut. But he got no further than the village of Abnud, down river from Karnak.

Just below Karnak, tragedy had overtaken ships in the little flotilla that had accompanied Desaix's expedition up the Nile, the river boat *Italia* among them. In addition to supplies, the *Italia* was carrying some three hundred blind and wounded soldiers, two hundred sailors and marines and a military band. On March 3, the boat, while beached, was attacked by two thousand frenzied Muslim warriors, many of them pilgrims from Mecca. They forced ashore those who survived their onslaught then obliged the band to play while, in the name of Allah the Merciful and to the accompaniment of martial music, they methodically sodomised, tortured and killed all the survivors, including the sick, blind and wounded. They then slaughtered the members of the band.

Two days later, on March 5, 1799, Belliard received news of the massacre. Although he had only a thousand men with him, many of whom were suffering from the usual trachoma condition, Belliard marched with his army to the attack. Three days later French Republicans and Muslims met near the village of Abnud, not far from the scene of the massacre. The mixed Meccan-Mameluke force stretched out in a line more than two miles long. Outnumbered by more than three to one the French infantrymen, with rage in their hearts, resolutely marched to the attack in their tight, square formations. They had only one gun, and fifteen cavalrymen rode along their flanks, facing at least three hundred and fifty Mameluke horsemen. The Meccans also had the artillery they had taken from the *Italia.* The French charged and took all the guns back.

The enemy, more efficient at massacring than at fighting, fell back. Some of the fleeing Meccans barricaded themselves in a large, fortified, brick mansion in the village. Belliard's men gave no quarter, took no prisoners. They threw burning material into the building, and turned it into an inferno. The Meccans, inside, desperately fought the flames, prayed, sang, hurled defiance at the Infidels, called on Allah for help, sallied out to attack the grimly merciless French, or tried to escape. The siege went on through the night. The Meccans had no water, either to drink or with which to fight the fire. They tried to beat out the flames by stamping on them or hitting them with their hands. By the morning it was all over. The French found thirty men still alive, so burned that if they moved, their skin burst open. Three Tunisian pilgrims on their way home were spared.

Later in March, Desaix, now near Asyut, defeated and destroyed an army of several hundred fellahin, while Murad and his horsemen waited on the sidelines to see how the fighting developed. Seeing it was not going in their side's favour, they galloped away to safety. In April, General Davout, out on a punitive mission with a few hundred cavalrymen, attacked an army of two thousand Arabs recruited by Murad Bey and killed most of them, for the loss of eight of his men.

Meanwhile, after the horrific little battle of Abnud, Belliard continued south to meet with Desaix, as he had planned. But first, he headed east to Kosseir, in order to block the flow of the Meccans coming into Egypt. His force amounted to only three hundred and fifty French infantrymen and some sixty friendly Bedouins. They left Qena on May 26, mounted on camels, covered the hundred and fifty miles in three days, and took Kosseir without a fight. Belliard stayed a couple of days in the down-at-heel little Red Sea port and then retired to Qena, leaving behind a garrison of Frenchmen, whose presence was sufficient to put an end, once and for all, to the Meccan intrusions and, as we read earlier, to beat off a British landing by Commodore Blankett's force three months later.

Murad Bey continued his will-o'-the-wisp career for a few more months, until October 1799 when Desaix, at the head of his camel corps, defeated him in a skirmish near El Faiyum. It is said that the old warrior, worn out, agreed to join the French. But he never made his expected appearance by the side of his old enemies. He simply vanished.

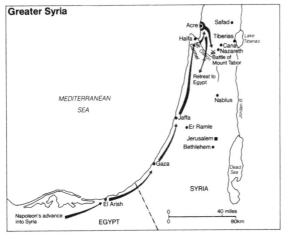

A DESTINY DESTROYED
The Syrian Campaign 1799

Before returning to Egypt to join General Desaix in his campaign against Murad Bey, Napoleon Bonaparte had been fighting the Turks in Syria. Back in February 1799, leaving the cheerful and cynical General Dugua in command in Cairo, the melancholic General Menou in charge of Rosetta, General Marmont holding the important port of Alexandria and trying to cope with the allied blockade, and General Louis Almeras at Damietta, Napoleon marched north, where Turkish troops were massing to attack him in Egypt. Four French divisions, one commanded by General Bonaparte himself, the others by Generals Reynier, Lannes and Kléber, thirteen thousand men in all, converged on El Arish, on the Egyptian-Syrian border, held by troops of the Ottoman Empire who were using it as an advance base for their planned invasion of Egypt.

General Bon and General Rambaud were also attached to the force, as was General Verdier whose courageous little Italian wife, refusing to be separated from her husband, accompanied him on the expedition. The one-legged General Caffarelli was in charge of the engineers, and General Dommartin in command of the artillery. The siege artillery, too heavy and cumbersome to drag overland but vital for attacks upon fortifications, had been sent by sea to be picked up by the French when they reached the vicinity of Acre.

It was an elite body of troops who laid siege to the fortress of El Arish where some fifteen hundred soldiers of the Ottoman Empire, mainly seasoned fighters from Morocco and Albania, were entrenched. Short of food and water, the outnumbered enemy surrendered to the French on February 18, after a ten-day siege, and were paroled on condition they went to Baghdad and no longer bore arms against the French. But there was a greater peril in the offing than these confused soldiers of Islam. When they entered the captured strongpoint, the French found one room full of stinking enemy soldiers dying of the plague. It was an ominous prelude to the campaign.

The French continued their hard-slogging march up the coast. Gaza, on the way, was taken without a fight on February 24 and, not far from Jerusalem, they occupied Er Ramble on March 1. The Muslims of Er Ramble had all fled the day before the French arrival, only the Christians remained, confident they would come to no harm from these fellow-Catholics, however renegade, from Europe.

The Christians in the next town to be taken, Jaffa, lived however to curse their co-religionists. The garrison refused to surrender when the enemy appeared outside the walls on March 3. The French launched their attack on March 7 and the town fell in the evening, after which some of the French troops ran amok and slaughtered many of the inhabitants, Muslims, Jews and Christians, without distinction.

The horror was compounded a few days later when Bonaparte ordered his troops to kill some two to three thousand Turkish troops who, holding the citadel, had surrendered on March 8 after promises by two of his aides that their lives would be spared. Only the Egyptians among the prisoners were spared and sent home. The others, mainly Turks, Algerians and Moroccans, were shot or bayoneted (to save ammunition) to death on the beach over the next two or three days. It is one of the few episodes of Napoleon's military career that have left an indelible stain on his reputation.

His apologists have tried to find excuses for him. His aides were not authorised to accept the Turkish surrender. True. Many of the men captured at Jaffa had already been captured at El Arish and had broken their parole by fighting against the French again, a capital offence under military law. True. There was not enough food to feed these prisoners. True. If he had freed them, they would probably have gone to join Djezzar Pasha's garrison at Acre to fight against the French again. True. The defenders of Jaffa had barbarically killed a French soldier who had gone to speak to them under a flag of truce, stuck his head on a pole and raised it over the citadel walls. True. All true, yet the fact remains that at this moment of victory Napoleon ordered the killing in cold blood of two or three thousand unarmed men. (Later, at St Helena, Bonaparte claimed that the number of men shot was 'about a thousand or twelve hundred'.)

Napoleon's justification can be summarised in two words: military necessity.

The day after Jaffa was taken, bubonic plague broke out in the French ranks. Its symptoms: large swellings (or *buboes*, hence the name) in the groin or armpits, bursting of the buboes, high fever, delirium, raging headache, pain all over the body, convulsions and, usually, death.

By March 9 the number of cases had risen to thirty-one.

The very word 'plague' carries fear and horror, and panic swept through the army. Bonaparte, as usual, remained cool. On March 11, disregarding the risk of contagion, he visited the victims in hospital and stayed one or two hours with them, comforting the sick and helping the doctors.

Three days later he left Jaffa to attack Acre. By then three hundred plague victims had to remain behind. On March 17, he arrived at Mount Carmel, near Haifa, from where he could look down on Acre on the other side of the bay, and where, to his dismay, he saw two powerful ships-of-the-line anchored offshore, seemingly waiting for him and his army. The Royal Navy was there.

The two vessels were the 80-gun HMS *Tigre* and the 74-gun HMS *Theseus*. With these ships, two old acquaintances return into our story: the stodgy New Englander, Captain Ralph Willett Miller, of the *Theseus*, who was with us about eight months ago at the Battle of the Nile, and that flamboyant and restless sailor, Sir Sidney Smith, now a commodore with his flag on the *Tigre*, as active as ever, always pushing himself into the most extravagant naval situations.

The confrontation in Acre was worthy of the man, although he could not have realised its full historical implications. For he now stood between Napoleon Bonaparte and what the general believed to be his destiny: the conquest of the East.

Mastery of the sea was to determine the ultimate fate of the military campaign General Bonaparte was now waging on land: the fate was to be defeat for the French, thanks to two warships floating in the water off Acre, this 'mud-hole' as Napoleon later referred to it. And Sidney Smith was to be forever, 'the man who made me miss my destiny.'

For Smith and Miller, the action at Acre was the second historic moment they were sharing. The first had been six years ago, on the day of the allied evacuation of Toulon, when they had tried to destroy the abandoned French ships in the harbour under the fire of Major Bonaparte's artillery. Now, once again, they were facing their old foe.

Commodore Sidney Smith had arrived only a few days before from Alexandria where he had taken command of the blockading naval force to the great annoyance, let it be said, of Lord Nelson who disliked him intensely – probably because Smith, a brash, tactless and presumptuous man who never paid excessive attention to military ritual and courtesies, had failed to show him the consideration to which Nelson felt entitled.

One of Sidney Smith's best friends was a French Royalist émigré who had helped him to escape from the Paris prison where he was held during the two years after his capture off the French coast in 1796, and who was now serving with him at Acre with a commission as engineer colonel in the British army. Louis Phélipeaux was a genius in the art of fortifications. He and Napoleon Bonaparte were old acquaintances. They had been cadets together at the military college at Brienne fifteen years ago. Bonaparte had joined the Republicans after the outbreak of the French Revolution. Phélipeaux had remained faithful to the king. Now on opposing sides, they faced each other across the battlements of Acre.

Just as Bonaparte arrived on the heights of Mount Carmel overlooking Acre, with perfect but disastrous timing, the French flotilla of nine small boats bringing Bonaparte's siege artillery hove into sight. The British battleships immediately pounced upon them. The French boats, with about forty small guns between them, had no chance against the heavy metal from the one hundred and fifty-four guns of the British battleships. Before Bonaparte's eyes, the British squadron not only captured six of the nine little French vessels but, what was worse, seized also the siege artillery and ammunition they were bringing, with which Bonaparte had planned to blast the walls of the town and citadel. Now, instead, these guns would be used against him. Bonaparte was discovering again, as after the Battle of the Nile, the importance of naval supremacy.

It was the Turkish commander in Acre, Djezzar 'The Butcher' Pasha, governor of the region, who benefited from Britain's might at sea and who, because of British help, turned the siege of Acre from expected defeat into a messy but momentous victory. Before the arrival of the British squadron, and of Phélipeaux, its Turkish defenders had been reconciled to the capture of the city with its ramshackle walls and fortifications that time and weather had gradually worn down, to the utter indifference of its lethargic rulers. After the British arrival, victory became inevitable.

Djezzar Pasha was a ferocious and ruthless old man who, after fleeing from his native Bosnia over a matter of murder, had begun life in the Middle East as a slave and then had joined the Mamelukes. His remarkable talent for murder went hand-in-hand with a masterly aptitude for intrigue, and the two, applied over the years as necessity required, brought him up into the ruling echelons of the Ottoman Empire, where such qualities were respected.

He was said to have strangled hundreds of opponents with his own hands. The rumours may have been an exaggeration, the figure may only run into dozens. Whatever the number, Sir Sidney Smith found

Djezzar the Butcher no gentleman.

Curiously, one of the most powerful political figures in Constantinople was a French woman from Martinique related to Bonaparte, Aimée Dubucq de Rivery, a cousin of Josephine. She had been captured at sea off the French coast by Algerian corsairs around 1780, and, because of her beauty, presented as a gift to the Sultan of Constantinople, the ageing Abdul Hamid I. She joined his harem where she spent most of her time, pink, pretty and naked, splashing around the baths with the other ladies of the harem. In due course, Aimée presented Abdul with a son, Mahmud. Abdul died in 1789 and she became a sort of Queen Mother, quite often influencing Turkish policy in favour of France – at least, until Bonaparte invaded Egypt.

This distant, exotic relationship was certainly not on General Bonaparte's mind when, without his artillery, he began the siege of Acre on March 1. It went on for more than two and a half months of numerous and bloody assaults and sorties. Both sides faced a common enemy: the plague. But, largely thanks to the work of Phélipeaux on the walls and battlements, even though the French occupied the town, they never broke into the citadel. They launched seven major assaults against the fortress, mined it, built trenches around it, tried to storm it with the use of ladders. It was all in vain. All the attacks were repelled by the Turks and their British allies.

Djezzar refused to grant a truce to bury the dead. The stench was appalling with rotting corpses littering the walls and courtyards surrounding the citadel. Furthermore, to the distress of Sir Sidney Smith who managed to save a few French enemies by keeping them as his guests on board his ship, the Turks cut off the heads of the French soldiers who fell into their hands. And since they received special bounty payments on each head brought in, Turkish soldiers even decapitated the dead bodies of French soldiers. The siege of Acre was a grisly affair.

Three generals were among the French dead: Rambaud and Bon, both killed trying to break into the citadel, and Bonaparte's great friend, Caffarelli. After losing his leg in Europe, he now lost an arm in Acre and died from his wound while having Montesquieu's *The Spirit of the Laws* read to him. A fourth general, the gunner Dommartin, died a few weeks later of tetanus. An ardent Republican, it was said he didn't give his best during the Syrian campaign as he feared Bonaparte was planning to be crowned king – of Persia!

Approximately one French soldier in ten was killed by the enemy or died of wounds, in all about 1,200 men. Another thousand died of disease, mostly of the plague. About 2,300 were wounded or returned seriously ill. The casualty rate in all was 4,500 out of 13,000 men, thirty per cent for three months of war. Even the trench warfare of the 1914-18 war was less of a holocaust.

On the allied side, Phélipeaux died on May 1, officially from ex-haustion but possibly from the plague. The thrifty New Englander Captain Miller was blown up when a pile of unburst enemy shells, which he had frugally collected on his ship with the intention of firing them back at the French, exploded. Miller and forty-five of his crew were killed. A few dozen British and a few hundred Turks perished in the fighting. But the big losses were nearly all on the French side, at least in the immediate area of Acre.

The fighting during the Syrian campaign, however, was not limited to the siege of Acre. Turkish regulars and local Arab tribesmen, at the call of Djezzar, were preparing to attack the French besiegers. They had to be dispersed. Four important battles took place in April 1799. Near Nazareth on the 5th, Junot put to flight an attacking Arab cavalry force which outnumbered his several times over. At Canaa, Kléber with fifteen hundred men routed a Turkish army of nearly five thou-sand on April 11. On April 15, Murat defeated another Turkish army of five thousand on the Jordan, near Lake Tiberias. On April 16, further south, near Mount Tabor, Kléber once again went into action with a small army of two thousand men. With Bonaparte's assistance in the last stage of the battle, he trounced a Syrian army of thirty-five thousand cavalry and infantry, for the loss of two men killed and sixty wounded.

Everywhere, that month, the French were victorious except in Acre. Tens of thousands of Druses and Lebanese Christians were ready to join Bonaparte and march on to Constantinople, or India, once Acre was taken, Djezzar captured and the British back at sea. But if Bona-parte did not take the town, his campaign would end right there. And that is what happened.

In mid-May, Turkish reinforcements poured into the citadel, brought in by sea in twenty transports from the island of Rhodes. The French were paying, once again, for their failure to rule the seas and now there was only one course left: to abandon the siege. On May 20 the long march back to Cairo began. The sick and wounded were given horses to ride. Everyone else, including Bonaparte, walked. General Boyer was sent ahead to announce their triumphant return. Napoleon Bonaparte had a great sense of public relations long before that art of masterly misrepresentation had become a highly-paid profession.

In his report to Lord Nelson, Commodore Sir Sidney Smith piously announced his victory to his devout chief. 'I am just returned from the Cave of the Annunciation where, secretly and alone, I have been re-turning thanks to the Almighty for our late wonderful success,' he wrote in a little note from Nazareth.

As for the French, they tramped wearily back through the desert to Egypt, giving thanks to no one and cursing Bonaparte. On June 14, that remnant of the French army from Syria still alive and fit to walk, reached the Egyptian capital and marched in through the Gate of Victory. Bands played, the garrison presented arms, every returning soldier wore a palm frond in his hat. They smiled and waved, pleased to have survived the plague and Djezzar's head-cutting soldiery. General Bonaparte raised his hat and saluted the Egyptian crowd who had gathered to watch his return. But no one was fooled. The people of Cairo, wrote a French officer, 'seemed extremely curious to discover how many of us were left.'

General Bonaparte was not thinking of marching on India that day. He was wondering how to make his way back to France.

THE GENERAL ABSCONDS
Egypt 1799

Beaten at Acre, before starting on his march back to Egypt, Bonaparte was already planning to return to France. Through the reports of travellers and the infrequent arrival of a newspaper or two, he had learnt that France was now at war with Austria again, as well as with the Russians and the Turks who had joined the fray after the Battle of the Nile. Europe was where the action was now, not Egypt. Egypt had become an aimless backwater, a place leading to nowhere, keeping General Bonaparte uselessly from where he should be: in the van of the fighting.

The Second Coalition, instigated and financed by Britain, had been formed just before Christmas 1798. Two hundred thousand French soldiers on the continent were now facing half a million enemy troops. The French were fighting General Mack's Neapolitans and Sicilians in southern Italy, Suvorov's Russians and Melas's Austrians in northern Italy, more Austrians under Prince Charles on the Rhine. An army of eighteen thousand men under the Duke of York, and Abercromby, was preparing to sail from England to join an equal number of Russians in Holland and northern Germany. The Russians were also in Turin and more Austrians in Milan. The Neapolitans had temporarily occupied Rome. The Austrians had defeated the French at Stockach on the Rhine and at Magnano and Cassano in Italy. The British were masters of the Mediterranean. Republican France, once again, stood alone against the kingdoms of Europe.

Bonaparte took two months to organise his secret departure. And fortunately he was able to leave Egypt, not with the memory of the Acre setback, but on the surge of a great new victory.

On July 14, 1799, a large Ottoman army which had been training for months in Rhodes, and included some of the troops against whom he had fought at Acre, landed in Aboukir Bay under the protection of British, Russian and Turkish ships. The next day Bonaparte, who had briefly joined Desaix in the pursuit of Murad Bey, was advised of the

Turks' landing and immediately rushed back to the coast to fight them.

He found the Turks installed in their thousands on the Aboukir peninsula. Bonaparte claimed there were twenty thousand of them, but that high number may have been chosen simply to enhance his victory. Others say there were only nine thousand. The true figure probably lies somewhere in between. Commodore Sir Sidney Smith was also present, in HMS *Tigre*. He wouldn't have missed a fight for any reason.

After landing and defeating the few French defenders on the shore, the Turks just stood around awaiting events. Bonaparte arrived ten days later with ten thousand troops. Joachim Murat's cavalry charged with such impetuousness that he drove right through the Turkish lines and captured their general, the elderly Mustafa Pasha, while the French infantry, under Lannes, was still far behind.

A couple of thousand fleeing Turkish troops managed to reach a nearby disused fort where they barricaded themselves in. Another couple of thousand were killed during the battle. A few more thousand, at least four thousand, drowned when, fleeing in terror, they tried to swim to the Allied ships offshore. Sir Sidney Smith sent the boats from HMS *Tigre* to pick up survivors, and took personal charge of a gig which pulled in several gasping, exhausted soldiers.

The Turks who had taken refuge in the fort, fearing they might be massacred, held out for a week without food or drink. One thousand of them died before the rest, weak from hunger and thirst, surrendered. Bonaparte gave them food and water and allowed them to go home. In this case there was no 'military necessity' for massacring them, as he claimed there had been at Jaffa. Total Turkish losses: about seven thousand dead.

After the battle, Sir Sidney Smith sent a sad little message to his superior, Lord Nelson, advising him, without any mention of the Almighty this time, of 'the entire defeat of the First Division of the Ottoman Army'. He also sent General Bonaparte a few recently received newspapers, from London and Frankfurt, just to show him the French were not doing so well elsewhere. Sir Sidney then went back to the blockade of Alexandria and Bonaparte returned to Cairo.

He only stayed in the Egyptian capital a week. By this time, prompted by the news in the newspapers of the recent French reverses, he decided to go back to France immediately. In a letter dated May 2, 1799, he had, moreover, received permission from the Directory to return, with or without his troops.

He only told a few intimates of his decision. Pauline Fourès was not one of them. Nor was General Kléber, who would succeed him to the command of the troops in Egypt. He knew his plan would antagonise many of the French soldiers – generals, officers and the rank and file – who would consider his departure a betrayal. He preferred not to hear their comments. Secrecy, also, was essential. Rumours of his plans might reach British ears, and lead to a tighter watch offshore by Sir Sidney's rather slapdash squadron, which found blockade duty dull.

In a few whispered, confidential conversations, he gathered around him the people he wished to accompany him: his secretary Bourrienne; four ADCs, including Duroc, and his stepson, Eugène de Beauharnais; three of the scientists, Monge, Berthollet and Denon; half a dozen generals; and a Mameluke, the Georgian Routstam, who was to be his personal servant for the next fifteen years. Admiral Ganteaume was in command of the two frigates in which they were to make their dash to France across a Mediterranean swarming with British ships.

Before sailing, General Bonaparte handed a sheaf of documents to General Menou, the commander in nearby Rosetta. They were mainly instructions addressed to General Kléber, whom he appointed to take his place as commander-in-chief of the Army of Egypt. There was also an order-of-the-day assuring the soldiers reinforcements would be coming from France, and a personal note to Kléber, asking him to make sure that General Desaix leave Egypt for France in November. There must surely have been a little *billet doux* for Pauline Fourès as well. Then, early on the morning of August 23, the two French frigates, the *Muiron* and the *Carrère*, raised anchor and, hugging the coast to avoid the patrolling British ships, headed in a westerly direction. Bonaparte, once again, was trusting himself and his future to the whims of winds and good fortune. And once again fortune smiled and the winds stood fair for Bonaparte.

The events that followed Bonaparte's departure from Egypt and arrival in France do not lie within the range of this book. It is enough for us to know that after an unadventurous trans-Mediterranean voyage, General Bonaparte and his party arrived on October 1 in Ajaccio, the town where he was born, for his last visit ever to his native Corsica. He remained for a week. He landed at St Raphael, on the French Riviera, on October 9. By the 16th he was in Paris. By the 18th, after a night of tears and pleading, he had made up with the unfaithful and distraught Josephine. By November 9, three weeks later, with the support of the politician Barras, his old acquaintance from the Toulon days, he ruled all France. His title was First Consul. The politicians Jean-Jacques Cambacérès and Charles Lebrun were Second and Third Consul. But the boss was unmistakably Napoleon Bonaparte.

One of his first actions was to send a message through the British blockade to his former comrades in Malta and Egypt, to announce that their former commander-in-chief was now the ruler of France and that he had not forgotten them.

MURDER IN THE WAY
Egypt 1799

General Bonaparte's carefully managed and secret departure had pre-
dictably incensed the French army in Egypt. Two people were particularly enraged. One, in the role of the woman scorned, was Pauline
Fourès, to whom he had said goodbye in Cairo after patting her on the
behind and telling her casually he was just off to Alexandria. The other
was General Kléber who was furious at finding himself in command of
an army marooned in a hot, dusty and dirty North African dump. In
Egypt the French were now virtually a besieged army, surrounded by
enemies on every side: to the north, from the sea, by the Royal Navy;
to the east by an advancing Turkish army, reported to be nearly eighty
thousand strong; to the south by the elusive Mamelukes; to the west,
by the cruel and endless desert and the cruel, erratic Beduin tribesmen.
Kléber had every right to feel outraged.

The Alsatian – he was from Strasbourg – didn't hide his feelings at
what he considered the trick Bonaparte had played on him. 'He's left
us with his breeches full of shit,' he roared with his strong Germanic
accent and in his usual earthy style. 'We'll go back to Europe and rub it
in his face.'

Kléber may have admired Bonaparte as a soldier but he had always
disliked him as a man. In addition, he now also disapproved of the entire Egyptian enterprise which he considered to have been utterly futile
and frivolous, aimed only at aggrandizing Napoleon Bonaparte's reputation. In this opinion he differed from his besotted colleague General
Menou who dreamt of a new France on the banks of the Nile and who
adopted his young wife's Muslim religion, after first making sure he
would not have to be circumcised. To integrate himself even more into
local life, this ludicrous man then changed his first name from Jacques
to Abdallah. He was the joke of the army.

Menou's conversion to Islam didn't impress the Turks. They just
wanted the French out of their Egyptian province, and a couple of
months after Bonaparte's departure several thousand of their troops
landed at Damietta. General Verdier pounced on them with less than a
thousand men, and once again the Turks were routed.

But the French army in Egypt, however numerous their victories,
could not win. Their position was not all that dangerous. It was simply
hopeless. They could hold out for many more months yet but their
very presence there had become meaningless. Victory for the French
was unattainable, even if they could not be defeated.

Kléber was a realist. It was now time 'for the two most civilised
nations of Europe to cease fighting each other,' he sensibly wrote to
Commodore Sir Sidney Smith. Sir Sidney, whose brother was on Lord

Elgin's staff at the British embassy in Constantinople, was delighted to step into the diplomatic arena and try to find an honourable way out of Egypt for his French enemies.

Just before his departure from Egypt, Bonaparte had written to the Grand Vizier in Constantinople, Yussef, who combined the position of Prime Minister of the Ottoman Empire and that of commander in chief of its armies, suggesting that since Turkey had been unable to recover Egypt by military means, it should try to do so by negotiation. 'France never intended to take Egypt away from you,' he claimed.

Even so, General Kléber limited himself, at first, to contacts with the British. He knew Commodore Sir Sidney Smith, hovering off the coast with his blockading squadron, was anxious to achieve a diplomatic *coup* by securing the French departure from Egypt. After writing him the pleasant little note already quoted, Kléber sent General Desaix and the chief French civilian official in Egypt, Monsieur Poussièlgue, under a flag of truce to see Sir Sidney aboard HMS *Tigre*. They were, of course, piped aboard and received with full military honours but also with genuine affability by the Commodore, who was always happy to have French guests on board, ally or enemy, to share his claret and on whom to try out his French.

The two emissaries remained three weeks on board, negotiating, with Sir Sidney virtually setting himself up as mediator between the French and the Grand Vizier, Yussef, now installed with his army at El Arish. The commodore received great encouragement from the British ambassador to the Sublime Porte, in Constantinople, the art-loving Lord Elgin, who had a double objective: to get the French out of Egypt and to remove the friezes from the Parthenon in Athens and ship them to London.

On January 13, 1800, Sir Sidney escorted his two French guests to the Ottoman headquarters for the conclusion of the Treaty of El Arish, which was signed a few days later. Under its terms, the French agreed to leave Cairo in forty days, to await transportation back to France in the ports of Alexandria, Aboukir and Rosetta. The Turks, well aware that they could not get rid of the French by fighting them, agreed to pay the French army two million francs to cover the cost of their occupation for another couple of months. Everybody drank mint tea, salaamed, and Sir Sidney and the two Frenchmen left, very satisfied with themselves. Sir Sidney, for his part, hoped the French soldiers would, on their return to France, give trouble both to the government that had sent them to a distant and unhealthy country, and to General Bonaparte who had abandoned them there.

But alas for the homesick French, they in fact had to wait almost another two years before returning home, for the British government refused to agree to any conditions save unconditional surrender by the French. Admiral Lord Keith, who had become commander-in-chief of the Mediterranean, was ordered to take no notice of any agreement between the French and the Turks.

While Kléber was still awaiting London's official reaction to the El Arish treaty, an envoy arrived in Cairo from Paris to announce to the Army of Egypt that their former commander-in-chief, General Bonaparte, was now the ruler of France.

The bearer of this momentous news, Colonel the Marquis Marie-Victor Nicolas de La Tour-Maubourg, as his name unmistakably indicates, was of an old and very aristocratic family. He had recently returned to France, after Bonaparte passed a law granting an amnesty to those who had fled abroad at the time of the Revolution. He was a friend of Lafayette and the First Consul had personally selected him to give his former comrades-in-arms the good news.

In Egypt, the marquis became Kléber's aide-de-camp and was with his chief when news of the British rejection of the Treaty of El Arish reached the French camp. Kléber roared like 'an infuriated camel' when he read Lord Keith's insolent letter.

In good faith, Kléber had already allowed the Grand Vizier's army, forty to seventy thousand strong, to establish itself at Heliopolis, a few miles from Cairo. That army now had to be made to leave. 'Prepare yourselves for battle,' he told his troops. He advised Yussef the truce was over and two days later, early in the morning, he attacked the vast Turkish horde with ten thousand French soldiers and sent it reeling back east. The Battle of Heliopolis remains one of the great feats of arms of these wars. It took Kléber one week to rid Egypt of all the Ottoman troops.

Romantic General Menou, who had opposed the signing of the El Arish pact as a French capitulation, felt obliged to send Kléber a lyrical letter of congratulation after his victory. 'Remember who you are and you will be the founder of a magnificent colony,' he wrote. He received a curt reply from the Alsatian. He had hoped, Kléber wrote, that the Treaty of El Arish would end 'the insane [Egyptian] enterprise'.

'You, General,' Kléber concluded bitingly, 'have your face turned towards the East. Mine is turned to the West. We shall never understand each other.'

While Kléber was chasing the Grand Vizier's shattered survivors back to Syria, another Turkish force nipped into Cairo. The populace, believing the French had been defeated, rose in revolt and, aided by the Turks, went on a rampage through the Christian quarters where the Greeks and Copts lived, raping, looting and murdering.

Kléber, back outside Cairo a few days later, on March 27, laid siege to the city. The mob murdered his emissary, sent under a flag of truce, and the French general then decided to starve the city into surrender. At Bulaq, on the edge of Cairo, which the French occupied, the population fought them with the usual frenzied, suicidal courage of Middle

Eastern combatants. One of the mob leaders, Al-Bashtili, was captured by the French who nonchalantly ordered his own followers to execute him. They did not do so gently but savagely beat him to death with clubs, presumably for losing.

On April 22, Cairo surrendered, the French marched in and the Turks, under escort, marched out. Less than two months later, on June 14, Kléber was a dead man, stabbed by a religious fanatic, a Syrian from Aleppo, a young clerk called Soliman. He was a *hadji*, which means he had made the pilgrimage to Mecca, and he had killed the Christian invader, he said, 'for the glory of God'.

Soliman, in Cairo, was executed by the usual local method of impalement. But first his right hand, the hand that had killed, was placed over a fire of red hot coals and roasted. A stake was then thrust through his body and planted in the ground. It took him four hours to die. The French were more merciful to three sheikhs who, knowing of his intention to kill the general, had failed to warn them. They had their heads cut off.

General Abdallah Menou, an excellent administrator but otherwise absurd, now became commander in chief of the French army in Egypt. Soliman, writer J. Christopher Herold points out, 'had killed the man whose sole desire was to end the French occupation of Egypt, and in his place he had put an imperialistic maniac who was determined to make Egypt a part of France.'

General Belliard was appointed to the Cairo command.

That same month, tireless old General Sir Ralph Abercromby, back from the West Indies and Ireland and a bout of campaigning against the French in the Netherlands, arrived in the island of Minorca, off the coast of Spain, to take over the command of British troops in the Mediterranean. He would be landing in Egypt in a few months at the head of a large army to fight the French again. In India, too, an expeditionary force, under Baird and Wellington, was being readied for Egypt. Troops from South Africa were preparing to leave Cape Town for the Red Sea port of Kosseir, and another Turkish army was being formed to join the assault. The times ahead were not to be restful for the French in Egypt.

CHAPTER SEVEN

Frigates and Privateers of the Eastern Seas

THE MANGOES OF ADMIRAL RAINIER
The Indian Ocean 1794-1796

The French frigates from Mauritius that General Bonaparte was awaiting in Suez in November 1798 never came. There were eight of them
altogether, and the flotilla had been under the command of Admiral
Pierre de Sercey since his arrival in the Indian Ocean just over two
years before.

When de Sercey sailed into Mauritius back in June 1796, the British
and the French had been at war for more than three years but in all that
time there had been only one clash in the Indian Ocean between their
two navies. The reason was simple: it took two to have a battle, the
French only had two frigates in the whole ocean and didn't like to fight
in case they lost them.

It is, in fact, surprising that the British had not as yet made any effort
to take Mauritius and the other nearby islands of Réunion and Rodriguez – the Mascarenes as they were officially called, from the name of
their Portuguese discoverer three hundred years before. The British
had enough ships and regiments in India to obliterate the small French
forces defending them.

The islands may not have been particularly dangerous to the British
but they were a nuisance. From his island fief Malartic, the French
governor, backed the enemies of Britain in India, notably Tipoo Sahib.
Secondly, these French islands, by their geographical position astride
the route between Britain and India, could interfere – if not with impunity, at least with considerable freedom – with the British sea-traffic
to the Indies. They could also become a serious threat to Britain's

growing communications with her new colony of New South Wales in Australia.

Furthermore, the activities of the French privateers operating out of Port Louis, in Mauritius, would have been in themselves a sufficient reason for a British invasion. From 1793 to 1801, the corsairs of Mauritius captured a hundred and twenty-six British merchant vessels and London insurers were ceaselessly clamouring for stronger British action against the French in the Indian Ocean.

And yet, thanks to privateering, Port Louis was allowed to become a flourishing little port and the Americans, with their strong business vision, opened a consulate there in 1794. In September 1796, three months after Admiral de Sercey's arrival, thirteen American ships sailed from Mauritius, laden with British merchandise captured by French privateers from Bombay and Madras-bound East Indiamen.

The corsairs were adept at their own branch of warfare, which always favoured boarding above gunnery. An undamaged ship and its cargo were worth considerably more than a shattered hulk and burnt and water-logged merchandise. Cannonballs could cause great depreciation to a ship, cutlasses didn't. Robert Surcouf was the most successful of all the privateers. When de Sercey arrived in Mauritius, Surcouf had recently particularly distinguished himself again in a swift cruise, as these privateer sorties were called, which netted him six prizes in a few weeks including the East Indiaman, *Triton*.

Surcouf was already a legend in his own day. Lord Keith, formerly Admiral Elphinstone of the Royal Navy, who commanded in Cape Town and who was in Madras at the time, was stunned by the loss of the *Triton*, and wrote an incredulous, bitter and windy letter to the Admiralty in London. The East Indiaman, he said, 'has been disgracefully captured by a small pilot vessel manned only with twenty-five Frenchmen. The number on board the *Triton* was a hundred and forty. The circumstance is unparalleled in the history of surprising events, and scarcely to be credited.'

The privateers notwithstanding, the islands of Mauritius were very vulnerable and could have been taken with little trouble. Isolated and with small populations, they could not have resisted for more than a few days. Mauritius had 60,000 inhabitants, 50,000 of whom were slaves, Réunion had 57,000, including 47,000 slaves. Rodriguez had maybe two or three hundred people, mainly black slaves. To the north, another group of French islands, the Seychelles, had a population of around 2,000 (no census was taken until 1803), of whom only a couple of hundred were white.

But British activity in the Indian Ocean against their French enemy during the early period of the war was minimal. After taking Pondicherry and forcing the French out of India, they contented themselves with blockading Mauritius and Réunion.

In 1800 however, the British did consider an invasion of the islands. That year Wellington, then a colonel, was asked to take command of an expedition from India against Mauritius but his force was later switched to Kosseir, on the Egyptian Red Sea coast, to fight Bonaparte instead. And to his intense chagrin, before the expedition sailed its command was taken away from him and given to his hated rival, General Sir David Baird. That narrative is for a later chapter.

The blockade of Mauritius was effective at first. It caused severe food shortages on the island – only rice was in plentiful supply – and considerable hardship and grumbling among the white settlers who, being French, enjoyed a good meal and were not getting it.

It was vital to break the blockade and bring in supplies. On October 11, 1794, therefore, the two frigates in the harbour, the *Cybèle*, 40 guns, and the *Prudente*, 36, with the support of a couple of small vessels, made a spirited attack on the heavier Royal Navy vessels patrolling offshore, the 50-gun HMS *Centurion*, and HMS *Diodemede*, 44. It was the first naval engagement of the war between French and British in the Indian Ocean and, incredibly, the French ships won. They inflicted such damage on HMS *Centurion* that that battleship was obliged to limp back to Bombay for repairs and, as it was too risky to leave HMS *Diodemede* on blockade duty alone, the smaller ship sailed back to Madras. The Mauritian blockade was over.

A few weeks before this engagement, Admiral Rainier had arrived in Madras from England to take over the East Indies station. Soon after his arrival news came of this British setback off Mauritius. What was considerably more worrying, he was next advised from London that the Dutch had deserted the British alliance and might soon join the French.

Now Rainier had more than just two French frigates to be concerned over. The Netherlands had large colonies – and large naval squadrons – in and around the Indian Ocean basin: the Cape of Good Hope in South Africa; Ceylon (today's Sri Lanka); Java, Sumatra, Amboina and the other islands of Indonesia; Malacca in Malaya. And worse was to come. Very soon afterwards Spain broke her connection with Britain also and joined the French enemy. Spain too had nearby colonies. Manila in the Philippines was one of the strongpoints of her overseas empire.

So the British admiral found himself facing not one but three enemies: the French, the Dutch and the Spaniards. France was the weakest of the three. The Spanish had three 74s and four slightly war-weary frigates in Manila. The Dutch had a powerful squadron in the East Indies: four or five battleships, half a dozen frigates and seven corvettes, brigs and schooners. Rainier had no reason to feel safe.

With his white hair and black bushy eyebrows, his tight, turned-down mouth and his severe little round glasses, the fifty-year-old

Admiral Sir Peter Rainier

Rainier looked more like a schoolmaster than a fighter, but he was not a man to dither in an emergency. He had fought in all five of the particularly tough actions off the Carnatic coast against the Bailli de Suffren in 1782-83. It was during this first stint in India that Rainier had acquired the passion for mangoes that, according to his sailors, kept him ashore instead of going to sea during that luscious fruit's short season.

But now was no time for mangoes.

Rainier, on hearing the news of the Dutch betrayal (or so he must have considered it), organised two expeditions to attack their colonies. One was bound for Malacca in Malaya, the other, with Rainier himself in direct command, for Trincomalee, in northern Ceylon, with its huge harbour and powerful base. Both surrendered. Then, when winds permitted, Rainier sailed for the Moluccas and occupied the islands of Amboina and Banda, making a fortune in prize money from the nutmeg and the cloves stored in their warehouses.

Another expedition, from England this time, arrived in June 1795 at the Cape of Good Hope, under the orders of Admiral Elphinstone, with Commodore Blankett as his second-in-command. The Dutch capitulated. For the future Lord Keith, it meant a further £64,000 in prize money.

The Indian Ocean 1796-1799

Meanwhile, back in France, the Directory, probably the most absurd government with which France has ever saddled itself, decided that the time had come to strike in the Indian Ocean. Admiral de Sercey was given the command of four frigates, and two corvettes and ordered to wage war against the British navy in the Eastern Seas and defend Mauritius. If, in view of the weakness of his force compared to the enemy's (six ships-of-the-line and at least a dozen frigates, corvettes and sloops), these orders seemed somewhat fatuous, he did not query them. He had just had a very close brush with the guillotine and did not wish to say anything that might place his loyalty to the Republic again in doubt.

His squadron consisted of the frigates *Forte*, 44, *Vertu*, 44, *Regénérée*, 36, and *Seine*, 36, a corvette, the *Bonne-Citoyenne*, and a brig, the *Mutine*. Most of the ships sailed from France on March 4, 1796. The frigates all reached Mauritius but the other two ships were captured by the British on the way. The frigates reached Port Louis, in Mauritius, in June. The two original frigates, the *Prudente* and the *Cybèle* were anchored in the harbour when de Sercey sailed in and were immediately added to his little flotilla. About eight hundred troopers, many of them West Indians, accompanied the Sercey expedition to reinforce the garrisons in the islands.

One wonders what de Sercey was really expected to do. He had absolutely no chance of defeating the British if they ever brought him to battle. Rainier's six battleships included three 74s, as well as two 64s and one 50. Another seventeen British warships were on call in Cape Town, recently captured from the Dutch.

De Sercey was anxious, nevertheless, to show his overlords in Paris that he was a zealous Republican. On July 21, a month after his arrival, he sailed from Mauritius with six frigates to attack Penang, a British base in Malaya.

De Sercey's first cruise was marked by a lot of mileage but no outstanding successes; just a few prizes, taken mainly in the Bay of Bengal, one inconclusive fight against a more powerful British squadron off Sumatra, a visit to the Dutch allies in the East Indies, and then back home to Mauritius. Penang, the original objective, was never attacked.

While de Sercey was carrying out this operation, a much more important engagement was taking place on August 17 a few thousand miles to the west, in Saldanha Bay, near Cape Town, where Elphinstone, lucky as usual, captured without a fight eight Dutch warships. Quite a bag, and no casualties on either side. It won Elphinstone his peerage as Lord Keith and added considerable more tonnage to the already overweight British navy.

The news officially reached India in April 1797 that Spain was now fighting on France's side, and had been since the previous October. The governor-general, Lord Wellesley (still smarting from recent official intimations from London that Lady Wellesley, his French ex-prostitute wife, could not join him in India), put his personal problems aside and ordered his soldiers and sailors to attack the Philippines.

A fleet of six ships-of-the-line, seven frigates and corvettes and eight heavily armed transports were ready by August to sail for Manila and invade the Spanish islands. The two thousand troops in the expeditionary force included the 33rd Regiment, commanded by Arthur, the future Lord Wellington, the governor-general's younger brother. It was not sheer nepotism. Wellington was already showing his talents as a soldier. But before the expedition could sail Lord Wellesley learnt that the Austrian Empire had made its peace with France and withdrawn from the war. That left only Britain, with Portugal, still fighting the French. In fear of an attack on India itself, Lord Wellesley therefore kept all his forces at home and postponed the attack on Manila.

Instead of an expeditionary force, two British frigate captains penetrated, and with ease, the defences of Manila; Captain Edward Cooke (nephew of Sir Sidney Smith), in the 44-gun frigate, HMS *Sybille*, and Captain Pulteney Malcolm (nephew of Lord Keith), of HMS *Fox*, had been sent to find out whether the Spanish ships in harbour were ready for sea and presented a threat to India.

We are now in January 1798 and for Captain Cooke there was a certain *déjà vu* quality to the operation. Nearly five years ago, Lord Hood had sent him into Toulon harbour to find out whether the French fleet would be friendly, just before the British took the town.

Cooke and Malcolm disguised their ships as French frigates, hoisted the French flag, pretended to be from de Sercey's squadron and in need of water and supplies. Both captains' minds were turned to prize money as well as to the glory, for two Spanish treasure ships were said to be in port, and the capture of a treasure ship could mean £50,000 or £60,000 for the captain of the lucky ship that took her. They coolly sailed up Manila Bay, watched by all the other ships in harbour, past Corregidor, to anchor in sight of three battleships and two frigates. The two treasure ships were, unfortunately, nowhere to be seen.

A Spanish boat from shore intercepted HMS *Fox* and a party of Spanish naval officers came on board to be entertained by Malcolm, who was a Spanish linguist. Cooke, who spoke French like a Frenchman, joined them and everybody drank a toast in Malcolm's cabin to the King of Spain, the Republic of France and the defeat of England.

The two British captains were able to find out that the Spanish fleet presented no threat: the ships were not in a fit state to put to sea for at least two months. When they learned that the treasure ships were in an unreachable location at Cavita, Cooke and Malcolm brought their prank to an end. Cooke, who had been passing himself off as a Commandant Latour, announced to their bewildered guests that they were his prisoners and seized three nearby gunboats. But, having sailed in under false colours, the two British interlopers had the grace to release all their captives before departure. They were, after all, gentlemen.

De Sercey meanwhile was scattering his ships all over the world. Two others had joined his six: the *Preneuse*, and the *Brûle-Gueule*.

Prudente stayed in Mauritius as part of the island defence force. *Brûle-Gueule* and *Regénérée* hovered off the coast of India. *Seine* and *Vertu* took three hundred men as reinforcements to Java. The tired and worn *Cybèle* was sent back to France, in dire need of repairs and a refit. Miraculously, in spite of her poor sailing qualities, she sailed through the British blockade and reached her home port. Then the *Seine* was ordered to take three hundred old and sick soldiers back to France. They were unlucky. *Seine* was attacked and taken by two British frigates in the Atlantic and every one of her crew and passengers ended up in the filthy, dark and disease-ridden British hulks. Two frigates, the *Vertu*, back from Java, and the *Regénérée*, which had been operating off India, were now formed into a small squadron commanded by Captain Charles Magon – he died a few years later at Trafalgar – and dispatched to the Philippines at the request of the Spaniards who did not have in the whole colony a single ship fit to make the long voyage to Europe. Their mission: to escort to Spain the two treasure ships, filled with gold, which Cooke and Malcolm had so valiantly and deviously hoped to capture in Manila harbour. On the voyage, Magon fought off two attacks by British warships in the Atlantic, reached Spain safely and received a jewel-encrusted sword of honour from the Spanish Crown as a reward for bringing the treasure home.

Four of de Sercey's squadron had been sent to Europe. The *Prudente*, in Mauritius, was the next to leave his command. A group of local merchants pressured Governor Malartic to sell them the frigate for conversion into another corsair commerce raider. This time they were unlucky. The *Prudente* was taken three months later, on February 9, 1799, and the investors lost all their money.

De Sercey now had three frigates left. The next casualty, three weeks later, was his former flagship, the 44-gun *Forte*, under the command of the elderly Captain Beaulieu le Loup. She was lost in the Bay of Bengal fighting Captain Cooke's HMS *Sybille*. The battle, which began shortly after midnight on February 29, 1799, lasted about two hours, the two ships firing at each other broadside to broadside at almost pistol shot range. *Forte* suffered appalling losses, with nearly half her crew casualties, and three hundred shots in the hull, all the masts and the bowsprit shot away. HMS *Sybille* came out of the contest in much better shape, with two of her three masts damaged and rigging and sails down, and with only five men killed and seventeen wounded. The unfortunate Captain Cooke was one of the victims. One shoulder and part of his chest shot away, he lingered in agony in Calcutta for three months and then died, another naval hero, like Faulknor in the West Indies, with his destiny unfulfilled.

Admiral de Sercey's squadron was now down to two frigates: the *Preneuse*, to which he had recently transferred his flag, and the *Brûle-Gueule*. The *Brûle-Gueule* sailed to Manila to join two Spanish battleships and two frigates in an intended attack on the East Indiamen tea convoy from China. The Spaniards wandered aimlessly hither and thither on the South China Sea, their crews of landlubbers unable to handle the sails. They didn't even sight the fleet of East Indiamen and, somehow, managed to make their way back to Manila. The *Brûle-Gueule*, having achieved nothing, returned to Mauritius. She was then ordered to take the ringleaders of a local rebellion to France for trial. The trial never took place. The end of the *Brûle-Gueule* was even more dramatic than that of the *Seine*. In sight of home, she sank in a storm off the coast of Brittany with nearly all hands.

The 36-gun *Preneuse* was the last survivor of the Sercey squadron. Her captain, Jean L'Hermitte, was an energetic skipper and he relentlessly crisscrossed the Indian Ocean in search of prey. He captured two East Indiamen in the Bay of Bengal, sailed to Java to pick up de Sercey and brought him back to Mauritius where the now virtually shipless admiral set up his command post for his one-frigate squadron. He took a contingent of French volunteers to Mysore, then sailed to East Africa where he fought the 24-gun brig HMS *Camel* and the 18-gun schooner HMS *Rattlesnake* in Delagoa Bay in Mozambique, successfully repulsed the 50-gun HMS *Jupiter* sent in his pursuit and was finally cornered off Mauritius by two ships-of-the-line, HMS *Tremendous*, 74, and HMS *Adamant*, 50, in December 1799. He ran his frigate onto the beach, his crew scrambled ashore to safety and Captain L'Hermitte, having lowered his colours in surrender, awaited with dignity, in the company of his officers, the prize-crew from the British ships who set fire to the wrecked French frigate and destroyed her. De Sercey's squadron had ceased to exist.

There was no more fighting in the Indian Ocean between British and French before the 1802 Peace of Amiens. The British were too concerned over the threat of Bonaparte to India from Egypt to bother with Réunion and Mauritius. The islands remained free and prosperous. The Spaniards continued to stagnate, untroubled, in the Philippines but the phlegmatic Dutch lost their colonies of Ceylon and Malacca in Asia and the Cape of Good Hope in South Africa.

CHAPTER EIGHT

Peace with America and Russia

THE FLAGS FLY AT HALF-MAST
1800

The fate of the French expedition in Egypt has to have been one of Bonaparte's concerns when he became First Consul and ruler of France, but it wasn't at the top of his list of priorities. He had more urgent problems to face, the chief one of which was the defence of France itself.

Until recently France's enemies had been converging from north and east, Russians and Austrians from Switzerland, Russians and British from Holland. A temporary respite had come, thanks to generals Masséna and Brune. Masséna, a dashing cavalry officer from Nice, threw back the Russians under Korsakov and Suvorov at Zurich and the Austrians, under the Archduke Charles, at Constance. Brune, another southerner, from Brives-la-Gaillarde, defeated the British and the Russians at Bergen-op-Zoom. The British, commanded by the Duke of York and General Abercromby, then endured the hardships of a calamitous winter retreat until they reached the safety of the British fleet, lying off the North Sea shore, which evacuated the surviving Redcoats to England.

The erratic Tsar Paul I, disgusted with his British allies who left, he said, most of the fighting to the Russians, and with his Austrian allies, who had done virtually no fighting at all, stomped out of the Second Coalition, began quarrelling with Britain over Malta, and flirted with Bonaparte.

But the Austrians had just been biding their time. A few months after Bonaparte took France over, they went on the attack, sending the

French armies tottering in Italy and Germany and obliging the First Consul to pick up his sword and become a warlord again. He took back Milan from the Austrians, met Desaix who had just returned from Egypt and, on June 14, smashed the Austrian army at Marengo after a touch-and-go battle which was only converted into a French victory by Desaix's arrival on the battlefield. With a long ribbon tied to his hat streaming in the wind behind him, Desaix charged to win the day for Bonaparte and to die on the same day that Kléber was murdered in Cairo, killed by a bullet that shattered his valiant heart.

In southern Germany, General Moreau, seconded by the brilliant young General Antoine Richepanse, a Lorrainer from Metz and a former protégé of Kléber, defeated the Austrians at Hohenlinden. General MacDonald, a Frenchman of Scottish ancestry, advanced into the Tyrol. General Brune was also on the attack in Austria. The Austrian emperor, possibly feeling that 1800 had not been his year, sued for peace in January 1801.

Overseas, 1800 had not been a vintage year for the French, either. The British held all the French West Indian islands with the exception of Guadeloupe – where the former black slaves, still very insecure about their newly-found freedom, were keeping their machetes sharpened in case the French reneged on emancipation, which they did. General Desfourneaux, evicted from the island, was now moping and fretting his time away in an army depot in France, and the black general, Toussaint L'Ouverture, had expelled and sent back to France the latest French commissioner in the island. With the aid of his two most capable Negro generals, Christophe and Dessalines, he had defeated the two mulatto generals Pétion and Rigaud, and would soon take over the former Spanish part of the island, Santo Domingo.

In West Africa the French outposts of Gorée and St Louis, in Senegal, governed by Colonel Blanchot de Verly, were again raided by British naval squadrons. Blanchot had been governor since 1787, before the Revolution, and the numerous attacks he had endured had never even dented his defences. But this time he had to abandon Gorée, defended by only ten white and thirty black soldiers and attacked that spring by British troops from four transports after a bombardment by three battleships and three frigates. Admiral de Sercey's frigate squadron had just lost its last frigate, the *Preneuse*, in the offshore waters of Mauritius. If the virtually defenceless island and nearby Réunion remained free, it was simply because the British didn't take the trouble to take them.

1800 is also the year that First Consul Napoleon Bonaparte began to include Australia in his wide vision of the world. In mid-year he asked the British government for 'passports', as the documents guaranteeing safe passage for ships were called, for the French explorer-sailor Nicolas Baudin. In those sometimes more civilised days, belligerents placed science and learning above warfare and gave the right to enemy ships to navigate without interference on their voyages of discovery. Baudin was to travel to the great southern continent with two corvettes, the *Géographe* and the *Naturaliste*. The mission was essentially scientific and exploratory and, as in the case of the Egyptian expedition, a group of scientists, about thirty, went on the voyage.

America was also on Bonaparte's mind. He wanted to restore France's empire in North America. Louisiana had been ceded to Spain nearly forty years before, and in July 1800 he ordered the French ambassador in Madrid to begin negotiations with the Spanish government on the retrocession of this immense territory to France. But it was first necessary to guarantee safe passage between France and New Orleans, and this meant not only ending the war with England but also the little nuisance Quasi-war with the United States which was continuing intermittently at sea. The most important encounter between the ships of the two countries occurred in February 1800 when Captain Truxtun, still in command of the USS *Constellation*, fought an indecisive action against the heavier-armed French frigate *Vengeance*.

Bonaparte sent out peace feelers to President Adams in the White House. When General Washington died just before Christmas 1799, the First Consul tactfully ordered all flags in France to be flown at half-mast. President Adams responded by sending three commissioners to Paris, and on September 30, 1800 the two countries agreed to a reconciliation.

Then there was India, for Bonaparte's experiences in Egypt hadn't killed this exotic dream which had been pursuing him since adolescence. For the moment other exigencies had pushed it into the background, but it soon came to the fore again with Russia's secession from its alliance with the British and Austrians.

MURDER IN SAINT PETERSBURG
1801

Tsar Paul I, unreliable as he was, believed that Napoleon Bonaparte was the man who brought order and sense into the incoherences of the French Revolution, and that the peril to Europe came, not from France, but more from the ambitions of a Britain anxious to prevent a settlement in Europe so as to keep France under pressure at home while she carved herself an empire overseas.

Bonaparte proposed to Tsar Paul that their two countries form a joint expedition to invade India. Enthused by the idea, Paul suggested that it should be led by General Masséna, whose victory over the Russian field-marshal Suvorov in Switzerland had much impressed him. The proposed venture was to be organised with thirty-five thousand French troops who would link up with an equal number of

Russians on the Volga and march on India. The Tsar ordered an advance guard of twenty thousand Cossacks to proceed south through Khiva and Bokhara, to await the bulk of the invading army on the Indus. Unfortunately Paul was murdered before the campaign began and his son, the new Tsar, the young, good-looking and idealistic (at least, at first) Alexander I, was uninterested at that time in these Indian projects. So Napoleon Bonaparte found himself without an ally, and the expedition was cancelled. But Bonaparte kept up his contacts in the Indian peninsula.

A M. Desoutes arrived from India as the personal envoy of General Perron to the First Consul in Paris, and a secret correspondence reportedly began between the two generals, with a third general, General Le Borgne, now more nobly called Count de Boigne (*le borgne* means 'one-eyed man' in French) as go-between and unofficial adviser on Indian affairs to Bonaparte. The involvement of Count de Boigne in these Indian plans is still a matter of conjecture, but certainly the governor-general in India, Lord Wellesley, believed in it. Two years later, in a letter asking that Sindhia's power and influence be reduced because of the possibility of the renewal of war between Britain and France, he told General Lake, former massacrer of Irish peasants and now commander-in-chief in India, that 'Mr de Boigne, Sindhia's late general, is now the chief confidant of Bonaparte. . . . I leave you to judge why and wherefore.'

But Bonaparte's projects for an invasion of India did not exclude Britain herself, only twenty tantalising miles away, from his thoughts and plans. Admittedly, Bonaparte had considered an invasion of England impossible only three years before, but in 1801 he curiously reversed his views and ordered the construction of a large fleet of invasion craft at Boulogne. The command was given to Admiral Latouche-Tréville, probably the most competent senior officer in the French navy. The British government, in July, sent warning of an imminent French attack to army district commanders all over the country. To quieten an alarmed public opinion, Britain's Channel coast was placed under the personal and direct command of Admiral Nelson.

But India and England, in 1801, were battlefields that only existed in the realm of Napoleon's hopes. The Mediterranean, Egypt and the high seas, that was where British and French were clashing and scattering each other's limbs, blood and guts over sea and sand.

CHAPTER NINE

The Mediterranean Stockade

THE ESCAPEES OF VALLETTA
Malta 1800

The Mediterranean in 1800 was British. From Gibraltar, on its outside western edge facing the Atlantic, Admiral Lord Keith reigned over a vast maritime domain that stretched all the way east to the Dardanelles. The White Ensign was the law of the sea.

Unfriendly vessels only traversed it at their own risk. Notably the French.

Early that year Jean-Baptiste Perrée, who had commanded the French flotilla on the Nile, sailed from Toulon with a small squadron of one ship-of-the-line, the 74-gun *Généreux*, survivor of both the Nile and Corfu, three frigates and a supply ship, to go to the relief of Malta. He had recently been promoted rear-admiral, but he didn't live very long to enjoy his new rank. On February 18, 1800, he ran into Nelson with four battleships and several frigates. Perrée was killed and the *Généreux* was taken. Eleven of the thirteen French battleships at the Battle of the Nile had previously been destroyed or captured in Aboukir Bay. Now it was 'twelve out of thirteen', as Lord Nelson wrote to Lady Hamilton after capturing the *Généreux*. 'Only the *Guillaume Tell* remains.' The *Guillaume Tell*, too, was a doomed ship.

Her turn came later. On March 29, the 80-gun battleship on which Admiral de Villeneuve had flown his flag at the Nile, tried on a dark and windy night to escape from Valletta. On this voyage, she was more a hospital ship than a battleship. Her lower decks were crowded with wounded and sick soldiers and sailors, many of them victims of Venus rather than of Mars.

HMS *Foudroyant* and HMS *Lion* went after her in distant pursuit. But right behind the *Guillaume Tell* was a little frigate, the 36-gun HMS *Penelope* which, under her captain, the brave and stubborn Blackwood, hung on like a grim little terrier dog. Firing whenever he could get alongside the larger ship, Blackwood downed two of her masts. From that moment, the *Guillaume Tell*'s hope of escape vanished as the two British battleships caught up with her in the stormy darkness.

On her dash to home and hospital in Toulon, the French battleship was commanded by Decrès, Napoleon's future minister of marine. As a minister, Decrès was to prove himself a rat, but as a fighting sea captain, he proved himself a hero that night. It was a contest of fearless men, fought in the dark seas, lashed by winds and spray and cannon fire, in a ship awash with blood. It began at 11.00 pm and it continued through the night until after sunrise when Decrès, pounded by three British ships and having lost two hundred of his men, surrendered. 'A more heroic defence is not to be found among the records of naval action,' a prominent British naval historian has written. The British battleships, heavily damaged, were unable to tow their prize back to the nearest Sicilian port.

Decrès's sporting English foes gave a banquet in his honour when they arrived in Palermo. At the end of the festivity Decrès, presumably a little drunk by this time and more than a little maudlin, congratulated Captain Blackwood and, to the embarrassment of his hosts, kissed the blushing Briton on both cheeks.

Malta, cut off from the world, surrendered in September 1800. It had resisted the British for two years. The Irish peer, Colonel Lord Blayney, hoisted the Union Jack over the ramparts and then left with his regiment to join Sir Ralph Abercromby's army, training in Minorca for the invasion of Egypt.

Just before Valletta fell, two of the French frigates in the harbour, the *Justice* and the *Diane*, survivors from Aboukir Bay, made a dash for the open sea on the last day of August. But only the *Justice* succeeded in reaching Toulon. She was now the only one of the vessels that had gone through the Nelson grinder at the Battle of the Nile still flying the Tricolour.

THE ACROBATS OF ALEXANDRIA
Egypt 1800-1801

Lord Nelson, by this time, weary of the Mediterranean, was back in England, in the company of Sir William and Lady Hamilton. In Paris, First Consul Bonaparte was working meanwhile on plans to get supplies and reinforcements across to his old companions still in Egypt.

Later that year, he ordered Admiral Ganteaume, who had brought him back safely from Egypt and whom he trusted, to lead a rescue operation to Alexandria. Ganteaume sailed from Brest for the Mediterranean on January 22, 1801 with seven ships-of-the-line, two frigates and five thousand soldiers as reinforcements for Egypt. It was the beginning of a strange game of hide-and-seek on the high seas in which Ganteaume, who appeared terrified of meeting the British fleet, was the only protagonist, hiding most of the time from an enemy that didn't even know he was there. Over a period of five months he made three attempts to take his troops to Egypt. All of them failed.

But at least he acquired a couple of consolation prizes on the way. His squadron first captured the frigate HMS *Success*, then on June 24 the 74-gun battleship HMS *Swiftsure*, off Crete. For the rest of the voyage the kindly Ganteaume spent much of his time trying to comfort her distraught captain, Ben Hallowell, veteran of the Battle of the Nile but now just a disconsolate skipper, appalled at the loss of his command.

Ganteaume's ships were not the only vessels that tried to break through to Alexandria carrying reinforcements. Various frigates were also making isolated efforts to reach the stranded French in Egypt. A few got through. Early in 1801, the *Justice*, after her escape from Malta, made a fast crossing with *Egyptienne*, another frigate. The two vessels landed thirteen hundred troops. Two other frigates, at about the same time, were also headed for Egypt. One, the *Regénérée*, from de Sercey's old squadron in the Indian Ocean, also reached Alexandria, where she put ashore the eight hundred troops she was carrying. The other, *L'Africaine*, 40, was intercepted on February 19 in mid-Mediterranean by HMS *Phoebe*, 44, commanded by the Londoner, Captain Robert Barlow, and captured after a particularly fierce action.

L'Africaine was transporting four hundred troops to Egypt who had the misfortune to be under the orders of our old friend from Haiti and Guadeloupe, the fire-spitting, sword-brandishing General Desfourneaux, now intent on new exploits in a new continent. But HMS *Phoebe* stood between him and his glory.

Desfourneaux insisted that his men line up on the top deck instead of staying in the relative safety of below deck. The army had to show that when there was fighting to be done, it didn't take second place to the navy. So the soldiers, not suspecting that many of them would soon be turned into scattered flesh, blood and bones, ran smartly up on deck, lined up along the bulwarks and, aiming their muskets along the top, waited for the order to fire on the *Phoebe*, well out of their range, as if she were a line of enemy infantrymen facing them on a battlefield.

General Desfourneaux waved his sword and shouted insults at the enemy across the water as cannonballs and explosive shell sliced through his soldiers' ranks. The net result of this display of useless republican martial valour was a casualty list for *L'Africaine* of more than two hundred dead and a hundred and forty-four wounded, a few hundred more widows and orphans in France, against one killed and twelve wounded on HMS *Phoebe*. Desfourneaux was hit in the chest, but survived. After two hours of sustained slaughter, *L'Africaine* struck her colours and the French, including Desfourneaux, were made prisoners.

Barlow was knighted for his victory and his daughter later married Nelson's nephew, the second Lord Nelson. Since Nelson had no legal offspring, his title went to Captain Barlow's descendants. As for Desfourneaux, this infuriating, indestructible man was up within a few weeks and was soon back in France, all set and ready to go and fight in another war in Haiti.

As the story unfolds of the last stand of the French in Egypt and of the efforts to bring them help, strange moments of light-hearted lunacy appear. While Ganteaume was hovering off the Egyptian coast with his typhus-ridden troops sweltering below deck and his sailors at action stations, prepared to blast the British out of the water or, far more likely, to be blasted out of the water themselves, another French vessel suddenly appeared off Alexandria.

But the British blockading force made no preparations to fight. In a cordial letter to General Menou, besieged in the city from land and sea, Admiral Lord Keith told Menou he would let the vessel through the blockade as its only passengers were a shipload of actors, actresses, musicians, comedians, singers, clowns, jugglers and acrobats sent by the French to entertain their troops in Egypt.

In an absurd exchange of correspondence with the British admiral, the French general, whose army was desperately short of food and supplies, gravely thanked Lord Keith for his consideration. But, he explained, in view of the present circumstances he was unable to invite the entertainers to Alexandria. Would therefore His Lordship, as 'a friend of the arts', kindly send the artistes back to France?

Which, one hopes, the courteous Lord Keith did.

CHAPTER TEN

The First Desert Rats

CHEERING FOR THEIR COUNTRY'S GLORY
Egypt 1801

On the first day of the British invasion of Egypt, March 8, 1801, seven thousand troops, the vanguard of a larger army yet to come, landed on the shores of Aboukir Bay.

We have been with its commander-in-chief, General Sir Ralph Abercromby, through his recent campaigns, notably on several West Indian islands, and in Ireland. Egypt was to be his last. His grave was only three weeks away.

Conspicuously absent from this invasion force was Admiral Lord Nelson, undoubtedly to the great relief of Lord Keith, in command of the fleet, who had found Britain's hero, in his role as the Royal Navy superstar, a difficult prima donna subordinate. Nelson was still back in England and had recently had a ghastly row with the tight-lipped, boring and now understandably indignant Lady Nelson who came straight to the point: 'Lady Hamilton or me.'

Fortunately for history, literature and the motion picture industry, romance triumphed over morality. Nelson chose Lady Hamilton, who was certainly a more congenial companion than this tedious, unmerry widow whom he had met and married in the West Indies. He never saw his wife again but he did call on his old friend and chief, the Earl of St Vincent, who found Nelson 'devoured with vanity, weakness and folly' and very changed in every way. 'Poor man,' St Vincent added sadly.

Lord Keith, during the Egyptian landing, flew his flag on HMS *Foudroyant*, with Captain Philip Beaver as his flag captain. The two were

188

old acquaintances. Keith, back in 1795, when in the Indian Ocean, had been very impressed with Beaver's handling of a ship-of-the-line, when, caught in a violent squall, she had been thrown on her beam-ends with her sails in tatters. The admiral, a few years later, asked Beaver to become his flag lieutenant, then his flag captain.

The ubiquitous Sir Sidney Smith was also present off the Egyptian coast that early March morning, as always very much the upper-class Englishman, and as always ready to talk about himself to anyone who cared to listen. The as yet uncaptured HMS *Swiftsure*, which Gant-geaume was to take three months later, captained by Ben Hallowell, and HMS *Minotaur*, under Captain Thomas Louis – reputedly a British descendant of Louis XIV – were the only two ships in the invasion fleet that had participated on that same spot, nearly three years ago, in the Battle of the Nile, both under the command of the same two captains.

James Hillyar, who had served as a seaman on HMS *Victory* in the Toulon campaign, was also at the landing. But now he was a commander, captain of the frigate HMS *Niger*. Lord Hood, impressed by his ability, had given him a commission in Corsica. Hillyar was a serious young man. He had been in the navy since he was ten and at the age of twelve had fought against the French in a naval engagement off Boston during the American War of Independence. He was now thirty-two, the main support of his mother, his sisters and a crippled brother.

The British soldiers, although they had known mainly reverses in their recent wars against the French, in North America, Toulon, Corsica, Flanders, Holland and Germany, were full of optimism as they waited to come ashore. 'There is a certain devil in the army that will carry it through thick and thin. . . . At no former period of our history did John Bull ever hold his enemy cheaper,' young Colonel Edward Paget wrote home the day before the landing.

An old personal adversary of Nelson, with whom he had exchanged bitter words in Corsica eight years ago, General Sir John Moore was among the first to land, along with his old quartermaster friend, Sir Hildebrand Oakes, now a brigadier-general.

Another reminder of Corsica was the presence in the landing party of the green-jacketed, black-gaitered, shakoed Corsican Rangers, some two hundred light infantrymen recruited from among the exiled pro-Paoli islanders, and commanded by Major (Temporary) Hudson Lowe, unbearably self-important in his new functions. Because he knew Italian – as a youth he had studied at the University of Pisa – Lowe had been put in charge of the Corsican contingent, and his main concern was to turn his temporary rank into a permanent one.

French guns fired repeatedly at the British boats as they approached the shore and casualties were fairly heavy. But with their accustomed

doggedness the British came on, singing and shouting 'hurrah'.
'Many a fine fellow breathed his last while cheering for his country's
glory!' wrote Captain Beaver in the fine patriotic style of the day.

Only two thousand French troops were on the beaches to greet the
British, thanks to General Menou's dilly-dallying. He was in Cairo
when the presence of British sails offshore was notified to him on
March 3, five days before the landing. Yet he did not bother to return
to Alexandria until March 12, four days after the British had disembarked. 'He was not a soldier,' Napoleon said one day, when asked
many years later his opinion of the general. Menou, in fact, was an ass.

The very first Briton ashore was Colonel Brent Spencer, a specialist
in what would be called in more recent wars, commando tactics. We
were with Brent Spencer when, a few years previously, he landed at
Tiburon, in Haiti, and captured a hundred and fifty soldiers. In Egypt
his only weapon was a walking stick, but he shouted so loudly, 'Get
away, you scoundrel, you!' and shook his cane so vigorously at a
French soldier taking aim at him with his musket that the latter,
according to the colonel's regimental history, obediently lowered his
musket, turned round and ran.

The first assault across the sand dunes on the two-mile stretch of
beach was made by two brigades, Moore's Reserve, led by Oakes,
which included the Corsican Rangers, and General Sir Eyre Coote's.
Coote, the reader will remember, was last with us storming the Morne
Fortunée in St Lucia, in the West Indies.

The French on the beaches, who were led by the Upper Nile campaign veteran General Friant, were driven back towards Alexandria.
According to some reports, the French were all drunk when the British
landed. In spite of this reverse Friant was one of the best French
generals of his day and he had replaced General Desaix as commander
in Upper Egypt.

Like all the other French soldiers in Egypt, from general down, with
the exception of the maniacal Muslim convert Menou, all that Friant
wanted probably was just to get out of Egypt and go home. This must
have been one of the most homesick armies in history. They had been
in Egypt three years and they had had enough of what now seemed to
them all a useless, purposeless campaign.

Friant and General Lanusse joined forces the day after the British
landing. Their combined strength, now around five thousand men, was
enough to slow down the British momentum. Near a fortress called
Mandora, they fought a successful delaying action in which they lost in
dead and wounded five hundred men to the British thirteen hundred.

As the French retreated westward towards Alexandria another
enemy appeared to the east: the Turks, marching down again from
Syria. They had been specially trained by General Koehler, our German gunner from Toulon and Corsica who introduced the Martello

towers into England. He had been sent to Turkey to teach the Ottoman army modern methods of warfare. Jaffa had become his grave –
and that of his wife whom he had taken along to show her a bit of the
world. They had both died there in December the previous year of
what was described as 'a malignant fever produced by filthy surroundings.'

Five thousand more Turks would also soon be landing in Aboukir
again, anxious to avenge their ignominious defeat there by Bonaparte
two years before.

Another front, now unattended by the French, would also soon
become active to the south, in the Red Sea region, where Blankett
would soon be turning up with his flotilla and a three-hundred-man
British army from Aden, the vanguard of five thousand more from
India and South Africa.

The British big squeeze was on. The French were caught, like a very
small nut in a very big nutcracker.

The main battle between British and French took place on March 21
outside Alexandria, among the ruins of the ancient Roman camp of
Canopus. The Battle of Alexandria, or Canopus as it is also sometimes
called, was a shattering French defeat for which the incompetent
Menou was completely responsible. Although he had then the numerical superiority in Egypt with 25,000 men, by his inaction he had
allowed the British to be superior on the battlefield: 15,000 men against
12,000. Under the illusion that he was a military genius, he then assailed
the British forces, superior in numbers, and lost a third of his men.

Menou attacked at five o'clock in the morning. General Moore was
wounded in the leg and had his horse killed under him. General
Lanusse, commanding the vanguard of the French infantry, was also
wounded but mortally. The five hundred cavalrymen of General Roizé
(he too was killed), dragoons and hussars, charged awkwardly across
the British positions, among the Roman ruins. They were repulsed
with heavy losses, caused particularly by the intense fire from the
Highland regiments and by the American loyalist John Stuart's Fifth
Brigade, made up largely of foreigners (Spaniards from Minorca,
French Royalists, Swiss and German mercenaries).

During the American War of Independence Stuart, a Georgian loyal
to the king, had fought as an ensign under Cornwallis in New York,
South Carolina, New Jersey and, finally, at Yorktown, and more recently against the French in Flanders and Holland. A thorough professional, he had managed to turn his disparate unit into one of the best in
Abercromby's army.

Edward Paget, who had been a colonel of the 28th Regiment (now
the famous Gloucestershires) since he was eighteen, was attacked
simultaneously in the front and rear. He saved his regiment by ordering the rear rank to turn round. His order is a classic of British infantry

discipline and coolness under fire. 'Rear rank Twenty-Eighth! Right about! Fire!' Ever since the Battle of Alexandria, soldiers of the 28th Regiment have worn regimental badges at the back as well as at the front of their caps.

Alexandria was General Abercromby's last battle. The old soldier, after a tussle with a French dragoon from whom he tore away his sword, was hit in the thigh by a bullet which entered the bone and could not be extracted. He was lifted on a stretcher and carried to HMS *Foudroyant* for treatment.

An officer raised Abercromby's head to make him more comfortable. 'What is it you are placing under my head?' the general asked. 'It's only a soldier's blanket,' answered the officer. 'Only a soldier's blanket,' retorted Abercromby, always concerned over his men's welfare. 'But a soldier's blanket is of great consequence to him and you must send me the name of the soldier to whom it belongs, that it may be returned to him.'

It was the last order he gave. Gangrene set in his wound, and he died a week later.

The Battle of Alexandria took a heavy toll in lives. More than 4,000 Frenchmen were killed or wounded. The British, who held the field, buried 1,040 French corpses and 250 British ones the next day. British wounded amounted to around 1,250.

After the battle, General Menou, over in the French camp, came to pay his respects to the dying General Lanusse. It was a mistake on his part. Lanusse was a hard-fighting man who did not suffer fools gladly. He blasted his commander-in-chief as an incompetent fool who should be working in the army's kitchens instead of commanding it. Then he died.

Menou, unshaken in his belief that he was a great general, retired with what was left of his army into Alexandria, from where he shouted defiance at the enemy, wrote long letters in praise of himself to the First Consul in Paris, wrote to General Belliard in Cairo that he must win or die, and, to please his Muslim wife and impress the locals, prayed five times a day to Mecca.

In the British camp, the ungracious and bilious-looking General Hely-Hutchinson took over the command of the army from the dying Abercromby. His soldiering had improved in the Netherlands since the Castlebar days.

On the day after Alexandria, on the other side of Egypt, on the Red Sea, Admiral Blankett arrived at Suez with a squadron of fifteen vessels, including HMS *Leopard*. Three hundred soldiers, commanded by a Colonel Lloyd and picked up at Aden, came along with the fleet. Blankett had first called at Kosseir to attack the French, but found it abandoned by General Donzelot's garrison. There were no French at Suez either.

Colonel Lloyd, on hearing that the British had landed in Aboukir, was anxious to march off with his little battalion to join them. But Aboukir, as the crow flies, is a hundred and seventy miles from Suez, and most of the route lies through desert or dry scrub country, a test for survival. Blankett ordered Lloyd to wait for some camels promised by the Turks. The camels did not arrive until three months later. Neither did the long-awaited British armies from Cape Town and Bombay. Events were moving faster around Aboukir.

Four days after the Battle of Alexandria, on March 25, the Turkish Capitan Pasha arrived at Aboukir from Rhodes with four thousand janissaries.

On April 6, Colonel Brent Spencer, still smartly wielding his cane, marched off with a mixed Turkish/British force to attack Rosetta, forty miles east of Alexandria.

On April 26, General Hely-Hutchinson with the Turkish Capitan Pasha, marched south at the head of an allied army along the left bank of the Nile to attack General Belliard in Cairo, leaving General Coote to besiege General Menou in Alexandria.

On May 1, another Turkish army, this time of fifteen thousand men, led by the Grand Vizier in person, arrived through Syria in Egypt, turned south up the right bank of the Nile, destination Cairo where an anxious Belliard was waiting.

On May 15, an army of five thousand French soldiers met the Turks in battle outside Cairo, failed for once to rout them, and returned to Cairo.

Two British fleets, bringing between five and six thousand more troops, were also at this time on their way to Egypt. Commodore Sir Home Riggs Popham, with a squadron from South Africa trailing behind him, was bringing from the Cape two thousand soldiers commanded by the New York loyalist Colonel Samuel Auchmuty who had fought as a young soldier at the 1776 battles of Brooklyn and White Plains (on the British side, for the Auchmutys were of loyal Scottish stock).

Another three thousand men under General Sir David Baird, Wellington's old rival, were on the high seas from Bombay. One thousand of them were Indian sepoys, making this expedition the first venture by Indian soldiers outside Asia. The remaining two thousand were British soldiers stationed in India.

Wellington had hoped to be given the command, but Baird outranked him, so to his distress and mortification he was named second-in-command only. Finally he did not even go. He became infected with a particularly obnoxious form of ringworm, called the 'Malabar itch' on the Bombay waterfront, which his doctor told him he had caught from sleeping in strange beds. The poor man was so busy scratching himself and taking baths of nitric acid to ease the irritation that he had to cancel his passage to Egypt. A fortunate event, as it turned out, for the ship on which he was due to sail went down with all hands. So Wellington was saved for the Peninsular War and for Waterloo.

Even without Wellington, Baird had some solid soldiers around him when he sailed for Egypt. Some of Wellington's duties fell on the stern and reliable Major Lachlan Macquarie, whom Baird had asked to accompany the expedition as deputy adjutant general. Macquarie, who had fought at Seringapatam against Tipoo Sahib, was actually not one of Wellington's favourites. The future victor of Waterloo considered the future governor of New South Wales 'a good man but a little undecided', a judgment which Macquarie's future conduct in Australia certainly does not bear out. The wild one-eyed Colonel Beresford was also in the British contingent from India. He now commanded the Connaught Rangers in garrison in India and was anxious to get back with his men into battle. Colonel John Murray, who had recently returned to India from Aden, went along as quartermaster general. He was another who did not enjoy Wellington's good opinion. 'He always appeared to me to want sound sense,' Wellington wrote about Murray when both were later fighting in Spain.

GO HOME, FRENCHMEN
Egypt 1801

In the meantime, General Hely-Hutchinson had two large French armies opposing him in Egypt, one of about twelve thousand men defending Cairo, and another of some eight thousand holding Alexandria – which General Menou was swearing he would defend to the death.

General Belliard, who was in charge of the defence of Cairo, was a more reasonable type. He didn't have to prove his courage or his professional qualities as a soldier. Promoted general on the battlefield by Bonaparte himself, he was not a man to dodge a fight, but he was not a man either to shed his soldiers' blood uselessly.

The Turko-British forces reached the outskirts of Cairo on June 16. There was virtually no fighting. Heavily outnumbered, Belliard surrendered eight days later. But it was not unconditionally. All that the French wanted was to go home. All that the British wanted was for them to leave Egypt. The British had the ships, so the two sides were made to understand each other. Belliard demanded and obtained conditions very similar to those rejected by Lord Keith at El Arish two years ago: his men's repatriation in their enemies' ships.

The ladies – and they included Pauline Fourès – were taken down the Nile to Rosetta in river boats. The fully-armed French were escorted through the delta on the two-hundred-mile journey to the coast by British and Turkish troops. The French liked to march to the bagpipe tunes of 'Highland Lassie' and at night French and British mixed quite

The Battle of Alexandria, 1801, fought among the ruins of Roman Canopus. The British were victorious, but both sides suffered severe casualties

happily by the campfires. They reached the coast on July 31 and by August 8 all had left for France. Meanwhile a furious General Menou, holed up in Alexandria, swore he would rather die than surrender.

It was while Belliard's army was marching cheerfully to the coast that Baird's army reached Kosseir from India and that Blankett received the camels for Colonel Lloyd's detachment at Suez. The colonel and his three hundred men climbed on to their awkward mounts and headed unsteadily across the desert for the British camp on the coast. But they were not used to either camels or desert conditions, ran out of water, saved themselves by downing the officers' madeira and finally reached the British lines only after losing nine troopers.

General Baird and Colonel Auchmuty joined forces at Kosseir and headed east from the port to Qena, then sailed down the Nile, too late for the siege of Cairo but in time to join the besieging army outside Alexandria.

The Egyptians were very impressed by the Indian soldiers' bearing and uniforms. Major Lachlan Macquarie fell into the arms of his brother Charles, a captain in the Highlanders, whom he hadn't seen for fourteen years, and met up again with General Lord Blayney and General Oakes, whom he had known in the Americas.

In the Red Sea, his job done, Admiral Blankett, worn and tortured by the gout, retired to Jeddah and died there on his ship on July 14 of exhaustion in the broiling heat of an Arabian midsummer day.

The siege of Alexandria continued for a few more weeks. Menou found it difficult to discontinue his warlike posturing. He had received a message that Admiral Ganteaume was on the way with reinforcements and supplies. But Ganteaume never appeared, so, late in August, the subdued French general reluctantly invited General Coote to lunch, served him horse steak (the only food available) and asked him for the same terms as those granted to General Belliard. Coote was delighted to oblige. But there was one more condition upon which the British insisted: at Lord Elgin's urging Menou was to surrender the Rosetta stone, the basalt slab inscribed by the priests of Ptolemy V around 200 BC which gave the key to the ancient Egyptian hieroglyphs. To the distress of the French scientists Menou, who was an uncultured clod, did so and the relic now stands in the British Museum in London instead of the Paris Louvre. The French ships in harbour were also part of the spoils of war. The British took over the *Regénérée* but the frigate *Justice*, the last French survivor of the Battle of the Nile, unexplainably went to the Turks.

While the Egyptian campaign was engaged in its final phases, the victor of the Battle of the Nile, Lord Nelson, was engaged in more distant naval occasions. On April 2, under Admiral Parker, he had sailed into Copenhagen to give the death blow to the Armed Neutrality League, recently formed by Russia, Prussia and the Scandinavian countries to defend themselves from British attacks against neutral shipping. He smashed the Danish fleet, anchored in the port, capturing or destroying five battleships and ten frigates. It was the Nelson Touch again, and the end of the Armed Neutrality League of the north.

On August 15 Nelson, now in charge of Britain's Channel defences, sent fifty-seven gunboats to destroy Admiral Latouche-Tréville's flotilla in Boulogne harbour, being readied for the invasion of England. The Nelson Touch was absent on that day. Nelson's force was beaten off after losing sixty-three men killed and wounded, one of the few times in his career when he was worsted by the French, or by anybody, for that matter.

By September 14, General Menou and the Alexandria garrison were on their way to France. The Egyptian campaign was over. It had lasted three years and two months. The Egyptians were now free of the French, but not yet free of their British liberators nor of their Turkish masters.

On October 1, in London, the preliminaries of peace were signed between the French and the British and the Peace of Amiens came into force five months later.

In France, General Bonaparte greeted the returnees from Egypt with stirring words. But, anxious to avoid a domestic scene, he sent General Duroc to meet Pauline Fourès on her arrival. She was forbidden to visit the First Consul but, as a consolation prize, was given a mansion in the country. She married a minor consular official, Henri de Ranchoup, and accompanied him to his first modest post, Santander, in Spain. She decided that life in Paris suited her better, wrote a novel *Lord Went-worth* which failed to cause any sensation, took up painting, went on a voyage to Brazil, began trading in tropical woods and kept many parrots and monkeys in her Paris apartment.

In later life, she befriended the painter Rosa Bonheur, much admired by the American multi-millionaire railroad and shipping magnate Cornelius Vanderbilt, who presented her gigantic 'Horse Fair' to the Metropolitan Museum in New York, where it still hangs at the main entrance to the galleries. Pauline Fourès died in 1869, aged nearly ninety, after what was undoubtedly a well-filled life.

The same cannot be said of Zenab, Bonaparte's first love in his Cairo days. Three weeks after the departure of the French from the Egyptian capital, she was summoned to appear before a Turkish court after sunset and accused of having used her charms on the French. Her father was charged with favouring her association with Bonaparte. 'I am innocent. I knew nothing about it,' he said. 'I regret what I did,' she said. He was found not guilty, she was condemned to death and an executioner smashed the back of her head with a large club. She was nineteen years old.

The Turks were more gentlemanly with the British. To show their appreciation for their help in ridding Egypt of the French, they gave the British ambassador, Lord Elgin, permission to remove all the useless statuary and friezes from the ruined Parthenon in Athens which, to their intense puzzlement, he was so keen to take away. Known as the Elgin Marbles, they are one of the glories of the British Museum in London.

PART TWO

The Peace of Amiens
1801-1803

During the war in Haiti local guerrillas, lightly-armed and highly mobile, were able to inflict terrible losses on the more heavily equipped French Republican soldiers

CHAPTER ELEVEN

Peace with England – War with Haiti

THE SAVIOUR OF THE WORLD
1801-1802

In 1801, as if a fairy had willed it with a magic wand, Britain and France decided it was time to stop fighting. The decision was founded largely on mutual exhaustion after eight years of war and motivated, on both sides, by a desire to rest for a while before starting to fight again. It was made easier on the British side by the resignation, in February, of William Pitt, who had become a personal symbol of resistance to the French. His friend and political ally, Henry Addington, then took over the cabinet.

Early peace negotiations were carried out through a Mr Otto, un-official representative of the French government in London whom Prime Minister Addington's Foreign Secretary, Lord Hawkesbury, first approached in the early months of 1801 to inquire if the newly appointed First Consul might be interested in peace between the two countries. Britain was, probably, even more war-weary than France and all the talk in England was about 'the blessings of peace', which be-came a very fashionable phrase.

Bonaparte needed peace as much as Britain, probably more. France was exhausted, blockaded at sea, cut off from the colonial world. The French colonies at Guadeloupe and Haiti were in revolt. In Haiti Toussaint L'Ouverture had recently proclaimed himself governor for life and was obviously manoeuvring for the island's independence. In Guadeloupe the new governor, Admiral Lacrosse, General Humbert's old friend from Ireland, was facing another rebellion, this time led by the army, largely black and mulatto, who sensed that slavery was on the way back. But the British blockade stood in the way of massive reinforcements from France, most of the French colonies had been lost to the British, and Egypt was fast slipping out of French control. The French population at home too, like the British, was tired of war. When Bonaparte heard – before the news had reached Britain – that Alexandria had fallen, he decided the time had come to arrange a peace with the British, and to do so without delay.

The preliminaries to the peace were approved on October 1, 1801, in London and Paris. From then on, relations between Britain and France became almost normal. On October 4, the first French envoy, General Lauriston (the grandson of a Scotsman) was sent to London bearing the French ratification of the new pact. Enthusiastic crowds in London, singing and cheering, after unhitching the horses of his carriage, pulled it all the way from the French Embassy in Portman Square to the Prime Minister's residence in Downing Street. Hawkers in the street sold little pictures of General Bonaparte labelled 'The Saviour of the World', 'The Restorer of Public Order' and 'The August Hero'. Everybody cheered Peace, and they hip-hip-hoorayed the name of Napoleon Bonaparte down Whitehall.

An indignant Nelson was aghast at this display of mass hysteria. 'There is no person who rejoices more in peace than I do, but I would sooner burst than let a damned Frenchman know it,' he wrote angrily to a friend.

In the preliminaries, the British agreed to return to France all her old captured colonies. London also promised to hand over the island of Malta to the Knights of St John and the French, for their part, undertook to evacuate Egypt (which they had, in fact, already done) and return it to the Ottoman government in Constantinople.

To the disgruntlement of Spain and the Netherlands, Britain, however, kept Trinidad and Sri Lanka – for another hundred and fifty years, in fact, until these two territories became independent and joined the United Nations! But they returned the other captured colonies and overseas territories, notably the Cape of Good Hope, Surinam, Curaçao, Malacca and the Spice islands of Indonesia to Holland.

Then Britain and France, with equal bad faith, set about rebuilding their war machines for the next, and plausibly final round of fighting. Napoleon, for his part, hoped the peace would last at least a full three years. He needed desperately to rebuild his navy, the key to the restoration of a French empire in the Americas and to the conquest of India. It was down to thirty-nine battleships and thirty-five frigates to Britain's two hundred and two ships-of-the-line and two hundred and seventy-seven frigates.

He sent General Andréossy, who had returned from Egypt with him, as his ambassador in London. Addington appointed his haughty and patronising former envoy in St Petersburg, Lord Whitworth, as ambassador to Paris. World-and-war-weary Lord Cornwallis ('I feel out of sorts, low-spirited and tired of everything') left Irish problems behind in Dublin and established himself temporarily in the dull little town of Amiens with his French opposite number, Joseph Bonaparte, Napoleon's eldest brother, to thrash out the details of what was to be known as the Peace of Amiens. After more than four months of negotiations, it was signed by the two countries on March 25, 1802, and it helped to maintain a tenuous peace between them for sixteen months. It finally broke down, largely over the question of Malta.

Well before the peace negotiations were completed, the British had assured the French they would not attack a large naval expeditionary force Bonaparte planned to send to Haiti, to regain control of this immensely rich but now rebellious and largely devastated colony. In fact London was delighted the French were taking Haiti in hand again. The British feared the example of blacks rebelling against white rule might be catching, particularly in their nearby colony of Jamaica.

Toussaint L'Ouverture had decreed that slavery was to be abolished forever and addressed a letter to the First Consul in Paris, from 'the first of the Blacks to the first of the Whites' which had infuriated Bonaparte. In his rage, he swore to tear away 'the epaulettes of every Negro officer in the colonies'.

For Bonaparte was not only planning to reimpose French rule on these mutinous black subjects but already preparing to reintroduce slavery in the French colonies. A new constitution was being drafted placing these tropical territories under a regime of special laws. The colonies were, from now on, to be ruled directly from Paris, and Paris meant Napoleon Bonaparte, who considered slavery essential to restore 'prosperity' – which meant, in most cases, money for white Frenchmen and slavery for black Africans. Whatever forward-looking ideas Bonaparte may have had for France and Europe, his only policy in the colonies was a great leap back into the past.

Slavery, as an institution, had the approval of many of the well-to-do. Not only in France. In England, just about this time, Lord Nelson was denouncing what he called the 'hypocrisy' of Wilberforce and other emancipists trying to have slavery outlawed in all British territories. Slavery, Nelson maintained, was essential to the well-being of Britain's West Indian colonies.

THE MASS GRAVE
Haiti 1801-1802

As from November 1801, now that the British navy was, so to speak, neutral, an expeditionary force of about 35,000 soldiers began to assemble in the ports of France. The naval side of the expedition, commanded by Admiral Villaret-Joyeuse, began to move in December in flotillas of transport escorted by twenty-one frigates and forty-one battleships, including five Spanish ships-of-the-line under the command of Admiral Gravina, Lord Hood's former associate at Toulon. Three Dutch capital ships were also in the fleet.

Bonaparte gave overall command of the Army of St Domingue, as it was officially called, to his brother-in-law, General Leclerc, Pauline's husband, appointed to the recently created post of captain-general in the colony. It was a deadly gift: Haiti was to prove a military and human calamity, worse even than Egypt.

Pauline accompanied her husband to Haiti and took their infant son along. To her mind, the expedition was just one, great, big party. She ordered a whole new wardrobe, engaged a string orchestra, hired a staff of half a dozen nursemaids to look after the baby, packed dozens of crates of furniture, china, glass and cutlery and set off for the New World full of good advice from her brother Napoleon and his wife Josephine who, being from Martinique, knew at first hand what she was describing.

A bevy of lovers, former and future, followed Pauline to the island where her antics were to cause a furore unfortunately outside the scope of this book. Three of the men who came into her notorious tropical life were the Toulon Terrorist, Stanislas Fréron, her first lover – at least, so it is said – when she was fifteen. He sailed to Haiti to be near her and died of yellow fever soon after his arrival. General Humbert, the conqueror (almost) of Ireland, shared her bed and her favours. So did General Boyer, the former camel-corps man in Egypt. Pauline, gossip said, was insatiable in the torrid climate of the island of Tortuga, where she spent most of her time and had many other lovers, particularly officers from the army.

As well as his wife, Leclerc took forty generals with him to Haiti, considerably more than the number who accompanied Bonaparte to Egypt. Some of their names we know already. There was no shortage of volunteers for Haiti. With the Peace of Amiens in force, it was now the only outlet for a Frenchman with a sword and the desire to use it.

General Dugua (who would die of yellow fever in October 1802), left for Haiti soon after his return to France from Egypt, where he had ruled over Cairo and caused several hundred prostitutes to be executed as a prophylactic measure against the spread of venereal disease. Within two or three months of their return to France from Egypt, he and Boyer had volunteered for service in the Caribbean. In Haiti, he became Leclerc's short-lived chief of staff. Desfourneaux, now quite recovered from his wounds on *L'Africaine*, raring to get back into action, returned to Haiti where he had already done an incredible six years' fighting, from 1793 to 1799. General Humbert's former commander for the Irish expedition, General Hardy who had never

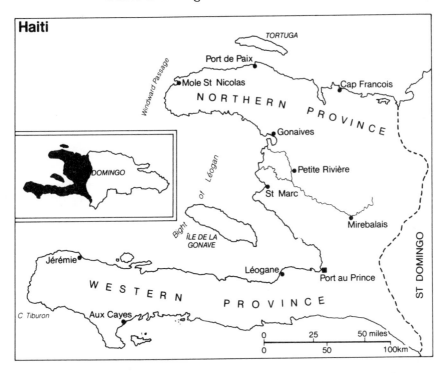

Haiti

TORTUGA

Port de Paix

Windward Passage

Mole St Nicolas

NORTHERN

Cap Francois

PROVINCE

Gonaives

ST DOMINGO

DOMINGO

Bight of Léogan

Petite Rivière

St Marc

Mirebalais

ÎLE DE LA GONAVE

Jérémie

Léogane

Port au Prince

WESTERN

PROVINCE

ST DOMINGO

C Tiburon

Aux Cayes

0	25	50 miles
0	50	100km

reached Ireland, to his misfortune did land in Haiti but lived only a few months – another victim of yellow fever in 1802. Humbert's second-in-command in Ireland, General Sarrazin, also went out to serve in Haiti where his murderous and scoundrelly conduct earned him a special mention by the historian Fortescue.

General de la Poype, whose capture of Mont Faron had been one of the main causes of the hurried British evacuation of Toulon, held the command of Mole Saint-Nicolas in Haiti. He survived the campaign to fight another day. So did General Clauzel, recognised by Napoleon as one of his ablest officers, promised promotion to marshal in 1815 but instead, after Waterloo, forced to flee for refuge to the United States. However, Generals Leclerc, Watrin, Debelle, and Jablonowski all died of yellow fever in 1802. Yellow fever, in fact, killed eighteen of the French generals in Haiti but, even so, disease spared them more than it did their men. Between 1801 and 1803, at least four out of five of the French soldiers serving in Haiti died of the Yellow Jack.

But the future, fortunately, is always a closed book and none of the appalling disasters that awaited the French expeditionary force in Haiti could be foretold as the ships sailed off a few days before Christmas 1801 to the cheers of the crowds on the seashore, the fanfare of the military bands and the delight of the young, departing soldiers at the thought of all the available pretty black girls in the faraway colony.

The First Consul, accompanied by Josephine, came to see his sister before the expedition sailed. He also had a pleasant word for Toussaint L'Ouverture's sons, Isaac and Placide, who were returning home after several years in France, and fondly said goodbye to his young brother, Midshipman Jerome Bonaparte, recently posted to the flagship *Le Foudroyant*. When the First Consul was to see him again, in 1805, Jerome was a commander and wed to a Miss Patterson, of Baltimore, a union which Napoleon, now Emperor and anxious to marry his younger brother into one of the ruling houses of Europe, promptly had annulled.

The first ships of the French expedition arrived off Haiti on January 20, 1802. Toussaint L'Ouverture, on his horse, watched the armada in the distance, turned to one of his aides and said tonelessly: 'We are doomed. All France has come to invade us.' He then galloped away to prepare the resistance.

The French, in whose cause he had previously fought, although somewhat ambiguously, were now the undoubted enemy, and he now had no allies. Britain, the traditional foe of France, was neutral – but only theoretically, for in the Caribbean context she was more friendly to the white French than to the black Haitians. On October 23, 1801, two months before the expedition sailed, Prime Minister Addington, during a three-hour walk around his Wimbledon estate, told the French representative, Mr Otto, that it was in the interest of both governments to destroy 'the jacobinism' of the blacks. 'We hope,' the British Prime Minister added, 'the number of troops you plan to send will be sufficient to establish order in your colonies.' On April 28, 1802 Admiral Duckworth wrote from Jamaica to Admiral Latouche-Tréville, now in command of the French naval forces in the West Indies, that 'all civilised nations' hoped for a French victory in Haiti.

Toussaint could count neither on help from the Spaniards, who were now France's allies, nor from the Americans, whose only interest in Haiti was to do business with whosoever was in power in the island.

One hesitates to plunge into a recital of the fighting in Haiti. Fighting is not the right word: slaughter and blood and hideousness and immense suffering was what it was all about. A narration of massacres, of treacherous deeds and bad faith, of civilisation's surrender to abomination, of eyes gouged out, limbs torn off, throats cut open, writhing victims burnt alive, of mass drownings, of hungry hounds hunting down runaway slaves and eating them, of groans, shrieks, pain and misery, of pregnant women disembowelled, infants bayoneted, of savagery and horror triumphant, and all, black, brown and white, guilty, equally guilty. Wading through an account of the Haitian campaign – waist-deep in dead and torn bodies and oceans of blood, and deafened by the shrieks of the tortured – one can only wonder at the depravity and sadism into which the entire human race can descend.

Far from these concerns of the future, the fickle, fun-loving Pauline looked with pleasure at the island scenery unfolding before her as the fleet approached the entrance to Port François and wondered which of her lovely dresses she should wear for the disembarkation ceremony. Her future home, she was told, would be the recently redecorated Government Palace with its colonnades and its garden and abundant flowers.

But awaiting the French ships at Cap François, the black General Christophe, Toussaint's envoy, was in no mood to be the perfect host. He belligerently informed Leclerc he could not enter the harbour without the governor-general's permission. If he did, the town would be set on fire. Leclerc disregarded the warning. The French ships moved into the harbour and Christophe's men immediately applied the torch to the houses, while the evacuated townspeople watched in dismay, but unprotesting, as their homes went up in flames. Christophe set his own mansion afire. When Leclerc landed, only fifty-nine of the two thousand buildings were still standing. Pauline's intended home was not among them. She found a more modest, temporary home in an old disused fort. Later, Leclerc set his wife up in an almost regal mansion on the island of Tortuga, a small island off the north-west coast of Haiti, free of yellow fever.

So began, with the firing of Cap François, two years of war in Haiti, a war of ambush, guerrilla fighting and siege. Leclerc sent one of his generals, Boudet, to occupy Port-au-Prince to the south, Desfour-neaux to Plaisance, Hardy to Dondon, Rochambeau to Fort Liberté, Humbert to Port-de-Paix and Kerverseau to Santo Domingo.

Humbert, facing Maurepas, one of the ablest of Toussaint's senior officers, promptly captured Fort Belair in Port-de-Paix defeating with five hundred men a force six times superior to his. But his enthusiasm overcame his caution and he pushed on a few leagues inland to be re-pulsed by Maurepas and thrown back to the coast, where he was joined by General Debelle.

Humbert and Leclerc were already manifestly at odds. Dissatisfied with his subordinate's handling of the situation at Port-de-Paix, Leclerc castigated Humbert in violent terms and transferred him to Port Margot, a small inland locality about twenty miles to the east, halfway between Port-de-Paix and Cap François. At Port Margot, Humbert came under Clauzel's command.

Faced with a powerful French army, many of Toussaint's generals foresaw defeat and came over to the French. Maurepas was among the first to answer an appeal by Leclerc to the rebels to join the French side, the side of freedom (no question of reintroducing slavery, of course) where their present military ranks would be retained and respected. But Toussaint's chief lieutenants, Christophe, Dessalines and Belair, remained – at least for the moment – loyal to their chief.

The first massacres were already under way. The captain of HMS *Nereide* from Kingston, Jamaica, who came on a goodwill visit to Cap François in March, reported back to Admiral Duckworth that the French had already executed eight hundred people. 'They shoot everyone they catch,' he wrote. The blacks were equally savage. That same month General Hardy, advancing in the region of St Marc, found the still warm bodies of a hundred white hostages, their throats cut by their fleeing captors.

Dessalines concentrated his forces near St Marc, around the fort of Crête-à-Pierrot. General Debelle attacked him in early March. The French were in a particularly vengeful mood. At nearby Vérrèttes they had just found eight hundred bloated corpses of men, women and children, massacred a few days previously by some of Dessalines's troops. General Hardy went in pursuit of the perpetrators, captured six hundred blacks and massacred them all. But the soldiers of a Polish regiment in French service refused to kill their prisoners.

More than twelve hundred Haitian soldiers took refuge in the fort of Crête-à-Pierrot. They were soon surrounded by ten times that number of French troops, but rebuffed all calls to surrender. For three weeks the French launched attack after attack against the fort. All were repulsed. Boudet, then Dugua, took command of the operation for a while. Both retired, wounded. Leclerc came up from Port-au-Prince. He too was unsuccessful. The mulatto General Pétion, fighting on the French side, tried to shell the fort into submission and failed. The black defenders sang the 'Marseillaise', to the bewilderment of the French troops besieging them, and flew flags of defiance from every corner of the fort.

The defenders, led by Lamartinière, a mulatto who could have passed for white, never surrendered. Short of ammunition, food, water and supplies, the survivors, about eight hundred in number, made their last sortie in the night on March 24 and escaped through the French lines into the countryside. But, just the same, the capture of the fort marked the end, temporarily, of Haitian resistance against the French. On April 25, 1802, Christophe and his army went over to the French. Ten days later Toussaint L'Ouverture, accompanied by General Hardy, rode into the Cap with a bodyguard of four hundred black dragoons for a meeting with Leclerc.

Toussaint lunched with the French general, who assured him that French intentions towards Haiti were pure. There was no question of reintroducing slavery, Leclerc said. But in spite of the host's studied joviality, it was not a great social occasion. Toussaint was glum. 'You can't get flour out of a sack of coal,' one French wit observed. It was not a great gastronomic occasion either. Suspicious that his hosts might try to poison him, Toussaint ate only a little piece of cheese and drank only water. He agreed to give up his command and retire to his plantation at Ennery. The black generals Dessalines and Belair during the next few days went over to the French. The war seemed over. Actually, it hadn't begun.

DIE, BLACK MAN I
Guadeloupe 1802

The catalyst that provoked a renewal of hostilities in Haiti a few months later was another rebellion, in the island of Guadeloupe, seven hundred miles to the east.

The previous year, even before sending Leclerc to Haiti, First Consul Bonaparte had named Admiral Lacrosse captain-general of Guadeloupe. Lacrosse was the hero of the *Les-Droits-de-L'Homme*'s lion-hearted battle in 1796 against two British frigates, described earlier.

Before leaving for Guadeloupe, Admiral Lacrosse had been advised in a very hush-hush fashion that – in time, but not right away – he would have to supervise the reintroduction of slavery in Guadeloupe. The obvious prejudices which Lacrosse constantly displayed towards the black and mulatto population of Guadeloupe led to widespread resentment. The island rose in revolt, not against France, but against Lacrosse. He was placed aboard a Europe-bound Danish vessel and ordered to leave.

Bonaparte's reaction to the expulsion of his captain-general was the Richepanse expedition: 3,500-men strong, it landed at Pointe-à-Pitre on May 6, 1802.

The selection of General Richepanse as its commander reflected the importance that Bonaparte attached to it, for he was regarded as one of France's most capable generals. His role at the Battle of Hohenlinden had perhaps made the difference between victory and defeat. Still only thirty-one, General Antoine Richepanse was the ideal man for difficult or perilous missions.

The situation in Guadeloupe seemed quiet enough when he arrived. To his surprise General Pélage, a mulatto whom he had been informed was a dangerous rebel, greeted him with respectful enthusiasm at Pointe-à-Pitre and with loud and vibrant shouts of 'Vive la France'.

It was a comedy of errors. Wielding alternatively the proverbial carrot and the stick, Richepanse affirmed that his troops were in Guadeloupe to re-establish French rule, to the uneasy bewilderment of the Guadeloupeans who had never considered French rule disestablished. The French general also assured the black islanders, who had been free for nearly eight years, that there would be no return to slavery. His secret instructions were, however, to bring it back as soon as practicable, and his tone, his postures and his shifty eyes undoubtedly betrayed his deceitful intentions to some of the black soldiers. They refused to embark as ordered on the frigates of the expedition, and instead disappeared with a few trusted officers into the wooded mountains.

How right their intuitions proved!

Those who boarded the warships were disarmed and packed into the holds. Those who fled into the mountains were able to fight and die like men.

Two names stand out in that forgotten, epic struggle: Major Ignace and Colonel Louis Delgrès. Unlike the Haitian Toussaint L'Ouverture, history has unfairly passed them by.

Ignace, a black soldier on garrison duty at Pointe-à-Pitre, was aghast at the supineness that General Pélage, whom he had always respected, showed towards the arrogant Richepanse. Ignace was a former 'maroon', an escaped slave who had fled into the hills as a youth and had come down to join the army and fight when emancipation was proclaimed in 1794. A born soldier, he helped to expel the British and, in due course, was made an officer. He was illiterate and reasoned by intuition. And his intuition told him that Richepanse intended a return to slavery.

He wasted no time. The very evening of Richepanse's arrival, he was off into the hills taking with him three hundred and fifty black soldiers whom he led south to the other main Guadeloupe town, Basse-Terre, to join the mulatto officer, Colonel Delgrès. He knew Delgrès would place loyalty to the coloured and black population of Guadeloupe above an abstract loyalty to a faraway Republic which was on the point of betraying them.

Delgrès's name is virtually unknown. It should be famous. As soon as he heard of Richepanse's arrival, and of the harsh and humiliating treatment being meted out to the black soldiers at Pointe-à-Pitre, he decided to fight. He assembled his men, and told the whites under his command he did not expect them to fire against their countrymen: they could deposit their arms and go away unharmed.

He answered Richepanse's call to the people of Guadeloupe for submission by his own proclamation which was posted on the walls of Basse-Terre. 'There are men,' it said, 'who can only visualise black men, or those of black origin, in the irons of slavery.'

General Richepanse, alerted to the revolt brewing in Basse-Terre, attacked the town on May 11. Delgrès, Ignace and their hundreds of supporters took refuge in Fort St Charles, the fortress which the British had called Fort Matilda a few years previously when they held Guadeloupe.

'There will not be the slightest undermining of the liberty which all French citizens, without distinction, enjoy,' General Richepanse promised in a new announcement pleading for the rebels to capitulate. But he was careful not to say that French citizenship was to be withdrawn from all Negroes and mulattos and that only men and women of pure white stock would be able to claim French citizenship in the future.

The capture of Fort St Charles was Richepanse's next concern. He had obtained from the governor of British Dominica, Sir Johnston Cochrane, mortars and ammunition and the bombardment of the fort began in earnest on May 17. Unable to hold Fort St Charles with only their few hundred men, Delgrès and Ignace smashed their way out four days later, and vanished into the hills in two separate groups. But the inevitable end was near.

Ignace made for the Grande-Terre, as the northernmost part of the island is called, and installed himself and his black followers in an old abandoned fort, the redoubt of Baimbridge, overlooking Pointe-à-Pitre. On the 25th, the French under General Gobert, a white officer born in Guadeloupe, and General Pélage attacked with artillery and troops. Within a few hours the defenders had run out of ammunition. Ignace kept the last bullet for himself. 'You will not have the honour of taking my life,' he shouted, and blew his brains out. Six hundred and fifty bodies, women as well as men – for wives and girl friends and sisters fought beside the men – were removed from the fortress. Two hundred and fifty of the defenders were captured. One hundred were shot the next day in the main square of Pointe-à-Pitre, and all the others two days afterwards.

Three days later, it was Delgrès's turn to die. He had led his column into the densely wooded and mountainous region of the Matouba, in the southern half of the island. On May 28, at dawn, Richepanse attacked the mansion in which the rebels were barricaded: their intention was to fight to the end, and they did.

Delgrès released a small group of white planters he was holding as hostages. He left a last quiet and dignified message. 'We can only now die bravely. Our death will bring renown to us, and we shall not perish entirely.' A large stock of explosives was then readied in the cellar.

Richepanse launched his last attack at three-thirty in the afternoon. The blacks who were fighting in the grounds of the estate retreated into the mansion. Some of the more exalted of the French soldiers fought their way into the building to fight hand-to-hand against the Negroes in the living-room and kitchens. Delgrès shouted 'Vive la liberté!' and the whole building exploded. There was not one survivor. Three hundred West Indian fighters perished in that instant.

The man morally responsible for the butchery was the First Consul himself. At his urging, the law restoring slavery had been passed in the legislative chamber in Paris on May 20, by two hundred and eleven votes to sixty. Liberty, equality and fraternity were now to be reserved for whites only.

Just over six weeks later, on July 8, French nationality was officially taken away from all blacks and mulattos in the island. All coloured men, with the exception of those who had served in the army, were ordered to return to the plantations where they had been working eight years ago and report to their former masters.

The repression began soon after the defeat of Delgrès. During the next few months, thousands were hanged, shot or beheaded, ten thousand according to some estimates. Three thousand were deported, dumped on uninhabited shores around the Caribbean, or sent to prison or to the army in France. Pélage, unwanted now that he had helped to break the Guadeloupe rebellion, was also shipped to France and jailed for fifteen months in Brest, then released without explanation or apology and taken back into the army. He was killed fighting Wellington at the Battle of Vittoria in Spain.

On June 8, Richepanse's second-in-command, General Seriziat, died of yellow fever. Richepanse followed him into the grave three months later, also from yellow fever. Fort St Charles was renamed Fort Richepanse in his honour, a name it still bears. Admiral Lacrosse came back to Guadeloupe and, for a few months, was supreme again in the island. In a brilliantly-lit ceremony on the night of August 8, to the applause of guests, planters, businessmen, army and navy officers, he officially declared slavery reinstated in Guadeloupe.

By now the island was no longer safe. Bands of armed Negroes roamed the interior, killing or robbing anyone who had the misfortune to fall into their hands. In retaliation, frightened and outraged whites attacked and killed innocent black and mulatto passersby in Basse-Terre and Pointe-à-Pitre. Savagery, under the paranoid Lacrosse, extended to the law. Two Frenchmen, Barse and Millet de la Girardière, convicted of being in league with Negro thieves, were sentenced to death. Barse was to be broken on the wheel and then burnt alive, Millet de la Girardière was condemned to sit astride the upturned blade of a guillotine in the public square. Millet hanged himself in his cell rather than undergo this horrifying ordeal, but Barse stoically suffered his fate. Thirty-two Negroes were executed with him.

Learning belatedly of Lacrosse's lapses into barbarism, First Consul Bonaparte replaced him as captain-general with the more moderate General Ernouf. Admiral Villaret-Joyeuse was appointed to the same function for Martinique and St Lucia, recently returned to France by the British under the terms of the Treaty of Amiens.

But meanwhile, over in Haiti, events were moving to a catastrophic denouement. Towards the end of July 1802, the frigate *Cocarde*, its holds filled with blacks being deported from Guadeloupe, sailed unobtrusively into Port-au-Prince harbour. Some of the prisoners on board managed to slip away during the night and swim to shore where they announced to those who came to their aid that General Richepanse had brought slavery back to Guadeloupe. Within a few days the news had spread all over the island and Haitians, who now knew what to expect from General Leclerc, prepared once again to fight.

DIE, BLACK MAN 2
Haiti 1802-1803

The fear of a return to slavery had been haunting the people of Haiti for months. Toussaint L'Ouverture had been very discreetly keeping in touch with the few rebels still resisting in the mountains. But some of his secret messages had been intercepted by the French. 'I am going to order his arrest. . . . I shall ship him off to Corsica for imprisonment,' General Leclerc wrote to Paris on June 6 after reading a letter from Toussaint to one of the rebel leaders. The next day the unsuspecting Toussaint, lured by General Brunet to a meeting, supposedly to discuss the harassment of his plantation workers by French soldiers, was surrounded by ten armed officers as he sat down for dinner. His hands and arms were tied and he was frog-marched to a waiting carriage, driven to Cap François and placed aboard the ship-of-the-line *Heros* which sailed a few days later for France.

'In overthrowing me they have only cut off the trunk of the tree of black liberty. Liberty will flourish again through its roots,' Toussaint observed philosophically to Captain Savary – the same man, who four years earlier, had taken Humbert to Killala to fight for the liberation of Ireland and who was now taking to exile and prison the man who had fought for the liberation of his country from an oppressive France.

There were however other blacks who, sent to France, ended up as 'Regiment Royal Africa', in the Neapolitan Army.

Shortly afterwards General Boyer seized seven thousand muskets from black peasants, but thousands more remained hidden. More were coming in, smuggled in by American ships trading off the coast.

Although weakened by malaria, Leclerc was determined to break the rebellion. 'All the blacks are persuaded by letters which have come from France, by the law which re-established the slave trade, by the decree of General Richepanse which re-established slavery in Guadeloupe, that the intention is to make them slaves again, and I can assure their disarmament only by long and stubborn conflicts,' Leclerc wrote to Admiral Decrès, the navy minister, on August 5. On the same day he sent a bitter letter to Bonaparte, which reveals the full deviousness of the plan to restore slavery. 'I entreated you, Citizen Consul, to do nothing which might make them [the blacks] anxious about their liberty until I was ready, and that moment was rapidly approaching. Suddenly the law arrived here which authorises the slave trade in the colonies, with business letters from Nantes and Havre, asking if blacks can be sold here. More than all that, General Richepanse has just taken a decision to re-establish slavery in Guadeloupe.'

Their wicked secret just hadn't been kept long enough. The rebellion spread. It spread into the black and mulatto regiments of the army. The first major defection occurred in August when a Negro brigade in French service mutinied. The entire force was condemned to death and the rebels were first obliged to watch the public executions of their wives. This was the signal for a second mass desertion from the French ranks. The Negro general, Belair, rode off with his army and joined the rebellion. A few days later, he naively walked into a trap, was promptly court-martialled and shot by a firing squad of Dessalines's men. For good measure so was his wife. They refused the traditional blindfold and died side by side.

The rebellion spread to the mulattos. Pétion and another mulatto general, Clairvaux, were the next to go. Christophe followed them after another massacre of twelve hundred disarmed black soldiers by the French.

Leclerc's black and mulatto soldiers were deserting and aligning themselves in rebel ranks. His white soldiers were dying of yellow fever. The hospitals of Cap François alone were losing a hundred soldiers a day. Leclerc sent piteous letters to Paris, begging for reinforcements, 'ten thousand men who must all come at the same time,' he stressed.

'To convey an idea of my losses: the 7th Regiment of the Line which arrived here with 1,395 men, today had only eighty-three half-sick men on duty and 107 in hospital. The rest are dead. . . . The 71st of the Line, originally 1,000 strong, has seventeen men on duty and 133 sick. . . . What general could calculate on a mortality of four-fifths of his army?' he asked despairingly.

The love life of his wife was another major worry for the unfortunate General Leclerc. He was well aware of Pauline's amorous capers on Tortuga island: a large Negro servant would carry her naked from her bath to the bedroom, where, General Boyer, among others, received what was then roguishly described as her 'favours'. Humbert succeeded him in her couch, a beautiful bed in the shape of a swan's nest, surrounded by mirrors.

By this time, Leclerc's sanity may have been leaving him. Christophe attacked him with six thousand men. Leclerc, in high malarial fever, left his bed to engage the rebel army and defeated it. Dessalines now absconded with his army and occupied St Marc. Only Cap François, Port-au-Prince and Les Cayes were in French hands.

In an insane move, perhaps to prevent any more defections among his black troops, Leclerc ordered a regiment of several hundred blacks, who had remained faithful to him up to this time, to be executed. He had them all tied together, thrown into the harbour and drowned. A few days later he caught yellow fever. A week later, on November 2, 1802, he died.

Accompanied by Pauline, who put on a great display of grief she probably didn't feel, Leclerc's body was shipped to France on the *Swiftsure*, the battleship that Ganteaume had captured from Ben Hallowell off Crete. Pauline, her hair cut to its roots in mourning ('It will grow again,' Napoleon said, unmoved, when he heard of his sister's sacrifice), wept as the coffin was hoisted aboard. Leclerc's secretary, Norvins, did not offer his condolences. The general's confidences to him, a month before he died, deterred him from paying his respects to the widow, he noted discreetly in his journal.

Humbert, expelled from the colony for financial intrigues, had sailed a few days before, Haiti destroyed his career. On Humbert's departure, his former foe, the black General Maurepas, took over command at Mole Saint-Nicolas and, after Leclerc's death, General Rochambeau became commander in chief of the army in the island. The men for whom Leclerc had been clamouring for months arrived as reinforcements from France soon afterwards and Rochambeau took the offensive in northern Haiti. The Cap François region was rapidly cleared of the rebels, then Port-de-Paix and St Marc were recaptured.

Rochambeau then embarked on a policy that can only be described as the deliberate extermination of blacks and mulattos. He started with his allies. The luckless General Maurepas was among his first victims. The black general and his family were arrested and taken to a ship in Cap François harbour. Maurepas was tied naked to the mast and the ship's carpenter nailed his general's epaulettes to his shoulders. He, and his wife and children were then bayoneted to death, and their bodies thrown overboard.

Rochambeau replaced Maurepas at Mole Saint-Nicolas with an old friend of Lafayette, the aristocratic Viscount Louis-Marie de Noailles, a veteran of both the Savannah and Yorktown campaigns of the American War of Independence. Leaving his wife in France (she was subsequently guillotined), Noailles had returned to the United States as a refugee in 1793, and lived for several years in Philadelphia. His family were among the largest land and slave owners in Haiti and he had returned to the island in 1802 to look over his estates. He met there his old friend from Yorktown, Rochambeau, and in December 1802 became a soldier again.

One would like to think that the gallant Noailles, supposedly a man of great personal charm, with active radical sympathies, raised some protest at the massacres that his old comrade was carrying out in Haiti. Six thousand blacks were reportedly taken to ships at anchor in the port of Cap François for execution. An eyewitness, one day, counted two hundred and forty bodies floating around one ship. Five hundred blacks and mulattos were hanged in the marketplace at Port-au-Prince. The blacks hanged five hundred whites in retaliation. Rochambeau ordered bloodhounds from Cuba to hunt the fugitive blacks in the forest, a practice widely followed by the Spaniards in their islands and by the British in Jamaica. The French commander-in-chief added a new refinement to the system. 'No ration allowances are authorized for the dogs. You will give them blacks to eat,' he told the officer responsible.

This policy of slaughter was deliberate. Rochambeau did not believe that any man who had enjoyed freedom would return to slavery unless sufficiently terrorised. General Kerverseau, who had fought under Toussaint L'Ouverture in the old days, and now commanded the troops in Santo Domingo, was aghast at the turn the fighting had taken. 'This is no longer a war,' he wrote to a friend, 'it is a fight between wild beasts. One has to be in a transport of fury to keep it up.' But, just the same, Kerverseau carried out Rochambeau's orders. 'I have to keep on telling the troops: it is no longer courage I want from you but rage. But one cannot stay in a rage indefinitely, and our common humanity makes us weep sometimes.'

Rochambeau was perhaps encouraged by a colonist who had written to Paris that if France wished to recover Haiti 'she must . . . destroy at least thirty thousand Negroes and Negresses – the latter being more cruel than the men. These measures are frightful but necessary.'

The massacres were still continuing when, in civilised Europe, on the morning of April 7, 1803, the great Toussaint L'Ouverture was discovered dead in his cold fortress cell in the Jura mountains, quite roomy, but no place for an ageing man from the West Indies. One of his last visitors had found him 'trembling with cold and illness, suffering greatly and having difficulty in speaking.' But his jailer, Major Baille, put an end to the visits of the doctor who occasionally attended him: 'The constitution of Negroes bears no resemblance to that of Europeans. I have dispensed with the services of a doctor and surgeon as they are of no possible use to him,' he explained in his report.

A little over a month later, on May 16, 1803, Britain broke the twenty-months-old Treaty of Amiens, the truce with France. She refused to evacuate Malta, as stipulated in the Treaty, while the French continued to occupy parts of Switzerland. France and Britain were at war again. With another break, in 1814, it was to last more than twelve years.

In Haiti, the rebel generals were informed that the British navy would now cooperate with them to expel the French. But it was to remain a strictly naval form of collaboration, offshore, not on land at all.

There was no question of sending British soldiers again to fight in the pestiferous, fever-soaked, death-ridden island, although we may be sure that the British officers sent to advise the Haitians of this new alliance did not explain their future role in such blunt terms.

CHAPTER TWELVE

The American Dream

HELLO LOUISIANA
1794-1803

The French empire across the Atlantic was not only Haiti and the other islands of the Caribbean. It was also Louisiana.

Nine years before the events described in the previous chapter General Georges Collot, the French governor of Guadeloupe, who surrendered the island to the British in 1794, had decided it would be wiser not to return to France when his captors released him on parole. The forty-three-year-old hussar and veteran of the American War of Independence made his way instead to the United States where he still had many friends and where there was no guillotine awaiting defeated French generals.

While he was in Washington, the Terror ended in Paris with the guillotining of Robespierre, and Collot returned to active service with a peaceful assignment in North America itself. The Directory, the new government of France, ordered him to go on an exploratory trip down the Mississippi to New Orleans. It was a nostalgic journey through territory that had been French until only thirty years before when Louis XV, out of friendship for his Bourbon cousin on the Spanish throne, had simply given it away to Madrid. It was a region where, in spite of the recent excesses of the French Revolution in Paris, the majority of settlers still felt strongly French.

During his trip down the Mississippi valley, Collot asked questions of everybody, studied the crops and the topography, pow-wowed with Indians, chatted with old French and more recent Spanish and American settlers. Everywhere he went, he noted down his observations in a little book.

It seems more than a coincidence that at about this time there arrived in Paris from the Mississippi valley the French-born chief of the local Creek tribe, Jean Le Clerc, more commonly known as Milfort. He had served in the French infantry during the War of Independence, deserted instead of going back to France when the war ended, and had wandered down south to settle among the Creek Indians in the lower Mississippi region.

A French thumbnail sketch of Milfort says he played an important part in the wars between the Creeks and the encroaching American frontiersmen pushing in from the north and east. In 1795, we find him suddenly in Paris as the envoy of the Creeks, probably prompted by Collot, demanding in their name that the French come back and take over their territory again.

The old, unfulfilled French dream of an American empire was coming to life again. Before the loss of Canada to the British and of Louisiana to the Spanish, France had ruled, if only nominally, over most of the vast and empty spaces of North America west of the Appalachians, all the way to the Rockies, up to the Great Lakes and the endless prairies, down to the Gulf of Mexico. Louisiana then was many, many times larger than the state which bears that name today.

It was plain from Milfort's rehearsed request that the French government had decided the time was ripe for the territory to return to France and thus restore France to her former eminence in the New World. Spain, partly occupied by French troops, haggled, hummed and hawed over the matter. It was not until Napoleon Bonaparte became First Consul and the no-nonsense ruler of France four years later that Spain finally agreed to let the territory go.

Weak and divided as Spain then was, she really had no option. But in exchange the French handed over to the Spanish royal family the Italian Duchy of Parma and Etruria, and there were many well-placed people in the Spanish court who were delighted at the deal.

Negotiations over the transfer of Louisiana continued between the two countries from July 1800 until its cession was confirmed by the Treaty of San Ildefonso, on October 1, 1801. When the people of New Orleans heard that Louisiana was becoming French again, they sang the 'Marseillaise' in the streets and coffee houses. For them it was a homecoming after nearly forty years of Spanish rule.

Napoleon had made peace with Great Britain in October 1801 and, a year earlier, with the United States with whom France had been in a state of half-war. The way to Louisiana therefore was now clear. The ocean between Europe and North America was wide open to commerce and travel again. The British navy was no longer in the way.

Strangely enough the Spaniards, and specially the court and government, were not displeased at returning the territory to the French.

Louisiana was a huge wilderness of snakes, swamps, prairies and wild Indians, with perhaps fifty thousand white settlers in all, and it was far from Spain. Tuscany, in delightful, highly civilised Italy and only a few days' travel from Madrid, had a population of over one million, and would bring its ruler a more than adequate revenue. 'Frankly, Louisiana costs us more than it is worth,' the Spanish foreign minister Mariano Urquijo wrote to his ambassador in Paris. Louisiana's deficit was trimming nearly $340,000 from the Spanish Treasury every year.

The Spaniards, moreover, were already worried over United States expansionism. Americans were beginning to swarm into the Mississippi region. In a period of just two months, in September and October 1795, Kentucky and Tennessee each received nearly thirty thousand new settlers, and these regions were only separated from Louisiana territory by a river's width. The Spaniards knew their big problem would be to keep the Americans out.

By 1800 the position had become even more troubling. 'It would be very useful to place a barrier between the Americans and ourselves, a barrier against their plans of colonisation, by means of a nation like France,' the Spanish foreign minister pointed out in his letter to his Paris ambassador, detailing the positive aspects for Spain of the cession of Louisiana to France.

Napoleon's new dream was taking shape. The dream was to build a new New France, to replace the old New France of Canada, lost to the British forty years before. This new New France would link the islands of the Caribbean, Martinique, St Lucia, Guadeloupe, Tobago, Haiti and the whole of the island of Hispaniola to the Mississippi valley, with New Orleans the vital point in the middle, and then on up north to Canada, skirting the Rockies to the west and the Mississippi River to the east, all the way to the Great Lakes and east down the St Lawrence River to Quebec and Acadia. It was a grand dream. It was not only a New France that would come into being. It was a New World, a French-speaking world. The other occupants of the North American continent, Britain, the United States and Spain, would be completely overshadowed. Napoleon's ambitions were never mean.

It is a matter of contention whether this North American dominion would have extended to Canada. Years later, when he was king of Sweden, General Bernadotte (to whom Napoleon felt under an obligation since he had married the Emperor's discarded girl friend, Désirée Clary, a Marseille soap manufacturer's daughter) claimed that Napoleon had once offered him the governorship of Canada when it was restored to French rule. And it is certainly unlikely, had the French won, that Napoleon would have allowed the British to continue ruling over the approximately two hundred thousand French-speaking Canadians in what is today the Province of Quebec.

There may be some doubt over Napoleon's intentions towards

Canada, but there is none about his plans to reoccupy Louisiana. On June 2, 1802, he wrote to Admiral Decrès, his navy minister, that he intended 'to take possession of Louisiana with the shortest possible delay.' A list of civil officers for Louisiana was drawn up, headed by a colonial prefect, Pierre Clément de Laussat. Some five thousand troops prepared for embarkation at Dunkirk. In August, General Victor, with whom we were last on his hospital bed in Toulon and whose cheerful disposition had earned him the nickname of *Beau Soleil* (Sunshine) was appointed captain-general of Louisiana, and given the command of the expeditionary corps and a salary of seventy thousand francs a year.

Napoleon Bonaparte forgot neither the native Indians nor the threat from the nearby Americans, particularly those whom he described as the 'Western Americans', the pioneers and frontiersmen who were already moving into the virtually untouched lands bordering the Mississippi River to the east, and who caused the Spaniards so much worry. 'We must also strengthen ourselves against the Western Americans by forming alliances with the Indian nations scattered on the east side of the river. The Chickasaws, Choctaws, Alabamans, Creeks, etc, are said to be entirely devoted to us,' the First Consul wrote in his instructions to Victor.

To cultivate Indian friendship was important, and a large quantity of presents for the Redskins were packed for shipment. They included two hundred special medals as gifts for friendly Indian chiefs and witch doctors. On one side the medal bore the effigy of First Consul Bonaparte. On the other, the words: 'To Loyalty'. Whose loyalty to whom is not clear.

Of more practical interest to the Indians would be the 5,000 muskets, 150 rifles, 20,000 pounds of powder, 1,000 swords and 5,000 tomahawks. There was enough there to do plenty of damage. Had Napoleon secured Louisiana, quite a few American scalps would have garnished the local Indian huts.

In October 1802 it was decided that the expeditionary force for Louisiana should leave from the Dutch port of Helvoet Sluys, near Rotterdam, instead of Dunkirk as originally planned. 'The First Consul desires you to depart without delay,' Decrès wrote to Victor. Because of supply problems the expected date of sailing, between November 22 and 27, was moved forward to the next month. 'The First Consul has ordered me to warn you that he desires you depart without delay,' Decrès wrote once more to Victor in November.

At Christmas the fleet was still not ready to sail. Victor was concerned as the winter threatened to be exceptionally cold, but he required two or three more weeks in which to bring up essential supplies from Dunkirk. Then the fleet could depart. But the fleet never sailed. Early in January the harbour waters froze and remained frozen until the end of February. The French ships could not stir from their anchorage. Relations between France and Britain were worsening. The First Consul had a dreadful row with Lord Whitworth, the British ambassador, at a public reception in Paris. The British fleet began patrolling off the Dutch coast.

These may have been months of inactivity in Helvoet Sluys for the French expedition but elsewhere, in Washington, Paris, London, Madrid, New Orleans and on the ocean, events were moving and messengers were rushing to and fro, as fast as the galloping hooves of horses and North Atlantic winds could make them.

In Spain, after finagling for better conditions, King Charles IV, with the connivance of his prime minister, Manuel Godoy, who slept with the Queen and styled himself The Prince of Peace, had at last signed on October 15, 1802, the Royal Order making over Louisiana to the French.

In London, in the usual lofty British diplomatic ambiguous tone, Lord Hawkesbury dismissed French accusations that the British ships were blockading the French expedition. The British naval vessels, he said, had been ordered not to make 'any movements or hold any language which could be regarded as being of a hostile nature.'

In the United States, President Jefferson viewed the reoccupation of Louisiana by France with great misgivings. 'The possessor of Louisiana is our natural enemy,' he wrote to Robert Livingston, the United States ambassador in Paris. The return of the French on the North American continent 'works most sorely with the United States,' he added. Never mind that it was largely with French money that the United States of America had won its independence twenty years earlier. National self-interest has no time for gratitude, as the Americans have since discovered for themselves. That's the way of the world.

'The day that France takes possession of New Orleans . . . we must marry ourselves to the British fleet and nation,' Jefferson told Livingston, in an obvious reference to a possible British-US alliance directed against France. Yet Jefferson was pro-French, or at least as pro-French as it is possible for an American to be, and a liberal who backed many of the principles of the French Revolution. But he didn't want France as a neighbour. France was too strong. Perhaps he too was already feeling the itch of 'manifest destiny' and wanted North America, all of it, for his fellow-Americans.

In the meantime, he authorised Livingston to offer $10 million to France for New Orleans and a strip of territory beside the Mississippi, and sent his friend and former law student James Monroe to Paris to assist the US envoy in his negotiations. Monroe already knew France well. He had been US minister in Paris from 1794 to 1796.

New Orleans, at the mouth of the Mississippi, had become a vital outlet for the United States of America. The port was used largely for shipping lumber, furs, cotton, tobacco and grain and, to the indignation of all, this navigational right (guaranteed by the 1783 Treaty of Paris) was temporarily suspended in 1802 by the Spanish authorities who were continuing, with France's accord, to govern the territory in the name of the still absent captain-general, General Victor.

His temporary replacement, De Laussat, arrived in New Orleans on March 26, 1803. He had come on ahead on the French ship, *Le Surveillant,* from the ice-free port of La Rochelle to represent France while Victor and his five-thousand-man army remained stuck in the Dutch ice.

Somewhere at sea, without sighting each other, the westward-bound *Le Surveillant* and an eastward-bound American brig passed each other in mid-ocean hundreds of miles apart. The United States vessel was taking to France President Jefferson's special envoy, James Monroe, to arrange the purchase of New Orleans from the French while the French ship was bringing Pierre-Clément de Laussat to New Orleans to take the city and territory over for France!

De Laussat was a minor politician who had survived the Terror and had then smartly backed General Bonaparte. He was not a widely-travelled man and Louisiana was his first colonial assignment. Judging by his comments when he reached La Rochelle, he had never even seen the sea until he came to board the ship that was to take him to New Orleans with his wife, children and official entourage. He was honest, clumsy and well-meaning.

The official French party included Colonel André Burthe, one of General Victor's staff officers, a cavalryman, wounded three times and a veteran of many campaigns. He had been sent ahead to prepare the ground in New Orleans for the military contingent.

GOODBYE LOUISIANA
1803

It must have been some time in March 1803, with war at hand and British ships off the Dutch coast, that Napoleon Bonaparte finally realised he had no chance of sending his army to Louisiana. Relations with Britain were becoming more and more tense. The Treaty of Amiens required the British to evacuate Malta, but they were refusing, and at the same time accusing France of maintaining troops in Switzerland, as well as in Italy and the Netherlands. The two countries were headed, once again, for war.

The First Consul concluded that since he would be unable to defend Louisiana against the British his only practical solution might be to sell the territory to the Americans. But first, on the evening of April 10, he summoned for consultation two of his ministers: Minister of the Treasury, François Barbé-Marbois, and Minister for the Navy and the

Colonies, Admiral Decrès.

Decrès, fat, cynical and supercilious, usually strongly opposed to distant military campaigns, this time spoke passionately in favour of fighting for Louisiana. He urged Bonaparte to keep Louisiana French. It was Barbé-Marbois who was in favour of selling. He thought the money would be useful. He had lived in America and his wife was American. The three men talked far into the night.

The next day, Bonaparte announced his decision: he would sell. But he would sell not only New Orleans, which the Americans were demanding anyway, but the whole of Louisiana, all the way from the Gulf of Mexico to the Great Lakes and to the Rockies. France was departing from North America, abandoning Louisiana as it had abandoned Canada.

'The British have twenty ships of war in the Gulf of Mexico. I have not a moment to lose to put Louisiana out of their reach,' Napoleon Bonaparte impatiently told the French diplomats who were negotiating with the Americans.

The British navy by its very existence and without even firing a shot won perhaps its most important victory of all time on the day of the famed Louisiana Purchase. But the victory was for the United States, not for England.

After Bonaparte's decision to sell the territory there remained one obstacle to the deal: Livingston, the American envoy to France. The American minister in Paris was empowered only to negotiate the purchase of New Orleans, not the whole of Louisiana. Barbé-Marbois, on the other hand, insisted that the sale was a package deal, New Orleans plus the rest of Louisiana, a territory as large as the then United States. It would double the size of the country. All for eighty million francs, just over eleven million dollars. It came to four cents an acre.

Startled and confused, Livingston asked for time to think. The next day Jefferson's friend James Monroe arrived in Paris. The timing was unplanned but for the Americans it was superb.

There was nothing small-minded about Monroe. He at once visualised the continental dimensions his country would acquire, literally between one day and the next. He gave his agreement immediately. The next three weeks were spent discussing the details.

The deed of sale – how better can we term the Louisiana Purchase Treaty? – was signed in Paris on April 30, 1803. On that day the United States acquired a territory nearly four times the size of France, covering in whole or in part thirteen of today's states: Louisiana, Arkansas, Missouri, Oklahoma, Kansas, Iowa, Nebraska, Minnesota, South and North Dakota, Montana, Wyoming and Colorado. Three weeks later Britain and France were at war.

Nothing Napoleon Bonaparte ever did had more far-reaching effects than selling Louisiana to the Americans. By thus propelling the

United States into the front rank of nations considerably sooner than would otherwise have been the case – maybe by a century or more – he transformed world history.

Barbé-Marbois's Pennsylvanian wife must have been delighted at the splendid and vast additions her husband had brought, by his advocacy of the sale, to the United States. There probably isn't one American in a hundred thousand who has heard of Barbé-Marbois. Yet he deserves a huge monument in Washington DC. No one has ever done more for US territorial expansion than he.

A number of people in France were outraged at the First Consul's disposal of the old French colony, named after one of the many Louis who had reigned over their country. Among the protesters were Napoleon's brothers Lucien and Joseph, both passionately in favour of keeping the territory for France. Before the sale was finalised they came to see Bonaparte and met him while he was in his bath. Their pleadings were to no avail. In his rage at having his decision disputed, Napoleon flung a bar of soap at his brothers and splashed them with water, and stormed out of the bathroom while his valet was frantically trying to put a towel round his naked body.

What his brothers and other critics hadn't understood was Napoleon's need for cash.

'I need money to make war upon the country that has the most money,' Napoleon had forcefully told Barbé-Marbois. He needed cash to finance the invasion of England. The City of London was most anxious to assist him. For a commission, of course, the Baring bank in London and the house of Hope in Amsterdam saw the complicated deal through to its final conclusion. The English banker, Alexander Baring, arrived in Paris on July 25, 1803, two months after war had broken out between his country and France, to organise the issue of the Louisiana bonds. The French minister of the treasury speedily obtained for him the required visa to return to England from where he was to sail by the first available vessel to New York to negotiate with his fellow-bankers in the United States the quickest deal possible.

So a British bank 'furnished the First Consul with $11,250,000 for waging war on its own country,' E. Wilson Lyon reminds us in *Louisiana in French Diplomacy*. Bankers practised multinationalism long before it became fashionable. After all, money – unlike corpses on a battlefield – has no smell.

As he had said he would, Napoleon Bonaparte used most of the proceeds from the sale of Louisiana to finance his proposed invasion of the British Isles. He armed, trained, equipped, fed and paid tens of thousands of men who didn't fight for two years but camped instead on the Channel shores, staring out across a few dozen miles of water to where the untested English enemy was preparing to repulse them. With the money, Napoleon also built thousands of invasion craft which never went to sea. Most of the boats rotted away with age. French Louisiana lies in the ooze and the mud at the bottom of Boulogne harbour.

And meanwhile poor, frustrated De Laussat had been strutting and posturing in New Orleans, sending his wife and three daughters to Mass every Sunday so that the good people of the town would understand that the Republicans taking over from His Most Catholic Majesty Charles IV of Spain were not a bunch of godless ruffians; shaking hands repeatedly with all the local notables; ignoring the rumours coming down the Mississippi about the sale of Louisiana to the Americans; assuring the patriotic Louisianans, so happy to be French, that France was here to stay . . . and wondering what was holding up the arrival of General Victor and his five thousand troops. But on August 8, De Laussat received a printed bulletin from Washington announcing that the United States had bought Louisiana from France. 'An impudent and unbelievable lie,' De Laussat wrote hopefully in a blustering but anxious letter to Paris, enclosing the printed document. Alas, as he soon learnt, it was no lie.

On November 30, the Spaniards ceremonially handed Louisiana over to the French. Three weeks later, on December 20, in a similar military ritual De Laussat passed it on to the two American representatives, the soft-spoken Governor Claiborne, governor of the territory of Mississippi who came down from Natchez for the ceremony, and General James Wilkinson, who was later involved in Aaron Burr's traitorous attempt to break the south-west away from the United States. The French flag was slowly hauled down and the Stars and Stripes raised on the flagstaff. The Louisiana Militia presented arms and one of its officers, accompanied by sixty of his comrades, carried the folded French flag to the downcast De Laussat and Colonel Burthe for safekeeping. 'We shall always remain attached to France,' he said. Many of the Louisianians were in tears. They were no longer French but American citizens and, to be frank, they didn't like it.

A similar ceremony was held on March 9, 1804, at St Louis, on the Missouri river, in Upper Louisiana. From St Louis that year, at the order of President Jefferson, the Lewis and Clark expedition set out to seek a route to the Pacific Ocean. The United States had become a continental power and, for France, the American Dream was over.

PART THREE

The Napoleonic Wars
1803-1814

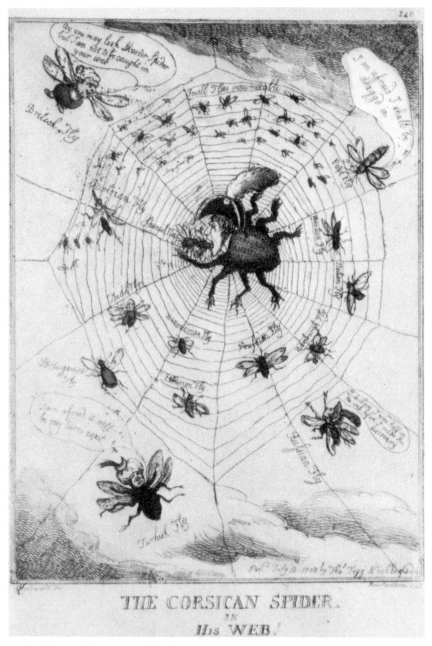

In this 1808 Thomas Rowlandson cartoon the voracious Napoleon gobbles up
Europe while Britain (top left) discreetly taunts him

CHAPTER THIRTEEN

The British Lion Growls

THE PONDICHERRY AMBUSH
India 1803

Britain and France both used the temporary Peace of Amiens to improve their position in strategic areas in Europe and overseas.

India was one of those areas.

Bonaparte was determined to re-establish a strong French presence in the subcontinent. Britain was equally determined to prevent it. Unfortunately for the French, Britain had the means of enforcing its policy. Bonaparte did not.

Even so, with Mediterranean cunning, the First Consul hoped to outfox the British. His first step, after the signing of the Peace, had been openly to send a contingent of two thousand French soldiers in March 1803 to garrison the colony of Pondicherry. Next, but now covertly, he proposed to coordinate the future actions of the French garrison with those of the mercenary General Perron, the French commander of Sindhia's powerful Mahratta army. A large number of young officers had been included in the French force that sailed for Pondicherry. Bonaparte's plan was to second many of these officers to General Perron in order to facilitate operations between the Mahratta and French armies.

The British, too, had their own scoundrelly plan ready. They were treaty-bound, by the Amiens truce, to return Pondicherry and the other French enclaves in India to French rule, but London sent instructions to Lord Wellesley to stall and dither and procrastinate and find reasons for not doing so. The Franco-British treachery in India was therefore mutual and in accordance with the best traditions of international diplomacy.

The British had been understandably concerned at the presence in the French contingent of a large number of former sepoy officers (who were intended to command future local recruits) but they were re-assured by the appointment of General Decaen to the command in India. Only thirty-four years of age, unknown and unconnected with any previous colonial ventures, General Decaen seemed unlikely to give trouble. 'I have had occasion to make the acquaintance of the general who is going out to take the command in Pondicherry,' Lord Whitworth, the British ambassador in Paris, wrote to his government on January 14, 1803. 'He is a young man, and bears a very fair character in private life, but possesses no very shining talents either as a general or a statesman. We may therefore conclude that, as far as he is con-cerned, it is intended rather to improve what possessions they already have in India than to extend them by conquest or intrigue.'

Quite obviously, even the cunning Whitworth had been fooled. He did not know that Decaen had volunteered for service in India because, as he told the First Consul, he hated the English and India seemed to be the most vulnerable place to go to fight them.

General Decaen sailed from Brest on March 6, 1803 – the troops under his command included a wretched battalion of confused blacks from Guadeloupe – and arrived in Pondicherry on July 11 in a small fleet made up of a ship-of-the-line, the 84-gun *Marengo*, three frigates and two transports, all under the command of Admiral Charles Linois.

Although an advance party from France, commanded by General Decaen's chief of staff, Major Binot, had been there for nearly a month, the general, to his intense annoyance, found the Union Jack still flying over the French colony and the British humming and hawing about obeying the Treaty of Amiens and giving up Pondicherry. A large British squadron (four ships-of-the-line, five frigates, two sloops) ostentatiously anchored close to the French ships. Aboard was Britain's top admiral in the region, the affable Sir Peter Rainier, com-mander-in-chief of the East Indies station, who looked like every-body's dutch uncle, but wasn't.

It appeared to the French as if they had sailed into a trap, but there was little they could do about it for the moment except imitate their English hosts, and stall. They did not know that Lord Hobart, secre-tary of state in charge of colonies and war in the Addington govern-ment, had sent several messages to Lord Wellesley explaining that a new war between France and the British seemed to be in the offing and that Wellesley therefore was to prevent the French from re-occupying their colony.

Decaen soon became aware of the reasons behind the tension, how-ever. On July 18 the fast brig *Bélier,* which had left France nearly two weeks after Decaen, arrived bearing urgent orders for the French to make for Mauritius forthwith, the renewal of war between France and Britain being expected at any moment.

Decaen had invited for breakfast the next day the British admiral whose grandfather, a French Huguenot, had taken refuge in England. Rainier had inherited his ancestors' gourmet instincts – we have already mentioned his fondness for mangoes. He was now looking forward to a tasty French *petit déjeuner*. But when he woke up, he discovered there would be no croissants for him that morning. The ungentlemanly Decaen, after carefully not cancelling the invitation, had sailed away secretly for Mauritius during the night. So had the whole French squadron. Some hundred and fifty French soldiers, who had preceded the main convoy with Major Binot, were stranded in Pondicherry. The posts held by these troops were immediately surrounded by British infantry and artillery but Binot, only sixty of whose men were armed, refused to surrender unconditionally so the British agreed to let them go back to France on condition they did not bear arms against Britain for a year. They all returned home and vanished into the Grand Army in Europe. Binot was killed at Eylau in 1807.

Following the orders Napoleon Bonaparte had given him, General Decaen continued to strive for the reconquest of India from his command post in the island of Mauritius. As a first step, in November, anxious to contact the Mahrattas, Decaen dispatched three secret agents to India: Captain Courson, a former sepoy officer, Lieutenant Durhone, and a former merchant in India, M. Doublet. They took a letter from General Decaen to General Perron, urging him to continue the fight against the British ('Prevent the Mahrattas from laying down their arms, that is the road for you to immortality'), and also Perron's commission as a general in the French army. They also carried letters from Decaen to Sindhia and to Holkar, rival Mahratta chiefs.

The journey of the three agents as they made their way on foot inland from near Goa was made particularly hazardous by Courson's blue eyes and conspicuous red beard, and by Doublet's dread of tigers. He was so scared of the beasts he refused to walk at night through the jungle, as they had originally planned in order to avoid meeting people. When stopped and questioned, they claimed to be French deserters on their way to join Perron's army, but their lie only took them as far as Poona, recently occupied by the British, who made them prisoners. They were all sent home after a few years and Durhone was killed in Spain during the Peninsular campaign.

Napoleon Bonaparte came up during the next few years with several new invasion plans for India. He had lived so long with his Indian dream, he could not bear for it to disappear. After all, to be another Alexander the Great was an attractive idea, particularly in that age of classicism when the study of the great deeds of ancient history was a normal part of education.

THE LAST PARTISANS
India 1803

The chief instrument of Lord Wellesley's success, outside of his own conniving mind, were two generals: his brother Arthur, the future Lord Wellington, and Sir Gerard Lake, the impeccably accoutred, blood-happy warrior, still insisting on his glass of claret at lunch and dinner, now revelling as much in slaughtering enemy Indian sepoys as he had enjoyed flogging, hanging and shooting Irish peasants a few years before.

The British campaign against the Mahrattas, aimed at destroying France's last major native ally in the subcontinent, was swift and surgical. It was greatly assisted by the divisions within the Mahratta camp itself: Sindhia, Maharajah of Gwalior, seemed to be in a perpetual state of hostilities with Holkar, Maharajah of Indore, while sundry other rajahs and maharajahs in the middle flitted hither and thither and sometimes even went over to the British side. To confuse matters still more, Sindhia and Holkar were allies in the final campaign against the British.

Discord was also rife among the European anti-British partisans. The non-French among them objected to the preferential treatment they felt French officers received from Perron. Within the French group itself there were further dissensions, with General Perron's second-in-command, General Bourquien (another deserter from the French navy who was now in command at Delhi), trying very hard to manoeuvre himself into first place. So determinedly, in fact, that Perron once considered having him murdered. The British could not have hoped for a more divided enemy.

The military campaign began in mid-August 1803 when General Lake, with an army of 10,500 men, invaded the northern part of the Mahratta dominion around Delhi, while Wellington came in from the south near Bombay. The French generals, whose Mahratta armies were centred largely near Perron's fief of Alighar in the Delhi region, found themselves fighting on two fronts.

For once, the able Perron seemed to lose control of the situation. His battalions were pushed aside at Coel, on August 2, and retreated to Agra, site of the famous Taj Mahal, while one of his senior officers, the ageing Colonel Pedron, was forced to retreat with his troops into the fortress of Alighar and prepare for a long siege.

The patriotic motive was very strong among these mercenary and exiled Frenchmen in India. France was the fairyland for which they fought. 'Remember that you are a Frenchman and that none of your actions must tarnish the reputation of our nation,' said a message from General Perron smuggled into the fortress for old Colonel Pedron.

Alas, Pedron had been fighting in India for forty-three years and was perhaps just too old and too tired to care any more. The fort was taken on September 4, after a resistance of only five days, with the Highlanders, bagpipes and all, leading the attack and fighting their way from room to room till the fort was entirely theirs. Pedron, 'an elderly man, clad in a green jacket, with gold lace and epaulettes', as the English historian Herbert Compton described him, sadly entered into the custody of the British.

If nothing succeeds like success, the corollary is equally true: nothing fails like failure. And a sense of impending defeat was strong among the Mahrattas and the French partisans, spreading gloom and breaking the will to fight.

Delhi was the next British target.

General Lake reached the outskirts of the capital on September 11. General Bourquien drew up his troops, which greatly outnumbered Lake's, with the river Jumna behind them. The British pretended to flee, the Mahrattas in their usual untidy way, pursued them shouting and cheering, the British suddenly turned round and charged, and the Mahrattas, utterly bewildered, fled back towards the river and were killed in their thousands. The victorious British entered Delhi three days later.

The emperor, who had once stood up and shouted at Clive, but now a blind, miserable old man 'seated under a small canopy, in a mockery of regal state,' as Herbert Compton described him, extolled the bravery of the British conquerors of his country, his new masters, and praised General Lake as the saviour of India.

While Lake was defeating the Mahrattas in the north, Wellington was doing the same in the south. The fortress of Ahmednuggur, one of the strongest in India, fell after a two-day siege and, on September 23, nine days after the fall of Delhi, Wellington won what was perhaps his greatest victory after Waterloo, at Assaye where his four thousand five hundred men routed Sindhia's thirty thousand Mahrattas.

It was the bloodiest fight of Wellington's career. One third of his force were casualties. And Wellington's victory was probably assisted by the speed with which the European chief of the Mahratta infantry, Colonel Pohlmann, removed himself from the battlefield. Colonel Pohlmann, a German from Hanover, was a brave man and it has been widely suggested he was bribed to flee the battle. He may also have been inspired by Sindhia who had disappeared even earlier.

If Pohlmann was guilty of treachery towards Sindhia at Assaye, he can be forgiven. Sindhia was often two-faced and treacherous towards his own men. A Teutonic *bon vivant,* Pohlmann probably scented the defeat of the Mahrattas in the offing and only wanted to continue the high life to which he was accustomed. He kept a harem, lived like an Oriental prince, dressed in purple robes, had a personal guard of

Mogul warriors and always travelled on his personal elephant.

For Sindhia, the passing bell was tolling. After more defeats at Argaun and Gawilghur the Mahratta chief who had given the British so much trouble made his peace with them on December 30, 1803. One of the most stringent terms of the new treaty between him and the British forbade him ever to hire again the services of a Frenchman for his army. The century-old Franco-British contest for supremacy in India seemed to be over. Actually, it wasn't quite over, not while Napoleon Bonaparte still ruled France.

General Perron, however, was no longer a participant in the struggle. He went back to Europe with what he had been able to save from his huge fortune, part of which was confiscated by General Lake. As a defeated general, Perron received only a cool welcome from Napoleon Bonaparte, now no longer a mere First Consul but Napoleon I, Emperor of the French. Napoleon felt that Perron should, somehow, have remained in India defending French interests there.

After Assaye, Wellington returned to Europe also. He had been in India since February 1797, seven years. 'I have served as long in India as any man ought. . . . I think there appears to be a prospect of service in Europe in which I should like to get forward,' he wrote to a friend. How right he was, and how forward he advanced! All the way to Waterloo.

Wellington was also anxious to meet again Kitty Pakenham, the sister of Captain Edward Pakenham, a bright Anglo-Irish girl who, at the urging of her family, had rejected him as an unsuitable suitor in 1793 when he was a poor captain. Now that he was a successful and well-known general, their opposition had vanished.

Kitty was in Ireland when he arrived in London, and he was not able to go over right away to meet her. They became engaged by mail although he had not seen her since his departure for India. In the intervening years she had had smallpox: her face was pock-marked, she had become very thin and consumptive-looking and had aged considerably. 'She has grown ugly, by Jove!' the startled Wellington whispered in a shocked aside to his brother when he met his fiancée again. But Wellington was a gentleman and his word was his bond. They were married a few months later in Dublin and lived unhappily ever after.

As for Napoleon Bonaparte in Paris, his Indian dream, somewhat battered by Wellington and Lake, lingered on. Perron had failed him. The French emperor, his destiny unfulfilled, would soon be seeking new assistance to realise his magnificent obsession. First, there would be General Decaen in Mauritius. Later, Tsar Alexander I of Russia, the son of Tsar Paul, would loom into view as a most suitable helper.

DIE, WHITE MAN
St Lucia and Haiti 1803-1804

The month before war broke out again between the British and the French Sir William Hamilton died in London. By his serene and dignified presence, the elderly diplomat had sheltered the illicit love affair between his wife and Lord Nelson. How the two romantics would now manage to remain together without his protection was the question all London was asking.

The renewal of war solved the problem: Lord Nelson went back to sea. His flag now on the 100-gun HMS *Victory*, he sailed to the Mediterranean with his squadron to blockade Toulon. He was downcast at leaving Lady Hamilton but ready, as ever, to do his duty. 'I can only pray that the great God in heaven may bless and preserve you,' he wrote her before leaving. God, for Nelson, was always nearby, approving everything he did, whether it was fighting Frenchmen or making love to Emma Hamilton.

In Paris, Napoleon Bonaparte was furious at the British decision to renew the war before he was ready for it. The French navy could only count on forty-three ships-of-the-line for immediate war service. Twenty-three others were under construction but were not yet ready.

On the grounds (denied by London) that two French merchant ships had been seized off the Brittany coast before the declaration of war, the First Consul ordered all male Britons between the ages of eighteen and sixty travelling in France to be arrested and interned. Ten thousand people fell into his net. When the news that Britain and France were once again at war reached the West Indies Nelson's friend, Sir Samuel Hood, now a commodore in Barbados, made immediately for the French island of St Lucia at the head of a small squadron. Ben Hallowell, on a visit from West Africa, accompanied him and had the pleasure of directing the landing of British troops on St Lucia on June 21, 1803.

After only one day of fighting, the British hoisted the Union Jack. It remained flying over the island for the next century and a half. There were a hundred and thirty British casualties. One of them was Wellington's future brother-in-law, Captain Edward Pakenham, hit in the neck by a half-spent bullet which forced him to carry his head at an angle until a few years later when, fighting in Martinique, another half-spent bullet hit him on the other side of the neck and straightened it out. It was one of the military medical sensations of the epoch.

Next target for the British was Tobago which was supposedly defended by General César Berthier, an arrogant, incompetent nincompoop who battened on his more gifted brother's eminence as General Bonaparte's chief of staff. Berthier agreed to capitulate with-

British soldiers take St Lucia from the French in 1803. The action lasted one day and
was almost as short and tidy as the picture suggests

out a fight but insisted that he and his troops march out with the
honours of war and be shipped back to France.

Martinique was left to later. So was Guadeloupe, where the stinging
memory of Victor Hugues was still too recent. So was French Guyana
where the nauseating Hugues was now governor, reintroducing with
ferocious cruelty the slavery which he had been at such pains to abolish
in Guadeloupe. 'I do what the government tells me,' he would answer
to those who reproached him for his volte-face. The Dutch colonies of
Demerara, Essequibo and Berbice were swept up by the British without casualties. It had all been, so far, nice and neat and easy.

The naval operations around Haiti, on the other hand, may have
been easy but they were neither nice nor neat. The extermination pro-
cess in Haiti had now gone into reverse, and it was the Negroes who
were slaughtering the whites. The British found themselves particularly busy saving their French enemies from their Haitian allies who
were determined to kill every French or mulatto man, woman and
child within reach of their musket butts. The British ships offshore
were lifeboats to the fleeing, panic-stricken French pursued by General
Dessalines's unleashed, bloodthirsty soldiery.

Much of the life-saving operation fell on the sturdy shoulders of the
American loyalist, Commodore John Loring, Massachusettsman to
the core and loyal to his king who, at the head of a small squadron sailing backwards and forwards between Cap François and Mole Saint-
Nicolas, saved thousands fleeing the fury of the surviving black
Haitians. Aghast at his reverses in Haiti, Rochambeau finally realised
he had only three options: to die fighting, to surrender to the blacks,
or to surrender to the British. He chose surrender to the British and
died fighting in Germany a few years later.

A large part of the French evacuation took place on November 30 when, under an arrangement made between the British and Dessalines, a whole flotilla of crowded French vessels sailed out of the harbour of Cap François, including three frigates, the *Surveillante*, the *Clorinde* and the *Vertu*.

One of the most spectacular rescues was that of the *Clorinde* which had on board no less than nine hundred people, including General de la Poype. She ran aground as she sailed out of the harbour and Dessalines's gunners ashore were preparing to fire red-hot shot onto her crowded decks when Lieutenant Nisbet Josiah Willoughby, a vile-tongued but courageous officer who was the bane of every captain on every ship in which he served, came alongside in a launch from HMS *Hercules*, climbed on board and hoisted the Union Jack, while another British officer rushed ashore to warn the furious Haitian artillerymen that the *Clorinde* was now British, therefore an allied ship, and would they please stop firing on her?

General Boyer, the Egyptian camel-corps man and Humbert's one-time competitor for Pauline Bonaparte's bed, was made a prisoner on that day. He was later exchanged for Lord Elgin who, as well as being British ambassador to the Sublime Porte in Constantinople, was also a general in the British army. Elgin had had the misfortune to be caught in France on vacation in the Pyrenees when the Peace of Amiens suddenly ceased.

In the Mole Saint-Nicolas (the British used to call it 'the Gibraltar of the Caribbean'), defended by the well-bred plantation owner General de Noailles, resistance continued until the last days of December 1803. Noailles was an aristocrat and a romantic of the old school. Gallantry was part of his nature and he seems totally out of place in this primitive war of annihilation. Yet it was types like his, removed by their title, wealth and connections from the dirt, strain and sweat of daily life who allowed slavery to flourish. Their fortunes were nourished by the blood, suffering and servitude of tens of thousands of unprotected, overworked and brutalised human beings. But Noailles was a brave man. He was not a fop, and he was not afraid to fight and die for his country.

He refused to surrender either to the British or to the Negroes. With a flotilla of schooners he managed to break out during the night, and a day or two later, on a blue swell, destination Havana, his lookout man signalled a sail to starboard. It was a 7-gun British brig, HMS *Hasard*. It was New Year's Day 1804. Noailles immediately attacked. He led the boarding party that took the brig over, but was severely wounded in the fighting and died in Havana a few days later.

With his departure, the war was ending in Haiti. It continued, however, in neighbouring Santo Domingo, where two French generals, Jean-Louis Ferrand and Joseph Barquier, had made their way to the city of the same name (today the capital of the Dominican Republic) to join General Kerverseau, in command of the region. Ferrand, a former trooper in the army of Louis XVI, had fought in Flanders. Barquier, a native of the attractive little French Riviera town of Antibes, was a veteran of the Army of Italy.

In the tense atmosphere that reigned in the city of Santo Domingo, the two new arrivals fell out with Kerverseau, arrested him, sent him back to France and fought on for another six years, against Dessalines's Haitian troops, against the Spaniards and against the British.

Total casualties of the war in Haiti are unknown. Figures vary with the sources. Probably some 55,000 French soldiers and sailors died, from fever or from battle. Even less precise statistics are available for the blacks and mulattos. In 1789 the coloured and Negro population of the colony was estimated at around 700,000. In the first census, taken in 1824, about twenty years after the war, the population numbered 351,819. Probably at least 350,000 blacks and mulattos – half the population – died during the war or were massacred by the French, the British, the Spaniards or their own people. Barbarism was the main winner in Haiti.

The holocaust continued after the French departure. The first victims were those French colonists who, anxious about their plantations or their local businesses, had imprudently remained after the French army's evacuation. On January 1, 1804, Haiti was declared free, black and independent and Dessalines – who considered the only good Frenchman was a dead one – decided that every French person still in the island, irrespective of age, sex or condition, should be killed.

The first massacre occurred at Jérémie on March 9. Hundreds were slaughtered on that day and their bodies were piled up in mounds and exposed to the jeering multitudes. During a week of slaughter, fourteen hundred were killed. The only white men spared were a few foreigners and priests. The remnants of General Jabolonowski's Polish brigade, still blockaded on the island, who had refused to take part in the massacre of prisoners, were also allowed to live.

Captain Perkins, of HMS *Tartar*, lying in Jérémie harbour, could do nothing to help his fellow-Europeans except watch the slaughter. 'Such scenes of cruelty and devastation have been committed as is impossible to imagine or my pen describe,' he wrote, overwhelmed, to Admiral Duckworth.

Dessalines left Jérémie on March 15 with twenty-five mules loaded with plunder and reached Port-au-Prince the next day. Eight hundred people were killed there in eight days and their bodies thrown into bogs and marshes to rot away. After more massacres in Arcahaie, St Marc and Gonaives, Dessalines reached Cap François where another two thousand were massacred. When the soldiers hesitated to kill the assembled women and children, the mulatto general Clairvaux seized a baby from one of the nursing mothers and smashed its head against a rock. To the stirring tune of a military march, the slaughter of the women and children then began.

So the war ended in Haiti. Dessalines, one of the maddest and bloodiest sovereigns in history, and there have been many, had himself crowned as Emperor Jacques I later that year. He was murdered in 1806. Christophe was elected president but Haitian society broke apart. Massacres continued, now on a strictly black-mulatto basis. In 1811, there emerged a Republican mulatto south with General Pétion as president and a Royalist Negro north with General Christophe, another insane, blood-soaked monarch as king, with the title of Henri I. He committed suicide in 1820.

Today, nearly two hundred years after independence, the Haitian tragedy is still not over.

THE GORÉE TAKEOVER

West Africa 1804

Black Africa was largely absent from the Napoleonic conflict. In the late 1700s and early 1800s it was still an unknown continent, touched only on its western, eastern and southern edges by traders and slavers. British, French, Portuguese, Dutch and Spanish slaving stations were dotted here and there on the west coast, mainly in what is now Ghana, the Ivory Coast, Benin, the Congo and Angola. The Arabs handled the bulk of the slave trade on the east coast, with its slave markets in Zanzibar, the Comores, Mombasa, Dar-es-Salaam and other places. The interior was still largely unknown. The European scramble for Africa was still nearly a century away.

In the age of Napoleon therefore, there was little rivalry in the Dark Continent between France and Britain. A little fighting took place in West Africa in and around the two French settlements in Senegal, St Louis and, just over a hundred miles to the south, Gorée. As we read earlier, a British squadron attacked and captured this last outpost in 1800, and was still holding it after the Peace of Amiens.

The governor of the French establishments, Colonel Blanchot de Verly, was on leave in France during the Amiens truce. His place in St Louis was taken by Colonel Lasserre, who turned the island just off the mainland into his personal business headquarters and signed an agreement with the local Fouta tribe chief to supply him with slaves. Against a yearly payment of twenty-eight gold guineas, a piece of red cloth, four ounces of coral, sixty-four pounds of gunpowder, ten muskets, a thousand musket balls, a snuff box full of cloves and a pair of scissors, the native ruler agreed to send his captives for trading to St Louis instead of the British settlement on the Gambia. St Louis was quite a substantial little town with a population of seven thousand, including six hundred whites, two thousand four hundred mulattos and free blacks and about three thousand black slaves. In addition to its French governor, it had a mayor, either free black or half-caste.

Colonel Lasserre introduced new regulations to divert all trade through a company directed by his wife. But he went beyond the accepted commercial practices when he imposed a head tax for his personal benefit on every slave shipped out of the colony. Outraged at this cut in their profits, the St Louis slavers put Lasserre aboard a schooner in 1802 and dispatched him to British-held Gorée. In August that year, Blanchot, now nearly seventy, came back from France, bringing with him a contingent of two hundred white soldiers, to add to the local garrison of thirty white and one hundred and forty black troops.

The war between France and Britain resumed in 1803 and Blanchot cooperated with Victor Hugues in Cayenne, in South American French Guyana, in setting up a network of privateers between the two colonies to harass British shipping across that stretch of ocean. The next year he led a one hundred and eighty-man expedition to recover Gorée from the British. After a short but tough resistance – the British suffered fifty-three casualties out of a force of a hundred and twenty – the defenders of Gorée surrendered and the outpost became French again.

Blanchot left one of his officers, Montmayeur, with a garrison of only twenty men to defend the settlement. But a few weeks later a British force of four hundred soldiers, accompanied by three hundred Irish convicts of both sexes, arrived at Gorée, not knowing it was in French hands again. The bewildered Montmayeur, faced with this overwhelming number of invaders, decided any form of opposition would be quite useless and surrendered to the first British officer he met.

Gorée was in enemy hands again but Blanchot went on defending St Louis against all marauding British ships. In July 1805 he also went to war against the Fouta chief who was not keeping to their agreement, but was sending his slaves to be sold in British Gambia.

Blanchot led the expedition inland and came back with six hundred Fouta prisoners who were sold as slaves. Blanchot and the native rulers made their peace and all was presumably quiet on the Senegal front when, on April 12, 1807, the tough old Frenchman suddenly died. Except for his recent home-leave in France, he had served continuously in West Africa for twenty full years.

While awaiting the arrival of a new governor, Colonel Pinoteau, Blanchot's second-in-command took over the running of the colony. But Pinoteau never arrived. Instead, two years later, the British attacked.

CHAPTER FOURTEEN

The Invasion Dilemmas of an Emperor

INDIA – THE MAURITIAN ENVOYS
1804-1805

General Decaen in Mauritius was close to Napoleon's Indian dreams. His short stay in India had convinced him that the British in the sub-continent were particularly vulnerable to an outside attack.

With only 20,000 white troops in an army of 140,000 men, the great majority Indian sepoys, some of doubtful loyalty, in a country as big as Europe, surrounded by large, potentially hostile armies of unfriendly princes and rajahs, Britain could be beaten, he said.

He was probably right. But the problem was how to get the French troops to India.

Decaen's first suggestion was modest. He asked Napoleon Bona-parte to send him four thousand troops backed by a squadron of four ships-of-the-line, four frigates and two supply ships. He proposed landing the troops near Goa and marching on Poona which could be reached in three days. The plan was hard-nosed, uncomplicated and practical and it could have worked.

Decaen, an optimist, foresaw a mass uprising against the British throughout India (it came, but half a century later), with the Mahratta confederacy in the van. Not knowing that Wellington and Lake had just smashed Sindhia and Holkar, Decaen sent his ADC brother-in-law, Captain Barois, to Paris with detailed plans of the proposed Goan operation.

Barois arrived in France in March 1804. The timing could not have been worse. Napoleon had two other major projects in mind at the time: to be crowned Emperor and to invade England. And two months

241

later the indomitable William Pitt returned to power in England.

The Corsican was already being presented to the British public as an ogre. The pious Lord Nelson, whose thinking usually reflected the basic instincts of his people, 'ardently wished', in a letter to a friend, that 'it would please God to take him [Bonaparte] out of the world.'

In a plebiscite the French voted by an overwhelming tally (3,572,329 to 2,569) for him to take over France as emperor of a new ruling dynasty. He was acclaimed as Emperor of the French on May 18, 1804 and was crowned on December 2 at the church of Notre Dame in Paris.

In these momentous days, the Indian suggestion of Captain Barois, freshly arrived from the tiny island of Mauritius in the Indian Ocean, seemed somewhat irrelevant and Napoleon listened to him with only half an uninterested ear.

Two other envoys from General Decaen arrived in Paris that year: a politician called Cavaignac, with a report on a journey he had made to the Arabian peninsula, and Stanislas Lefebvre, a young army officer.

Lefebvre had lived in India for eight years and was one of the few Europeans who had visited Vietnam where his uncle, a missionary, was bishop. He knew the East well and was an intelligent, articulate and enthusiastic proponent of French India. He arrived in Paris while the city was preparing for the Emperor's coronation, but Napoleon did find time to discuss with him French prospects in India.

Lefebvre suggested an alliance between France and the Pathans and Afghanis, on the northwest frontier of India. With the Mahrattas now out of the fighting, France would need more than the four thousand men originally proposed by Decaen: fifteen thousand French troops in India could secure victory, Lefebvre said. Because of the size of India and the wide dispersal of their army, the British could never put more than fifty thousand men in the field at any one point, eight thousand British soldiers, the rest of them Indian sepoys of dubious loyalty.

The invasion of England was proving impossible to organise. After his coronation, therefore, Napoleon's restless mind, spurred by the suggestions from the Mauritian envoys, turned again to the neglected East. Already, in January 1805, only a month after his coronation, he was beginning to visualise a great new expedition to the Indian subcontinent: no less than twenty-six thousand men. Twenty thousand French troops and three thousand allied Spaniards would sail for India aboard twenty transport vessels accompanied by supply ships from Brest, Rochefort and Ferrol in a vast convoy escorted by thirty-three ships-of-the-line and nineteen frigates. Another three thousand troops would be picked up on the way from Decaen's fiefs in Mauritius and Réunion.

Asked for his advice, the pessimistic Admiral Decrès, whose main trait was lack of enthusiasm for any of Napoleon's distant projects, cautiously and sytematically tore the whole plan to pieces. 'You would need for such a project to succeed that the man responsible for carrying it out be of such strength of intellect, will and energy that I do not know of such a person in your Majesty's navy,' he declared in a grammatical style as tortuous and convoluted as he was himself.

General Decaen, forlorn and abandoned on Mauritius and eager to go campaigning in India, sent a fourth emissary, Colonel d'Arsonval. Napoleon was in Italy when d'Arsonval reached Paris in April 1805 and Decrès, anxious to dampen Napoleon's fervour for India, made sure the colonel never left the French capital. He forwarded Decaen's latest project by army couriers to the Emperor in Italy, hoping this latest set of proposals would be buried and forgotten in one of the Emperor's files. To Decrès's dismay, Napoelon wrote back proposing September as a suitable date for the start of an expedition to India. But, caught up in the European conflict, Napoleon subsequently shelved the project.

When Napoleon arrived back in Paris in July, he found yet a fifth envoy from the disgruntled General Decaen who was still longing to break out of his Mauritius island outpost and win honours and glory on the battlefields of India. This time the go-between was General Decaen's younger brother, René, a naval officer serving as his ADC. He was no luckier than his predecessors. Napoleon, perhaps under Decrès's crafty guidance, had once again cooled on the Indian invasion plan. He bluntly told young René Decaen he would never send less than twenty thousand men on such an expedition, and that he could not spare that number of men at the moment.

Quite obviously India was no longer in the foreground of the Emperor's thoughts. The War of the Third Coalition, with Britain, Austria, Russia, the Two Sicilies and Sweden ranged against France, was looming. Always adaptable and ready to change his plans to fit the circumstances, Napoleon temporarily abandoned his Asian and England invasion plans and, on August 24, 1805, wheeled his army at Boulogne – which he had financed from the proceeds of the Louisiana sale – and marched it east to the other end of Europe, to crush the Austrians at Ulm in October and they and the Russians at Austerlitz, in Slovakia, on December 2. Napoleon was now master of Europe. At Ulm, the Austrians lost ten thousand men killed and wounded, and another twenty thousand surrendered. At Austerlitz, the Austrians and Rusians lost twenty-seven thousand men.

The news reached the British Prime Minister William Pitt just before Christmas. 'Roll up that map,' he said, pointing to a print of Europe on the wall. 'It will not be wanted these ten years.' Tired, ill and dispirited, Pitt died the next month. He was succeeded as Prime Minister by his foreign secretary, Lord William Grenville.

But in the meantime, Nelson had fought, won and died at Trafalgar.

The West Indies 1804-1805

After quickly seizing St Lucia and Tobago on the renewal of the war with the French, and helping the blacks to expel them from Haiti, Britain lapsed into naval somnolence in the West Indies. There was just one memorable feat to Britain's credit in 1804: the capture of Diamond Rock, a conic island, infested with deadly fer-de-lance snakes, rising almost perpendicularly six hundred and fifty feet out of the sea seven miles off the Martinique port of Fort-de-France.

Commodore Samuel Hood had spotted it one day from the quarter deck of HMS *Centaur* and decided, there and then, it would be a good place to set up a gun battery to harass French ships sailing in and out of the port.

The undefended rock was occupied by the British on January 7, 1804, christened 'HMS Diamond Rock', strangely listed as a seagoing sloop in the Royal Navy, and 'crewed' by a naval detachment of five officers and a hundred and sixteen men, nearly all of them gunners, under the command of James Wilkes Maurice, the son of a Devonshire revolutionary who had named his son after John Wilkes, the British radical leader. The boy had joined the Royal Navy at the age of fourteen as an apprentice seaman and through sheer grit and competence had risen to commissioned rank.

The armament of Diamond Rock, which he now 'captained', consisted of six guns: three 24-pounders, one perched perilously halfway up the rock, two on the beach, one carronade and two 18-pounders, each gun weighing at least two-and-a-half tons, which had been hoisted to the top by an intricate system of pulleys.

The presence of this peculiar British bastion off the coast of Martinique enraged Napoleon and in 1805 he ordered, as part of his diversionary tactics for the invasion of England, a general nuisance offensive in the Caribbean which included the elimination of the Diamond Rock 'bump', as he called it.

Two French squadrons, one under Admiral Missiessy, the other under Admiral Villeneuve, swept in from across the Atlantic and, although they did not do much damage, made the British aware of their presence by a few pugnacious and profitable raids.

The purpose of diverting the French warships across the Atlantic to the West Indies was to incite the British into sending their European-based fleets after them. According to Napoleon's convoluted project, while the British ships were hunting the French in the Caribbean, Villeneuve and Missiessy would then nip back east to Europe, meet at a pre-arranged spot and, backed by the Spanish fleet and by Admiral Ganteaume's squadron from Brest, sail up the Channel to escort the

French invasion fleet to the English shore. Britain would be occupied and the English goose, Napoleon reckoned, would be cooked.

It was all very cunning, but far too complicated, and it ended as a gigantic game of hide-and-seek in which large French fleets roamed around the ocean seeking and not finding each other.

On January 17, 1805 Admiral Villeneuve slipped out of Toulon with eleven battleships and nine frigates, carrying some 6,500 troops, under the command of General Lauriston who had been First Consul Bonaparte's first envoy to London when the British sought peace in 1801. He evaded Nelson's blockading squadron and, shadowed by two of Nelson's frigates as far as Ajaccio, then sailed south. His destination: the West Indies. Foxed once again, as he had been in 1798 by the Egyptian expedition, Nelson decided the French fleet was heading for the Middle East and scurried off in the direction of Alexandria.   Two days after leaving Toulon, appalled by the sloppy handling of his ships by the inexperienced crews, Villeneuve held a conference with General Lauriston. The general was equally appalled that his army was at the mercy of untrained seamen who had no idea how to cope with the sails of their ships. He gladly agreed when Villeneuve timorously suggested they should return immediately to Toulon. Villeneuve crept back with his unattacked squadron into port on January 21 while Nelson, all sails set, was heading east to intercept him off the Egyptian coast!

Admiral Missiessy had more success with his crews and ships. Six days before Villeneuve sailed out of Toulon, he had slipped through the British blockade with five ships-of-the-line and three frigates from Rochefort, on the Atlantic coast, and headed for the Caribbean to meet up with Villeneuve's vessels from the Mediterranean. Aboard his fleet was also an army contingent, 3,500 men this time, led by General Joseph Lagrange, veteran of the Army of Egypt and one of Josephine's many former lovers, whom the Emperor was doubtlessly pleased to ship off to more distant conquests in the West Indian islands.

Napoleon's original plan for the invasion of England was not just grand. It was grandiose. It combined wide sweeping army/navy operations in five seas and oceans – the Mediterranean, the North and South Atlantic, the Caribbean and the Channel – with precisely-timed attacks on half a dozen West Indian islands, a landing in West Africa, another in South America, the takeover of a South Atlantic island, the gathering of several fleets, French and Spanish, in the Caribbean, in mid-ocean and off blockaded continental ports, and all to culminate in a massive combined attack on England!   One thousand of General Lagrange's three thousand five hundred troops in Missiessy's squadron were to be dropped off in Martinique, another thousand in Guadeloupe, to strengthen existing garrisons in those islands, several hundred more were to be left in Santo Domingo to reinforce General Ferrand's besieged army and Diamond Rock was to be quickly seized.

be quickly seized.

Malaria and yellow fever permitting, Missiessy was also ordered to retake St Lucia and to occupy the British island of Dominica. His squadron was then to head for the British-occupied Dutch colony of Surinam on the South American mainland there to await the arrival of Villeneuve's fleet from Toulon with more troops under General Lauriston.

Lauriston's soldiery had numerous and formidable tasks facing it too. First of all, after passing through the straits of Gibraltar, eighteen hundred men of the army contingent were originally supposed to head south to recover Gorée in Senegal, then to go on to take the island of St Helena, needed as a base by French privateers and frigates in the southern hemisphere that otherwise could only use Mauritius in the Indian Ocean. (The Gorée and St Helena projects were later shelved.)

Having shed some of its vessels on that mission, the rest of Villeneuve's fleet was to sail on to Cayenne, pick up the vigorous Victor Hugues, to be the future governor of Surinam, join Missiessy off that Dutch colony, take it from the British, and harass British shipping and islands in the Caribbean. Then both fleets would sail back to Europe, attack the British ships blockading the port of Ferrol, in north-west Spain, link up with the squadron there, and appear in July off Rochefort with at least twenty ships-of-the-line. Admiral Ganteaume would then emerge from Brest with another twenty battleships and they would all converge towards the Channel, escort the invasion fleet and attack and take England.

It was a great programme on paper – mathematically precise but utterly exhausting, and quite impractical. Napoleon forgot that ships are not regiments, that sails depending on wind power are not as reliable as soldiers' legs, cavalrymen's horses and the wheels of guns and wagons. Above all, he underestimated the power and efficiency of the Royal Navy.

In mid-February 1805, more or less on schedule, avoiding the guns of Diamond Rock, Admiral Missiessy sailed into Fort-de-France with General Lagrange's men. From then on, nothing happened as planned.

After his Martinique landfall, General Lagrange made the British island of Dominica his first military target. On February 21, General Sir George Prevost, Governor of Dominica, had the biggest surprise of his life when Roseau, the capital, was suddenly attacked by a French army, supported by three battleships and a number of brigs and frigates. Prevost had already fought against the French in St Lucia and St Vincent and the *Dictionary of National Biography* describes him as 'well intentioned and honest'. An amiable gentleman and a loving family man, Prevost had one major defect as a soldier: he was a ditherer, 'cautious to a fault', his biographer says, and when he lost, he still considered himself the winner.

The French, he wrote in his report, 'were successfully driven back' when they landed. This impression of victory was spoiled, however, two lines further on when he described how 'despite their spirited conduct', the defending British troops were 'compelled to fall back' and when, in the next line, he 'deemed it prudent' to allow the town of Roseau to capitulate.

Prevost then retired to another part of the island and sent a letter to Lagrange thanking him for his 'humanity and kind treatment' of his wife and children. The French, more interested in plunder than glory, collected a £7,000 ransom from the occupied capital, broke into the government stores and took whatever they could carry, seized twenty vessels in the harbour, kidnapped a number of Negro slaves (some of whom were later returned from Martinique) then five days later, as suddenly as they had come, sailed away again.

The inhabitants of Dominica, very impressed by the thoroughness of the French looting, thereafter always referred to 1805 as 'the Lagrange year'.

On the 27th, Lagrange arrived off the island of St Kitts and went through the same procedure as before. The British troops, as outnumbered as they had been in Roseau, retired into the hills while the French plundered and ransomed the town. The inhabitants of Basse-Terre, capital of St Kitts, more wealthy or perhaps more frightened than those of Roseau, managed to put together £18,000 and the French sailed away again, taking with them five merchant ships then lying in port.

Admiral Missiessy's Caribbean cruise sounds more like a pirate raid than a war operation. The islands of Montserrat, Nevis, St Eustace, were also each visited in turn and each provided its quota to the French war treasury. Missiessy then sailed back to Martinique on March 12 to await Admiral Villeneuve's arrival.

But Villeneuve failed to arrive.

Instead a message came from Paris saying Villeneuve was still in Toulon and intimating that Missiessy should return as speedily as possible to France to take part in the invasion of England.

Although urged by Admiral Villaret-Joyeuse, Captain-General of Martinique, to occupy Diamond Rock before returning home, Missiessy refused to do so, fearing the operation might take too long.

On the way home, following instructions, he did call on March 27 at Santo Domingo, from where nothing had been heard for nearly two years. He found the town still in French hands and a French army under the orders of General Ferrand, debilitated but resolute, fighting off a Haitian force led by the bloodthirsty General Dessalines.

Missiessy's opportune arrival saved Ferrand and his army from destruction by the Haitian horde. When the Haitian leader saw the sails of the French squadron hovering off the coast, he simply gave up the siege and went home.

Missiessy left Ferrand a few hundred men as reinforcements. The French in Santo Domingo were to fight on for another four years, virtually alone, in turn against the Haitians, the Spanish and the British.

Meanwhile new orders to the now absent Missiessy arrived in Martinique from Napoleon I by a fast brig. Written one month after the last message it now told Missiessy that Villeneuve had broken out of Toulon and was on his way to join him. Napoleon ordered Missiessy to wait in the West Indies until the end of June if necessary for Villeneuve's arrival, and to join forces with him for a grand return to the Channel and the invasion of England.

By the time the Emperor's instructions reached Martinique, Missiessy and his fleet were sailing east back to Europe and on May 20 he arrived in Rochefort harbour, most happy at the fast time he had made on the homeward trip. But Napoleon was most displeased to see him. His fast return to Europe and his failure to combine forces with Villeneuve's fleet had jeopardised the Emperor's invasion strategy. And Missiessy hadn't even captured Diamond Rock! 'I choked with indignation when I read Missiessy had not taken the Rock,' the Emperor wrote furiously to Decrès, the minister of marine.

On May 14, six days before Missiessy's arrival in Rochefort, Villeneuve had sailed into Fort-de-France to find his colleague gone. The slowness of communications, coupled to Napoleon's frequent changes of plans and to Missiessy's eagerness to do quickly what he thought was the Emperor's will, were all combining to defeat Napoleon's meticulous invasion plans.

Villeneuve's fleet was the biggest display of naval might ever assembled in Fort-de-France. With his flag on the 80-gun *Bucentaure,* Villeneuve had under his direct command eleven French ships-of-the-line, six frigates and two corvettes, and was also accompanied by seven Spanish battleships, a frigate and two brigs, commanded by Admiral Gravina who had joined the French admiral at Cadiz. Still aboard were some six thousand troops of General Lauriston, intended for the recapture of St Lucia and the capture of a few British islands.

The day Villeneuve reached Martinique Admiral Nelson was in Madeira, trailing the French admiral across the Atlantic, after failing to find him in the Mediterranean. He had surmised rightly that Villeneuve was making for the West Indies and not Egypt after all, and was in pursuit with ten battleships and three frigates.

The stage was being set for the greatest naval battle in British and French history. But the encounter was to be not in the West Indies but off the south-west coast of Spain, five months later, at Trafalgar.

Meanwhile Villeneuve decided to get rid of 'the Diamond Rock bump' and attacked the British garrison on May 29 with a naval force of two battleships, a frigate, a brig and a schooner, under the command of a valiant Breton sailor, Julien Cosmao-Kerjulien. The landing force was under General Lauriston, seconded by Major Boyer de Peyreleau. The bluejackets awaited the assault in caves and crags up the mountain side, from where they poured down an intensive fire on the French attackers who were more scared, however, of the aggressive and venemous fer-de-lance snakes than of their British foes.

British casualties were tiny (two killed, one wounded) but the defenders were short of food, short of ammunition and, most important under a direct, vertical, tropical sun, short of water. 'Several of them fainted for want of water, and obliged to drink their own,' wrote Lieutenant Maurice in his report. They surrendered after two days and shortly afterwards left on a French ship flying a flag of truce, on parole, for Barbados, to be greeted by the recently-arrived Admiral Lord Nelson.

A couple of days later, another French admiral, Charles Magon, arrived in Fort-de-France with two battleships, to be followed a day afterwards by a frigate bringing a new set of orders from Napoleon to Villeneuve. Admiral Ganteaume, currently blockaded in Brest, would be joining him shortly with his squadron, Villeneuve was told. Wait for him until June 20, then sail back to Europe, the order added. (As it turned out, Ganteaume was never able to break out of Brest.)

There is something particularly ludicrous about this gathering of French squadrons in the West Indies in order to take part in the invasion of England, thousands of miles away across the Atlantic. It is not surprising that the whole enterprise ended in calamitous failure. Napoleon was undoubtedly a brilliant soldier. But a naval strategist he certainly was not.

Napoleon planned his invasion of England for August. A total of 167,500 soldiers were poised in northern French ports, ready to sail with 9,149 horses in 2,345 boats. In the meantime he wished to confuse the enemy by widely scattering the ships that would later escort and protect the invasion fleet on its journey across the Channel. The grand invasion plan was a landlubber's plan, devised by a man unused to the problems of the sea.

Nelson, unlike Napoleon, was a naval strategist. His plan was to bring Villeneuve to battle, right there in the West Indies . . . if he could find him. On his arrival in the Caribbean, the British admiral had been informed, quite wrongly, that Villeneuve had sailed to Trinidad. Hoping to repeat the grand exploit of the Battle of the Nile, Nelson rushed south – only to find, on his arrival in Trinidad on June 3, the harbour of Port-of-Spain quite bare of French and Spanish ships. He immediately turned back north and made for Barbados, to arrive just before Lieutenant Maurice's defeated contingent from Diamond Rock, and to learn of Villeneuve's latest fleet movements.

Villeneuve, for his part, heard of the dreaded Nelson's arrival in the West Indies almost simultaneously as he received new orders from

Paris. For the French, the name of Nelson carried with it a heavy whiff of defeat. There and then, after consulting Gravina (who had met Nelson when they were allies in Toulon), Villeneuve decided to sail with his squadron back to Europe immediately, rather than risk a battle in the Caribbean which might imperil the Emperor's English invasion plan. He disembarked many of Lauriston's soldiers – but not the general – in Martinique and sailed off to France.

Nelson did not know where Villeneuve had gone. 'Whether the enemy's object is to attack Antigua or St Kitts, or to return to Europe, time will show,' he said. But his intuition soon told him Villeneuve's destination was France, or Spain, and three days behind his prey he returned across the Atlantic to southern Europe, from whence he had so recently come. Thus the campaign – to be later called the Trafalgar campaign – moved out of the West Indies back to Europe towards its slow but inevitable conclusion off the Spanish coast.

Once convinced that Villeneuve was heading for Europe, Nelson dispatched the frigate HMS *Curieux* to England, to inform the Admiralty. In doubt as to whether Villeneuve's destination was Rochefort in France, or Ferrol in Spain, the Admiralty ordered the two relatively weak fleets of Admirals Calder and Stirling, patrolling in the Atlantic, to combine to meet their numerically stronger opponent. Villeneuve and Gravina came up against their fifteen ships-of-the-line when they reached European waters on July 22. In an inconclusive engagement, Calder captured two Spanish ships. On the 25th, the combined Franco-Spanish fleets entered the ports of Ferrol and Corunna.

'Sail and do not lose a moment, and with your combined squadrons, enter the Channel. England is ours. We are all ready. Everything is on board. Get here for just twenty-four hours and all is accomplished,' the Emperor wrote hurriedly to Villeneuve when he heard the Franco-Spanish fleet was back in Europe.

But Villeneuve and Gravina were not the only admirals back in Europe. Nelson was back also. He had been pursuing Villeneuve along a route further south and had arrived in Gibraltar on July 20. Finding that his quarry was nowhere around, Nelson headed north five days later to join Admiral Cornwallis's Channel Fleet off Brest. The brother of Lord Cornwallis, Admiral Cornwallis was known in the British Navy as 'Billy Blue'. Calder and Stirling had joined Cornwallis the day before. The senior British admiral now had no less than thirty-six battleships under his direct orders. Off Cadiz, Collingwood was blockading the Spanish port with another three.

By a singular twist of fate, it was not the French ships that were now assembled in the Channel for an attack on England, but a mass of British battleships. These, instead of being scattered as planned by Napoleon, were all together in the right place and at the right time to prevent the French invasion! The Emperor's involved and convoluted naval strategy had turned completely against him.

Unable to find any French ships to fight, Nelson stayed with Corn-wallis's fleet only a few hours. On August 18 he came to anchor in Spithead. It was his first visit home in two years. The next day, he hurried to Lady Hamilton's side.

A few days earlier, on August 13, Villeneuve had prepared to sail from northern Spain for the French port of Brest but, informed that three dozen British warships were waiting to pounce on him and his fleet off the French coast, he turned south and sailed with his twenty-nine battleships to Cadiz. General Lauriston, who was doing his best to stiffen the admiral's wilted morale, said afterwards that Villeneuve was talking all the time 'about his olive trees and how pleasant life is in Provence.'

By this time, with summer ending and the autumn storms approaching, and with growing Austrian hostility towards France, it became plain to Napoleon that his English invasion project was doomed. Cursing Villeneuve and the navy, Napoleon left Boulogne on September 3 and headed east. Austerlitz was at the end of his journey. Villeneuve was less lucky. Trafalgar lay at the end of his voyage.

Unaware that Britain was no longer threatened, the British Admiralty sent a messenger to Lord Nelson on September 2 at the Merton country house in Surrey where he was staying with Lady Hamilton. England is now ready to go to the attack, the First Lord of the Admiralty, eighty-year-old Lord Barham, told him. Would Lord Nelson be willing to take command of the fleet assembling around Collingwood's ships off Cadiz? We all know the answer.

The evening of his departure, on September 13, Nelson noted in his diary: 'At half-past ten drove from dear, dear Merton, where I left all which I hold dear in the world, to go to serve my King and Country.' All he held dear in the world were Lady Hamilton and their daughter Horatia, and all the emotions he felt at that moment come through the restraint of his prayer: 'May the great God whom I adore enable me to fulfil the expectations of my country,' he added. Perhaps because we know of Nelson's impending fate, God does not appear this time as an intruder into the world of weaponry and blood, where he has no place as an accomplice, but as the last trusted friend of a doomed hero. The next day Nelson sailed from Portsmouth on HMS *Victory*.

On September 28 he arrived off the southern coast of Spain and took command of the more than thirty British ships-of-the-line blockading the port where Villeneuve and his fleet had taken shelter.

Ten days previously, on September 18, Napoleon had named Admiral Rosily, a specialist in charts and navigational problems, as a replacement for Villeneuve. At the same time he inexplicably ordered Villeneuve to sail with his fleet to Naples to reinforce the French army in southern Italy! The minister of the navy in Paris, Admiral Decrès, deliberately failed to notify Villeneuve of the upcoming change in command, but on October 20 Villeneuve heard by chance that Rosily was coming to take over his ships and was already in Madrid on his way south. After writing a bitter letter of reproach to Decrès, Villeneuve decided to sail before Rosily's arrival. His honour was at stake. At seven o'clock the next morning, the first ships of Villeneuve's fleet, taking advantage of a favourable wind, appeared outside Cadiz harbour and were immediately spotted by the watching Royal Navy.

The French van was led by Rear-Admiral Magon who had fought against Rodney off Dominica in 1780, against Hood and Graves at the Chesapeake in 1781, and in de Sercey's squadron in the Indian Ocean. The whole fleet came up behind him.

Because of the temporary absence of six British ships in Gibraltar, the numerical odds were slightly in favour of Villeneuve's eighteen French battleships and fifteen Spanish versus twenty-seven British. But the British had Nelson, and he alone was worth a squadron.

The battle was over by four-thirty in the afternoon. Casualties were enormous. It was one of the hardest fought encounters in the history of naval warfare and remains one of the proudest epics in two thousand years of British history.

British losses in ships were nil, although nine of their ships were badly battered. But none struck or were sunk. The French lost nine ships, including the old *Swiftsure* that Ganteaume had taken from Ben Hallowell in the Mediterranean a few years before. The Spaniards also lost nine battleships. Total French and Spanish casualties amounted to 2,600 dead, and 4,400 prisoners including Villeneuve. The dead included the tough Magon, killed in action, and the gallant Gravina, died of wounds. British losses were 1,600 dead and wounded.

Nelson, the great Nelson, was among the dead, shot through the spine early in the battle by a sniper from the rigging of the *Redoubtable*. 'God be praised, I have done my duty,' he said as he lay dying. But, a mere mortal after all, his last thoughts were as much for the woman he loved as for the God he adored. 'Take care of my dear Lady Hamilton. Take care of poor Lady Hamilton,' he said to his flag captain, Hardy, a few minutes before he died. 'I leave Lady Hamilton and my adopted daughter Horatia as a legacy to my country.' His country gave him a great funeral. But England treated the last wishes of its greatest sailor as shabbily as it did, a few years later, the defeated emperor he had hated and fought. England, not the England Nelson loved and for whom he had fought and died, but another England, priggish, ungenerous, bigoted and unctuous, rejected his own. To those who stood high in the councils of state, Lady Hamilton was the flaw that had marred his greatness. Nelson dead, she was not a responsibility to be assumed but a fat ageing strumpet, who drank too much and laughed too loudly, an encumbrance fit only to be pushed aside.

Nelson's dismasted flagship, HMS *Victory*, is towed into Gibraltar harbour after the victory at Trafalgar in 1805

Abandoned, Lady Hamilton died ten years later, from drink and misery, alone in a squalid room across the Channel in Calais, in the land of Nelson's enemies, where she had gone to escape merciless creditors.

Horatia, Nelson's love child, grew up into a prudish Victorian woman. She married a clergyman and never spoke of the father of whom she should have been so proud.

CHAPTER FIFTEEN

The Continuing War at Sea

SWEEPS IN THE EASTERN SEAS
1803-1805

Historians are inclined to consider the Battle of Trafalgar as marking the end of naval warfare during the Napoleonic Wars. In fact, the naval war between France and Britain went on for several more years, notably in the Caribbean, the Atlantic and the Indian Ocean.

After Europe and the West Indies, the Indian Ocean became the most important theatre of war where British and French forces clashed during these two decades of conflict.

The nature of the war in the Eastern Seas – I am indebted to C. Northcote Parkinson for the choice of this evocative name to describe that vast area of ocean that covers our planet all the way from the Cape of Good Hope to the Pacific – was essentially different in every way to the conflict in other areas.

It differed, first of all, by its immensity. It must have covered well over a quarter of the world, including some of its most exotic, tropical areas. The fighting was therefore considerably more scattered, stretching all the way from South Africa to the Philippines. British and Americans also clashed in the South Pacific. Being a naval war mainly, without the multitudes of land armies, the fighters were numbered only in thousands, but we shouldn't underestimate the importance of the eastern naval war zone, just because of the fewer men involved. After all, the Battle of Britain in 1940-41 was fought by only a few hundred men, but it was one of the decisive battles of history.

The final British success in the Eastern Seas turned a large part of the southern hemisphere into a British-dominated area for nearly a century and a half, and the Indian Ocean into a largely British lake.

Mauritius was the centre point of this vast and watery battlefield. From its vantage point in the middle of the Indian Ocean, astride the great maritime routes to and from India and China, French raiders – corsairs and frigates – harassed British shipping and caused severe losses to British trade. Mauritius was also important, strategically, as the main French base in the entire region, the spot from which Napoleon might, one day, launch an invasion of India. It could also become the springboard for a French attack on New South Wales. Its very existence, as a French territory, was a perpetual threat to British imperial ambitions.

It was the expulsion of the French from India that made Mauritius the main French bastion in the southern hemisphere. General Decaen had become, in 1803, captain-general of all French settlements east of the Cape of Good Hope. These now only added up to the Mascarenes, the Seychelles, a few island dots here and there, such as Diego Garcia, and the trading post of Tamatave, in Madagascar.

There were three main islands in the Mascarenes: Réunion, Rodriguez and Mauritius which remained the main base thanks to its natural harbours and the favourable winds, vital for sailing ships, that blew on and off shore.

It is from this small Indian Ocean island base, with a force of only between three and four thousand soldiers for defence and Admiral Linois's diminutive squadron (three frigates and a battleship, his flagship, the *Marengo*), that Decaen began his war against the British Empire.

Linois opened the conflict on October 18, 1803, when he sailed on the first of three trans-ocean sweeps. His most important assignment was to capture the China tea convoy that would be sailing from Canton in early February, as it did each year. His next priority was to strengthen the allied Dutch in the East Indies and he took along some two hundred soldiers as reinforcements for Java. On the way, Linois captured a large merchantman and attacked and captured Fort Marlborough, which protected the British settlement at Bencoolen in southern Sumatra. He seized a British trading vessel anchored in the bay and burnt the East India Company's warehouses, filled with opium, pepper and camphor. He suffered his first casualties in Sumatra: a lieutenant named Fleuron and a drummerboy were both killed fighting ashore.

After the Sumatra incident, the French soldiers were taken and deposited in Java. Major Jauffret took over the command of the French army contingent in Java and remained behind, with the other battalion officers, to serve alongside the Dutch.

Advised by an American sea captain in Batavia that the China tea convoy in Canton was ready to leave, Linois set all sail with his squadron to intercept it at Pulo-Aor, in the Malacca Straits, on February 14, 1804. The attack turned into a farce. Thanks to the ingenious and courageous tactics of the convoy commander, Commodore Dance, Linois mistook the four or five leading vessels, camouflaged with painted guns and naval standards, for ships-of-the-line. Convinced he had stumbled onto a powerful naval squadron, Linois hastily made off, ignominiously chased by the disguised merchant ships, playing their role right to the end! Dance returned to England a hero and received a £5,000 bonus from the delighted insurers of the convoy. Poor Linois became the laughing stock of Paris and London.

His squadron sailed on two more sweeps in the Indian Ocean, both with mediocre results. On his last cruise, however, he captured the East Indiaman *Brunswick* with a cargo of cotton she was taking from Bombay to Canton. During this last cruise the *Marengo* had a short and sharp encounter with the 74-gun HMS *Blenheim*, with Admiral Troubridge aboard, which Linois wisely broke off when he became aware he was dealing with another battleship and not an East Indiaman. The French admiral then decided he was wasting his time in the Indian Ocean and decided to return home by the Cape of Good Hope and the island of St Helena, with the *Marengo* and two of his three frigates, the *Belle-Poule* and the *Atalante*, leaving the *Sémillante* (Captain Motard) to continue her career in the Indian Ocean.

The *Atalante* failed to reach the Atlantic. She was driven ashore and wrecked near Cape Town in a storm on November 3, 1805. The survivors, about two hundred and fifty, joined the defence force of the Dutch governor of the colony, General Janssens. The *Marengo* and the *Belle-Poule* sailed into the south Atlantic and cruised dismally around for about three months, short of food, their rigging in tatters, capturing nothing more sensational than a couple of British slaving ships.

Near the Canaries, on March 13, 1806, in the middle of the night, his two ships fell in with a fleet of unknown vessels. Linois, it is said, anxious not to repeat his error of Pulo-Aor, decided it must be a convoy of merchantmen, immediately rushed into the middle, attacked ... and found himself in the midst of Admiral Sir John Borlase Warren's squadron of battleships and frigates!

After a fierce five-hour battle, adjudged by many to be the stoutest Linois ever fought, the *Marengo* and the *Belle-Poule* were forced to surrender. The battleship, pounded by the 98-gun HMS *London*, was a bloody, shattered hulk before Linois agreed to strike his colours. Sixty of his men were killed, and eighty-two wounded.

Himself wounded in the right leg, Linois was taken to England and held a prisoner for eight years.

A few months before Linois's departure from the Indian Ocean, Captain Bergeret, who had many friends among British sailors, including Matthew Flinders the explorer, and Admiral Sir Edward Pellew, had taken command in Mauritius of the locally-built frigate, the *Psyché*, and sailed her to the east coast of India to attack shipping in the Bay of Bengal.

Bergeret was widely known and respected by his enemies, for his chivalry and kind treatment of prisoners and as the (losing) hero of the lone, long fight of the *Virginie* against Pellew off the Lizard back in 1796. When Admiral Pellew now arrived to take over the Indian command from Rainier, he was very interested to learn that his old friend (for the two men had so become after the *Virginie*'s surrender) was again in the offing. But he wasn't in the offing for long. On February 14, 1805 Bergeret lost again to a British warship, the more heavily armed HMS *San Fiorenzo* (her broadside weighed 934 lbs against the *Psyché*'s meagre 432 lbs).

Bergeret, as usual, put up a courageous fight and did not surrender until after a five-hour fight in which fifty-seven of his men were killed and seventy wounded. The *San Fiorenzo* had twelve men killed. Bergeret was taken to Trinchomalee as a prisoner of war and Pellew came to meet his old French friend at the dockside, to commiserate with him at his second defeat by a ship under his command, and then to take him home as his guest!

After the capture of the *Psyché*, the *Sémillante* from Admiral Linois's old squadron was for a short time – if we except a few minor vessels – the only French naval unit in the Indian Ocean. A month after Bergeret's capture Captain Motard sailed from Mauritius in the *Sémillante* to advise the Spaniards in the Philippines, in case the news hadn't reached them yet, that their country was now at war with England and was France's ally. In August Motard was attacked in San Jacinto Bay, in the San Bernardino Straits, by the 38-gun HMS *Phaeton* and the sloop HMS *Harrier*, 18, both down from the Malayan island of Penang. Although outgunned, the *Sémillante*, 36, beat off the enemy attacks after a three-hour fight in which she lost four men killed and ten wounded. HMS *Phaeton*, badly battered, retired to Macao for repairs.

THE BATTLE OF SANTO DOMINGO
1806

This almost unknown battle is considered, after Trafalgar, Britain's greatest naval victory over the French during the Napoleonic Wars.

The protagonists at Santo Domingo were the Frenchman Admiral Corentin de Leissègues with five ships of-the-line, two frigates and one corvette, and the Englishman Admiral Sir John Duckworth, commander-in-chief of the Jamaica station, with seven battleships.

Leissègues has already come into our story. In 1793 he had escorted the abominable Victor Hugues to Guadeloupe and had then helped to defend the island against Admiral Jervis's counterattacks. Now an admiral, he had just landed a thousand troops as reinforcements for General Ferrand in Santo Domingo when the British, on February 6, 1806, less than four months after Trafalgar, pounced on his unready fleet. Only his smaller vessels escaped. Duckworth captured three of the French battleships and drove the other two ashore where they were burnt and destroyed.

Total French casualties amounted to around fifteen hundred. The British losses were, as usual, far fewer: seventy-four killed and two hundred and sixty-four wounded. Two captured former French battleships were part of Duckworth's fleet: his second-in-command, Captain Louis, commanded the old French *Franklin*, which had fought at the Nile and was now HMS *Canopus*. The second ex-French ship was HMS *Donegal*, the former *Hoche*, which had been taken with Wolfe Tone on board off the coast of Ireland in 1798.

The victorious Duckworth was a troublesome officer to the Lords of the Admiralty for, as well as being a fine sailor, he was an astute businessman. He had recently been court-martialled for turning one of his frigates into a cargo ship to carry what was described as an 'immense' quantity of merchandise from the West Indies to Britain. At his trial, Duckworth insisted that this merchandise consisted solely of 'presents' for friends and relatives, and the court martial chose to accept this explanation, even though the list of 'presents' filled many pages. The fact is that like many of the army and navy officers of the period, British and French alike, Duckworth was a rogue.

After the Battle of Santo Domingo, Leissègues managed to return to France and was appointed to the command of the port of Venice. The British government conferred a baronetcy on Louis and a Knighthood of the Bath on Admiral Sir Alexander Cochrane, who was third-in-command. There were no rewards, however, for Duckworth who was presumed to have rewarded himself enough through the 'presents' he had brought back to Britain. But he obtained a consolation prize. The City of London, quick as always to recognise its own, gave him the freedom of the city and a valuable sword of honour.

THE BATTLE OF THE ATLANTIC
1805-1807

While most French ships were blockaded in Toulon and the French Atlantic ports, now and again some managed to break out into the Atlantic on expeditions that would be the precursors and the inspiration of similar German navy commerce raiders in the 1914-18 and 1939-45 world wars.

The Breton Commodore Zacharie Allemand, with his flag on the 110-gun *Majestueux*, sailed out of Brest in 1805 and in a wide-sweeping mission captured forty-two merchantmen and four warships, including the 54-gun ship-of-the-line HMS *Calcutta*.

That same year Captain Jean L'Hermitte, who had once commanded the frigate *Preneuse* in Sercey's squadron in the Indian Ocean in the 1790s, broke out of Lorient at the end of October, ten days after Trafalgar, for an eleven-months cruise in the south Atlantic in which he captured some fifty British vessels.

In 1806 another French squadron sailed out of Brest under the orders of Admiral Jean-Baptiste Willaumez, another veteran of the Sercey squadron. With his flag on the *Foudroyant* and at the head of a squadron of eight vessels, he led one of the longest and most useless cruises of the war. For fifteen months he zigzagged across the Atlantic, down to the Cape of Good Hope, up to Brazil, north to the West Indies, then across and up and down again. Total bag for all this frenzied activity: seventeen merchantmen captured and the British island of Montserrat in the West Indies ransomed.

In the Bahamas, one of Willaumez's more undisciplined subordinates, Captain Jerome Bonaparte, of the 74-gun *Vétéran*, tired of the whole useless cruise, left the squadron, returned to Europe without orders and on the way home captured six merchantmen. For this unruly escapade, Jerome was promoted rear-admiral but, to the French navy's silent relief, soon resigned his commission and began two new careers, as a general and as King of Westphalia.

In the Caribbean the great era of the privateers was over. The Guadeloupe experience of the nineties, which had been such a financial (if somewhat criminal) success was just a memory. There were a few eminent corsairs still sailing these seas but privateering no longer had the zest of former years and was often more like piracy. The privateers enjoyed the facilities of New Orleans, now a United States port, for a while, but that privilege came to an end with the appointment in 1807 of a new naval commanding officer, Commander David Porter, Truxtun's former midshipman.

Weary of the exactions of foreign corsairs in nearby American seas, Porter succeeded in having two of the French and one of the Spanish privateers that used New Orleans as a base of operations condemned and sold by a local court. From that moment, New Orleans's status as a haven for French privateers ceased.

In 1807 Britain captured Dutch Curaçao and the Danish Caribbean island of St Croix. Slowly the French West Indian islands were being strangled. But in Santo Domingo, to the hoarse and tired singing of 'La Marseillaise', Ferrand and his disease-ridden army were still holding out, and in the Indian Ocean, a handful of decrepit and rundown French frigates were causing substantial losses to British trade, British insurers and British naval prestige.

CHAPTER SIXTEEN

The Indian Dream Lingers

THE TEHERAN CONNECTION
1807

In the spring of 1807 Napoleon's Indian invasion plans came to life again in the ancient Finkenstein Castle in Poland, which he was romantically sharing with Maria Walewska, the twenty-two-year-old Polish countess he had met only four months previously, at a ball in Warsaw.

She had reluctantly abandoned her aged husband at the pleadings of Polish leaders, desperate at the disappearance from the map of Poland, partitioned between Russia, Prussia and Austria. Aware of the French Emperor's interest – he was thirty-eight at the time – in the beautiful, blonde aristocrat, they had begged her to forget her Christian morals and the teachings of her youth to become the mistress of the man who alone could restore Poland to its former greatness. So, tearfully and patriotically, she consented to the sacrifice . . . and then fell madly in love with her seducer.

In May a delegation from the King of Kings, Fath Ali, Shah of Persia, was sent to Finkenstein Castle to meet the Emperor of the French and conclude a pact with him. The Shah wanted Napoleon's help in the recovery of the province of Georgia, lost recently to Russia, a country that was also at war with France.

Napoleon immediately perceived the advantages to him of such a pact. Persia, on the southern edges of Russia, could carry out diversionary attacks against their common enemy. But, above all, Persia was India's neighbour on its western borders and could be useful to him if he invaded the subcontinent.

Isfahan, the old Persian capital and site of probably the most beautiful mosque in the world

On May 4, France and Persia signed the Treaty of Finkenstein in the great hall of the old castle, a strangely sombre setting for such an exotic event. Napoleon undertook to provide the Persians with arms, to send officers to Teheran to train their army in modern methods of war and to help his new allies recover Georgia from the Russians. In return Persia (or Iran, to give it its modern name) agreed to declare war on England, to obtain the cooperation of the Afghans in a French attack on India, and to provide bases and supplies for a French naval squadron in the Persian Gulf.

For the Persians, the Finkenstein pact was essentially about Georgia. For the French, the whole inspiration was India.

Within a month Napoleon had a seventy-man mission on its way to Teheran. It was led by General Gardane, an old soldier who had begun his military life eighteen years before as a gunner in the French coastal artillery. Gardane left Warsaw in early June and arrived in Teheran four months later.

His main job was to train the Persian army and to prepare plans for the invasion of India. One of his officers, Lieutenant Fabvier, set up a foundry in Isfahan, the old Persian capital and the site of what is probably the most beautiful mosque in the world. The Shah bought twenty thousand muskets and leased the island of Kerth to his new French allies, and two of Gardane's officers, Captains Verdier and Lamy, set about turning the Persian army into a fighting force capable of marching alongside the French into India. Gardane and his officers examined the country from the Persian Gulf to the Caspian Sea and studied maps to locate the best invasion routes from Europe into India. The French expeditionary force would number twenty thousand men, Napoleon had told Gardane. They would arrive in Persia either by marching overland from the Syrian town of Aleppo, or by ship round the Cape of Good Hope to a port on the Persian Gulf. Gardane's extensive travels, investigations and enquiries prompted him to suggest the best route from Europe might be from Aleppo to Baghdad, Basra, Bushir, Shiraz (famous for its roses), Yedz and Herat. Since a large part of the country through which the invading troops would have to travel was desert or semi-desert, Gardane did his work thoroughly and came up with a second possible route on the Basra-Herat lap, through Hamadan and Khorasan. He also suggested yet a third route to Herat, this time through Trebizond. The march from Aleppo to the Indus River would take seven to eight months.

Herat, now located in north-west Afghanistan, east of the Iranian town of Meshed and close to the frontier, was to be the central point of departure for the invasion of India. From Herat, the route lay through Kabul and Peshawar. Gardane advised Napoleon he could probably rely on the aid of the warlike Sikhs, once his troops reached the Punjab, and he suggested this overland attack be combined with a landing near Bombay by Decaen's troops from Mauritius.

Events in Europe were, however, to transform this whole strategy. For the Emperor Napoleon and Tsar Alexander made peace.

On June 14, a little over a month after the signature of the Finkenstein Treaty with the Persians, Napoleon defeated the Russians at Friedland. Shortly afterwards, a subdued Alexander met the French Emperor at Tilsit. 'I hate the English,' the petulant young Tsar said. 'Well, why are we fighting then?' a delighted Napoleon exclaimed.

THE TILSIT VISION
1807-1808

The two sovereigns set up a vast and comfortable raft in neutral territory, in the middle of the Niemen River between their two armies. They dined, talked and socialised for three weeks. They discussed Napoleon's recently proclaimed Continental System aimed at closing European ports to British trade. They discussed the British Orders-in-Council which gave the Royal Navy the right to search vessels on the high seas for goods destined for France. And they also discussed India. If Britain did not sue for peace by November, Napoleon suggested, Russia should become France's ally, and both countries should then march together against India.

Fascinated by the vigour, clarity and personality of the French emperor, the young and impressionable Tsar agreed.

There was just one major barrier to this grandiose strategy: Napoleon was now the ally of Russia's enemy, Persia, and in the Treaty of Finkenstein there was a clause which stated specifically he would help Persia to retake Georgia, occupied by the Russians three years earlier.

Napoleon, who so often accused his British enemies of perfidy in their international relations, was no novice himself in the art of double-dealing. Russia was stronger than Persia and it soon became clear – notably to the Persians themselves – that the Emperor had no intention of helping the Shah at the risk of antagonising the Tsar. Napoleon was quietly preparing to renege on the Treaty of Finkenstein.

In 1808, far from trying to dislodge the Russians from Georgia, he was trying in fact to inveigle them into a joint attack on India. On February 2 that year, two months after Gardane had reached Teheran and before Napoleon had yet received his envoy's report, the Emperor wrote to the Tsar: 'A Russo-French army of fifty thousand men, including perhaps a few Austrians, marching via Constantinople into Asia, would no sooner appear on the Euphrates than it would throw England into a panic. . . . The blow would be felt in India, and England would be on her knees.'

In faraway Teheran the Shah, conscious of this Franco-Russian flirtation, was fast becoming aware that he could not rely on Napoleon to recover his lost province of Georgia and he listened instead to the honeyed reasonings of the British envoy Sir Hartford Jones, sent in all haste from London to wean him away from the French alliance. Sir John Malcolm, one of Wellington's best friends, also hurried over from Calcutta to pour convincing arguments into the Shah's ear. The realistic French, outbid, knew they had no more to offer Persia, and – discreetly not clearing it first with Napoleon – went home.

THE DREAM FADES AWAY (ALMOST)
1809-1812

Later, back in Russia and far from Napoleon's charisma, Alexander became less enthusiastic about his French connection, and notably over the proposed joint enterprise against India. But Napoleon's Indian malady, for so it seemed to the men around the French emperor, notably Decrès, persisted. Now without Persian or Russian allies, Napoleon was considering a purely maritime expedition.

Trafalgar notwithstanding, the French navy was still a powerful instrument of war. As he reminisced to Dr O'Meara, in St Helena: 'In Brest I had as many as fifty-six sail-of-the line . . . I intended to distribute thirty thousand soldiers in forty of these ships, eight hundred in each ship and only four hundred sailors. There would have been a proportionate number of frigates and other smaller vessels. Ten of the battleships would have been old and of little value. The ships would also have taken on board six to eight hundred dismounted cavalry, some artillery, provisions for four months and everything necessary for an army to take the field. They were to make their way as best they could to Mauritius, where they would have watered and provisioned afresh, landed their sick and taken on board other troops to replace them, with three thousand blacks forming colonial regiments. They would then have proceeded to India, and have landed in the nearest possible place so as to allow the Mahrattas, with whom I had an understanding, to join them. . . . After landing, they were to burn ten old ships, and divide the crews among the rest of the squadron's vessels, which would then have been fully manned. They would then sail in various directions, and do you all possible damage in your settlements.' As for the army which had landed on Indian soil, 'left to itself, but under the command of a resolute and capable leader, it would simply have repeated the prodigies which we know about, and Europe would have learnt about the conquest of India as it learnt previously about the conquest of Egypt.'

It was a brave plan but that is what it remained. India stayed out of reach while the frustrated Decaen on Mauritius raged against a fate that left him stranded on a small island in the middle of the Indian Ocean while the great actions of the war happened elsewhere.

General Sir John Moore, veteran of many battles, killed outside Corunna in Spain in 1809, after the bitter 250-mile retreat from Salamanca

Europe, which had never been a dream but always a reality, soon held Napoleon's full attention again. Europe was where his enemies were, all round him. He was soon caught up in two campaigns, one against the Austrians which culminated in the Battle of Wagram in July 1809, and one on the Iberian peninsula where his main opponent was at first the now legendary General Sir John Moore, our friend from Corsica, St Lucia and Egypt, to be replaced after his death by the even more legendary Wellington, the Wellington of Seringapatam and of Assaye.

India, once again, inevitably, slipped into the background. But now and again it came to the fore and a word here, an uttered thought there, remind us that the dream had not entirely vanished. As late as 1812, just before he set out on the calamitous invasion of Russia, Napoleon casually remarked in an aside to Narbonne, the French ambassador in Vienna: 'The road to Delhi is through Moscow.'

Was it India that really lay at the end of the long march to Moscow that he was about to undertake? Many of his soldiers certainly believed it. Their horizons had no limit and, in the bivouacs at night, they talked of the wonders that awaited them after they had taken Moscow and marched south. How romantic India must have seemed, with its maharajahs and minarets and palaces and fakirs and elephants and snake charmers to those lads from Burgundy, and Brittany, and Flanders and the Dordogne. It wasn't far, no place was far for them, just a few thousand miles away.

There is a letter, quoted by the writer Alan Palmer, that survived from one of the soldiers of that doomed campaign. 'We are going to Greater India. It is three thousand leagues from Paris,' a young French infantryman wrote to his parents at the start of the great march. Taking Moscow was to be just an incident on the way. The domes of Delhi were at the end of the journey. Nothing seemed impossible to the soldiers of Napoleon.

But the Indian dream had to end somewhere, and it ended in the Russian snow.

CHAPTER SEVENTEEN

The Giant Southern Lands

AUSTRALIA – 'TERRE NAPOLÉON'
1802–1808

Not even Australia, away over on the other side of the globe, escaped completely untouched by the Anglo-French rivalries and conflicts. The recently-founded convict settlements of Norfolk Island and Port Jackson, in what is today Sydney, lived in incessant expectation of a French attack. In 1803 Governor King of New South Wales armed and equipped the Loyal Parramatta and Sydney Associations to protect stores and buildings in case the New South Wales Corps that policed and guarded the colony had to go and fight French invaders. Even as late as the War of 1812, the local authorities were convinced of the imminence of a French invasion. And now that Britain and the United States were also at war, the Americans would of course participate in the landing too.

A dreamer and a man of action at the same time, Napoleon was intrigued by that recently discovered and still largely unknown antipodean continent. One of the books he had taken to read when he left on the Egyptian expedition was *The Voyages of Captain Cook*. On his return from Egypt, after the *coup* that made him First Consul, he sent the French navigator, Nicolas Baudin, with two ships to explore this southern land. In those days, wars did not interfere with explorations. Explorers were universally helped and, in Port Jackson, Baudin and his exhausted crews were welcomed and fêted by their hospitable enemies.

Baudin had always specialised in exploration and in scientific voyages. Emperor Francis II of Austria had sent him to India in 1788 to bring back tropical plants for the glasshouses in the royal gardens of

266

Schönbrunn, and even during the French Revolution he had continued his exotic voyages, most recently to Indonesia, China and the West Indies.

Baudin had surveyed the southern coast of the continent in what are today the states of Victoria, South Australia and Western Australia, named it 'Terre Napoléon', a pointer perhaps to high expectations which were, however, never fulfilled. His presence greatly worried the British colonial authorities in New South Wales.

An envoy from Governor King of NSW intercepted Baudin in November 1802 on King Island, north of Tasmania, to prevent the French claiming it and to hoist the Union Jack. 'You're too late,' Baudin told the envoy mockingly, 'Tasman the Dutchman was here a hundred and sixty years ago.' Baudin then assured the envoy he had no intention of declaring Tasmania French – but, he added mysteriously, he did not know what his government might do. Soon afterwards he sailed for France taking with him two black swans from Western Australia for Bonaparte's wife, Josephine, and saplings of eucalyptus trees and of mimosa, or wattle as the locals called it. They were planted in the south of France and still embellish the French Riviera today.

Meanwhile, perplexed colonial leaders in Sydney pondered what Baudin's ambiguous words could mean. Governor King feared that the Frenchman might establish a settlement on the Australian mainland in the Bass Straits as well as in Tasmania and the worried British promptly occupied sites near the present cities of Hobart and Melbourne. For the next few years, first to forestall the French then out of sheer habit, Royal Navy ships scurried round the coast of Australia planting their flag here and there. Before long the English were the sole owners of the entire continent.

Baudin was probably never, himself, strongly motivated by the imperialist urge. Anyway, he died in Mauritius in September 1804 from sheer exhaustion, possibly largely brought on by his bad temper and his constant bickering with the scientific members of his staff and with his officers.

Some members of his expedition, notably the botanist François Péron and the surveyor Louis de Freycinet, were stirred by other ambitions than the pursuit of geographical knowledge. At least, the reports they made to Governor Decaen in Mauritius on their arrival there tend to show they had taken full advantage of old Sydney's open-hearted hospitality to do some spying on the side.

Péron described his natural history outings around Port Jackson as 'merely a pretext'. The real purpose of his little expeditions, he now claimed, had been to spy out the land and gauge Port Jackson's defences. 'My opinion . . . is that it should be destroyed as soon as possible' with the help of the rebellious Irish convicts, he wrote. 'Today we could destroy it easily. We shall not be able to do so in twenty-five years time.' He drew a map of Port Jackson which was later on Napoleon's desk in Paris. The conquest of the colony would be 'very easy to accomplish,' Freycinet agreed, and the French attack should be made preferably through nearby Botany Bay.

Péron was certainly right about the feelings of the Irish convicts. Those at Castle Hill, near Parramatta, revolted the next year. The New South Wales Loyal and Associated Corps, after a forced overnight march, engaged the wretched, largely unarmed rebels, killed nine, and recaptured most of the rest. Five were subsequently hanged.

Napoleon was perhaps remembering Péron's and Freycinet's advice when, in 1809, he directed General Decaen in Mauritius to attack and 'take the British colony of Port Jackson, where considerable supplies can be obtained.' Unfortunately for Napoleon, when this message reached Mauritius, that island had itself just been attacked and taken by a British expeditionary corps from India. So Sydney remained British and Mauritius became so.

Australia never did become a battleground, it just loomed off-stage and the war largely passed it by. In 1806 it even lost its big chance to send an expeditionary corps into battle overseas when General Craufurd, in Cape Town – as recounted in another chapter – instead of heading east to Sydney to pick up troops of the New South Wales Corps and convict pioneers for an attack on Valparaiso in Chile, headed west to Buenos Aires.

For the next three years, until 1807, convict ships continued to arrive in the colony, unharmed by the French corsairs and frigates then based in Mauritius. The route the convicts followed along the Roaring Forties was considerably south of these French vessels' normal operating region and it would have been difficult anyway for the French to deal with the cargoes of these British ships, mainly petty criminals and underprivileged subjects of King George III. What could they have done with them? They would only have added to the considerable problems with which Governor Decaen already had to cope. By 1809, there were more British prisoners on Mauritius than French troops.

There was only one notable war incident involving these convict ships, and that was in 1797 when some French prisoners of war, who had been virtually impressed from the British hulks into the New South Wales Corps, mutinied on the convict ship *Lady Shore*. The Frenchmen were guarding, presumably to the mutual pleasure of each, sixty-six women (and one lone male) prisoners being transported to Botany Bay. Shouting 'Vive la République' the French guards killed the ship's captain, Mr Willcocks, and took over the *Lady Shore* a few miles off the River Plate in South America, helped by the other guards, nearly all Irishmen and Germans.

The rebels sailed the ship into Montevideo harbour where the female convicts disappeared into local society and perhaps gave the River

Plate region the first hint of the English tone which it has since displayed in spite of its Spanish affiliation. What happened to most of the Frenchmen involved in the mutiny is one of history's lesser mysteries. Several of them were former sailors of the corvette *Bonne Citoyenne* captured off Cape Finisterre in March a year earlier. Presumably they made their way back into French service. One of them, Jean-Baptiste Prévot, was captured again by the British who, two days before Christmas in 1799, one cold foggy morning, hanged him for the murder of the captain of the *Lady Shore*.

Had he been luckier, Prévot might have been sent Down Under, as Australia was beginning to be called. That was the fate of quite a few French prisoners of war. Two of them, François de Riveau and Antoine Landrien, transported to Sydney in 1800, became the first wine growers in Australia. But they had travelled all the way to New South Wales for nothing. Their wine was almost undrinkable.

Australia also played an inglorious role in the Napoleonic Wars as a dump for British soldiers and sailors guilty of misconduct or cowardice. The most notorious case concerned the 18-gun HMS *Carnation* captured by the smaller French vessel, the *Palinure*, off Martinique on October 3, 1808. The captain of the British ship was killed early in the battle and all the other officers were severely or mortally wounded. When the *Palinure*, in the favoured French fashion, came alongside to board, the officerless, panic-striken *Carnation* survivors rushed below deck to hide rather than fight it out. They were afterwards all tried for misconduct in the face of the enemy. A Royal Marine sergeant was hanged and thirty-two seamen and marines transported to New South Wales to start a new life as convicts.

One Englishman who had a good reason not to retain the kindest memories of his travels in the southern hemisphere, and of the French in particular, was the navigator Matthew Flinders who did most of his exploration around the Australian coast at about the same time as Baudin. In fact, the two men met on the southern coast, in what was marked on the maps as Encounter Bay. Flinders called at Mauritius on his way home, where Governor Decaen showed himself considerably less hospitable than Governor King of New South Wales had been to Baudin.

In a fit of contrariness that lasted six and a half years, Decaen held Flinders a prisoner on the island on the flimsy grounds that the name of the ship (*Investigator*) indicated on the passport issued by the authorities in France was not the same as the one which he was now commanding (*Cumberland*). He simply rejected as invalid Flinders's explanation that he had changed vessels as HMS *Investigator* was no longer seaworthy.

Decaen, anyway, boasted that he 'hated' the British. His anglophobia, as ridiculous as Nelson's francophobia, may explain his perversity.

Also Flinders personally antagonised the Frenchman. He may have been the type of Briton, once widespread but now mercifully rare, who felt that foreigners should be put in their place, so he kept his hat on his head when ushered into Decaen's office. 'This British officer introduced himself with great arrogance with his hat on his head,' Decaen wrote indignantly later. Quite obviously, the two men disliked each other on sight. Decaen, who had recently heard from Péron and Freycinet about all their spying in and around Sydney, probably looked upon Flinders as a similar undercover agent – but on the enemy side.

The British explorer was relegated to a country mansion where other British officers were housed, given an allowance of 450 francs a month, and told to wait. Decaen steadfastly refused to release him, even when ordered from Paris to send the Englishman home. Matthew Flinders's long stay on Mauritius was made a little less intolerable, one hopes, through the fellowship of several French officers, including young Lieutenant Charles Baudin (no relation to the explorer).

In 1808, Baudin's right arm was carried away by a cannonball during the fight between Captain Motard's *Sémillante* and HMS *Terpischore*. On the French frigate's return to Mauritius, it was Flinders by his friendship and advice who helped young Baudin surmount the deep depression into which the French officer had fallen at the thought that his naval career had come to an early end.

SOUTH AFRICA – THE BLUEBERG COMMANDOS
The Cape 1806

South Africa, in the days of Napoleon, meant the Cape of Good Hope. The rest of the country was a vast no-man's land, or rather a black man's land. The Cape was white: mainly Dutch and French Huguenot. The Dutch had been there for a hundred and fifty years, the Huguenots – who had also arrived from Holland – about a hundred. The British had occupied the colony after Lord Keith's victory at Saldanha Bay in 1796 and had regretfully gone home after returning it to Holland, now known as the Batavian Republic and the ally of the French Republic, at the Peace of Amiens in 1802.

A pleasant, honourable but incompetent soldier, General J. W. Janssens, was in command of the Dutch army at the Cape. The forces under his command were as unimpressive as he himself. Most of his troops were not Dutch, but recruited from all over Europe, and steadiness and reliability were not their outstanding virtues. They numbered around 2,200 men and were as disparate as the Foreign Legion, but without its fighting quality. They included a battalion of Waldeckers, made up largely of Hessian, Austrian and Hungarian mercenaries, a couple of nominally Dutch battalions but, in fact, an assortment of international riff-raff: Poles, Bohemians, Flemings, Walloons, French, with a few

Dutch thrown in, mostly inducted into the army straight from prison. There was also a small corps of dragoons and a company of gunners, also largely foreign-born, which reportedly included several Americans.

With this ragbag force of third-rate fighting men the Batavian Republic hoped to hold, and to keep out of Britain's rapacious hands, one of the most pleasant lands of the world, vitally located on the route to India, China and Australia, with a balmy climate and a fertile soil.

The Dutch didn't have a chance. In September 1805, while Nelson was preparing to confront the French at Trafalgar, another British expedition was being prepared to meet the Dutch in battle and take the Cape of Good Hope from them. The man in charge was another admiral, the busybody Sir Home Riggs Popham.

Popham was of a most restless character. His career was as odd as it was variegated. He tried (unsuccessfully) to make a fortune with a shipment of tea on a voyage from China, he carried out (successfully) extensive surveys of coastlines (West Africa), ports (Calcutta) and islands (Penang). He sued (successfully) his superiors at the Admiralty, he tried (unsuccessfully) to blow up the sluices at Ostend to halt the French advance in Flanders, he was presented with a gold snuff box by Tsar Paul I and a diamond ring from the Tsarina for some obscure service he rendered Russia, he invented the flag signal code which Nelson used at the Battle of Trafalgar to tell his sailors that England expected every man to do his duty, he picked the brains of the Venezuelan patriot Miranda to discover the best business opportunities in South America, and we shall be with him shortly when he leads an expedition to what is today called Argentina and Uruguay, without the permission of his government, to take those territories from the Spaniards.

Admiral Popham's task force on the South African expedition was made up of three 64-gun battleships, a 50-gunner, two frigates, a corvette and a sloop, in addition to a force of seven thousand soldiers under the command of an old friend from India and Egypt, the recently-knighted General Sir David Baird. This huge, gangling Scotsman had returned to India after the Egyptian expedition but, we are told, threw up his command in disgust when Wellington, the governor-general's brother, was appointed over him during the Mahratta war. Muttering violent invectives against nepotism, Baird returned to England, where he had not set foot for nearly a quarter of a century and was given the command of the Cape expedition.

In November 1805, while Popham was heading for the Cape from England, Linois was heading in the same direction from Mauritius. He lost his frigate, the *Atalante*, in Cape Town's Table Bay when a merchant ship broke from its moorings during a storm, smashed into the French frigate and drove it ashore. Around two hundred of the shipless survivors were added to the Dutch garrison and placed under the orders of General Janssens.

The wrecked *Atalante* was joined a few days later in Cape Town by another French vessel, the 30-gun *Napoléon*, a privateer captained by the Breton corsair, Malo Lenouvel. He arrived in Table Bay on December 12 after a successful cruise off the East African coast in which he captured several valuable merchantmen.

The two French ships were both in Table Bay when, on the evening of January 4, 1806, Admiral Popham's fleet dropped anchor in nearby Losperd's Bay. While messengers rushed to the Cape to advise General Janssens of the enemy's arrival, the British landing began under the command of General Baird.

Baird was seconded in this campaign by a brace of other generals: Samuel Gibbs and the old Etonian Sir William Lumley, seventh son of the 4th Earl of Scarborough, a genuine old-style aristocrat who had served in Egypt and taken part in the siege of Cairo. As for Gibbs, he was an army old-timer who had already served in Corsica, Flanders and Martinique. For those who have always looked upon the Napoleonic Wars as a European conflict, let me add that Java was next on the fighting itinerary of this globe-trotting army officer and that it was an American bullet that ended his life, outside New Orleans in 1815.

The Earl of Tyrone's bastard son, the one-eyed General William Beresford, now nearly middle-aged at thirty-eight, bursts again into our pages after previous appearances in Toulon (he was acting marine officer on one of the warships), Corsica and Egypt, where he had already served under Baird. He was in command of the British first brigade and age hadn't mellowed him. He was, as usual, longing to get into the middle of the fight, just an Irish brawler in spite of his noble (if illegitimate) birth and his general's epaulettes.

The wind was fresh and the waves were high when the invasion fleet reached the vicinity of an inlet on the coast some fifteen miles from Cape Town, north of Table Bay. On January 5, fearing the high seas might prevent him landing, Baird diverted Beresford and the 38th Regiment, in all between nine hundred and a thousand men, to Saldanha Bay, about forty miles north. He planned to sail there himself with the rest of the army on the next day but the winds eased on the 6th, and the main landing took place between Robben Island and the Blueberg mountain, as originally planned.

Janssens was coming up from Cape Town to meet the invaders but by the time he reached the beach-head, on January 7, the British were all ashore. The sea had been more deadly than the Dutch to the British. One of the landing boats overturned in the surf and thirty-six Highlanders were drowned. The only enemy to meet the British were a small, unhappy company of part-time militia burghers who, under the

View of Cape Town in 1806, from the deck of a British warship. Inset below: the
battle at nearby Blueberg which led to Cape Town's capture by the British

threat of the naval guns, kept well out of range but managed to fire a
few shots that killed one unlucky British soldier and wounded four
others.

Beresford, meanwhile, landed unopposed up in Saldanha Bay and
marched off south to join the rest of the expeditionary force.   The
Baird army comprised the cream of Britain's soldiery: Highlanders
and some of the best British regiments of the line. Nearly 6,500 strong,
they outnumbered the defenders by just over three to one. Janssens
could only oppose to the highly professional, cohesive and disciplined
British his motley force of half-trained men: the 400 Waldeckers, 224
mounted civilian burghers from Cape Town, two Dutch battalions,
each of about 400 men, a contingent of some 100 bewildered slaves
from Mozambique, a small company of Malays, 300 Hottentot tribesmen and 240 French sailors and marines from the *Atalante* and the
Napoléon, commanded by the frigate's skipper, Captain Beauchêne.

The engagement between Janssens's and Baird's armies, described
by the *Standard Encyclopedia of Southern Africa* as 'one of the most
important milestones of South African history', is known as the Battle
of Blueberg from the nearby mountain. The Waldeckers, all four
hundred of them, took to their heels and ran at the first British charge
(they all later joined the British army en masse). Only the French, the
Hottentots and some of the Cape Town burghers stood and fought

back, killing fifteen of the enemy and wounding two hundred. By the evening the fighting was over, Janssens's casualties amounted to 337. The list included 188 Dutchmen, 110 French, seventeen Hottentots, ten Malays, eight Mozambicans and four Cape burghers.

While Janssens and what remained of his force melted into quaintly-named Hottentot's Holland, the territory just south of the Little Karroo mountains east of Cape Town, General Beresford, cursing at having missed the battle, joined Baird's weary and thirsty army marching in the baking midsummer heat towards Cape Town.

Three days after the Battle of Blueberg, the British took the city without a fight. Eight days later, Janssens came in from the countryside and surrendered.

Admiral Popham was jubilant. Forgetting Baird's major contribution to the victory, he considered he had conquered a great, new colony for Britain and won a great new market for British businessmen. But his ambitions were not over.

Before his departure for the Cape, Popham had met and discussed with Miranda, the South American revolutionary, the great possibilities of trade with that continent, now slipping out of Spain's withered hand. France, Popham claimed in a memorandum to the British government, was getting, through Spain, two-thirds of South America's £20 million exports. Now was the time for Britain to invade Latin America.

The smell of easy conquest and easy money was in the air. Wellington, back in England, was also preparing a British naval and military expedition to the Orinoco region, in the north of South America.

Having, so to speak, conquered South Africa, Popham now planned, without orders and without informing his government, to conquer South America. But first, he needed soldiers. General Baird had those, so he had to persuade the general to help him.

SOUTH AMERICA – THE POPHAM SCHEME
Uruguay and Argentina 1806-1807

Spanish South America, weak, rich, and almost defenceless, seemed ripe that year for the picking.

It wasn't only Britain who was interested. So was Napoleon. British and French interests flowed into the Latin American void which followed the political, military, naval and economic weaknesses of Spain. Its allegiance, whether to Britain or France, was unsteady as the Spanish throne itself. There were three competitors for the kingship: father Charles IV and son Ferdinand VII playing for the throne as if it were a game of musical chairs until, in April 1807, Napoleon stepped in, forced both kings out of the game, gave them a couple of castles in France and brought in his brother, Joseph, as king.

South America in the early 1800s

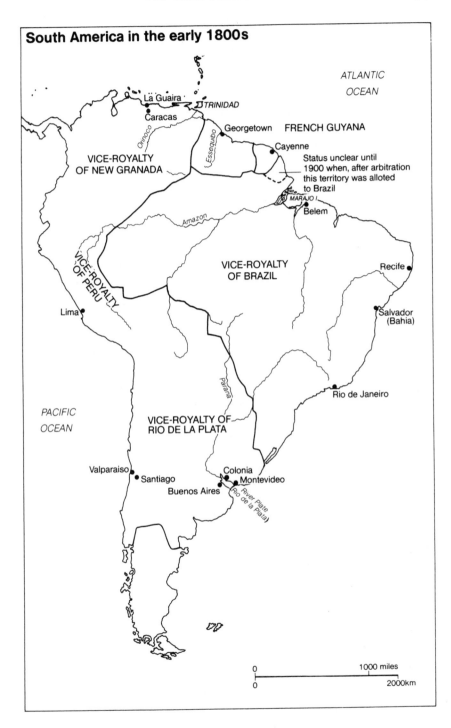

ATLANTIC OCEAN

La Guaira
TRINIDAD
Caracas

Orinoco

Georgetown   FRENCH GUYANA

Cayenne

VICE-ROYALTY
OF NEW GRANADA

Essequibo

Status unclear until
1900 when, after arbitration
this territory was alloted
to Brazil

MARAJO I.

Amazon

Belem

VICE-ROYALTY
OF PERU

VICE-ROYALTY
OF BRAZIL

Recife

Lima

Salvador
(Bahia)

Parana

Rio de Janeiro

PACIFIC
OCEAN

VICE-ROYALTY OF
RIO DE LA PLATA

Valparaiso
Santiago

Colonia
Montevideo

Buenos Aires

River Plate
(Rio de la Plata)

0   1000 miles

0   2000km

But, even before then, while Spain was fighting for her soul, her Latin American colonies were left to fend for themselves. These were happy days indeed for those who, like Popham, enjoyed fishing in troubled waters.

The British were, thanks to him, the first on the scene. Now was Britain's chance to seize Latin America. The capture of Trinidad a few years before had been the first step, but the next step, and by far the most important, was the capture of the Cape of Good Hope, and it was Admiral Popham who provided first the brain, then the muscle, for the enterprise.

This Elizabethan-style adventurer had set his mind on conquering South America and, needing soldiers, immediately after the capture of Cape Town, he buttonholed General Baird and poured into the Scotsman's eager ear wild proposals of conquests and riches in South America – straight across the ocean, there to the west, just a few weeks' sail away.

The opulent halls of the great banking houses were as much Popham's natural element as restless ventures, bold proposals, raging seas or tropical horizons. Nothing and no one daunted him. His brain, always whirling with a hundred different schemes, had for some time been fired with an amazing, simple, direct, outrageous and utterly unscrupulous idea which, if successful, was sure to make him one of the great names of British history . . . and one of the wealthiest men of his times. His plan was to attack the Viceroyalty of La Plata in South America, occupy Buenos Aires and Montevideo and the hinterland, snatch the pampas from feeble and groggy Spain and provide Britain with new, unlimited opportunities of domination and trade in Latin America.

The whole scheme reeks of imperialism at its arrogant best, but also of adventure and patriotic ambitions, gain and booty – in both the fire-and-sword tradition of Drake and Hawkins and of the voracious spirit of the sharp-toothed City of London barracudas.

Captivated by Popham's super-salesman talk, and by visions of unlimited prize money, Baird was convinced. He obligingly provided a regiment of nine hundred and fifty men with General Beresford to lead them, and the expedition sailed away on its freebooting expedition on April 1, 1806.

On the way to South America, the expedition called at St Helena where the glib Popham talked the governor of the island into lending him four hundred men and, on June 14, the convoy reached the mouth of the River Plate.

The original idea had been to take Montevideo. Its defences were stronger than expected, however, and Popham decided to head instead for Buenos Aires, reputedly more weakly-held and where, Popham was informed, a vast treasure was stored, awaiting shipment to Spain.

The Spanish viceroy, the Marquis Rafael de Sobremont, was attending the theatre on the evening of June 24 when advised that a British naval squadron had arrived offshore. He hurriedly went home to his palace to pack his clothes, his wife's jewellery, and his treasures and then fled from the city. The next day General Beresford landed at the little town of Quilmes, a few miles south of Buenos Aires and, at the head of an army of 1,560 men, marched to the city and captured it and its 50,000 inhabitants, virtually without a fight. One British soldier was killed and twelve wounded.

General Beresford assured the sullen people of Buenos Aires that private property would be respected and, having thus quieted the fears of the business community, he proceeded to plunder the town of the gold and specie belonging to the Spanish government.

Admiral Popham was also busy. In a letter intended to be posted up at Lloyd's Coffee House where City of London businessmen regularly met for their mid-morning break, he advised them that the conquest of the South American capital now 'opens an extensive channel for the manufactures of Great Britain'. Everyone present on the day cheered and the grateful City of London awarded the absent Admiral a jewel-encrusted sword of honour for his 'gallant attempt to open up new markets'. 'Buenos Ayres at the moment forms part of the British Empire', exulted *The Times* when the news reached London in September. Popham meanwhile had loaded the loot from Buenos Aires aboard HMS *Narcissus* and shipped it hurriedly to England where it filled six wagons.

Before the booty arrived, however, when news of the unauthorised attack on Buenos Aires reached London, the British government sent an official admonition to Baird and Popham for acting without orders. But at the same time it found the opportunity of expanding the British Empire too good to miss. Along with the rebuke to Popham it also sent several regiments to the River Plate, just to make sure the British troops already out there held on to their illegally acquired conquest.

But by now, in the River Plate viceroyalty, after the quick and surprise victory of the British, a new Spanish army was preparing in Montevideo, across the river, to fight the invaders. This new army was organised and led by a French naval officer in Spanish service, Captain Jacques de Liniers, who had assumed command of the Spanish and native Creole insurgents. It consisted at first of only six hundred men, composed largely of Catalan immigrants, with a nucleus of regular soldiers and a few companies of local militia. The force grew to some thousand men with the addition of three hundred Spanish navy sailors and of seventy-five French seamen from a privateer commanded by Captain Mordeille, a corsair from Marseille. Pierre Gicquel des Touches, who had been an ensign in de Sercey's squadron in the Indian Ocean, then in Baudin's expedition to Australia and was now a privateer, also joined the insurgent force. So did a young Italian immigrant, Manuel Belgrano, who later rose to be a general and whose name is particularly remembered today after the sinking during the Falkland Islands war of the Argentine cruiser named after him.

De Liniers and his little army left Montevideo on the night of August 3, 1806, crossed the River Plate unseen by Popham's ships and attacked Buenos Aires on the 10th, after having been joined by volunteers from the city who streamed out to join his forces. The fight lasted two days. After suffering 165 casualties – of whom 101 were killed – Beresford surrendered and Admiral Popham removed his ships discreetly down the river. The British occupation of Buenos Aires had lasted less than six weeks.

Under the terms of the capitulation the British were to be sent home, but the angry Spaniards and Creoles, whose casualties amounted to several hundred, refused to agree to their departure. The British prisoners were scattered in several Argentinian towns and villages. Beresford and his second-in-command, Colonel Denis Pack – the officer who, eight years before, had escorted the captured Humbert to Dublin after the French general's defeat at Ballynamuck – were assigned residence at Lujan, eighty miles from Buenos Aires.

Meanwhile, unaware that General Beresford had capitulated, reinforcements were on their way from both Britain and South Africa to the British army in Buenos Aires.

The first reinforcements, 2,200 men under the command of Colonel Backhouse, sailed from Cape Town in August, three weeks after the surrender. On arrival at the River Plate on October 13, Backhouse was greeted by a desperately anxious Admiral Popham, striding up and down the quarterdeck of his ship, his squadron intact but all his army now prisoners in Spanish hands.

In the circumstances, Colonel Backhouse sensibly decided to do as little as possible. He seized the post of Maldonado, on the north shore of the River Plate, about eighty miles east of Montevideo, and sat down to await events and more troops.

The latter came three months later, on January 5, 1807, in the persons of the American loyalist, General Auchmuty and four thousand men from Britain. Auchmuty – with whom we were last in Egypt – also brought with him an order for Admiral Popham to return to England and face a court martial for abandoning his post in Cape Town. Auchmuty, restless and energetic, immediately decided to mount an expedition against Montevideo. The British attacked the town ten days later and took it on February 3 after an eighteen-day siege which cost the British over four hundred casualties. The Spaniards lost eight hundred in killed alone, and two thousand were made prisoner.

Auchmuty was shortly afterwards joined in Montevideo by Beresford and Pack who had escaped from their place of confinement.

Beresford, feeling bound by his parole, asked to be sent home but Pack, angry and rebellious, decided to continue the fight against de Liniers and the Spaniards.

Buenos Aires was Auchmuty's next target but before attacking the now well-defended capital he decided to await the expected arrival of more reinforcements under General Robert Craufurd.

Craufurd, a specialist in light infantry tactics, had left Falmouth in September with 4,500 men on a rather bizarre supporting expedition bound for Valparaiso, in Chile, via Cape Town and Sydney, Australia. His orders were to pick up troops from the New South Wales Corps and a couple of hundred convict pioneers in Botany Bay and then proceed across the Pacific to Chile, take Valparaiso, march over the Andes and link up with the victorious British troops in Buenos Aires, a thousand miles from the Chilean coast! News of Beresford's surrender reached Cape Town while Craufurd was there and, instead of sailing to Australia and Chile, he was ordered to sail directly to the River Plate, to reinforce Colonel Backhouse's and General Auchmuty's forces.

But in the meantime, the British government – headed since Pitt's death in January by Lord William Grenville, the former foreign secretary – for obscure reasons appointed a new commander-in-chief, General Whitelocke, to replace General Auchmuty in Montevideo. Auchmuty was a first-class soldier. Whitelocke was an arrogant, vulgar and pretentious nonentity.

Bringing a further 1,800 troops, Whitelocke reached Montevideo on May 10, Craufurd in mid-June. He and his men had been in their wretched ships for nine months! After Craufurd's arrival, Whitelocke's command came to 8,500 men, all based on the northern bank of the River Plate. The British held Montevideo and Maldonado. Pack, in command of a battalion, held the outpost of Colonia, some hundred and fifty miles west of Montevideo. But the south bank, centred on Buenos Aires, was under Jacques de Liniers's firm control.

Whitelock launched his attack on June 28. Six thousand British troops landed in an isolated swamp at Ensenada, some thirty miles east of Buenos Aires and, after slogging their way through mud and water, sometimes armpit-deep, reached the outskirts of the town four days later.

Another defeat lay ahead. Whitelocke, like Prevost in Dominica, was a ditherer. When he saw Buenos Aires, he swore he would never send his troops into such a trap: narrow streets, overlooked by flat-roofed houses from where, behind parapets, the enemy could shoot at will at the unprotected British troops. He then did just what he had said he would never do: on July 5 he broke his troops into several columns and sent them into the city from thirteen different directions.

Inside, de Liniers was awaiting the British. In those days Buenos Aires, laid out in rectangular, regular blocks, was about two miles long from north to south, and a mile from east to west, with its eastern side along the river-front where several vessels, including that of Gicquel des Touches, lay anchored with their guns pointing up the streets, waiting for the intruders to arrive. Trenches were cut, barricades set up, and some seven thousand men took up their positions at the windows, on the rooftops and around the bullring. The Redcoats blundered in.

It was a bloody defeat for the British. Hopelessly entangled in the little streets, they were fired on from every side by multitudes of unseen snipers. Four hundred were killed in a few hours, six hundred and fifty wounded and two thousand surrendered. Whitelocke capitulated and agreed to return to Britain with all his surviving troops.

The crestfallen British were allowed to remain in Montevideo for two months. Whitelocke asked that a gaggle of British merchants who had accompanied the expedition should be permitted to remain longer, to do some business on the side but de Liniers contemptuously rejected this idea.

The River Plate campaign was a disaster for the British, and notably for General Whitelocke. This undistinguished and unfortunate officer went home to be court-martialled and expelled from the army in disgrace, unfit to hold any further command. When dreams end as nightmares, the cost can be high for those who have no place to run for cover.

As for Jacques de Liniers, he was appointed viceroy, but tantalisingly and disappointingly for such an ambitious man, only on a temporary basis, while awaiting the appointment of another official from Spain.

This was the moment for the Emperor Napoleon I to come on the scene and he entered with considerably more finesse than his British predecessor, Admiral Popham. After all, his brother Joseph was already on the point of becoming King of Spain, so Napoleon could try to direct Latin America into the French sphere through Joseph. But first, he decided, he would see what Jacques de Liniers could do in Buenos Aires.

Compared to Britain's massive military effort, his diplomatic method was very discreet. But it turned out to be equally futile.

SOUTH AMERICA – THE SASSENAY MISSION
Argentina 1808

De Liniers, in spite of his years of service for Spain and his royalist background, was a great admirer of Napoleon and less than a week after the British defeat at Buenos Aires, he wrote a long letter to the French Emperor, describing the battle and expressing his personal sympathy for the leader of France. Napoleon was never a man to let an opportunity pass, so he filed the letter and awaited the right moment to make his move. It came the next year, in May 1808, when his brother was on the throne of Spain. Napoleon sent the Marquis de Sassenay as his special envoy to Buenos Aires to win de Liniers over to the new king. An aristocrat and former émigré, the marquis knew de Liniers well, had lived during a part of his exile in Buenos Aires – and had fought for the British against the French Republicans in Haiti. Before returning to France, under First Consul Bonaparte's amnesty law, he had worked as a supercargo on a brig trading between Wilmington and the River Plate where he and de Liniers, two Frenchmen of breeding stranded among the riff-raff of the Americas, had immediately become friends.

When the marquis arrived in Buenos Aires on August 13, de Liniers made it clear in a conversation with his old friend that the high esteem in which he held the Emperor Napoleon might link him more closely to the new (Spanish) dynasty (Joseph Bonaparte's) where his fate would be clear, instead of in the current uncertainty in which he lived. For he was viceroy only provisionally and his position was very tenuous. His first loyalty was not to South America, and not particularly to the Spanish Bourbons but to Spain, his adopted country.

In very guarded language, de Liniers was telling de Sassenay that if he were made viceroy for life he would be willing to give his allegiance to Joseph I, of the Spanish House of Bonaparte, instead of to Ferdinand VII, of the Spanish House of Bourbon.

On the completion of his mission in Buenos Aires de Sassenay was supposed to travel onward to Chile and Peru to gauge these colonies' feelings towards the installation of Joseph on the Spanish throne. But he was instead arrested by suspicious Spaniards in Montevideo on August 19, a few days after his meeting with de Liniers and, in spite of his compatriot's efforts to have him freed, kept in irons in a dark cell for ten months, with only bread and onions for food. At the end of 1809 he was shipped to Spain in a British warship and held in a rotting, waterlogged hulk with other French prisoners in Cadiz. On a windy night, on August 15, 1810, the French prisoners in the old hulk cut the moorings and drifted into nearby French-held territory and freedom. After more than two years' absence, the Marquis de Sassenay returned home to his wife and children.

As for Jacques de Liniers, he found himself caught in the middle of the violent controversies that raged between the Spanish-born colonists and the native-born Creoles over the future of the territory. A Frenchman, he was regarded – like de Sassenay – with suspicion by both rival factions and on January 1, 1809, on the day of the local elections, crowds gathered in Buenos Aires's Plaza Mayor shouting: 'Down with de Liniers the Frenchman!'

That month a new viceroy arrived from British-held Spain and de

Liniers retired to his estate in Cordoba. He was executed by firing squad the next year for his loyalty to his adopted country, Spain, by the men he had led to freedom and who now wanted independence as well.

The expeditions to Argentina and Uruguay and the abandoned Chilean campaign had 'by no means exhausted the projects of the British War Ministry for South America' sardonically comments the historian Fortescue. It now instructed General Wellington, just back from India, to open a new theatre of war in Latin America, this time in Mexico, and on two fronts: Atlantic and Pacific. Troops from the West Indies and Britain would attack on the Atlantic coast, troops from India on the Pacific side.

Wellington worked out an elaborate two-pronged assault: by nine thousand white and Negro troops in the Caribbean and by five thousand British troops and Indian sepoys around Acapulco. He suggested further that the troops from India, in a side campaign, also land in the Philippines and capture Manila, and that those from the West Indies seize Venezuela from Spain as well as Mexico.

The idea of Venezuela absolutely fascinated the British government, suffering at the time from an acute attack of imperial dementia, and this proposal received top priority. A Venezuelan expedition, nine thousand men in all, was assembled in the Irish port of Cork. The project, of course, received the enthusiastic support of the Venezuelan patriot, Francisco Miranda, and Wellington left London for Ireland to take over his new command and sail to the Orinoco. Wellington's campaign in Venezuela would have been a wonderful chapter in any history of the Napoleonic Wars. Unfortunately the Spaniards in Spain chose this moment to revolt against the French occupants of their country and called for British help. Spain was to be no longer an enemy but an ally. The British decided not to liberate the Venezuelans from the Spaniards but to liberate the Spaniards from the French instead.

So, after a stormy meeting with the outraged and betrayed Miranda, Wellington sailed in July 1808 to Corunna instead of to Caracas. The Peninsular War began.

'You will be lost,' Miranda in his rage and frustration shouted at Wellington at their last meeting in the street as the embarrassed Briton walked away as fast as he could from the unpleasant scene. Poor Miranda, never was a man more wrong. The Peninsular War was to be one of Wellington's greatest triumphs.

So the British never took Venezuela. Neither did the French. The same month, an imperial envoy, Lieutenant de Lamanon, skipper of the 16-gun sloop *Serpent*, arrived at La Guaira, the port area for Caracas, to inform the people that Joseph was now their king and Napoleon their friend.

De Lamanon only managed with difficulty to escape lynching by the outraged crowd, shouting their loyalty to King Ferdinand. The *Serpent* sailed away, only to be captured the same day after a short and sharp engagement by the 40-gun HMS *Acasta*, commanded by Captain Philip Beaver, which was standing offshore, awaiting the Frenchman.

Napoleon and the British were both thwarted in Latin America. But though Spanish America escaped enrolment into the British Empire, it played a great role in the next decades of British commercial expansion and it achieved this role through Portuguese Brazil.

The Portuguese, more lucky than the Spanish, managed to slip their royal family out of their threatened country in 1808 under the protection of a British fleet commanded by Sir Sidney Smith who was always around when there was some interesting action under way. The royal family, the Braganzas, established in Rio de Janeiro the foundations of the future Brazilian empire – how else can we call that huge country covering half of South America? – and made its passage from colony to independence relatively painless.

The British ambassador to the Portuguese court, Lord Strangford, who accompanied the royal family to Rio in 1808, arrived in Brazil with instructions to make it a depot for British manufacturers in South America.

We recall that when Admiral Sir Home Riggs Popham had 'conquered' Buenos Aires he promptly advised London businessmen of the great new opportunities with which the British occupation of the River Plate region provided them.

Was that all that these dreams of empire meant in the end: selling pots and pans, woollens and cottons and insurance policies? It is a saddening and sobering thought. And it does lack glory. The glory was only for those who fought for their flag, shouting 'England forever' or 'Vive l'Empereur'. They died – painfully – and made history. Others lived – splendidly – and made money.

CHAPTER EIGHTEEN

Mayhem in the Middle East

THE HEAVY GUNS OF THE DARDANELLES
Turkey 1807

Neutrality is risky in wartime. Belligerents hate neutrals, sometimes more than they hate the enemy. During the Napoleonic conflicts both Britain and France found other nations' neutrality an obnoxious obstacle to the normal conduct of war. Neutral objections to the high-handed methods of the belligerents were regarded as an intolerable intrusion. Neutrals were a nuisance.

The Ottoman Empire, of which Egypt was part, had been neutral in 1798 and General Bonaparte invaded this province without the slight-est compunction. Three years later Britain had objected to Danish par-ticipation in the armed neutrality of the north. Nelson thereupon sailed punitively into Copenhagen and destroyed or captured fifteen Danish vessels.

In 1807 these two neutrals at each end of Europe began again to dis-turb Britain.

Turkey was the first to come into Britain's gunsights, largely because of the smouldering hostilities between the Ottoman and Russian empires, for, since the formation of the Third Coalition in 1805, Russia was Britain's ally and in the confusing revolving door of shifting alliances that marked Turkish policy, the Sublime Porte in Constantinople, after its short war against the French, was now friendly to Paris. It had, in fact, requested French military help to for-tify the Dardanelles. French soldiers were the new paladins of Con-stantinople. A soldier, General Sébastiani, was French ambassador in Constantinople. With him were a military mission led by artillery

Colonel Maximilien Foy, and the engineer Major François Haxo, both of whom were to finish their Napoleonic careers as generals at Waterloo. An additional force of three hundred gunners was on its way from France to train the Turks manning the forts along both shores of the Dardanelles and the sea of Marmora.

The British were anxious to prevent the Turks from going to war against their Russian ally. The best way, according to straightforward British thinking, was to disarm them, or at least to take their ships. So in February 1807, Admiral Duckworth, back in the Mediterranean from the Caribbean, was ordered to break through the Dardanelles to Constantinople and force the Turks to surrender their fleet of twelve battleships and nine frigates. It was to be a repeat of Nelson's 1801 Copenhagen performance.

The Russian Admiral Seniavin, based in Corfu, was ordered to join Duckworth in the attack. He arrived with his eight ships off the island of Tenedos, at the entrance to the straits, only to find that without waiting for his allies, the impatient Duckworth had sailed in with his squadron of seven battleships and two frigates and his flag aboard the 100-gun HMS *Royal George*.

In typical RN fashion, Duckworth was rashly planning to attack and capture a fleet larger than his own. The British had long known about 'the Nelson Touch'. They were now about to hear of 'the Duckworth Touch'.

Admirals Louis and Sir Sidney Smith (again!) were also taking part in the raid, under Duckworth's orders, Smith aboard HMS *Pompée*, captured at Toulon, and Louis on HMS *Canopus*.

With magnificent effrontery, the British warships entered the straits soon after dawn on February 19, with HMS *Canopus* leading the fleet. Two Turkish forts fired on the British as they drew into the narrow waters causing some casualties among the crews: six dead and some fifty wounded. The ships of a small Turkish squadron – a 64-gunner, four frigates and several smaller ships – were at anchor off Nagara and immediately opened fire on the intruding British naval force.

While the rest of the squadron sailed on, the irrepressible Sidney Smith, once again delighted to be in action, anchored within musket shot of the Turkish ships, captured a corvette and a gunboat and drove the rest ashore. A British landing party spiked the guns of a fort and then returned to their ship, and Sir Sidney rejoined the rest of Duckworth's squadron having lost seventy-two men in killed and wounded in the seven-hour affray.

Sailing past Gallipoli, Duckworth and his fleet reached Constantinople the next evening and anchored eight miles from the city. The raid so far had been a strictly naval operation. It now turned into a diplomatic charade in which Duckworth was completely outfoxed by the devious Turks.

'No negotiations with the Turks should continue more than half an hour,' Admiral Collingwood, commander-in-chief of the British Mediterranean fleet had warned Duckworth. But there followed, from the morning of February 21, an eight-day exchange of correspondence and dithering between Duckworth and the Turks. British politicians and diplomats may have been adept at perfidiousness, British admirals definitely were not.

Admiral Duckworth, in his first note to the Turks, bluntly demanded the surrender of their fleet, and insisted on a reply, not in half an hour as Collingwood had advised, but at sunset the following day. The Turks refused to allow his envoy to land so Duckworth sent a second note, giving the Turks half an hour to reply. No reply came so Duckworth sent a third note at midnight, warning the Turks against 'warping their ships-of-war into places more susceptible of defence, and in constructing batteries along the coast.'

While the Ottomans were procrastinating, Colonel Foy and the other French military experts were travelling overland down the straits, setting up the Turkish guns along the shore and readying to greet the British ships on their return trip.

No reply or Turkish envoy came on February 22. On the 23rd, the frustrated Duckworth sent another note to the Turks, the fourth, giving them until 'very early in the morning' of the 24th if they wanted to save Constantinople 'from the dreadful calamities which are ready to burst upon it.'

Unmoved, the Turks on the same day arrested a British midshipman and four apprentices from HMS *Endymion*, as they were on their way to get provisions in a jolly boat. Duckworth demanded their immediate release. The Turks refused to free them.

In the morning of February 27, under the personal direction of General Sébastiani, Turkish janissaries began to put up a gun battery on a small island within firing distance of the British ships. A detachment of Royal Marines was sent ashore to disperse them but, outnumbered, were forced to retire, losing seven men killed and nineteen wounded. By the next day Duckworth was in a state of semi-panic over the reinforced batteries the Turks were erecting, under French supervision, along the shore. He visualised his squadron, bottled up in the Dardanelles, obliged to surrender ignominiously to the Turks. On March 1, without any more ado and any more notes or threats to the Sublime Porte, Duckworth tamely sailed away to run back to the welcoming wide waters of the Mediterranean, past the heavy gauntlet of the Turkish batteries along the way.

Heavy is certainly the right word for the operation. The Turkish guns from Gallipoli and other points along the shore fired huge missiles of rounded rock, some of which weighed half a ton, compared to the heaviest British 32-pounders. One of these projectiles, nearly seven feet in circumference, exploded the powder boxes stored in the lower deck of HMS *Standard*, killing and wounding fifty-five men. Another stone shot, weighing eight hundred pounds, carried away the cutwater of HMS *Royal George*. The wheel of HMS *Canopus* disappeared into tiny fragments when one of these enormous shots swept across her deck. All the ships, with the exception of Sir Sidney Smith's lucky HMS *Pompée*, emerged into the Mediterranean with large holes in their hulls.

One hundred and sixty-seven men were killed and wounded on the return passage.

The Russian Admiral Seniavin met the still shaken Duckworth off Tenedos and suggested the two fleets join up and force the Dardanelles again to Constantinople. But Duckworth, aghast at the thought of facing those projectiles once more, refused to go back and sailed away to Gibraltar to present his report to Collingwood and show him the huge holes in his ships.

The Russian was more successful than Duckworth. He waited outside the straits for the Turkish squadron to appear. The two were about of equal strength and he pounced upon the Ottoman fleet with his ten ships-of-the-line off the island of Lembos. Three Turkish battleships and one frigate were sunk or captured, including the 84-gun *Sedd-ul-Bakir*. Aboard, Seniavin found the midshipman and the four apprentices who had been prisoners of the Turks for four months and were miraculously still alive.

The British were soon to suffer a second setback at the hands of the Turks in the Middle East, this time in Egypt where, to forestall what they claimed was an imminent French threat, they occupied Alexandria in March. In fact, it wasn't just a setback: it was a minor disaster which cost hundreds of British soldiers' lives.

THE ROSETTA TRAP
Egypt 1807

By this time Napoleon Bonaparte, 'Boney' as he was unaffectionately known to his British foes, had long been not only the main British bogeyman but also a most convenient scapegoat, for his imperial plans (real or imaginary) always served as a suitable screen, or excuse, for Britain's own imperialist designs.

A few intimidated remnants of the French fleet, skulking in the harbours of Toulon and Cadiz, were all that was left of France's Mediterranean squadrons, destroyed, shattered, sunk or captured at Trafalgar. But, the British maintained, the French threatened Egypt. So, just as Bonaparte had done in 1798, they had decided to occupy Alexandria and the other Egyptian Mediterranean coastal cities while assuring the Sublime Porte of the purity of their intentions.

On March 6, a few days after Duckworth's exit from the Dardanelles, a British army of some six thousand men (including a thousand Sicilians and a thousand Germans) sailed from Messina for Alexandria, where they arrived ten days later. The Egyptian port, weakly defended, surrendered on the 21st.

General Alexander Mackenzie Fraser, who commanded the army, was a Scotsman, like so many of the British army officers of his day. He was fifty-five years of age, 'an open, generous, honourable Highland chieftain', a fine soldier but a dreadful general. Hence, after the recent Dardanelles disaster, another disaster lay ahead.

On March 29 he sent sixteen hundred men under his even less able second-in-command General Wauchope, a Scotsman too, to attack and take nearby Rosetta. Wauchope was one of those no-nonsense, officers who believed that the sight of a British uniform should be enough to terrify the enemy and provoke him into immediate flight or surrender. No artillery was needed, he said. The gates of the town were open. No defenders could be seen along the walls. He didn't send any scouts ahead to investigate. It was a waste of time. He barked an order or two and marched at the head of his troops into the narrow and crooked little alleys of the town.

It was exactly as Buenos Aires was to be three months later. Suddenly, from every window and from every rooftop, a withering fire was poured down upon the British who could neither take shelter nor find a target upon which to fire. Four hundred men were killed, including General Wauchope. The rest made their way out of Rosetta as best they could and back to Alexandria. The Turkish soldiers then went about methodically cutting off the heads of all the dead and wounded (including General Wauchope's) and placing them on spikes along the road leading into town, for the delectation of passersby.

To wipe away this disgrace, General Fraser decided upon a second attack on Rosetta, to be led by General William Stewart, yet another Scotsman. This time 2,500 men, including elite Highland regiments, were in the attacking force. They reached the walls of Rosetta around mid-April, carefully abstained from marching in and, instead, surrounded and laid siege to the town.

Unfortunately the besiegers were outnumbered by Turks from outside, both infantry and cavalry, who attacked the British positions on April 21st and cut the besieging force to pieces. About a thousand Britons were killed, another thousand fled and the remaining five hundred surrendered.

Survivors chaotically made their way back to Alexandria where the Irish surgeon, Captain Barry O'Meara, later Napoleon's friend and physician on St Helena, attended to the wounded in what had been General Menou's stables during the French occupation.

Thanks, of all people, to the French consul in Rosetta, M. Drovetti, to whom General Fraser later wrote a warm letter of thanks, the British prisoners were well-treated by the Turks. Fraser, not knowing what else he was supposed to be doing in Egypt besides occupying Alexandria, remained there until mid-September when he capitulated, recovered his prisoners and, like the French six years before, shook the sands of Egypt forever from his feet. The only lasting result of the expedition were a few hundred spiked British heads rotting in the sun outside Rosetta.

Britain carried out one more attack against a neutral that year, and this time it was a huge success. Fearing that Denmark might cede her fleet to France, the British Foreign Minister George Canning ordered the Danes to hand their ships over to the British navy. The Danes refused and in late August 1807, a British fleet sailed to Denmark under Admiral Lord Gambier, while a British army under General Lord Cathcart – with Wellington in command of a brigade – landed near Copenhagen.

The outnumbered and outgunned Danes surrendered. Sixty-nine ships, including sixteen battleships and ten frigates, were captured. On land Wellington had 172 casualties and was one of the three British commissioners to countersign the Danish capitulation. British naval losses were nil. Danish army and navy casualties amounted to approximately 540. The booty carried away from the city filled a hundred British ships, and most of Copenhagen was burned to impress the natives. Denmark joined Napoleon and for a while Britain had a naval guerrilla war on its hands.

Gambier, let it be said in passing, was not a great warrior. He preferred a desk at the Admiralty to the quarterdeck of a ship-of-the-line, and the singing of hymns to the roar of guns. In whatever ship he commanded, morning, noon and evening prayers were *de rigueur*.

During these wars missionary activities continued unabated in the most distant parts of the world. In the late 1790s, while assigned to the Admiralty, Gambier gave so much help to some London Missionary Society people in obtaining the supplies they required before sailing to the South Seas that the grateful Captain Wilson, of the missionary ship *Duff*, gave the name of Gambier to a group of islands he discovered in the South Pacific. The Gambier Islands are now part of French Polynesia and the French nuclear bomb-testing site, Mururoa, is their nearest neighbour.

CHAPTER NINETEEN

Trespassers in the Far East

HARA-KIRI IN NAGASAKI
Japan 1808

Several countries in south-east Asia played a role in the Napoleonic saga, notably Indonesia, the Philippines and Malaya. The events that took place in Manila and Indonesia, particularly in Java, are narrated elsewhere in this book. In the Malayan peninsula the British had established themselves in Penang a few years before the war as the first step towards the gradual takeover of the whole country, and during the war they seized Malacca from the Dutch.

In the Far East, China and Japan also figured fleetingly in the conflict. The Napoleonic war led to several suicides in Nagasaki and to one Royal Marine casualty in the port of Canton.

The Japanese casualties resulted from an impromptu visit by the British frigate HMS *Phaeton* into Nagasaki bay one fine October morning in the year 1808.

The unauthorised arrival of this ship, commanded by Captain Fleetwood Pellew, the nasty son of Admiral Pellew, was greeted with dismay by the local officials. Japan, at the time, was closed to all foreigners except the Dutch who were, at regular intervals, allowed into the port of Nagasaki to trade. Holland was allied to France and Sir Edward Pellew's twenty-seven-year-old son wished to see whether any Dutch ships were around to be taken as prizes.

Pellew discovered nothing, peremptorily ordered the Japanese to deliver water, food and a few goats and cattle to his ships and sailed away the next day. But ashore there had been consideable face-losing during the past twenty-four hours. The governor of Nagasaki and his five top military commanders, having shown themselves unable to cope adequately with this unexpected foreign intrusion, all honourably committed hara-kiri by cutting their bellies open with their samurai daggers. Three Japanese interpreters, being of a lower social order, were ordered to go and drown themselves as a gesture of atonement. And so the Napoleonic Wars passed over Japan.

THE CANTON AFFRAY
China 1808

It was the Chinese turn the next month to become involved in what must have seemed to them the totally incomprehensible Round Eyes' war.

Admiral O'Brien Drury, Admiral Pellew's recently arrived replacement as commander-in-chief of the Indian station, a stern but humane man, was urged by officials of the East India Company to seize Macao, a weakly-defended trading outpost on the Chinese coast near Canton which the Portuguese, Britain's allies, were occupying with the permission of the Chinese emperor.

The ostensible reason for this little act of aggression against an ally was to save Macao from the French, although Napoleon had no military or naval forces, except for an occasional frigate, for thousands of miles around.

Drury gathered off Penang his invading force, made up of several transports, HMS *Dedaigneuse*, a former French frigate captured seven years ago off Portugal, and once again, the *Phaeton*, just back from its Nagasaki jaunt. Admiral Drury sailed off to Macao with his little fleet and a thousand British sailors and marines, a force large enough, he hoped, to impress the Portuguese who had virtually no military force in the settlement. As expected, the Portuguese wrung their hands helplessly and allowed their powerful and threatening allies into Macao. At the insistence of the East India Company's representatives, anxious to protect their tea business with a show of naval strength, Drury then agreed to push upriver to Whampoa, the port area of Canton.

Well aware of his great numerical inferiority to the Chinese, and concerned lest a badly-timed shot might precipitate a general action with them, Drury, brave but prudent, rowed up the last stretch of the river in his admiral's barge with just a small escort. His plan was to meet the local Chinese commodore and discuss seriously with him, perhaps over a cup of East India Company tea, the French threat to China, which happened to be non-existent.

Drury's appearance on the river did not, however, please the Chinese. Thousands of screaming Orientals lined both banks and pelted the silent and dignified British admiral and his sweating rowers with stones, bits of wood, rotten fruit and vegetables, anything on which they could lay their hands. A flotilla of Chinese navy junks, moored across the river, fired one shot, and one only, at the intruders. It went right over their heads and fell harmlessly in the water. A Royal Marine was struck on the head by a stone. He was the only British casualty.

There were no Chinese casualties. To his credit, Drury never fired back at 'this strange and almost totally defenceless rabble', as he described them in his report to the Lords of Admiralty. No Chinese commodore was on hand to greet him, so Drury decided that a dignified withdrawal was in order, and he retired to his squadron.

Sometime later, the Chinese emperor, in a haughty letter, advised Drury that he was quite able to defend his realm against the French without British help, and as Macao had been leased to the Portuguese and not to the British, he requested Drury to get himself and his fleet out of there.

Drury, a reasonable man, sailed away. Thus, as he wrote in his report, ended 'the most mysterious, extraordinary and scandalous' affair of his career.

When China wakes the world will tremble, Napoleon once said. Perhaps Drury had subconsciously felt during his few days in China its immense latent power and had preferred to do nothing to wake the giant who was to lie dormant for another century and a half.

CHAPTER TWENTY

The British Lion Roars

THE CAYENNE ASSAULT
1809

In late 1808 the British began to wonder why the French were still masters of most of their colonies even though Britain was mistress of all the seas.

In spite of their difficulties in shipping supplies and sending reinforcements overseas, the French had only lost St Lucia and Tobago, and that had been five years ago. Guadeloupe and Martinique were still defiantly free; Santo Domingo, besieged and surrounded by hostile blacks and Spaniards, was still French. Frigates and privateers operating out of Mauritius and Réunion were still pestering British shipping in the Indian Ocean and resting and recreating in the Seychelles. More privateers, operating out of Senegal and French Guyana, were active in mid-Atlantic. French army detachments, allied to the Dutch, were helping to guard Java.

In Europe too, Napoleon's control of the continent – except for rebellious Spain – had rarely been more complete. He was Emperor of the French and King of Italy. His brother Louis was King of Holland. Another brother, Joseph, was King of Spain – although his elevation to the Spanish throne had brought about the Peninsular War. His youngest brother, Jerome, after a disastrous stint as a naval officer, was now King of Westphalia in Germany, and his sister Caroline was married to Joachim Murat, King of Naples. Prussia was crushed and dismembered. Then Austria, after her defeat at Wagram in 1809, was obliged to become France's ally.

In the Iberian peninsula, the French had forced the British army, under Sir John Moore, to evacuate Spain after the long retreat to Corunna. The gallant Moore was killed covering the evacuation and the irascible General Sir David Baird, Wellington's old rival in India, took over the command and had his hand shot off in the fighting.

Later Wellington led all the British troops in Spain and Portugal, and the Peninsular War remains, after Waterloo, the finest of his triumphs. Now that Nelson was lying in his vault in St Paul's and no longer available for public adulation, Wellington took his place as Britain's Public Hero No. 1.

The records are more discreet about Wellington's private life at this time. His marriage with Kitty Pakenham rocked along and she had given him a son, Richard, a couple of years previously. Her disorderly habits as a housewife infuriated him and he would write her bitter letters of reproach over trifling unpaid household bills. She lived in an agony of self-reproach over her bookkeeping failures. His relations with her brother, the affable Colonel Edward Pakenham, were better and the two men were good friends, although Wellington always said his brother-in-law, Ned as he called him, could have done with a few more brains.

Napoleon too, about this time, was having great personal problems and 1809 was in fact an important year in his life. First, since Josephine had failed to give him a child, he divorced her to her great anguish, and prepared for his second marriage with the eighteen-year-old Archduchess Marie-Louise, the nice, well-rounded, blonde, blue-eyed daughter of Francis I, Emperor of Austria, an alliance which he hoped would seal the legitimacy of the upstart Bonaparte dynasty in the haughty royal circles of Europe.

Second, in the face of all these Napoleonic successes and pretensions the time had come, Britain decided, not only to fight France at her doorstep, in Spain, but also to wrest her colonies from her – and, particularly, to put an end once and for all to French threats to British domination of the Caribbean, and of India, Australia and the Eastern Seas.

It was in South America, in French Guyana, that the French colonial collapse began.

Cayenne was the first French tropical town to fall to the British assault, in this case acting in conjunction with their Portuguese allies in Brazil.

The peripatetic admiral, Sir Sidney Smith, was commander-in-chief of the expedition, although this time he exerted his command from faraway Rio de Janeiro. He seemed to be all over the world. After taking part in Duckworth's mishandled expedition up the Dardanelles, he had rushed to Lisbon in November 1807, to command the convoy that transported the mad Queen Maria I of Portugal, her regent son Joao VI and the Portuguese court and government to exile in Rio de Janeiro while the French armies, under General Junot, occupied the

Portuguese capital.

After his arrival in Brazil, Sidney Smith had remained in the South Atlantic as commander in chief of the South American Station where he spent most of his time quarrelling violently with the British minister to the Portuguese court, Lord Strangford, over the extent of his command, which Sir Sidney claimed included Buenos Aires (important because of the prize money involved). However, he did find time between abusive letters to the British diplomat to order Captain James Yeo, of HMS *Confiance*, to attack and take Cayenne. This French tropical town defended by four hundred French regulars, with six hundred part-time militiamen and two hundred blacks, was the next obvious target.

Yeo first went to Belem, the Brazilian port at the mouth of the Amazon, where he was joined by two Portuguese vessels, the 24-gun brig, the *Voador*, and the 64-gun *Infante Don Pedro*, and a force of some eight hundred Portuguese and Brazilian soldiers under Lieutenant-Colonel Manoel Marques. One of Marques's officers, the Amazonian Tupi chief, Lieutenant Goncalves, covered in red 'roucou' pigment from head to foot, was later to play a prominent part in the surrender of Victor Hugues to the allied force.

The *Confiance*, along with the two Portuguese ships, seized a French post on the Oyapok River on December 8, 1808 and, a week later, attacked another post on the Appruage River, farther north. In those days, French Guyana extended all the way down to just above the north shore of the Amazon River, and its governor, Victor Hugues, the former bloodthirsty master of Guadeloupe, had been as busy reinstating slavery there since 1800 as, in the previous years, he had been eradicating it in Guadeloupe.

Cayenne was a colourful little town. Indians from the whole region used to come and go around the French colonial settlement as they wished and no one paid any particular attention to the roucou-tinted Goncalves when he strolled, in his plumes and half-naked, into town one morning. But, just the same, the servants in the governor's mansion were surprised when he walked in and was received by the governor himself. Goncalves warned Hugues that Cayenne would soon be attacked and advised him not to resist too much, otherwise the colony would be taken over by the British instead of the more neighbourly Portuguese. Then he strolled away again, and rejoined his unit in the Portuguese army.

The joint British and Portuguese expeditionary force landed at the Mahury River estuary, east of Cayenne, on January 7, 1809. Yeo, leading a party of marines and bluejackets in ten canoes, took the strong point of Fort Diamant for the loss of only six men, wounded. The Portuguese under Major Joaquim Manoel Pinto carried the gun battery of Degard de Cannes. Three days later Hugues was asking for terms.

French resistance had been slight, perhaps because of the advice given
by Goncalves to Hugues. Sixteen men were killed on the French side.
Portuguese losses amounted to one man killed and eight wounded.
There were twenty-four casualties among the crew of HMS *Confiance*.

French Guyana became part of Brazil and remained so for five years,
until the new Portuguese governor Joao Severiano Maciel da Costa returned the colony to Louis XVIII, who was by then back on the
French throne. But the Portuguese kept about half of Guyana, all the
land south of the Oyapok River down to the Amazon. It is now part of
the Brazilian territory of Amapa. The Brazilians, friendly to France
but a little suspicious, still discriminate against French citizens in
Amapa. It is the only part of Brazil where, to this day, no Frenchman is
allowed to own property, a curious but lasting side-effect of the
Napoleonic Wars.

The treacherous, opportunistic Hugues who had caused so many
deaths and so much distress, who had ordered so many horrible executions in Guadeloupe, returned to Guyana after the war to attend to his
business interests. There he caught leprosy, went blind and died in misery and want. However hideous his sufferings, he deserved them all.
Let that be his epitaph.

THE MARTINIQUE ATTACK
1809

The fall of the island of Martinique followed the month after
Cayenne's. A vast British armada of forty-one vessels, commanded by
Admiral Alexander Cochrane with his flag on the 98-gun HMS *Nep-
tune*, sailed from Barbados on January 28, 1809 with an accompanying army of ten thousand men under General George Beckwith –
another specialist, like his friend Craufurd, in light infantry tactics.
Aboard the old HMS *Pompée*, Commodore George Cockburn, arrogant and condescending as ever, was second-in-command of the naval
squadron. Also present at the landing was Captain Beaver's HMS
Acasta which six months before had captured the *Serpent* off the coast
of Venezuela.

Two days later the invasion fleet arrived off Martinique, meagrely
defended by a force of 2,400 regulars plus the usual ineffective militia.
There were also a few French naval bits and pieces around to defend the
island: the 40-gun frigate *Amphitrite*, the *Diligente*, 18, and the *Carnation*, 18, a captured Royal Navy vessel.

Wellington's brother-in-law, the slightly stupid and very brave
Colonel Edward Pakenham, was in the landing. He still carried his
head at a stiff angle from the musketball that had hit him in the neck
during the fighting for the island of St Lucia six years ago. He was hit in
the neck again, this time from the other side. His head was jerked back

into its normal upright position, and he thus became from then on one of the medical freaks of the British army.

The British carried out three landings: 3,000 men at Pointe Sainte-Luce, 600 at Cap Solomon and 6,500 on the north side of Baie Robert under Sir George Prevost, former captain-general of Dominica.

There were no French troops to oppose the landing, only a few hundred local militia who gathered uneasily near the beaches, watched the British arriving in their thousands, shrugged their shoulders at the helplessness of it all, went home, took off their uniforms and went back to their daily civilian tasks as planters, clerks, traders, artisans and shopkeepers.

The fighting for Martinique took just over three weeks and cost the British five hundred and sixty men.

Although, since the collapse of the Peace of Amiens, British and French had been at war for six years, the British had never yet taken one of the famed French eagles, the almost sacred standards which Napoleon's soldiers carried in battle and swore to defend with their lives. It was in Martinique that the British captured their first Napoleonic eagle and they immediately and jubilantly sent it to England to show to the king.

Fort-de-France, after a five-day bombardment, fell on February 24. The bag of French prisoners came to over two thousand.

After capturing Martinique, the British seized the nearby tiny Saintes islands in April. Only Guadeloupe remained to be taken in the West Indies, but it was a name which, since the Victor Hugues days, carried a horrible flavour of terror, of fierce, desperate fighting, of carrion and death, of decapitated heads grimacing in a last spasm of fear as they rotted in the tropical sun. The British hesitated to attack. It was not until nearly a year later that General Beckwith took the offensive.

THE SANTO DOMINGO AFFAIR
1808-1809

Napoleon's efforts to inflict his brother Joseph on the Spaniards as their king misfired not only in Spain but also in the Spanish colonies, which turned en masse against their former French allies. French and Spanish were now enemies and General Ferrand's troops in Santo Domingo suddenly found themselves in the middle of a hostile people.

The French general received his first intimation of this new situation on August 10, 1808 when an envoy sent by the Spanish governor of Puerto Rico advised him that their two countries were now at war. Shortly afterwards Spanish forces landed in the eastern part of the island of Hispaniola and the French who in their time had been rather revolutionary themselves, complained that the very air of Santo Domingo became 'impregnated with revolutionary miasma'. A new Spanish captain-general, Don Juan Sanchez, was appointed to direct the war against the French in Santo Domingo.

On November 7 the over-confident General Ferrand, with only five hundred men, attacked a Spanish army of twelve hundred infantry and six hundred cavalry at Palo Hincado on the Seybo River. The Spaniards waited until the French had deployed into lines, then poured a withering fire into them. Many of the French were killed or captured. The desperate Ferrand blew his brains out rather than surrender.

His second-in-command, General Joseph Barquier, a military hospital administrator, now took over. He retired back into the city and declared it in a state of siege. The Frenchmen, numbering around two thousand, were surrounded by a well-entrenched Spanish army. A British fleet came to join the besiegers and hovered offshore. Occasional schooners broke through bringing supplies to the French but the only food regularly available to them was a wild local plant called *gualliga* which, to be made edible, had to be boiled for six days.

On March 15, 1809 the French, more hungry than usual, called for a truce which Don Juan Sanchez refused, telling the French to put their trust in God. On May 11 eleven British ships-of-the-line took up their position outside the harbour and called upon the French to yield. When they prevaricated, eight of the guns from one of the battleships were landed and positioned ashore. On June 1 the shelling began. The French remained firm.

The next day four Royal Navy launches, each with forty men on board, came into the harbour to attack some anchored French boats. The French sank one, killing all on board but one. The others withdrew. On June 11, sixty women and children evacuated the town by sea to escape the deadly British bombardment. On the 20th Don Sanchez again asked the French to capitulate. Barquier again refused. On the 27th the British General Carmichael landed with fourteen hundred men and joined the Spaniards. On July 6 the French surrendered. The previous day, in Europe, Napoleon had won the Battle of Wagram. It was a splendid victory but finally it gained the Emperor nothing while the French defeat at Santo Domingo lost France one of the richest territories in the Caribbean.

On July 11, 1809, General Barquier, Carmichael and Sanchez had breakfast together and afterwards, under the terms of the capitulation, Barquier's honourably defeated little army embarked on parole. Most, black man and white, soldier and civilian, went to New Orleans, some six thousand including women and children. Some two thousand were white. Some ultimately returned to France, others stayed in Louisiana. Many of the Santo Domingo veterans were to fight against the British again five years later, at the Battle of New Orleans, this time under the Stars and Stripes.

THE FALL OF GUADELOUPE
1810

Admiral Cochrane and General Beckwith sailed from occupied Martinique in January 1810 to take Guadeloupe. Beckwith had seven thousand troops. The French general Ernouf had some three thousand men to defend Guadeloupe, which included regulars, semi-trained militia and untrained blacks.

The British landed at several points on the island on January 27, 1810 and gradually made their way over rugged mountain terrain, through weak resistance, to Basse-Terre where Ernouf hoped to make his stand. But by this time most of his army had been demolished and, in this final confrontation, he had only one regiment of the line to oppose to the entire enemy force.

After a couple of days' skirmishing the French white flag went up on February 3. In a week's fighting, the British had suffered three hundred casualties, including fifty-two men killed. The French lost between six and eight hundred. Another eight hundred French soldiers vanished into the bush to escape capture and 1,309 were shipped to the hulks and prisons of England.

Beckwith then rapidly took over the few Dutch islands in the Caribbean, the sugar trade was assured, and the West Indies ceased to be one of the major theatres of war.

Sweetening the tea of an Englishman had proved expensive in terms of human life. Since that first attack on Martinique way back in 1793, in terms of human life it had meant slavery for hundreds of thousands of black plantation workers and death for tens of thousands of British sailors and soldiers – perhaps as many as a hundred thousand including all the smaller islands and Haiti.

Trying to strangle British trade had been just as devastating for the French. Perhaps a hundred thousand of them also lost their lives in these pestilential spots where Club Méditerranée resorts now flourish and topless bikinied Parisian girls strive for a quick tropical suntan.

All the islands in the Caribbean remained under the control of Britain, or her ally Spain, until the end of the war – with the exception of the Haitian part of Hispaniola, partitioned between mulattos and blacks, where violent civil war intermittently raged.

THE SENEGAL SURRENDER
1809

The depredations of the privateers based in St Louis, in the French colony of Senegal, doomed that isolated colony also.

As we read in an earlier chapter, one of the two French settlements in

Senegal, Gorée, had been accidentally taken from the French by a convict ship in 1804. The governor, Colonel Blanchot de Verly, never bothered subsequently to send an expedition from St Louis to retake it, perhaps because he was too old – sixty-seven at the time – and lacked the energy to do so after twenty-seven years in the tropics. He died three years later and his second-in-command, Captain Levasseur, took over St Louis and awaited the arrival of Blanchot's successor, Colonel Pinoteau. Pinoteau failed to arrive but the British did, two years after Blanchot's death, and it took them less than a week to conquer the rest of Senegal.

The British expedition was organised from Gorée. Major Charles Maxwell, who commanded the small British garrison there, and Captain Edward Henry Columbine, RN, who was the senior officer in the establishment, decided to combine forces and capture the French outpost. The naval support came from two frigates, a brig, a transport, a schooner, and a number of even smaller vessels all assembled to give the appearance of a larger and more heavily armed force than was the case.

Major Maxwell led a troop of a hundred and sixty-six soldiers drawn from the Gorée garrison and the expedition sailed on July 4, 1809 reaching St Louis three days later. Three hundred and thirty sailors, soldiers and marines landed on the 8th. The British ships bombarded the French positions and by the 13th it was all over. The French garrison surrendered and Senegal was ruled by Britain for the next five years.

St Louis and Gorée were restored to France after the return of the exiled Louis XVIII, and it was the wreck of the frigate *La Méduse*, bringing French Royalist troops to reoccupy the colony, on a sandbank off the Senegalese coast that inspired Gericault's famous painting 'The Raft of the Méduse' that hangs in the Louvre Museum in Paris.

Senegal became the springboard for French colonialism in Africa and it is from there that much of the continent absorbed the culture and values, notably the cuisine, which distinguish French-speaking from English-speaking Africa. Anyone who, in the equatorial heat at noon, has been offered toad-in-the-hole for lunch, followed by bread-and-butter pudding as dessert, two well-known English delicacies, will know exactly what I mean.

THE IONIAN SIREN CALL
1809-1810

By a secret clause in the 1807 Treaty of Tilsit, the youthful Tsar Alexander I, who was then still under the influence of Napoleon, had ceded France the Ionian islands; since a joint Russo-Turkish force had defeated and expelled the French in 1799, these had been officially known by the awkward name of Septinsular Republic.

Although nominally a tributary and vassal of Turkey the islanders, mainly Christian orthodox by religion, had naturally turned to the Tsar for support and the islands had become a virtual protectorate of Russia. But Alexander had been happy to hand them back to the French in 1807 to please his friend the Emperor.

Napoleon, delighted at their return, sent a mixed French-Italian force to occupy the islands and appointed as governor the fussy, insufferable General César Berthier, formerly in command at Tobago. Napoleon was anxious for the islands to fall within his control quickly and Berthier arrived in Corfu on August 3, 1807, only three weeks after the signing of the Tilsit Treaty. But his sharp, vexatious manner made him as disliked by the Greeks of Corfu as he had been by the West Indians of Tobago and in March the following year he was replaced by General Donzelot, 'a man of talent and integrity' as a British contemporary called him, who had served recently against Prussia and Russia, and who was with us earlier, fighting against Murad Bey with Desaix up the Nile Valley.

Donzelot's first eighteen months in Corfu and the beautiful Ionian isles were idyllically peaceful. But in the autumn of 1809, the American loyalist general, Sir John Stuart, who commanded the British in Sicily, sent an army to establish a bridgehead at the entrance to the Adriatic, on the Ionian islands of Zante and Cephalonia, which were defended by five hundred French and Italian soldiers.

General Sir John Oswald, a soldier of wide Mediterranean experience, sailed from Palermo on September 23 at the head of eighteen hundred troops, reached Zante a week later and first sent a landing party ashore of six hundred Corsican Rangers under his second-in-command, Colonel Hudson Lowe. There was no fighting. The outnumbered garrison capitulated promptly to the British – or perhaps one should say, more correctly, to the Corsicans. For Hudson Lowe, it was a welcome little victory. He had recently ignominiously surrendered the island of Capri to the French.

Oswald, leaving Hudson Lowe and his Corsicans fraternising with the locals on Zante, then sailed on to Cephalonia, held by two hundred men who also surrendered without resisting the invaders.

General Oswald deserved these easy victories. He was a capable soldier, had fought in 1794 in Martinique, Guadeloupe and St Lucia, been wounded in Holland, blockaded Malta, fought in Calabria and in Egypt a couple of years before. A handsome man, over six feet tall, he had attended the same military school at Brienne as Napoleon, but just after the future Emperor of the French had left for the army. At Brienne Oswald became a lifelong friend of Bourrienne, Napoleon's future secretary.

The capture of these two islands had been so simple that Oswald sent one of his officers, twenty-five-year-old Captain Richard Church, with some British infantry and Corsican Rangers to attack two other islands in the group, Ithaca and Cerrigo, hoping they would fall just as easily into British hands. They did. Both capitulated without firing a shot.

After securing Ithaca and Cerrigo, Church raised a regiment of light Greek infantry to defend the islands, to the anger of the nearby Turks on the mainland: they feared that these tough soldiers might become a spearhead for future Greek independence from Turkish rule.

General Oswald was aware that the two French-occupied islands to the north, Santa Maura and Corfu, might attack the weakly-held British islands. So, five months later, on March 22, 1810, he resumed the Ionian campaign by invading Santa Maura at the head of 2,500 men.

The attacking British army included Hudson Lowe with his Corsican Rangers, Church with his light Greek infantrymen fighting under the Greek flag, two companies of Royal Marines and some German mercenaries.

Santa Maura was defended by a thousand French regulars and by Greek irregulars. Half of the latter deserted to the attackers' Greek standard. General Louis Camus, who commanded the French troops, fought a delaying action which cost the British a hundred and thirty casualties, while his men retreated into the fortress of Amaxichi.

There was only one way to beat the French, strongly entrenched within their casemates, and that was to batter them into submission. After nearly ten days' bombardment, General Camus's men were ready to give in. On April 16, eight hundred survivors marched out, leaving two hundred corpses behind them.

The Ionian Islands, however, were not fully vanquished. General Donzelot was still holding the most important of all, Corfu. With four thousand French soldiers defending it, it was considered too strong to be attacked. In consequence Donzelot was still holding out four years later when Napoleon abdicated for the first time in April 1814 and left for Elba.

Louis XVIII, who now ruled France, ordered General Donzelot to surrender Corfu to General Sir James Campbell, the new commander of the British forces in the Ionian Sea. A disciplined soldier, Donzelot obeyed. But he rallied to Napoleon when the Emperor escaped from Elba in March 1815, and he followed him to Waterloo and final defeat.

As for General Camus, he was captured in Russia during the retreat in 1812 and died from exhaustion a few months later, perhaps thinking of those enchanted Greek islands of mythology in the warm, blue Adriatic, so different to the cold, snowy, vast wasteland where he lived out his last miserable months.

CHAPTER TWENTY-ONE

The Indian Ocean Campaign

THE HAMELIN DIVISION
Mauritius 1808-1809

The record of the French frigates that sailed the Eastern Seas during the Napoleonic Wars provides one of the few inspiring pages of the French naval history of this period. The British historian Clowes recounts some of their adventures and actions in his history of the Royal Navy and even praises, at last, the 'remarkable skills' (the words are his) and the seamanship of their crews.

Consider the 40-gun *Canonnière* (ex HMS *Minerva*) commanded by Captain Bourayne, who successfully fought off two British battle-ships, HMS *Tremendous*, 74, and HMS *Hindustan*, 50, off the coast of East Africa. With his seasoned crew he then sailed to Manila, across the Pacific to Acapulco in Mexico, back to the Philippines and finally on to Mauritius. The whole expedition – the word seems singularly appropriate for such a long voyage – took from May 1806 to July 1808, more than two years. The purpose of the voyage to Mexico was to bring back to Manila a three-million piastre cargo of coins required in the Philippines for specie, as none of the Spanish ships in Manila harbour was in a state to undertake the voyage. On the return journey, after repelling HMS *Fox* and HMS *Caroline*, in Manila harbour, Bourayne sailed back to Mauritius on March 19, 1808 (the sick sailors of his crew all replaced by Filipinos), captured three British vessels off the coast of Sumatra and was back in Port-Louis on July 13, just in time to celebrate Bastille Day the next day. Two months later the *Canonnière* captured the 22-gun HMS *Laurel* after a brisk ninety-minute fight off the French island. Adjudged unfit for further service, she was sold a few

The Battle of Grand Port. Attack on French frigates by *Nereide* at the battle of Grand Port, Mauritius, 2 August 1810

months later, disarmed and sent back to France with Captain Bourayne aboard as passenger. She was captured and so was he. He remained in captivity in England for four years.

One of the few occasions in naval history when a ship was forced to surrender because it ran out of ammunition occurred on March 8, 1808 when the French frigate, *Piemontaise*, commanded by Captain Jean Epron, had to strike to HMS *San Fiorenzo* after a forty-eight-hour fight off the coast of Sri Lanka. The *Piemontaise*, when she struck, having no more cannonballs to fire, had suffered a hundred and forty-one casualties, fifty-nine of whom were dead. HMS *San Fiorenzo* lost thirteen men killed and twenty-five wounded. One of the dead was her new captain, George Hardinge, struck by grape shot.

The raiding by the French naval frigates and by the privateers continued for years in the Indian Ocean to the despair of shippers, merchants and insurers in India and Britain. Between 1803 and 1810, no less than a hundred and twenty-seven British merchant vessels, many of them East Indiamen, all captured by the handful of French ships operating in these waters, were brought into the two ports of Mauritius. Others were taken to Réunion and to Java. Still others were sunk or ransomed. British businessmen who needed a scapegoat blamed first Admiral Rainier for their losses. After his departure, Admiral Pellew became the target of their often vicious verbal attacks. They could not understand why the large British army and navy in India did not occupy the weakly-defended island of Mauritius, from where nearly all the French raids originated.

Neither could Napoleon.

Decaen's brother René, sent to Paris again as the captain-general's envoy, was summoned on January 27, 1808 to appear before the Emperor. 'Why haven't the British taken the island?' Napoleon asked him brusquely.

René Decaen replied that the British knew how militarily weak Mauritius was, but, he added, it owed its security to Napoleon's unpredictable moves in the Middle East and on the European continent which kept the British off-balance, fearful of an attack on India.

The British remained aloof for another couple of years. A new governor-general had arrived in India the previous year. It was Lord Minto, better known to us as Sir George Elliot, the dismal former commissioner in Toulon and viceroy of Corsica, raised to the peerage after his two failures, perhaps as a consolation prize. Lord Minto, who fancied himself as a military strategist, was concerned over the continued French presence in the Indian Ocean and was determined to bring it to an end.

In 1809, there were four new French frigates in Mauritius and their arrival had caused British merchants great concern and despondency. The latest newcomer was Captain Jacques Hamelin, who had commanded the *Naturaliste* in Baudin's expedition to Australia. After his return to France, he was one of the few officers who had managed to serve with a certain amount of dash in the dead-end Boulogne invasion fleet, by making occasional sorties when British ships were hovering offshore.

He was now in command of what the worried British called 'the Hamelin Division', composed of the four frigates *Manche*, *Caroline*, *Bellone* and *Vénus*, and two corvettes, one of which, the *Victor*, was commanded by Motard's able former First Lieutenant, Abel Roussin.

The other corvette, the *Créole*, had recently accompanied Hamelin on his flagship, the *Vénus*, to Sumatra where the two French vessels had destroyed the British post of Tapanoly. Hamelin, soon afterwards, captured three prized East Indiamen. The *Bellone* had recently captured the Portuguese Goa-based frigate, the 52-gun *Minerva*, almost a battleship. The *Caroline* had recently taken two Indiamen.

Five large, powerful, well-armed and well-laden East Indiamen captured in one year! That was too much for the Company to accept. Mauritius, 'that nest of pirates' as outraged British businessmen called it, must be taken.

SUICIDE FOR THE GENERAL
Réunion 1809-1810

From 1809, British strategy seemed motivated by one single worldwide purpose: attack, attack, attack. Spain, the West Indies, South America, West Africa, the Ionian islands, the Mascarenes, everywhere, at sea and on land, the British were on the offensive.

Considering the distances between these various battlefronts and the slowness of communications, these near-simultaneous assaults across the world must have been largely coincidental. But, even so the timing chanced to be excellent.

Everywhere, or nearly everywhere, the French were heavily outnumbered. Superiority – having the most men at the same place at the right time – is always the aim of a good general, and British military leaders knew their trade by now. 'It may be a politic idea to indulge, but an imprudent one to put into practice, that an Englishman can beat several Frenchmen at any time,' wrote an English writer in the nineteenth century. An Englishman may have felt that he was worth three Frenchmen but, as these campaigns show, the Redcoats often managed wisely to outnumber their enemy by three to one, and even more.

Among British targets, one of the most important that year was undoubtedly Mauritius, in the Indian Ocean.

'It is difficult to assign a reason why this measure [against Mauritius] has not been resorted to before, for the island has for many years nourished a vile nest of buccaneers against our Oriental commerce,' indignantly noted Captain Beaver in his diary on August 23, after his posting to the invasion fleet.

The first stage in the campaign against the Mascarenes (Mauritius: 700 square miles; Réunion: 980 square miles; Rodriguez: 40 square miles) began early in 1809 when the governor-general of India, Lord Minto, ordered the army and navy to take Rodriguez. The purpose was to establish a base from which to attack the two larger islands, about 300 miles from it.

In May 1809, a four hundred-man expedition, half British, half Indian sepoy, sailed from Bombay under the orders of Lieutenant-Colonel Keating. But there was no fighting on Rodriguez when the Anglo-Indian force landed on August 4. The entire population of the island consisted of three Frenchmen and eighty black slaves who grew vegetables for Mauritius and Réunion.

Once on Rodriguez, the restless Colonel Keating laid his plans next month to attack Réunion. He joined forces with Commodore Josias Rowley who, with his flag on the 38-gun HMS *Boadicea*, was in command of the small Royal Navy squadron that blockaded the French islands.

HMS *Nereide*, 36, and HMS *Otter*, 18, along with HMS *Boadicea*, sailed from Rodriguez on September 16. The two other ships were commanded by two of the most obnoxious officers in the Royal Navy, Captain Robert Corbett, for HMS *Nereide*, and Captain Nesbit Willoughby, in HMS *Otter*.

Corbett may have been a fighter but he was a detestable individual, hated by his crew. In 1808, when in command of HMS *Nereide*, his crew had issued a complaint of cruelty and oppression against him and had later mutinied. Ten men were condemned to death, but nine were finally pardoned after an investigation revealed that floggings were an almost habitual punishment on his ship, with knots tied in the cat-o' nine-tails to make the suffering more severe. Corbett was then himself court-martialled but, as was usual in the case of officers, found not guilty.

We have already seen Willoughby in action, heroically in Haiti, and more prosaically in the Dardanelles. In spite of his courage, Willoughby was one of the problem officers of the Royal Navy. An obstreperous and arrogant man, he had already been court-martialled four times (and was to go through a fifth trial) for insubordination, disobedience of orders, disrespectful behaviour, treating his captain with contempt, and most recently for cruelty. All his transgressions, except for the last, were rather endearing but this last one was not, for his victims this time were crewmen, not his superiors.

Captain Bligh, at his worst, was an angelic choirboy compared to Willoughby whose floggings were notorious throughout the squadron. 'I shall flog like hell,' he used to tell his cowed crew. 'I like to punish a man . . . as much as going to have my breakfast.' Charges of cruelty had finally been proferred against him the previous year in a complaint presented by the ship's company 'one and all'.

His five-day court martial, in February 1809, had found him not guilty, although he obviously was. But officers in those days, always terrified of mutiny, never failed to defend their own against accusations from the lower deck.

Corbett and Willoughby were joined off Réunion a few days later by the 64-gun battleship, HMS *Raisonnable*, and a frigate, HMS *Sirius*, 36, arriving off the little town of St Paul, in Réunion on September 21.

The soldiers, Royal Marines and bluejackets who formed the landing party – six hundred and four men – took the town by surprise early in the morning, seized the frigate *Caroline* and a few other vessels that were at anchor in the harbour, and chased out the garrison, only of company strength, while the unfortunate general in charge of the island's defences, General Nicolas des Brulys, wrung his hands in despair and wondered what to do.

Des Brulys was a tragic figure in the sequence of events that followed during the next few days. Once a brave and capable officer, twice wounded in the fighting in Flanders and Belgium in the 1790s, and before that an ensign with a French sepoy regiment in India, he had been imprisoned in Paris during the Terror and held in prison under the shadow of the guillotine for eighteen months. He had never recovered from the experience.

Feeling that with the small defence force he commanded, only six hundred men, he just couldn't cope with the situation, and afraid of being called back to Paris to face another vengeful tribunal, General des Brulys decided suicide was the only solution. His first impulse was to blow himself up and he tied two sausage-like bags of gunpowder round his neck. Then he decided to cut his throat with his razor instead. His wife found his body in the early hours of September 25. The shrieks of the unfortunate woman woke up his staff officers who were sleeping nearby. They could only view the general's corpse with dismay, try to obtain a truce from the British, bury him and consider their next move.

It was the British who moved. They emptied the warehouses, burnt what they could not take, loaded up their ships and sailed away, promising to be back. They kept their promise nine months later.

In Mauritius, General Decaen realised his island was now gravely threatened. The British were at Rodriguez, a few hundred miles away, and he now knew how weak his land forces were. But at least his frigates, all skippered by capable captains and manned by brave and resolute crews, could prove dangerous in any invasion attempt, in particular *Vénus*, *Bellone* and *Astrée*, the latest arrival from Cherbourg. They each carried 40 guns.

The *Vénus* was commanded by Captain Hamelin, not unfamiliar with these waters since he had been Nicolas Baudin's second-in-command in the expedition to Australia. The captain of the *Bellone*, Victor Duperré, had entered the navy from the merchant service during the Revolution, and had served in the West Indies. Captain René Lemarant de Kermadiel, of the *Astrée*, had also served in the Indian Ocean, and more recently had fought at Trafalgar.

These officers were no longer the unpractised, diffident sailors of previous years: they were of a younger generation and had been fashioned in the fire of republican and imperial combat, with already more than fifteen years of war service. They respected their Royal Navy foes but they were not afraid of them. In many respects they resembled, in their confidence and their ardour, their counterparts in the United States Navy who, in single combat, were soon to prove themselves often the equals and sometimes the superiors of the British. But unfortunately for the French, their own naval renaissance came too late to influence the course of the war at sea.

Réunion was again the target of the British in early July 1810. This time they not only raided the island. They invaded it and occupied it.

The British army, whites and sepoys, four thousand men strong, was still under the command of Keating, the navy was under Rowley's orders. Two vessels, recently arrived in the Indian Ocean, had joined the squadron: the 36-gun HMS *Iphigenia* (Captain Henry Lambert), and HMS *Magicienne* (Captain Lucius Curtis), another 36-gun frigate. Willoughby was now in command of HMS *Nereide* – her previous skipper, Captain Corbett, had gone to England to take over HMS *Africaine*, the former French frigate captured long ago off Gibraltar with General Desfourneaux and his four hundred men on board on their way to Egypt. Captain Samuel Pym commanded HMS *Sirius*. Under Duckworth, he had fought the French at Santo Domingo.

The French troops, pathetically few in numbers in Réunion, were under Colonel Sainte-Suzanne. Only one-third of his troops, a hundred and fifty men, were soldiers of the line. When the British sails were seen, the soldiers trotted round on shore, keeping the ships in view so as to be at the right spot when the enemy landed. This simple strategy unfortunately failed to work, for the British landed at three different points, on July 7 and 8.

The British hero of the day was thirty-three-year-old Captain Willoughby. He had, three weeks before, suffered severe injuries during an exercise when a musket exploded in his face. His lower jaw was shattered, his neck so torn that the windpipe was showing. But undaunted, his face and neck covered in bandages, shouting and swearing in spite of his lacerated throat, Willoughby organised the attack near the port of St Marie on July 7 and led ashore the landing party of four hundred sailors and a hundred and fifty soldiers.

Soon the British were teeming over the island. The outnumbered French went through the motions of defence but St Denis surrendered on the 9th and with the fall of St Paul the next day all resistance was over. The campaign had lasted three days and ninety-seven British soldiers had been killed or wounded.

Mauritius, a hundred miles to the north-east, was the next British objective.

THE BATTLE OF GRAND PORT
Mauritius 1810

After the British occupation of Rodriguez and their 1809 raid on Réunion, Decaen had hurriedly sent his ADC brother-in-law Captain Barois to Paris for the second time (his first visit had been in 1804 just before Napoleon's coronation, when the future Emperor had been much too busy to be interested in General Decaen's problems), to warn Napoleon now that unless reinforcements soon arrived in Mauritius, the island must inevitably fall to the British. He only had two thousand men to defend it.

Barois reached the French capital in February 1810. His timing was again disastrous. His arrival once more coincided with the approach of a great ceremonial occasion. This time he found the Emperor too engrossed with his forthcoming marriage to Princess Marie-Louise of Austria to be interested in General Decaen's Mauritius survival plans.

It was not until June 1810 that the Emperor found the time to look into the Mauritian question. He had been married two months and he now told Barois he might quite soon send fifteen hundred men to reinforce Decaen.

If Napoleon was slow to move, the British were not. Only one month after capturing Réunion they attacked Mauritius. The first landing took place on August 13, 1810. Captain Pym, acting as commodore, led the British naval squadron in HMS *Sirius*. HMS *Neireide*, HMS *Iphigenia* as well as a small 14-gun sloop, HMS *Staunch*, took part in the operation. Colonel Keating led the army detachment of one hundred and twelve soldiers. Their target: the Ile de la Passe, an islet at the entrance to the harbour of Grand Port, on the south-east side of Mauritius.

The British plan was to seize the Ile de la Passe and hold it as a propaganda centre from where to subvert the whole of Mauritius with political pamphlets telling the people, notably the always vulnerable, money-minded business community, why they would be better off under British rule than French. Psychological warfare is by no means a twentieth-century innovation. Ile de la Passe was also to provide a base from which to launch what we would call today commando raids against the main island.

Five boats under Captain Lambert's first lieutenant, Lieutenant Henry Chads, rowed quietly in under cover of darkness to attack the islet's small French garrison, which surrendered after killing and wounding twenty-five of the British attackers. Captain Willoughby, 'the most insatiable fire-eater in the king's navy' (as Fortescue describes him), then took over the command of the islet. He wasted no time. He established a garrison of fifty British grenadiers and four days later led in person a battalion of soldiers, marines and bluejackets twenty miles into enemy territory, distributing subversive literature to the bewildered locals. More propaganda raids followed on August 18, 19 and 20. Willoughby had become the Royal Navy's PR officer in the Eastern Seas.

On this last day, five strange sails were seen approaching Grand Port from the open sea. Willoughby, just back from his pamphlet raid, hastily hoisted the French colours on the fort – a legitimate stratagem in those days, as long as you did not fire until you had raised your true colours – and the unsuspecting ships sailed into the harbour. They proved to be two 40-gun French frigates, the *Bellone* (Captain Duperré) and the *Minerve* (Captain Bouvet), the 22-gun corvette

Victor (Captain Morice) and two East Indiamen prizes, the *Windham* and the *Ceylon*.

The French sailed right into the trap Willoughby had laid for them. It was just after lunchtime and Duperré's vessels were entering the pass into the harbour, just a few cable-lengths away from the fort, when the French flag flying above it suddenly came down, the White Ensign went up and the little *Victor* received a volley that shook its timbers. The fort then began to fire on the *Minerve*, killing several of her crew, but she sailed past the guns and on into the harbour where she anchored out of range.

Disregarding the gunfire, most of the other French ships followed and anchored a few cable-lengths from the *Minerve*. The first part of the Battle of Grand Port had ended almost as soon as it began.

Across the stretch of quiet, blue water, Frenchmen and Englishmen stared at each other and prepared for the next round of what was to be more an untidy, ferocious and murderous brawl than a naval battle.

There was not much room for manoeuvre in the limited inner reaches of the harbour, but both sides called for reinforcements: Duperré sent a messenger overland to Decaen in Port Louis where Hamelin and his squadron were on call. The frigates *Manche*, *Vénus* and *Astrée* prepared to sail as soon as they heard the British enemy was at Grand Port. Willoughby sent a cutter to warn Commodore Pym that he was no longer alone in Grand Port.

The British commodore was already aware of the changed situation. One of the French prizes, the Indiaman *Ceylon*, had reached the safety of the harbour, but the other, the *Windham*, had tried to flee and made for the open sea where she was captured by HMS *Sirius*.

An uneasy peace prevailed in the harbour the next morning, August 21, as the two foes confronted each other. Grand Port is a treacherous roadstead, with unexpected shoals and reefs scattered under its quiet surface. Duperré, who did not know the harbour, asked Bouvet, a local man, to take charge of the battle preparations. Bouvet ordered all the buoys marking the passages to be removed so as to hinder the British.

The next day, the 22nd, Commodore Pym in *Sirius* entered the harbour in the morning intending to join Willoughby's *Nereide*. But Pym's pilotless ship piled up on an underwater shelf in the shallows and it took until the next morning to get her off. As HMS *Sirius* was refloated, Pym and Willoughby were joined by HMS *Iphigenia* and HMS *Magicienne*, and at 4.40 pm the British frigates slowly and majestically moved into formation to attack.

In line of battle, like capital ships, the British frigates, four in number, their sails down and pushed only by the breeze on hulls and rigging and by the gentle currents of the bay, headed for the French squadron anchored in a cove in the north-west of the harbour, just a few hundred yards north of the town of Mahébourg where the whole population gathered along the waterfront to watch the coming battle.

The French ships, anchored close to the shore, prepared to repulse the enemy: two French frigates, a corvette and captured East Indiaman, against four British frigates. The British had every reason to feel confident of victory.

The second and vital round of the Battle of Grand Port was about to begin.

The sun was beginning to go down when, at 5.30 pm on August 23, the French ships fired their first broadside at the approaching British frigates advancing hesitatingly over the unmarked waters. On HMS *Sirius*, the watch failed to see the outline of the underwater shoals and the frigate, for the second time in two days, came to rest against a rock. The same accident then befell HMS *Magicienne*, but they were both near enough the French ships to continue firing. Only HMS *Iphigenia* reached her allotted spot without incident, about twelve hundred feet away from the French ships, which she could pound with all her starboard guns.

The French ships were also in trouble. The British fire cut ropes holding the anchored ships and they all drifted several cable-lengths towards land, with now only part of their artillery usable against the British. The corvette *Victor* drifted right out of the battle and took no part in it. The *Minerva* could only use four of her main guns, and five on the quarterdeck; the ex-Indiaman *Ceylon* was only able to bring nine of her guns to bear against the British.

HMS *Nereide*, some six hundred feet off the *Bellone* and abreast of her French enemy, lost her cable and drifted perilously close to all the French ships which then turned all their attention on her.

One of her first casualties was Captain Willoughby. A splinter struck his left cheek and tore the eye out of its socket. Then his first lieutenant was killed. Four other officers were also killed or wounded. More than 220 of her crew of 280 were casualties, including ninety-two killed. Willoughby, shouting and ranting, helplessly watched his ship and his men die in the night battle. At the start of the action he had defiantly nailed the Union Jack to the mizzen masthead in a 'victory or death' gesture, so typical of the man. The rigging of the mast was now shot away and although he wanted to surrender there was no way of climbing up the mast to tear the flag down. And while it flew, the French kept pounding his ship. Finally Willoughby ordered the mast to be cut down with axes. This last order may have lacked dignity, but at least it was effective. The mast crashed down on the deck, with the defiant flag attached to it, and the French then accepted Willoughby's surrender and stopped firing.

Aboard the French ships, Duperré was wounded by a round shot and handed the command of his flotilla to Bouvet, who moved his flag to the *Bellone*, leaving the command of the *Minerve* to his first lieutenant, the capable Abel Roussin.

Bouvet now concentrated the French squadron's fire on HMS *Magicienne* and at daylight on the next day, the 24th, the full extent of the French victory became apparent. The mastless, shattered and surrendered HMS *Nereide* lay a cable-length from the *Bellone*, her decks covered with corpses. HMS *Magicienne* and HMS *Sirius* were aground in midstream, the *Magicienne* firing an occasional defiant and useless shot. The guns of HMS *Sirius* were silent. Pym moved his crew over to HMS *Iphigenia*, while the French sailors watched with interest but without interfering. At eleven o'clock HMS *Sirius* blew up. HMS *Magicienne* went on firing intermittently until 5.00 pm when her captain transferred the survivors to HMS *Iphegenia* and blew his ship up too.

Of the four proud British frigates which had sailed in a few days ago, only the now overcrowded HMS *Iphigenia* remained afloat, preparing courageously but hopelessly for battle again.

The rest of the operation was mainly one of cleaning and tidying. For the next couple of days the French were hard at work refloating their ships. During the night of August 25, French sailors went aboard HMS *Nereide* and, in the words of the ship's log, 'committed the bodies of the slain to the deep.' It must have been an unpleasant task. There were many of them and, in the tropics, bodies rot quickly.

The two French frigates, seconded by a more lightly captured Indiaman, had destroyed or captured three more heavily armed British frigates. The second round of the Battle of Grand Port was over.

The third round was short, virtually eventless and totally bloodless. It began with the arrival in Grand Port on August 27 of Hamelin's squadron from Port Louis and ended the next day, after a few hours of negotiation, with Captain Lambert's surrender of HMS *Iphigenia*.

The British toll was now four frigates. French casualties were given as thirty-seven killed and a hundred and twelve wounded. Some seventeen hundred British soldiers, sailors and marines became prisoners of war, including four Royal Navy captains: Pym, Willoughby, Curtis and Lambert. The French victory was complete and the Battle of Grand Port deserves its inscription on the Paris Arc de Triomphe.

The British frigate squadron in the Indian Ocean was virtually destroyed and the people of Mauritius understandably believed that the threat to their island was over. Decaen, although he now had more prisoners to guard than soldiers to defend Mauritius, planned to go on the offensive and recapture Réunion and Rodriguez from the British.

In their elation, the French forgot that the British still had lots more ships and lots more soldiers in India and Cape Town. They were to appear in force in November. But meanwhile the French were to win two more frigate victories, two quick come-and-go frustrating battles in which the final victor was the unshakeable British mastery of the seas.

HMS *Africaine* and HMS *Ceylon* played the losing roles in these two engagements.

VANISHED VICTORIES
The Indian Ocean 1810

After the Battle of Grand Port, the command of Commodore Rowley in Réunion was reduced to three ships only: his own frigate the 38-gun HMS *Boadicea*, the 16-gun HMS *Otter*, and the 16-gun HMS *Staunch*. The old HMS *Iphiginia*, now rechristened without much imagination *L'Iphigénie* and captained by Bouvet, arrived off Réunion to blockade the British-held island on September 9 with the 40-gun *Astrée*, and the 14-gun brig *L'Entreprenante*. On the same day, HMS *Africaine*, with Captain Corbett in command, arrived back from England at Rodriguez on its way to India. When he learned the news from Grand Port, Corbett immediately sailed to join Rowley's squadron in Réunion.

By September 12, Corbett was off Réunion and joined Commodore Rowley's squadron in pursuit of the blockading French ships.

Speedier than her consorts, HMS *Africaine* drew ahead, overtaking *Astrée* and *Iphigénie*. With the usual Royal Navy bravado, Corbett engaged the two enemy ships while HMS *Boadicea* was still four miles behind.

Corbett had perhaps forgotten that these French sailors of the Eastern Seas were redoubtable foes and within a short time his ship was in shambles, with forty-nine men killed and a hundred and fourteen wounded. Corbett was among the casualties. A round shot carried away his right foot, a wooden splinter smashed his thigh and he died from his wounds shortly afterwards. His delighted crew heaved his body overboard. The fighting had started at 2.20 am and at 5.00 am the *Africaine* surrendered. Casualties on the two French frigates amounted to forty-five.

For the French it was a shortlived respite. Pym's three-ship squadron caught up with them seven hours later and the *Astrée* and the *Iphigénie*, outgunned, had to abandon their prize. It was an anti-climatic end to a great battle, the fifth straight victory in a few days by the Mauritian squadron. The sixth came four days later.

On September 18, another British frigate appeared in the Mascarenes. She was the 32-gun HMS *Ceylon* (not to be confused with the East Indiaman of the same name recently captured by the French).

HMS *Ceylon* had sailed from Madras to join Commodore Rowley, bringing with her General John Abercromby, the late Sir Ralph's son, and his staff. His mission: to invade and occupy Mauritius.

General Abercromby was eager to get into battle. He had just spent five years as a prisoner in France. He had been on holiday on the continent when the Peace of Amiens ended in 1803. Promptly arrested, he had only been released in 1808 in exchange for a French general captured by Wellington in Portugal. He was anxious to make up for these years of absence from the battlefield by distinguishing himself in action. Now was his chance.

He very nearly bungled it, or at least HMS *Ceylon* nearly did it for him, by getting herself captured that afternoon after a running fight against Captain Hamelin's *Vénus* in which both frigates were heavily damaged and suffered severe casualties. *Ceylon* struck and a downcast Abercromby became a prisoner of the French again. But fortunately for the British general, Commodore Rowley and his little fleet were not far away and four of these vessels caught up the next day with *Vénus* and the corvette *Victor*, which was trying to tow the much larger HMS *Ceylon* to Mauritius.

When Rowley's squadron appeared, the *Victor* cast off the *Ceylon* and made all sail back to Port Louis. The *Vénus* struck, and General John Abercromby, after one of the shortest captivities on record for a general, resumed his command.

The *Vénus* was taken into the Royal Navy but the British considered her name too suggestive, too flippant – too French, in short – and renamed her HMS *Nereide*. The old *Nereide*, the one Willoughby had recently commanded, was now flying the French flag, so the two sides now each had their *Nereide*. A third French *Néréide*, also a frigate, will arrive from France early next year. Sorting out all these ships can certainly become very confusing.

The obnoxious Captain Willoughby, former skipper of HMS *Nereide*, vanishes from our story in this chapter. But not from history. Sent back to England he was, as custom and naval ritual demanded, tried by court martial for the loss of his ship and 'most honourably acquitted' of any wrongdoing. With one eye gone, his face torn and battered, his jaw smashed, he looked more fit for disposal than for the service of His Majesty. The Royal Navy admirals took one look at him and, to his great annoyance, decided he was unfit for further duty. So he went to Russia, joined the Russian army, was taken prisoner by the French during the retreat from Moscow and, in a situation when life expectancy was not high, not even for the best armed and warmest clad Frenchman, managed to survive the long winter trek back to France as a captive of the beaten, harassed, starving and frozen French army. He was held a prisoner at Péronne, from where he managed to escape in 1814. In 1841, twenty-seven years later, he was named ADC to the young Queen Victoria. He was then sixty-three years old, and still unmarried. No woman could have stood him for a husband.

THE BRITISH ARE BACK
Mauritius 1810

British troops were pouring in from India, to Rodriguez and Réunion, to join General Abercromby's force. The invasion of Mauritius was inevitable. General Decaen had a total force of some two thousand men at his disposal, only thirteen hundred of whom were soldiers of the line. The rest were militiamen of the National Guard, civilians called upon to serve for short periods of emergency, unreliable, often unwilling to fight and always unwilling to die. His troops also included five hundred Irishmen recruited from among captured British naval and merchant ship crews.

By November over 10,000 British soldiers were massed on the offshore troopships. A squadron under the command of Admiral Bertie arrived from Cape Town. Captain Beaver was in charge of the landing operations. French naval supremacy in the Mascarenes, which Decaen had anticipated after the Battle of Grand Port, had never materialised. The British were back, and in force.

The invasion fleet, no less than seventy ships in all, sailed from Rodriguez on November 22, 1810. Among the invaders we must note the name of Captain James Hillyar, of the frigate HMS *Phoebe*. Hillyar and the *Phoebe* were to prove a nemesis to the French in the Indian Ocean and, a few years later, to the Americans in the Pacific during the War of 1812.

The British reached Mauritius on the 29th and the landing was made on the north-eastern extremity of the island, where they had been least expected. There was little that General Decaen, with his scanty two thousand men, could do to stop them. Needing every volunteer he could find, he called on all to serve, and among those who came forward was old Admiral de Sercey, who was still living in retirement there. The British prisoners on the island, more numerous than their captors, stood around with folded arms, grinning. They knew their captivity would soon end. Defeat came inevitably and soon. The capitulation was signed on December 3, 1810, after only five days of resistance. Some seventy of the British invaders were killed and nearly a hundred wounded.

General Abercromby, an honourable man like his father, granted General Decaen generous terms and agreed to repatriate the defeated French troops.

A couple of Royal Navy ships sailed on to Madagascar the following month, where the French commercial agent Sylvain Roux held a small post at Tamatave defended by twenty-five soldiers, and took it over without a fight.

Mauritius was never to be French again. It remained British for a

In November 1800 a British invasion fleet landed 10,000 troops on Mauritius. The 2,000 French defenders were quickly defeated

century and a half and then attained independence. Réunion is still French today, no longer a colony but an overseas department. It recently contributed a prime minister to France, Mr Raymond Barre.

Meanwhile, a squadron of three frigates was preparing to sail from France to Mauritius, part of the reinforcements for the island Napoleon had promised back in June: the *Clorinde*, the *Renommée*, and, to confuse the reader, the third *Néréide* in the Indian Ocean. Captain Barois, a recent envoy to the Emperor Napoleon I, was a passenger aboard the *Renommée*, returning happily to his island home. An unpleasant surprise awaited him on his arrival.

THE LAST FRIGATES
Mauritius and Madagascar 1811

On February 2, 1811, two months after Mauritius had fallen, a fact still unknown to Paris of course, the three frigates, each of forty guns, sailed from Brest carrying a few hundred troops as reinforcements. The squadron was under the command of Captain François Roquebert, who commanded the *Renommée*. Captain Jacques St Cricq commanded the *Clorinde* and François Lemaresquier, the *Néréide* which, to avoid any mixup with the other two *Nereides* in this chapter, we shall call *Néréide* III.

Captain Roquebert's squadron had orders to sail to Java if Mauritius was no longer in French hands. The three frigates, on reaching Mauritian waters, cautiously approached the Isle de la Passe on May 6 and were told by two Negro fishermen that the British were now masters of the colony. Almost immediately, the French ships spotted three

British vessels in the offing. Two were frigates, Captain Hillyar's HMS *Phoebe*, 36, and HMS *Galatea*, also of 36 guns. The third was the 18-gun brig HMS *Racehorse*. A third British frigate appeared, HMS *Astroea*, also of 36 guns, commanded by Captain Charles Schomberg.

The French ships had but one sensible course of action: flight. Obviously Mauritius was no longer the place for them. But they had been three months at sea and needed to replenish in food and water, so they had to find a new landfall before making for distant Java.

Captain Roquebert decided to head with his consorts for Tamatave, in Madagascar, which with luck might still be French and, if not, would in any case be weakly held.

Captain Schomberg, who took command of the British ships, guessed their destination and intercepted them at dawn off the Malagasy coast. In the battle that followed both Roquebert and Lemaresquier were killed and their ships heavily damaged. *Néréide* III suffered a hundred and thirty casualties, *Renommée* lost a hundred and forty-five. The *Clorinde*, pusillanimously, stayed out of most of the fighting and only had a dozen killed and wounded. The unlucky Captain Barois had an arm torn off by a round shot on the *Renommée*. The *Renommée* struck, the *Clorinde* made off for faraway France, and the *Néréide* III managed to escape towards Madagascar.

Schomberg stubbornly followed her with his little squadron, found *Néréide* III at anchor off Tamatave, with Lieutenant Ponée, her valiant first lieutenant, now in command and determined to defend himself and his ship to the end unless the British accepted the terms under which he would capitulate. The British agreed to repatriate Ponée and his crew to France and *Néréide* III then surrendered and Schomberg returned to his duties in Mauritius. The grandson of the German Hebrew scholar, Meyer Lower Schomberg, was to continue his distinguished career in the Royal Navy, to receive a knighthood and to become commander-in-chief at the Cape of Good Hope.

In Mauritius the Royal Navy added to its lists the two French ships surrendered to Captain Schomberg: *Néréide* III was renamed HMS *Madagascar* and the *Renommée* became HMS *Java* and the command given to Captain Lambert, recently released from captivity after the French capitulation on Mauritius. Nine months earlier Lambert had lost HMS *Iphigenia* to the French at Grand Port. Eighteen months later he was to lose HMS *Java* to the Americans off Bahia during the War of 1812.

CHAPTER TWENTY-TWO

The Indonesian Finale

RAFFLES SHOWS THE WAY
The East Indies 1810-1811

Java became a French colony in July 1810. After the fall of Mauritius it was the only colony where the Tricolour flag was still flying. Everywhere else in the world French sovereignty had been eliminated – except in Europe, of course, where the Pax Napoleonica now reigned.

The frontiers of France had been stretched all the way up to the outskirts of Hamburg in the far north and down to the outskirts of Naples in the far south. Austria and Prussia were now her allies. Only Britain, Portugal, the islands of Sardinia and Sicily, the tiny, obstreperous Kingdom of Montenegro on the Adriatic and huge, disillusioned Russia were now at odds with the French Emperor. But there was virtually no fighting anywhere, except in Spain.

Britannia ruled the waves and overseas the French empire, except Java, was under British occupation. We must except the island of Hispaniola. Haiti was now black, independent and torn by civil war. The eastern part of the island had been returned to its Spanish masters. And, in South America, French Guyana seemed to have become part of Brazil.

Java, anyway, had become French only recently. It had long been Dutch. Then Holland had been annexed to France after the abdication of King Louis of Holland in July. Dutchmen had become Frenchmen and Dutch colonies had also become French. But all except Java and a few other Indonesian islands, had been occupied by the British.

Java had always been preoccupied by the British threat from India. It was so more than ever now that it was French.

The island defences had been strongly fortified by the previous governor, General Daendens, known for his loyalty to France and his tough methods. His *pièce de résistance* was Fort Cornelis, an entrenched camp about a mile long and four to seven hundred yards wide, running from north to south a few miles south of Batavia. It had been carved out of the jungle and plantation and, hemmed in between the wide Batavia River on the west and the Skoddan canal in the east, was defended by two hundred and eighty pieces of artillery spread among eight strong batteries: four batteries at the northern end formed the base of this strongpoint's defences.

The Dutch said it was impregnable.

General Daendens had arrived on the island in 1808 on the French privateer *Virginie*, commanded by Captain Pierre Gicquel des Touches. The French corsair had stayed on as commander of the naval forces in the island, now reduced (after a few unfortunate encounters with the British) to a flotilla of gunboats, used mainly to suppress the activities of the local Malay and Filipino pirates.

Daendels remained in Java until April 1811 when a new governor landed in the island. It was none other than General Janssens, former Dutch governor of the Cape of Good Hope. He was the personal choice of Napoleon, who liked the man personally. The Emperor, however, remembering Janssens's defeat at the Battle of Blueberg a few years ago, had called him in before his departure. 'Remember, Sir, that a French general does not allow himself to be captured twice,' the Emperor reminded him. But Napoleon must have been well aware that Java, defended by only ten thousand troops, of whom fewer than two thousand were Europeans, would not withstand an assault by the British if the latter were determined enough.

Janssens had sailed from France a few days before Christmas 1810 in a flotilla of two frigates, the *Méduse*, 44, the *Nymphe*, 32, and the corvette *Sappho*. The flotilla carried a few hundred French light infantrymen and two senior French officers, the Peninsular veteran General Alberti, and General Jumel, who had fought at Marengo and in Haiti, neither known as a military genius. They arrived in Java in the spring of 1811.

In India, meanwhile, great plans were afoot in the British camp. An enterprising young official of the East India Company, Stamford Raffles, after serving in the former Dutch colony of Malacca in Malaya, suggested to Lord Minto that Java should be taken. Encouraged by the recent rapid conquest of the French islands of Réunion and Mauritius, and anxious to make a name for himself as a conqueror of the East, Lord Minto had not only acquiesced in the idea: he announced he would go in person to Java.

The command of the expedition was given to the loyalist American, General Samuel Auchmuty who, as commander-in-chief in Madras, had come a long way from his New York days as an impecunious loyalist ensign. The defeat inflicted on the British in Buenos Aires had, however, made him cautious, too cautious perhaps.

Army personnel numbered more than twelve thousand men, half of them British, the other half Indians, mainly high caste Rajput warriors. General Rollo Gillespie, the pushing and aggressive Ulsterman, was to command the army in the field. He was as high-spirited as ever but since his Haitian years had fought only in India. The war against Napoleon had completely passed him by. Colonel Samuel Gibbs (with us in the 1806 Cape of Good Hope expedition) took command of one of the brigades.

In the fleet (four ships-of-the-line, fourteen frigates and seven sloops and corvettes) that escorted the expedition, were two old acquaintances: Captain Fleetwood Pellew, still in command of HMS *Phaeton*, and Captain James Hillyar, still in HMS *Phoebe*. They sailed from Madras and Calcutta in April. After a stopover in Penang, the fleet headed south for Java. The target was Batavia (Jakarta today), a fever-ridden spot, surrounded by swamps.

Already, back in 1810, Admiral Drury's ships had seized several islands in the Dutch East Indies, notably Amboina and the Moluccas. Drury had since died and his place had been taken by Commodore William Broughton. But, adjudged too fussy and too cautious, Broughton was replaced before Auchmuty's expedition reached Java by the more enterprising Admiral Sir Robert Stopford, a veteran of the San Domingo, River Plate and Copenhagen campaigns.

The British, somewhat groggy after their four-months voyage, landed on August 4 near the undefended village of Chillingching, twelve miles east of the capital. Auchmuty, obsessed, it is said, by the disasters that had overtaken the British army (and himself) when it attacked Buenos Aires five years before, was reluctant to plunge ahead and take the nearby unprotected town. After a prudent, unopposed, four-day advance along the coast, battered only by the scorching, tropical sun, the British took Batavia without a fight on August 8. But the advance had been too slow. When they entered Batavia, part of the town had been set on fire and the warehouses, which contained so much tropical produce, flooded. The streets were full of broken bags of coffee and sugar, enough, quaintly wrote an eyewitness, 'to have made an English washerwoman weep.' British hopes of huge prize-money diminished.

General Janssen was relying on the unhealthy climate on the coast to decimate the enemy European troops rather than his own ramshackle part-French, part-Dutch, part-Javanese, part-Celebes, part-Moluccan army. Language difficulties between Dutch, French and Indonesians resulted in chaos in the transmission of orders. Moreover, some of the French, recently arrived, were not familiar with the uniforms and sometimes confused foes and friends. General Alberti, astride his charger, burst into the British lines one morning and, taking some soldiers in green jackets for Dutchmen, shouted to them: 'Follow me!' One of the 'Dutchmen' aimed his rifle and shot him down.

After the capture of Batavia however, Janssens moved with his troops into the entrenched camp of Fort Cornelis. His plan was to entice the enemy and shatter him against the fort, with its redoubts and two hundred and eighty guns.

The enticement was successful. On August 10, Auchmuty and his troops under General Gillespie reached the approaches to the camp into which the whole of Janssens's army had now moved. Janssens prepared to survive the inevitable assaults and send the broken British army back to India. But, in the end, it was the wrong army that was broken: his own.

The most kindly way to describe Janssens is as a courteous, affable and likeable man. But, as an army commander, he was totally ineffective. More a fussy administrator than a warrior, he was the wrong man, at the wrong place, at the wrong time. When his attention had first been called to the presence of the British ships offshore, instead of preparing tactical countermoves he continued to busy himself designing new epaulettes for his officers.

TO STORM THE PROUD CORNELIS
Java 1811

The siege of the impregnable Fort Cornelis lasted twelVe days. Its beginning can be dated from August 14 when the British established themselves on the north face of the enemy lines and cut a path through a pepper plantation to bring up material and supplies. It lasted until August 26. Its great hero was undoubtedly Gillespie who won for himself the unofficial title of 'the bravest man in the British army'. For several days the siege consisted mainly of artillery duels between the two sides. Most of Janssens's gunners were fierce and reliable Celebes islanders. The British artillerymen were largely Royal Marines and naval gunners, some from Captain Beaver's ship, HMS *Nisius*. On the long voyage from Mauritius Beaver had passed the time studiously reading his way from A to Z through the *Encyclopaedia Britannica*.

There were gallant feats of arms – mainly on the last days, and notably by Gillespie who, at dawn on August 26, aided by a deserter, broke by stealth through the French defences, and took two redoubts at the point of the bayonet. Worn out and racked by fever, Gillespie then fainted in the arms of one of his officers but, on recovering consciousness, went back to the attack and, leading the charge, captured a third redoubt as well as overcoming tough resistance by General Jauffret who was taken prisoner. 'In the whole history of the army, no man has ever distinguished himself so signally in any one engagement as did Rollo Gillespie at the lines of Cornelis,' wrote Fortescue. But that was written in the 1890s, before World Wars I and II.

The only major feat of arms by the French worthy of record was the suicidal destruction of the redoubt's powder magazine by two self-sacrificing officers, Majors Holsman and Muller, who blew themselves and some two hundred of the enemy into eternity. Major Holsman had long ago said that if the British ever took the redoubt 'they would all go together to Paradise.'

The capture of these three redoubts, the key to the defence of Cornelis, caused a major panic among the defending native troops. The bulk, six thousand in all, surrendered. Others fled south into the jungle, ignoring the pleas and the orders of their French and Dutch officers. Some of the officers also took part in the general exodus. 'I saw,' wrote a witness, 'more than one officer tearing and stamping on the tricolour emblem to which he had sworn fidelity, and crying out to the British: "I am not French, I am Dutch!"'

The battle for Fort Cornelis, forgotten today, was viewed in its day as one of the great feats of arms of the British army. Casualties were heavy: 2,000 on the French side, 630 for the British. Two French generals and more than 230 other officers were captured. Forty French and Dutch officers were killed, 63 wounded.

Generals Janssens and Jumel escaped. Jumel, who had hidden himself in a swamp, was later captured by some Royal Marines from Cap-

Boarding parties from the British sloop, HMS *Procris*, capture five French gunboats anchored off Java in 1811

tain Beaver's ship at nearby Cheribon while Captain Hillyar, in HMS *Phoebe*, was taking over the fort of Tagal.

French resistance was not quite over. On September 3, the twelve hundred men of Javanese Prince Prang Wedono's colourful mounted legion, and Javanese militia from Soerkarta and Jokjakarta, joined Janssens's survivors. These exotic, rickety allies and what remained of the Fort Cornelis garrison attacked Colonel Gibbs's disciplined soldiery on September 16 and were easily repulsed. In the ensuing rout, many of the Indonesian soldiers, presumably weary of fighting the white man's battles, massacred the officers who tried to stand in the way of their flight.

Two days later Janssens capitulated. He could only oppose to the victorious British army some forty Dutch and French officers, including Captain Gicquel des Touches defending the fort of Reinbang, some twenty Celebes artillery men without artillery, a few dragoons, the loyal and magnificently accoutred Prince Prang Wedono and his two sons, one solitary gun and a few gunners from the Prince's native army, commanded by one lone, staunch French lieutenant. This force represented all that was left of Napoleon's Army of the East. The two French frigates, *Nymphe* and *Méduse*, managed to slip by the watching Royal Navy ships and made their way back to France.

Janssens went back on parole to France, to be absolved of all blame for his defeat by Napoleon himself, whose generous and forgiving mood was perhaps inspired by an important event that happened the month after the battle for Java: the birth of a (legitimate) son and heir. Jumel, after three years as a prisoner of war, returned to France in 1814. Captain Beaver died humiliatingly of constipation in Cape Town eighteen months later. General Gillespie was killed fighting the Gurkhas in Nepal. Auchmuty handed over his Madras command to General John Abercromby, and was appointed commander in chief in Ireland where he died shortly after his arrival from a fall from his horse.

Lord Minto appointed young Raffles, who had suggested and inspired the expedition to Java, to the post of lieutenant-governor of the island. But, in spite of Raffles's protests, the island was returned to the Dutch after the war and the young administrator went back to Malaya.

Deprived of one island, Raffles bought another, from the Sultan of Johore, at the southern extremity of the Malayan peninsula where he founded in 1819 a trading outpost for the East India Company. It was called Singapore.

PART FOUR

The War of 1812

The British captured Washington in 1814, and burned the city in revenge for the
American burning of Toronto the year before

CHAPTER TWENTY-THREE

The Imperial Dawning of the USA

CANADA! CANADA! CANADA!
1812-1814

The War of 1812 between Britain and the United States, an offshoot of the Napoleonic conflict, was the first real demonstration of armed American imperialism in action.

'Free trade and sailors' rights' were the causes for which the Americans ostensibly went to war against Britain. The call for 'free trade' was a protest against Britain's latest Order-in-Council which prevented Americans from trading with countries hostile to Britain. The protest about 'sailors' rights' concerned the impressment of American sailors into the Royal Navy, one of the more odious British practices of the war. But these maritime problems were not the cause for America's declaration of war against Britain, they were only the excuse for it. The New England seafaring states of Massachusetts and Connecticut were adamantly against the war, although their sailors suffered the most from British violations at sea, and the real American motive for the war was imperial: more land, more territorial conquests. To the north Canada, defended by Britain. To the west the Indian territories, defended by the Shawnee chief Tecumseh.

The United States' 'manifest destiny', still unexpressed, was already bursting out of its breeches, and God, so recently Nelson's ally, was now, unexplainably, in the Americans' camp as well, urging them to occupy lands which belonged to Britain. Bible in hand, the American 'war hawks', as they were called, were claiming their divine right to conquest. 'The waters of the St Lawrence and the Mississippi interlock in a number of places and the Great Disposer of Human Events [i.e.

God] intended these rivers should belong to the same people,' intoned one politician from Kentucky. 'This great outlet of the northern world [the St Lawrence] should be at our command for our convenience and future. The Author of Nature [i.e. God] has marked our limits to the south by the Gulf of Mexico, and on the north, by the regions of eternal frost,' clamoured another, from New Hampshire.

Not all American politicians waved the Bible and the sword. Congressman John Randolph, of Roanoke, Virginia, professionally anti-Madison, was aghast at the prospect of war against Britain as France's unofficial ally. 'Bound to France,' as he described it, 'as Sinbad the Sailor was bound to the putrefying corpse of his deceased wife.'

With the usual Anglo-Saxon, anti-French gut reaction, many Americans, most of whom were of British descent, found any alliance with their former French allies quite repugnant. They also feared that Napoleon was pressuring them into joint actions against Britain. In Hartford, the *Connecticut Courant* warned its readers: 'Be on your guard, the appointment of French officers to the command of our soldiers has commenced. During the last week, two Frenchmen, one in New London, and the other at Norwich, received commissions from Mr Madison, one as a captain, the other a lieutenant, in our army.' (James Madison was then President of the United States.)

The Americans were quite unreasoningly suspicious. Napoleon, as he later told Admiral Cockburn, the first governor of his island prison, had been ready to lend 'any number of ships-of-the-line Mr Madison might have desired, if American seamen could be sent to man them, and take them away.' But Mr Madison wanted and asked nothing from the French. The Americans were never allies in this conflict: they were at best co-belligerents, and not cooperative ones at that. The Stars and Stripes over Canada, divinely ordained, was what the War of 1812 was about for many Americans.

The sharp-tongued Randolph of Roanoke, the most feared orator of his day, knew that sailors' rights were the last concern of those who clamoured for war. For no one really cared about British impressment except the kidnapped sailors and their families. 'Agrarian cupidity, not maritime right, urges this war,' Randolph thundered in Congress. 'We have heard but one word, like the whippoorwill, but one eternal monotonous tone: Canada! Canada! Canada!'

Canada and the Indian territories of Michigan were the immediate targets and soon all the land to the west and to the south-west would be targets too, to the limits of the seas, the lands of the Indians and the Spaniards. The 'manifest destiny' was in the offing, with its Monroe Doctrine corollary.

It is as the first, clear budding of the American imperial spirit that the War of 1812 is particularly interesting. The war has otherwise retained an indistinct character, and its very name is a misnomer. Its last battle was not fought until 1815. Many Americans, notably in New England, were totally opposed to the war and called it 'Mr Madison's War'. Apart from its naval aspects, distressing to the British with American privateers active in the English Channel, the War of 1812, finally, was simply the dawn of United States imperialism in North America, just as the wider Napoleonic conflict was the prelude to Spanish decolonisation in Latin America.

The United States declared war on Britain on June 18, 1812. This was a vital year for Britain and her allies in Europe, the year of Napoleon's disastrous retreat from Moscow, and of the British victory at Salamanca in Spain won by Wellington – thanks largely to the dash and courage of his brother-in-law General Sir Edward Pakenham. But even though Wellington entered Madrid on August 12, with King Joseph in full flight back to France, the Peninsular War was to continue for another year and a half.

In North America, the British and the Americans were to confront each other on the Canadian border for the next three years. In 1814, two new fronts opened: one in the Chesapeake-Washington region, the other on the Gulf of Mexico. But for most of the war, it was the northern zone alone that counted.

SEESAW IN THE NORTH
US/Canadian border 1812-1814

Several thousand American militiamen, stiffened with regulars, were assigned to the Canadian invasion. Three times during 1812 – in June, October and November – American armies tried to invade Canada. Each attack failed. After the first, it was the British who crossed into the United States and occupied Fort Dearborn, on the site of present-day Chicago, while in the October attack, aimed across the Niagara River at Kingston, the New York militia commanded by General Van Ransselaer actually refused to enter Canada, claiming they had been recruited for service in the United States only. And the militia again refused to move into Canada in November. The cry of the war hawks was obviously of limited resonance.

Detroit saw another American setback. General William Hull, sixty years old and tired, decided not to fight when attacked there by the British, and surrendered to a mixed force of around four hundred Canadians under General Brock and six hundred Indian warriors led by Chief Tecumseh.

On another part of the long frontier between the two countries, an American force under General Dearborn took the town of York (later to be renamed Toronto) while another general Winfield Scott (later a candidate in the United States 1852 presidential elections) went on to attack Fort George on the Niagara River with four thousand men, forcing the numerically weaker British to evacuate their wooden log fortress.

The British governor-general of Upper Canada now made his entry on the battlefield, and he was none other than General Sir George Prevost whose main qualities, as we saw on the West Indian island of Dominica a few years ago, had been procrastination and timidity. They were to be so again, as the British prepared in their turn to invade the United States. In May 1813, Sir George launched an amphibious attack against Sackett's Harbor, at the eastern end of Lake Ontario, with the naval part of his operation under the orders of Sir James Yeo, of Cayenne fame, now a commodore and commander-in-chief of the British naval forces on the America lakes. Prevost had already routed the Americans when, a ditherer once again and tortured by doubt over the outcome of the fighting, to Yeo's fury he sounded the signal for retreat.

The British plan to invade what was then the north-west of the United States (present-day Ohio, Michigan, Indiana and Illinois) required the control of the Great Lakes which provided an easy route deep into enemy territory. And this British invasion scheme suffered a severe setback when, on September 10, 1813, Captain Oliver Hazard Perry attacked with his squadron of nine ships the smaller (six ships) but slightly more heavily armed British squadron on Lake Erie, and defeated it. 'We have met the enemy and they are ours,' he jubilantly wrote to Washington afterwards.

This US naval success made it possible for General William Henry Harrison (future ninth President of the United States), to cross the lake with an army of 4,500 men, recapture Detroit and, on October 5th, defeat the British and their Indian allies at the Battle of the Thames River, in which Tecumseh was killed.

The American had retaken control of the threatened north-west from the British. Now a fourth assault against Canada was launched from Lake Champlain.

It failed as badly as the previous American attempts. The British recaptured Fort George on the Niagara River, and burnt the town of Buffalo on the southern shore of Lake Erie.

The situation on the northern frontier was thus a stalemate. Then in July 1814, more than two years after the start of the war, thirteen hundred Americans led by Generals Jacob Brown and Winfield Scott routed a slightly larger British army at Chippewa, north of Buffalo and on the other side of the Niagara River.

But Chippewa was a dead-end victory. Only three weeks later, the Redcoats forced their enemy off the battlefield at nearby Lundy's Lane, within walking distance of Niagara Falls. The defeated Americans retired to Fort Erie, subsequently salvaging their pride by fighting off a spirited British attack there.

The dithering General Sir George Prevost and the angry Commodore Yeo now make their final appearance in this narrative. The British made a new attempt to invade the United States on September 6 when Prevost came with eleven thousand men from Montreal down Lake Champlain, the traditional invasion route from the north into New York State. The immediate objective was Plattsburgh, on the western side of the lake. The British troops were escorted by a squadron of warships and twelve gunboats, led by Captain Downie. The American squadron, commanded by the brilliant young Lieutenant Thomas McDonough, was about equal in size.

Downie, killed early in the two-hour battle, fought at anchor. McDonough forced the four British ships to surrender. When Prevost, already fighting in the outskirts of Plattsburgh and on the point of victory, heard of the British ships' defeat, he ordered his army back to Montreal. Outraged again, Commodore Yeo wrote to the Admiralty in London demanding that Prevost be court-martialled. The timorous British general died, some say of chagrin, some of dropsy, while awaiting his trial.

Both for the British and the Americans, the military campaign on the Canadian-American border had in fact been deadlocked from beginning to end. Neither country could invade the other and Canada and the United States have been at peace ever since, each indifferent to the other while all the time pretending to a warm mutual friendship. In the turbulent context of international relations, this remains a most healthy relationship.

THE WHITE HOUSE BURNS
Washington and Baltimore 1814

While British and Americans were fighting on the Canadian border, the war against France had continued in Europe until April 1814. Britain and her allies won notable victories in Spain, Russia and Germany, and finally invaded France itself. In April 1814 Napoleon abdicated. The Empress Marie-Louise and her infant son fled to the safety of her father's court in Vienna where she became the mistress of the Austrian Count Niepperg while her husband, the formidable Napoleon, now reduced to the role of a cuckold, languished in exile in the Mediterranean island of Elba, not far from his native Corsica.

More British troops, released from the war in Europe, now became available for combat in North America. The British added three new fronts in the United States: in Maine; in the Chesapeake region where General Robert Ross, backed by Admiral George Cockburn, landed in August 1814 with five thousand experienced troops; and on the Gulf coast where the British arrived in December 1814 not knowing that peace was to be signed that month between their country and the USA.

The troops in the Chesapeake were commanded by General Robert Ross, 'the perfect model of the Irish gentleman... humane and brave' as one of his American prisoners was later to describe him. They landed at the small port of Benedict, on the shores of Chesapeake Bay, on August 16 to be met on arrival by the bombastic Admiral Sir George Cockburn, who had been blockading the coast and raiding the local townships and villages for the past fifteen months, busy earning his prize money. When he met Ross, he had just been on a slave-raiding trip to Florida where he had kidnapped a number of black slaves and taken them to Barbados for sale.

Unlike General Prevost, his counterpart to the north, General Ross was no ditherer. His orders were to attack Washington and, after defeating an American army at Bladensburg, that was exactly what he did. Within eight days of his arrival he marched, with a vanguard of two hundred men, into the undefended capital on August 24 and, in retaliation for the burning of Toronto and under strong pressure from the malevolent Cockburn, set fire to the Capitol. The British went to the White House, rapidly evacuated just before they arrived, had dinner, then burnt the building down and went on to set fire to the Treasury, the War Department, the State Department and other public buildings that took their fancy. They stayed in Washington briefly then marched back, untroubled, to their base at Benedict. Toronto was avenged.

The burning of Washington was not an act of which the gallant Ross was proud. His days, anyway, were numbered. On September 14, the British sailed up the Chesapeake to Fort McHenry, within a few miles of Baltimore, where the general hoped to set up his winter headquarters. British guns were firing on Fort McHenry while the lawyer Francis Scott Key, watching the bombardment and stirred by the sight, jotted down the words of 'The Star-Spangled Banner' destined to become the American national anthem. General Ross rode towards a copse of oak trees and was scanning the enemy positions with his telescope when a bullet hit him in the chest. He cried out 'Elizabeth', the name of his wife, and died. His body was placed in a barrel of rum and shipped home in HMS *Tonnant*, the old Battle of the Nile veteran.

The American flag flying over Fort McHenry never came down. Baltimore was never occupied, and Ross's army went on to fight in New Orleans and Waterloo.

THE MARQUESAS EPISODE
The South Seas 1813-1814

One of the most colourful naval episodes of the War of 1812 is the Pacific Ocean cruise of the USS frigate *Essex*, 32, commanded by Captain David Porter who first entered our story as a midshipman in the

USS *Constellation* in the fight against the French *L'Insurgente*, in 1799. In March 1813, the USS *Essex* rounded the Horn and sailed into the Pacific. During the next twelve months, the *Essex* captured thirteen prizes, all but one – a Peruvian privateer – British whaling ships. Porter also became involved in a Polynesian native war between cannibal tribes in the island of Nuku-Hiva in the Marquesas islands, and on November 19, 1813 told the man-eating natives assembled around the four-gun fort built by his sailors of watercasks and mud: 'You are now Americans.'

He followed up the acquisition of these new US citizens with a formal declaration of annexation. 'Our rights in this island being founded on priority of discovery, conquest and possession cannot be disputed,' the declaration said. The United States, unbeknown to its government, was now in the colonial race, alongside Britain, France and the other European colonial powers. But the US State Department never honoured Captain Porter's subsequent report 'with any appropriate notice', Porter's biographer, Archibald Douglas Turnbull, tells us, and thirty years later, the Marquesas islands, including Nuku-Hiva, all became French. It was not until towards the end of the century that the United States, formally and strongly entered the colonial race in the Pacific with the annexation of Hawaii, the Philippines, Guam and the eastern Samoan islands.

The *Essex* cruise came to an end on March 28, 1814 in a dogged fight off the Chilean port of Valparaiso against HMS *Cherub* (18) and HMS *Phoebe* (36), captained by the ageing and much travelled Sir James Hillyar, who has accompanied us through many pages since his first appearance at Toulon twenty-one years ago. The *Essex* surrendered after losing fifty-eight killed and sixty-five wounded out of a crew of two hundred and fifty-five. HMS *Phoebe* came out of the battle almost unscathed, with five men killed and ten wounded. One of the *Essex* survivors was Porter's adopted son, David Farragut, then a midshipman of thirteen, destined to become one of the great names of US naval history and, forty-eight years later, a hero of the Civil War battles of Mobile and New Orleans, two cities that also figured largely in the War of 1812.

THE BATTLE OF NEW ORLEANS
Louisiana 1814-1815

After Napoleon's abdication and the accession of King Louis XVIII to the French throne, the British government appointed Wellington, fresh from his victories in the Spanish campaign, to the post of British ambassador in France. He was joined in the French capital by Kitty, his wife, but unfortunately, although she was the sister of his friend Edward Pakenham, he couldn't stand the sight of her. She was a frump, a bore, she had no taste, and he preferred the company either of con-

tinental ladies or of junior officer's wives. In the best British upper-
class fashion, he carried on his affairs with impeccable discretion. There
was rarely any scandal attached to any liaisons he may have had, unlike
the notorious Horatio Nelson–Emma Hamilton romance, which all
England had sniggered over. Wellington inherited, one is tempted to
say 'by right of conquest', two of Napoleon's former mistresses, both
on the stage. One was the Italian opera singer Guiseppina Grassini,
the other Mademoiselle George, of the Comédie Française. Years later,
the French actress admitted to friendship with both the French emperor
and the British general and of the two, she used to say, 'the Duke of
Wellington was much the stronger.' Bully for Britain!

Wellington also enjoyed meeting his former enemies from the field
of battle. They were, after all, in the same business: war. Wellington
liked to gossip with them about their common profession. He was on
particularly friendly terms with General Foy, brave and distinguished,
whom he had fought against recently in Spain. It was Foy who had
trained the Turkish guns a few years ago on Admiral Duckworth's
squadron in the Dardanelles.

Foy liked and admired Wellington, but he remained a Bonpartist
and to him the British were still the enemy, and Bourbon kings and
princes were 'the very humble valets of England'.

'Oh, Napoleon, where are you?' he once wrote despairingly in his
diary, appalled at the arrogance of France's foreign masters. This attitude was widespread among the French during the occupation of their
country by foreign troops. The government in London, well aware of
the intensity of these feelings, feared that their best soldier and most
eminent public figure might be murdered. To get Wellington out of
harm's way, therefore, the British Prime Minister, the Earl of Liver-
pool, offered him the command of the British expeditionary force in
North America. But the British hero was totally uninterested in going
to America, so the command was given instead to General Pakenham.

Pakenham hadn't been very keen to leave Europe. 'I think I have
escaped America and shall consider myself vastly fortunate in having
been spared of such a service,' he wrote to his mother in June. But
when given the command, he loyally obeyed orders and sailed for New
Orleans, taking with him as second-in-command General Gibbs, veteran of various European campaigns as well as of South Africa, Java
and India. As for Wellington, to save him from an imaginary French
assassin's dagger, he was sent to Austria to represent Britain at the
Congress of Vienna.

The semi-tropical Gulf coast, towards which Pakenham was now
sailing, was the third major theatre of war to open in North America
after the Canadian border conflict and the Chesapeake and Washington battles.

The British had first appeared in the Mexican Gulf in August that year, in the little Spanish port of Pensacola. A small squadron and an army detachment of around a hundred men had taken over the virtually undefended settlement for 'the purpose', in the words of Lieutenant-Colonal Edward Nicholls, commanding His Britannic Majesty's forces in the Floridas, 'of annoying the only enemy Great Britain has in the world, as France and England are now friends.' That enemy was the United States. Colonel Nicholls recruited several hundred Indians, dressed them up in British army uniforms and sent out proclamations to the people of nearby Louisiana and of Kentucky, calling on them to rebel against the 'faithless and imbecile government' of the United States. Neither the Kentuckians, stout Americans to the core, nor the Louisianians, nursing their old French enmities against England, responded except with curses.

But Colonel Nicholls, a busybody, was still anxious to raise the local people against the Americans, so he next sent envoys to the freebooters of Barataria Bay islands near New Orleans. Most of these tough and unrecommendable specimens were more or less renegade Frenchmen, former sailors and soldiers who, through the vicissitudes of war, had been cast into the swamps and bayous of the Mississippi delta as refugees, outlaws or exiles and had turned to semi-piracy, smuggling and slave-trading for a living. They usually claimed to be privateers fighting for the (non-existent) Republic of Carthagena, in present-day Colombia. They were, in fact, just a bunch of ruffians, harried and hated by American authorities, led by a charismatic leader of great presence called Jean Laffite, probably a native of Bayonne in the southwest of France. They were French to their very heartbeats and if they hated the Americans they hated the British more.

With a remarkable lack of insight, Nicholls tried not only to recruit these rough-and-ready rascals into British service, but he also revealed what he believed to be future British plans to them: an attack on Mobile to be followed by one against New Orleans. Mobile was then defended by an irascible, peppery general called Andrew Jackson (destined to become the seventh President of the United States) who lived in a perpetual state of bad temper and who, Jefferson once said, 'could not talk without choking with rage.'

Colonel Nicholls offered Jean Laffite a captain's commission in his forces and gave him fourteen days to think over the offer. But to Laffite the British were still the enemy. He not only warned Governor Claiborne in New Orleans of the impending attacks but also offered to fight with his men in defence of the city.

The British never reappeared at Barataria. But, as they had told Laffite they would, on September 12 a force of one hundred and thirty Royal Marines and six hundred red-coated Seminole Indians attacked Fort Bowyer at Mobile. During the attack, a British frigate ran aground and had to be abandoned. The British then retired temporarily from the scene and the Indians went back to their families. Jackson, meanwhile, had been rampaging through the territory. He marched on Pensacola in early November with some regular troops and Tennessee volunteers, three thousand men in all, and took it from the Spaniards on November 7. Four days later he was back in Mobile where a letter was awaiting him from New Orleans: the British would soon be attacking the Louisiana city and Governor Claiborne needed his help. A few days later Jackson marched out of Mobile, and headed west to New Orleans.

His force was not the only army bound for New Orleans. A vast British army was also on its way on the high seas, made up largely of Highland veterans from the Peninsular War and from the Cape of Good Hope. In command was General John Keane, a veteran of the Egyptian and Spanish campaigns.

They sailed from Plymouth, 4,400 men in all, on September 18. Their intentions did not seem entirely military, for the British ships were carrying also an imposing civilian establishment which, it might be reasonable to infer, intended to remain in Louisiana and administer the territory after Britain had won it. Possession is, after all, nine-tenths of the law.

The British expedition first called at Jamaica where they were joined by three thousand men who had fought under Ross in Washington and Baltimore. On November 26, the British fleet of some sixty ships sailed from Jamaica bound for New Orleans under the command of Admiral Cochrane.

Britain's anticipated reconquest of North America was about to begin. Admirals, generals, captains, junior officers, NCOs, petty officers, privates and bluejackets were already trying to calculate how much prize money they would make from the thousands of bales of cotton, bags of sugar and other merchandise that reputedly filled the warehouses of the city. So anxious, it is said, was Admiral Cochrane to get his hands on all this booty that he disregarded the tactical requirements of the landing in order to anchor as close as possible to the city warehouses. Wellington later blamed the Admiral for the disastrous British defeat which was to follow.

On December 2 General Jackson's army marched into New Orleans. Creoles and French rushed to join it. One of Jackson's first recruits was General Amable Humbert who had left France, where he was kept in idleness, for the United States to offer his services to the Americans. Humbert, in these intervening years, had become a heavy drinker. His speech was often blurred and, in the words of a contemporary, he had 'the crimson cheeks and scarlet nose of one who has never been scared of alcohol.'

Since New Orleans, with its eighteen thousand inhabitants, was one of the most important French-speaking cities in the Americas, Humbert had naturally gravitated there. He lodged in a local inn and late every morning would sally out in his full general's uniform, his sword clanking by his side, to spend the rest of the day drinking and playing dominoes in one of his two favourite bars, the Café Thiot or the Hotel de la Marine.

General Jackson, no mean soldier himself, took a liking for this rough, drinking, fighting man and placed him on his personal staff.

Other Frenchmen and Creoles were rapidly trained and formed into fighting units. Major Jean Plauche, a Creole, commanded the Battalion of Orleans volunteers, the most professional unit in the state. French and Creole officers organised other militia units of carabiniers, dragoons and chasseurs. Half of the twenty-eight guns of the American artillery were manned by veterans of Napoleon's armies and Creoles, while more than half of Jackson's force was made up of American regulars, and included also redoubtable Tennessee frontiersmen in blanket coats and slouch hats, and Kentuckians, all of them great marksmen. They confidently awaited the coming of the British.

General Pakenham himself was still on the high seas on his way to Louisiana when the first land skirmish took place between Americans and British on December 22. Nearly two thousand recently landed Britons, under General Keane and Colonel Thornton (who had led the British attack at Bladensburg, on the way to Washington), clashed with an American patrol up one of the bayous. On the 23rd, the British reached the plantation of Gabriel Villeré, only nine miles from the city, and made him a prisoner. But Villeré, a major in the Louisiana militia, escaped and managed to reach Jackson's headquarters to warn him of the presence of the British. Jackson immediately marched against the enemy and forced them to retire behind a levee along the river.

The next day was Christmas Eve and the Americans and British prepared for battle, while in the faraway Belgian city of Ghent on that same day British and American negotiators signed a treaty ending the war.

On Christmas Day General Sir Edward Pakenham finally landed. He was not pleased at what he found: a British army, in the words of Fortescue, 'cooped up on an isthmus three-quarters of a mile broad between the Mississippi and the swamp. In front was Jackson's fortified position. On the river were the enemy's armed vessels, flanking the only possible line of advance; and in the rear was the lake and the sea.'

But Pakenham was not a man to be daunted by adverse conditions. He destroyed a troublesome American armed schooner on the river, and, as a tryout, attacked Jackson's line with two columns of troops on December 27. They were repulsed by the Baratarian artillery, commanded by Beluche and Dominique You.

The Americans were also measuring the enemy's strength. General Jackson sent out Humbert with an escort of Tennessee cavalry to look over the British positions from a safe distance. But the smell of approaching battle, and perhaps the presence of General Pakenham, who had been a young officer in Ireland the year of Castlebar, were too much for Humbert. In the best early republican tradition, the French general raised his sabre and shouted 'Charge!' But the Tennesseans, more realistic and possibly less drunk, galloped the other way and the crestfallen Humbert had to turn and hurry back to his companions.

1815 opened with a barrage by thirty British guns. Pakenham was hoping to blast his way into New Orleans on New Year's Day with artillery alone. In spite of the bombardment's intensity, casualties were few. Artillery had failed, so Pakenham decided to take New Orleans with a massed frontal enemy assault. Reinforcements were expected and they arrived on January 7: two thousand five hundred veterans from the Peninsular campaign under General John Lambert. The attack was fixed for the next day.

On January 8, just before daylight, the British attacked the American positions defending the approaches to New Orleans on both sides of the Mississippi. General Jackson had gauged the main British assault would come on the north bank (at this point the Mississippi, which twists and turns across the delta before reaching the sea further south, runs almost in a straight west to east direction) and he was right. His position was virtually impregnable. He had built, behind a canal and a dry ditch, a mile-long five-foot high parapet, strengthened with pointed pieces of wood fencing, behind which he had lined up 4,700 of his 5,500 men. To avoid the possibilty of circumventing the defences, the breastwork extended at one end into the Mississippi river, and at the other into an impenetrable swamp.

The most uncomfortable feature of the Americans' position was the mud behind the parapet, which was often knee-deep. But wet feet were preferable to a bullet in the stomach or in the chest, and the Americans were relatively safe from the British unless the Redcoats climbed over the parapet and attacked them in hand-to-hand combat, for which ladders and fascines were required.

Bringing this equipment up was to be the role of the 44th British Regiment of the Line. Their colonel, Thomas Mullens, was most unhappy over his dangerous assignment and was heard to grumble that his men had been ordered to execution. In fact, General Pakenham was ordering virtually his entire command to execution. The attacking Redcoats would have to cross open ground, swept by artillery and rifle fire for several hundred yards, almost helpless targets for the Americans safe behind their parapets.

General Gibbs led the assault along the swamp edge, Keane moved along the Mississippi bank. In the American lines, nearly five thousand rifles and thirteen pieces of artillery were firing continuously at the advanced massed British infantry. In spite of their appalling losses, the

British marched steadily on, in close ranks, until the few survivors reached the American lines where they stopped and stood helplessly. The 44th, instead of bringing the scaling ladders and fascines, had scattered. The Americans, snug behind their embankment, fired down into the mass of bewildered Britishers. General Pakenham, seeing the plight of his men, rushed forward to encourage them, took his place in the front line and cheered them on to nowhere. A bullet hit him in the right arm but he took no notice of his wound. When his horse was killed under him, he asked for another. He then ordered his troops to retire about three hundred yards to regroup. They then marched heroically and uselessly back to the attack, Pakenham, Gibbs and Keane at their head. Pakenham was hit by another rifle ball, in the thigh this time, and his second horse was killed. He fell into the arms of one of his officers and was hit a third time, in the groin. He died a few minutes later, under a tree, shaded by Spanish moss. Immediately afterwards, Gibbs was mortally wounded. At the other end of the British line, Keane was wounded in the neck and carried back unconscious. The fight lasted twenty-five minutes. More than eight hundred and fifty British troops were dead or mortally wounded. Another two thousand five hundred were injured. Total American casualties were about fifty, in both dead and wounded. British courage had been outstanding. So had General Pakenham's stupidity. So had the Americans' shooting.

On the other, south, side of the river, the secondary battle went Britain's way. The American general, David Morgan, and his Kentuckians fled when the British, under Colonel Thornton, charged. Jackson, seeing their difficulties, sent Humbert across the Mississippi to take command. But Morgan and his officers refused to accept orders from a 'foreigner' and Humbert stalked away in a fury. Fortunately, for the Americans, at that moment Thornton realised that the British army on the north bank of the river had, for all practical purposes, ceased to exist. For fear of finding himself outnumbered and surrounded, he moved back to his original positions. The Battle of New Orleans was over.

As a consolation prize, the British attacked and captured Fort Bowyer in Mobile, in mid-February, and General Lambert, who was now commander-in-chief, was planning a new attack on New Orleans from Mobile when news of the Ghent peace treaty finally reached the belligerents. The British sailed back home. As they neared the English shore near Plymouth, the first ships encountered a fishing boat a few miles from land. 'Anything new?' they shouted down at the fishermen as they passed. 'Yes, Bonaparte is back in France,' the fishermen shouted back. The survivors of New Orleans then knew their fighting days were not yet over.

Their next battle would be Waterloo.

PART FIVE

The Hundred Days of 1815

BLÜCHE, THE BRAVE EXTRACTING THE CROWN OF ABDICATION FROM THE CORSICAN BLOOD HOUND.

Napoleon off to his first place of exile, Elba, after his 1814 defeat by the Prussian general, Blücher. Cartoon by Thomas Rowlandson

CHAPTER TWENTY-FOUR

The British Lion Kills

CHARGE, MY HEROES, CHARGE
Waterloo 1815

Napoleon tired very quickly of life in Elba. The eighty-six square miles of the little island could not encompass the ambitions and restless energy of the man who had ruled France and much of Europe and controlled the destiny of a large part of the world although, now forty-six, he was looking somewhat portly, had a paunch and was beginning to lose his hair.

On February 26, 1815 he quietly said goodbye to his mother and sister Pauline, who were visiting him, and slipped away from the island aboard the brig *Inconsistent*. 'I shall reach Paris without firing a shot,' he told his followers. The Hundred Days, the last phase of the Napoleonic Wars, had begun.

He landed at Golfe Juan, between Cannes and Antibes on the French Riviera, on March 1 and began his march north with his personal army of 1,050 men who had followed him from Elba in six smaller ships. Louis XVIII hurriedly sent troops to intercept him under the orders of Marshal Ney, who promised he would bring the invader back in an iron cage. But glory had returned to France. From Ney down, the soldiers all rallied to the Emperor. Along his route to the capital, the French acclaimed the man in the grey army-coat and black cocked hat who was bringing back with him France's lost pride. By March 20 he was outside Paris. Fat, gouty Louis XVIII rolled wheezily into his carriage and fled north to safety.

The crowned heads of Europe, garbed in silk robes, retrograde and faint-hearted, trembled once again for their debased thrones and their extortionate privileges. The Allies, gathered in Vienna, declared Napoleon an international outlaw and formed a new coalition against the man they could only hope to defeat by mass action and crushing superiority. The most powerful adversaries of Napoleon, the Britain/ Russia/Prussia/Austria quartet agreed each to put 150,000 men in the field against him until he was beaten. From London, the Foreign Secretary, Viscount Castlereagh, wrote to Wellington in Vienna offering him the command of the British army in Flanders. Wellington immediately set out for Brussels.

Napoleon was starting his new reign surrounded by enemies determined on his downfall. History books may have condemned him as the aggressor, but history knows he was now the prey. Initially Napoleon only had 200,000 soldiers and he certainly did not want war. He wrote an appeasing letter to the Regent in London (the future George IV was standing in for his father, George III, now quite mad). The letter was returned unopened. He wrote to the Emperor Francis in Vienna, his father-in-law, and received no reply. European royal society was defending its own, and its own was the dumpling Louis XVIII. Napoleon was a usurper. Whether the French wanted him as Emperor or not was of no consequence to the sovereigns of Europe. They were determined to inflict their Bourbon cousin on France.

Napoleon met the challenge immediately. The danger came from the north, in Belgium, where a vast 250,000 man Allied army, composed of 120,000 Prussians, 23,000 British and 6,500 men of their attached King's German Legion, 30,000 Netherlanders, 15,000 Hanoverians and 6,500 Brunswickers, was massing to invade France. The Prussians were under the command of Field-Marshal Blücher, seventy-three years old. The British, the Netherlanders (both Dutch and Belgians), the Hanoverians and Brunswickers made up the army of Duke of Wellington. The Iron Duke, as he was known already, winner of so many battles, was about to win his greatest.

Forced to fight, Napoleon on June 14 marched into Belgium with 120,000 men. After two hard encounters at Quatre Bras, against the British, and at Ligny, against the Prussians, he obliged the enemy to withdraw and encamped on the road to Brussels on June 17. He prepared to do battle the next day, now with 72,000 men, against the 68,000-strong Anglo-Dutch-German army, just south of the village of Waterloo. The bulk of the remainder of his troops, some 32,000 men, a few miles to the east under Marshal Grouchy, were trying to catch up and engage Blücher's much larger Prussian force, about 70,000 men strong.

Blücher was trying to join Wellington at Waterloo and blocking, or delaying, this Prussian army was vital for the French. If the Prussians succeeded in joining with Wellington, Napoleon's original slight superiority in numbers on the Waterloo battlefield would be transformed into a heavy inferiority.

The battle of Waterloo is too well known to require detailed retelling here. But a summing-up is in order. It was, after all, the last vital battle of the Napoleonic wars and many of the soldiers we have encountered in this narrative played their part in it, including of course the two main protagonists, Napoleon I and the Duke of Wellington, who met here for the first and last time in battle.

The battlefield stretched across four miles of rolling countryside from east to west, and a couple of miles from north to south. The Allied line extended across the road leading to Brussels, the French were to the south of their enemy, in a parallel line to them.

After a diversionary attack on the Chateau of Hougoumont estate on the eastern edge of the battlefield by troops under Napoleon's youngest brother, General Jerome Bonaparte, four divisions of General d'Erlon's First Corps in the centre were to storm the enemy positions facing them.

Because heavy rain during the night turned the ground into a quagmire, Napoleon put off the Hougoumont attack, which was to herald the start of operations, until eleven o'clock. This delay, as it turned out, probably cost the Emperor the battle. . . and his throne. He was not, anyway, at the top of his form that day nor did he seem at any time to be in full control of the situation. It is said he was suffering from a very unglamorous and painful ailment, particularly for a man who had to sit for several hours on a horse: haemorrhoids.

Napoleon, before ordering the first main attack, sent his chief engineer, General Haxo, to check whether the enemy had erected field fortifications for their defence. Since we were last with him eight years ago fighting with the Turks against the British in the Dardanelles, Haxo had served in Spain, Germany and right through the Russian campaign. He had managed to survive an attack of typhus, a shell splinter in the chest and imprisonment in Hungary.

There were no parapets, Haxo reported when he came galloping back after his inspection. The enemy had only cut down a few trees and laid them across the Brussels road. Then, just before d'Erlon attacked at 1.30 pm, the French captured a Prussian horseman carrying a message to Wellington informing the British commander that Blücher was on his way . . . and Blücher's arrival would mean another seventy thousand men against Napoleon!

Napoleon immediately prepared to fight on two fronts, to the north and to the east. He ordered the Sixth Corps, under General Mouton, Count Lobau as he was known, a total of eleven thousand men, to take up positions east at the village of Plancenoit, to prepare to meet the Prussians who would be hitting the French on their right flank, and he ordered d'Erlon to move against Wellington to the north with four massed divisions – about sixteen thousand men in all – including the

2nd division, commanded by General Donzelot who, until last year, had been successfully defending Corfu.

D'Erlon's infantry advanced shouting 'Vive l'Empereur', an easy target for the British, German and Dutch marksmen on the crest of the slopes and for the Allied artillery that mowed them down. They reached the Allied line where stood the Anglo-Hanoverians of General Picton. The hard-swearing, rough-talking Picton had served with Abercromby in the West Indies and with Wellington in Spain, and was one of the Iron Duke's best generals. But Waterloo was his last battle. In the furious melee that followed the irruption of the French troops in the British lines, Picton was killed, shot through the head by one of Donzelot's men.

General Lambert, just back from New Orleans, moved in quickly to strengthen the line with his brigade. Nearby, General Pack's division was also hard-pressed. Pack, since Buenos Aires, had been fighting in Spain where he had acquired no less than eight wounds. At Waterloo, under relentless French pressure, his Gordon Highlanders began to waver but, after a charge by the British heavy cavalry at around three o'clock in the afternoon, d'Erlon's attack was broken. The Scots Greys, however, galloped too far into the French lines, were cut off and roughly handled.

By this time the Prussians were appearing in growing numbers on the French right. The risk, for the French, was the old one of a walnut caught between the two sides of a nutcracker, one side Wellington's army, the other Blücher's Prussians. A quick victory was absolutely essential for Napoleon. But each move he made had to be well timed. At three-thirty the French cavalry, led by the impetuous Marshal Ney, charged against the British squares, but with no infantry or horse artillery support. 'It's too soon,' stormed Napoleon when he saw the cavalry charging without waiting for his orders.

There was one New Orleans veteran on the French side: General Burthe who had seen the Tricolour lowered in 1803 and the colony handed over to the United States. Now, at Waterloo, he was leading his cavalry division into battle. The French cavalry were so closely packed that each horseman's stirrups touched those of the man next to him. Their horses were sometimes lifted off the ground and carried forward by the charging line, their hooves frantically stirring the air, wonderful targets for the incredulous gunners and infantrymen on the other side. Over the British lines, the cool order went out: 'Prepare to receive cavalry!' The infantry formed squares, the gunners fired their volleys into this mass of approaching equine and human flesh and then hurried for shelter inside the squares. The infantrymen, formed along four sides in four ranks, fired, reloaded, fired.

The slaughter of Frenchmen and horses was horrific. The useless and heroic attacks went on for two hours. Five times the French cavalry

**Waterloo
18 June 1815**

To Waterloo

To Chain

Mont St. Jean

PRUSSIAN
I CORPS

Marbe
Braine

HOUSEHOLD AND
UNION BRIGADES

VANDELEUR

Braine L'Alleud

VIVIAN

CHASSÉ

Papelotte

La-Haye
Sainte

Frischermont

D'ERLON'S
CORPS

PRUSSIAN
IV CORPS

Hougomont

GUARDS

NEY'S
CAVALRY

REILLE

JEROME

BACHELU

La Belle
Alliance

NEY'S
CAVALRY

IMPERIAL

GUARD

Plancenoit

Rossomme

PRUSSIAN
II CORPS

Key
Allies   French

Infantry   Infantry

Cavalry   Cavalry

0   1000 yards

0   1000 metres

charged. Four times Marshal Ney's horse was shot under him and four
times he mounted a fresh steed and charged again.

Heavy smoke covered the battlefield through which horses and
horsemen would suddenly appear and disappear like wraiths lost in a
shrieking hell. At the end of each charge the French cavalrymen would
swirl around the squares, shouting insults at the British infantrymen,
only a few feet away from them but out of reach behind their wall of
pointed bayonets. Cavalry attacks alone cannot break disciplined
squares. Horses are less stupid than believed, and are well aware that
bayonets are dangerous.

The Duke of Wellington, inside one of the squares, asked an aide
what time it was. 'Twenty minutes past four,' replied the officer. 'The
battle is mine and if the Prussians arrive soon, the war will be ended,'
said Wellington.

But still the insane French cavalry charges went on. As the cavalrymen cantered away after each charge to regroup and charge again, the
British gunners would dart out of the squares where they had been
sheltering, return to their guns, load, aim and fire again, turning horses

and men into broken, dispersed bits of bone, flesh, guts and muscle.

There is a story that during a lull in the battle one of the British gunners, standing by Wellington, spotted Napoleon sitting astride his white charger, a mile or so across the fields, and asked for permission to fire at the French Emperor. Wellington did not approve of the suggestion. 'No, no!' he replied, 'Generals commanding armies have something else to do than shoot at one another.'

On the right flank, where Count Lobau was facing the Prussians at Plancenoit, the French flank was now under heavy attack from General von Bulow, commanding the van of Blücher's Prussian troops. Prussian artillery was also coming into action. Before any more Prussians arrived, the French must smash through Wellington's lines ahead of them. General Foy's infantry brigade now came heavily into the fighting, too late, and were cut to pieces by the British artillery.

The farm of La Haye Sainte, a key defence point covering the centre of the British line, was now the focus of the French attacks, with Donzelot's division in the lead. After half an hour of desperate fighting the French occupied the building, only forty of the German defenders surviving. The time was now around 6.30 pm. The Allied line, after repeated buttings, was cracking. Many Allied soldiers had fled the battlefield towards Brussels, shouting that the battle was lost.

General von Zieten's First Prussian Corps, about thirty thousand men, emerging out of the woods near the village of Ohain to link up directly with Wellington's army, was met by a mob of Allied fugitives. Von Zieten assumed that Wellington had lost and prudently began to march back east, to the main Blücher army. The Iron Duke hurriedly sent his liaison officer, Colonel Muffling, across to von Zieten to bring him and his army back. 'The battle is lost unless the First Corps returns,' Muffling pleaded. Von Zieten nodded, wheeled his troops round and joined the Allied line. Napoleon now had to fight the Prussians in front of him as well as on his right flank. It was the beginning of the end.

The time was now about 7.00 pm. The battered French, fighting on two fronts, were bolstered for a few minutes by the rumour that Marshal Grouchy was on his way to join them with more than thirty thousand men. The weight of his troops would swing the battle to the French, and as more and more Prussians were spotted on the distant skyline, the deceived French shouted enthusiastically 'Voici Grouchy! Vive l'Empereur!' In a final bid for victory, Napoleon sent into the fray the dreaded Imperial Guards, the most feared soldiers of Europe, the men who never lost a battle and who, throughout the day, had been kept in reserve.

To the muffled, monotonous beat of drums, they advanced towards the enemy, six thousand five hundred men in all, in their tall bearskin hats, steady and in close ranks, the elite of the world's armies, in columns of eighty men across. At their head walked General Friant, now fifty-seven years old, son of a wax polisher, Count of the Empire, a soldier since 1782, wounded six times in action, veteran of Fleurus, the Tagliamento, the Pyramids, the Nile valley, Aboukir, Heliopolis, Alexandria, Austerlitz, Auerstadt, Eylau, Ratisbon, Wagram, Smolensk, the Borodino, Montmirail and Craonne.

The Belgian General Chassé, until last year fighting in the French ranks, tried to intercept the Guards and was thrown back. Three battalions of Brunswickers fled. Two battalions of Sir Colin Halkett's Hanoverian brigade, badly mauled in the fighting, were swept aside.

Along the Allied line, the order went out to the British infantry: 'Lie down and wait.' The men slid down into the barley field, behind the slopes where they were sheltering. To the attackers, they seemed to have disappeared. Only the gunners, British and German, remained standing and in sight, pouring shot into the apparently unshakeable French ranks. Marshal Ney, riding with them, fell as his fifth horse was killed that day. He picked himself up, and marched alongside Friant.

Wellington approached General Sir Peregrine Maitland, commander of the First Brigade of Guards. He waited until the French line was only fifty yards away, advancing slowly and deliberately, almost solemnly, towards an enemy they could not see. 'Now is your time, Maitland,' the Iron Duke said quietly. The order went briskly to the British Guards: 'Stand up Guards! Make ready! Fire!' Two thousand Englishmen stood up and fired. In the next five seconds, three hundred Frenchmen dropped dead, hundreds more were wounded.

Friend and foe were suddenly blended in a furious, brawling mass. In twenty minutes, twelve hundred French Guards were killed or wounded. And suddenly, to the horror of their watching comrades, the unthinkable happened. The Imperial Guard was retreating.

The French soldiers were at last aware that the thousands of troops streaming in from the east were not Grouchy's Frenchmen: they were Blücher's Prussians. Among the bewildered, shaken and weary French, nearly a third of whom had already been killed or wounded, one massive shout was heard: 'We have been betrayed!' Then came the horrendous cry: 'Sauve qui peut!' Napoleon was no longer the master of his troops. Panic was.

The British and Prussian lines had merged, the French were now streaming away from the battle in hordes. Probably some fifty thousand corpses and wounded too injured to move lay around the battlefield, at least half of them were French.

Wellington, his hat high in his hand, was waving his troops forward. Admiral Sir Sidney Smith, who somehow managed to be always where the action was, even if it were many miles from the sea, rode up to Wellington in his hour of triumph to congratulate him on victory, shook his hand and then went to help some of the abandoned French wounded on the battlefield. He had been visiting Belgium as a tourist when the battle started and had ridden up to Waterloo to 'see the fun'.

Marshal Ney, a broken sword in hand, his uniform covered in blood and mud, was still fighting, trying to find a soldier's death on the battlefield, plunging into every mêlée around him. But he survived Waterloo and was shot as a traitor to France a few weeks later by the vindictive, victorious Royalists. The ashen-faced Napoleon drove away from the battlefield towards Paris where the never-say-die General Desfourneaux, nearly sixty now, but still fighting fit and sputtering contempt for the enemy, had taken over the defence of the hills of Montmartre, should the Allies progress that far.

The Allied victory and the abdication of Napoleon were now inevitable. On June 22 the Emperor abandoned his throne, hopefully but unsuccessfully in favour of his son. A week later, at Malmaison, after spending a long time alone in the room where Josephine had died, he kissed his mother goodbye and, accompanied by a few faithful officers, drove in a carriage to the Atlantic port of Rochefort. Two frigates, the *Méduse* (Captain Ponée) and the *Saale* (Captain Philibert) were waiting to take him or escort him to the United States. But offshore a British squadron, made up of the old 74-gun HMS *Bellerophon*, and three 20-gun corvettes were on guard. Their mission: to intercept the French Emperor if he tried to flee, capture him and take him to England.

Captain Ponée, determined to die for the Emperor (he had fought the Schomberg squadron off Madagascar in 1811), suggested Napoleon take passage on the *Saale* while with the *Méduse* he diverted British attention by attacking and boarding HMS *Bellerophon*. The proposal was insane but the *Méduse*'s final fate would have been more heroic in this hopeless enterprise than her ghastly end on a West African sandbank under a Royalist captain, the following year. Napoleon turned it down. It would cost too many lives, he said.

British mastery of the sea once again triumphed, and capitulation to the British was, finally, the only course left for Napoleon. The British are a generous and hospitable race and they will not fail a vanquished monarch who throws himself at their mercy, the Emperor convinced himself. Exile in England would be tolerable, even enjoyable.

On July 15, in the late evening, the Emperor walked up the gangway of HMS *Bellerophon*, raised his hat, bowed to her captain, Frederick Maitland, and said: 'Sir, I am come on board and I claim the protection of your Prince and your laws.' But, at the end of his voyage, it would not be England that awaited him but a sordid, unhealthy, rat-infested little South Atlantic island, and a gimlet-eyed goaler, Sir Hudson Lowe. At Torbay, the amiable, affable Lord Keith came on board to announce to him that England was not his final destination but St Helena.

Resistance was over. France was now in the hands of the hated Royalists. But the last battle of the Napoleonic wars was still to be fought. Already twice blood-drenched, by Victor Hugues and by General Richepanse, Guadeloupe was to bleed a little more.

THOSE BLOOD-SOAKED HILLS
Guadeloupe 1815

But this time the Caribbean island did not provide the setting for an execution yard or massacre. This last clash in arms for the loyalty of Guadeloupe was more an affray than a battle, a courteous if murderous exchange of the civilities, bullets and cannonballs required by military honour.

Neither Martinique nor Guadeloupe had shown much royalist zeal after the Bourbon king regained his throne. However, Martinique, now governed by the Count of Vaugiraud, a former émigré, came under tighter royalist control than Guadeloupe, where Admiral Linois, who had served the Emperor loyally and bravely if not always very efficiently, ruled in the king's name. The army garrison was commanded by another ex-Bonapartist, General Boyer de Peyreleau who, seven years ago, had led the assault against the island 'HMS' Diamond Rock, and had since fought in Germany and Russia.

When news of Bonaparte's return to Paris had reached the islands, three months late, Martinique not surprisingly remained faithful to King Louis XVIII, but in Guadeloupe the king was dispossessed and Napoleon proclaimed Emperor.

The commanders of the British forces in nearby Barbados, General Sir James Leith and Admiral Sir Philip Durham – two of our old acquaintances also – wisely waited before taking any action. In mid-July came the news of Waterloo. The British military and naval leaders then issued a joint proclamation calling on the French in Guadeloupe to lay down their arms and accept their king's sovereignty in the island. They politely sent a copy to Admiral Linois first, advising him they would be landing shortly.

The British sailed from Barbados in late July with six thousand men. Curiously, however, the expedition, composed entirely of British and West Indian troops, was operating not in the name of the Prince Regent but for His Most Christian Majesty King Louis XVIII.

On arrival off Guadeloupe, Admiral Durham sent his aide-de-camp under a flag of truce to see Linois, offering him, if he were acting under constraint, the protection of the Royal Navy. Admiral Linois, an honourable man, politely declined the British invitation.

The British, as was their fashion in these island operations, landed at three points on Guadeloupe. The first landing, on August 8, was at Anse St Sauveur, in the southern part of Basse-Terre, by some eight hundred and fifty Royal York rangers who met a little half-hearted opposition by five hundred French defenders on the beach who soon decamped under the fire of the British warships. The bulk of the French troops were concentrated, with General Boyer de Peyreleau, at the next point of the British attack, at Grande Anse. French artillery tried to prevent General Leith from landing with some two thousand troops but the British reached shore for the loss of only one gunboat. After some sharp fighting, the French retired into the hills overlooking the sea and all the fighting stopped as night fell.

The third and final landing was made in the morning of the 9th near Basse-Terre while the troops that had landed the previous day were fighting with the French in the hills. Some fifty British troops were killed and wounded. But there was no alternative to surrender for the French. They knew Napoleon was now a prisoner in British hands and that Louis XVIII was their lawful sovereign. Their present battle was not a fight to the death but a gesture of rage against the harshness of fate which had destroyed their venerated Emperor.

During the night, in the middle of a torrential, tropical downpour, Admiral Linois sent one of his officers to General Leith to ask for capitulation terms. In the morning, the Tricolour flying over the French camp was slowly lowered. Admiral Durham, who as a lieutenant aboard HMS *Spitfire*, had seen the first French flag lowered in surrender in 1793, was now seeing the last surrender. The war was over. The slaughter and the bloodshed had ended not in the fury and magnificence of the fields of Waterloo but in a forgotten affray in the forest-covered mountains of a small West Indian island.

Admiral Linois and General Boyer de Peyreleau were ordered back to France to be court-martialled for treason and rebellion against their king (they were both ultimately pardoned). Linois, as an indicted felon, was ordered to make the Atlantic crossing with his wife aboard one of the overcrowded transports, to face his trial in Paris. But Admiral Durham insisted he and Madame Linois travel back in comfort in his own, more spacious ship. When Linois came on board, the British admiral told his French captive that 'from what he had heard of Linois's kind treatment of English prisoners he had taken during his command of the French squadron in India, he had every wish to grant him any indulgence in his power. For this,' Durham added in his memoirs, 'Linois seemed most grateful.'

After twenty-two years of war, hatred and bloodshed, human solidarity could still triumph.

Epilogue

NAPOLEON BUONAPARTE.

Napoleon in 1821, after six lonely years of exile on St Helena, a few months before
his death. Drawn by one of his guards

CHAPTER TWENTY-FIVE

The Words of a Soldier

So ended the first world war. Britain and her colonies emerged and expanded and became in due course the British Empire, the largest, the strongest and the wealthiest the world has ever seen. It covered a quarter of the globe and lasted nearly a century and a half.

The acquisition of colonies had consistently been one of Britain's major, if unacknowledged, war aims. The gains were impressive: Cape Colony in South Africa changed its allegiance from loyal Dutch to disloyal British. Dutch Malacca, in Malaya, also became British and Raffles founded Singapore a few years later as a trading post to rival Jakarta. In India the defeat of the French generals and of France's native allies made India safely British until after the end of World War II. In the antipodes, the British settlers in New South Wales, fearful of a French takeover in Tasmania, gradually occupied the whole Australian continent. Sri Lanka, once Portuguese, then Dutch, also came under the Union Jack. So did a large slice of Dutch Guyana in South America. So did the Spanish colony of Trinidad which the British had hoped to use as a base for the conquest of that southern continent. So did the French islands of St Lucia and Tobago in the West Indies, and Mauritius, the Seychelles and the tiny strategic islet of Diego Garcia in the Indian Ocean. There were other island acquisitions here and there, not only, as we have seen, Malta and Corfu, but also Heligoland in the North Sea – taken from the Danes – and Ascension and Tristan da Cunha, in the south Atlantic. Between 1792 and 1815 the British imperial domain doubled in size.

So did, may we repeat, the United States, through its purchase of Louisiana, a territory Napoleon felt unable to defend against potential

355

British raiders. But after the war, the French recovered Martinique and Guadeloupe in the West Indies, the cod-fishing islands of St Pierre and Miquelon off Newfoundland, the island of Réunion in the Indian Ocean, its West African enclaves of Gorée and St Louis, its territories in India and half of French Guyana.

The long-range effects of the Napoleonic Wars were shattering to the established order in Central and South America as well. The sale of Louisiana turned out to be a disaster for Mexico. A French-ruled Louisiana would have been a buffer between the dynamic, acquisitive and assertive United States to the east and the weak and troubled Iberian lands to the west and south-west. The French departure opened the way for the Americans who over the next four decades and in the name of their 'manifest destiny' took half of Mexico for themselves, all the way west to California and south through Texas to the Rio Grande.

The whole of Spanish America, in fact, was shaken by Napoleon's invasion of Spain, his removal of its legitimate king and his replacement by Joseph Bonaparte. Spanish America, cast adrift, learnt the habit of independence. So did Brazil. By chasing the Portuguese royal family out of Lisbon to Rio de Janeiro, Napoleon opened wide this gigantic country to European influences and gave the royal House of Braganza a South American root which greatly facilitated the early and bloodless accession of the country to independence.

The Dutch recovered Java and prospered in the East Indies. The Portuguese less so in Angola, Mozambique, Goa and its other enclaves here and there, after the loss of Brazil. The US and Russian empires grew until they reached the Pacific shores and beyond. The Spanish and Turkish empires went on slowly dying until they finally expired, the Spaniards' in Manila Bay in 1898, blasted by the guns of Dewey's fleet, the Turks' lingering on until after World War I.

The man responsible for so many of these global upheavals, Napoleon Bonaparte, died in 1821 – six years after Waterloo – in his shabby, forlorn cottage in St Helena, harassed to the end by his snarling gaoler. His last words were those of a soldier. 'At the head of the army,' he said, and died. In England Wellington, a symbol of the military calling at its honoured best, became, alas, one of the most reactionary prime ministers Britain has ever known. He governed his country with an uneven hand from 1828 to 1830. Born the same year as Napoleon, he outlived his old enemy by thirty-one years.

General Andrew Jackson, whose troops had killed Pakenham, Wellington's brother-in-law, at New Orleans, was elected president of the United States in 1828. Unlike Wellington (and also unlike a current British lady Prime Minister, unlike a recent ex-actor US President and unlike a recent right-wing French Prime Minister) Jackson did not believe in government for the good of the rich and the powerful but, we are refreshingly told by the Columbia-Viking encyclopedia, 'for the good of the small man, of the frontier farmer and the backwoodsman, the laborer and the mechanic'. After his presidency, he retired to his estate in Tennessee where he died in 1845.

Our story calls for one last obituary. General Amable Humbert, lost soldier of France, died alone in his dingy hotel room in New Orleans on January 4, 1824. 'A sense of honour remained deep within him, in spite of his lapses,' the French consul in Louisiana wrote to his foreign minister in Paris, announcing the general's death.

Were Humbert's last thoughts, one wonders, for Pauline Bonaparte whose promiscuous love had destroyed his military career and ruined his life? Or were they for Castlebar, the only French victory on British home soil since the Battle of Hastings in 1066? 'A brilliant feat of arms has assured him a place in our history,' the consul wrote to Paris. He was wrong. The Battle of Castlebar has long been forgotten by the French who have a short memory and by the English who remember only their victories.

Bibliography

ANDERSON, R. C. *Naval Wars in the Baltic*, London 1669

ARCIENEGAS, GERMAN, *Caribbean, Sea of the New World*, New York 1946

AUGUSTE, MARCEL BONAPARTE AND CLAUDE BONAPARTE, *La participation étrangère à l'expédition française de Saint Dominique*, Quebec, Canada 1980

BAEYENS, JACQUES, *Sabre au clair – Amable Humbert, Général de la République*, Paris 1981

BAINES, EDWARD, *History of the Wars of the French Revolution*, London 1817

BAINVILLE, JACQUES, *Napoléon*, Paris 1931

BARBER, NOEL, *Lords of the Golden Horn*, London 1973

BARROW, JOHN, *Life and Correspondence of Sir Sidney Smith*, London 1842

BEARD, CHARLES A. AND MARY R., *The Rise of American Civilisation*, New York 1939

BENNETT, GEOFFREY, *Nelson the Commander*, London 1972

BENOIST-MECHIN, *Bonaparte en Egypte ou Le Rêve inassouvi*, Paris 1978

BERNARD, J. F., *Talleyrand*, New York 1975

BESSON, MAURICE, *Les aventuriers français aux Indes*, Paris 1932

BLACK, J., *An Authentic Narration on Board the Ship Lady Shore*, Ipswich 1799

BLAINEY, GEOFFREY, *The Tyranny of Distance*, Melbourne 1966

BOIGNE, COMTESSE DE, *Mémoires*, reprinted Paris 1982

BONNEL, U., *La France, les Etats Unis et la guerre de course, 1793-1815*, Paris 1961

BORDONOVE, GEORGES, *Les marins de l'An II*, Paris 1974

BROGAN, HUGH, *Longman History of the United States of America*, London 1985

BRYANT, ARTHUR, *The Years of Endurance 1793-1802*, London 1944

BRYANT, ARTHUR, *The Years of Victory 1802-1812*, London 1945

BRYANT, ARTHUR, *The Years of Elegance 1812-1822*, London 1954
CARTER III, SAMUEL, *Blaze of Glory – The Fight for New Orleans 1814-1815*, New York 1973
CHANDLER, DAVID, *Napoleon*, New York 1973
CHANDLER, DAVID, *Dictionary of the Napoleonic Wars*, London 1979
CHANDLER, DAVID, (edited by) *Napoleon's Marshals*, London 1987
CLOWES, SIR WILLIAM LAIRD, *The Royal Navy*, London 1903
COLLET, OCTAVE, *L'Ile de Java sous la domination française*, Brussels 1909
COMPTON, HERBERT, *A Particular Account of the European Military Adventurers of Hindustan*, London 1893
CRONIN, VINCENT, *Napoleon*, London 1983
DAVIS, EDWIN ADAMS, *Louisiana – The Pelican State*, Baton Rouge 1959
DIESBACH, GHISLAIN DE, *Histoire de l'émigration 1789-1814*, Paris 1975
DRONKERS, J. M. G. A., *De generaals van het koninkijk Holland 1806-1810*, The Hague 1982
DUGGAN, JAMES, *The Great Mutiny*, London 1966
DUHAMEL, JEAN, *The 50 days – Napoleon in England*, Coral Gables (Florida) 1970
DUPONT, ADMIRAL MAURICE, *L'Amiral Willaumez*, Paris 1987
DURANT, WILL AND ARIEL, *The Age of Napoleon*, New York 1980
EDWARDES, MICHAEL, *Glorious Sahibs*, London 1968
ELLIS, M. H., *Lachlan Macquarie*, Sydney 1973
ESPOSITO AND ELTING, *A Military History & Atlas of the Napoleonic Wars*, New York 1914
FAIVRE, J. B., *L'expansion française dans le Pacifique*, Paris 1953
FARRÈRE, CLAUDE, *Histoire de la Marine Française*, Paris 1962
FITCHETT, W. H., *How England Saved Europe*, London 1899
FORESTER, C. S., *The Age of Fighting Sail*, New York 1956
FORTESCUE, SIR JOHN, *A History of the British Army*, vols 4-10, London 1906-1920
FORTIER, ALCÉE, *A History of Louisiana*, New York 1904
FROST, ALAN, *Convicts and Empire*, Melbourne 1980
GRAHAM, GERALD SANDFORD, *Great Britain in the Indian Ocean*, Oxford 1967
GRAHAM-YOOL, ANDREW, *The Forgotten Colony*, London 1981
GRUPPE, HENRY E., *The Frigates*, Amsterdam 1979
GUENIN, EUGÈNE, *La Louisiane*, Paris 1904
GUILLEMIN, RENÉ, *Corsaires de la République et de l'Empire*, Paris 1982
HARBOTTLE, THOMAS, *Dictionary of Battles* (revised and updated by Georges Bruce), New York 1975
HEINL, ROBERT D. JR AND GORDON, NANCY, *Written in Blood*, Boston 1978
HENRY, DR A., *La Guyane Française, son histoire 1604-1946*, Cayenne 1981
HERBERT, A. P., *Why Waterloo*, New York, 1953
HEROLD, J. CHRISTOPHER, *Bonaparte in Egypt*, London 1962
HEROLD, J. CHRISTOPHER, *The Age of Napoleon*, New York 1968
Historical Dictionary of Argentina, London 1978
HORNE, ALISTAIR, *Napoleon, Master of Europe 1805-07*, London 1979
HOWARTH, DAVID, *Sovereign of the Seas – The Story of British Sea Power*, London 1974

JABARTI AL- ABD-AL-RAMMAN, *Journal d'un notable du Caire durant l'expédition française 1798-1801*, Paris 1979
JAMES, C.L.R., *The Black Jacobins*, London 1982
JENKINS, E.H., *A History of the French Navy*, London 1973
JONES, J.R., *Britain and the World 1649-1815*, London 1980
KEEGAN, JOHN, *The Face of Battle*, London 1976
KEEGAN, JOHN AND DARRACOT, JOSEPH, *The Nature of War*, New York 1981
KEMP, PETER (edited by), *The Oxford Companion to Ships and the Sea*, London 1976
KENNEDY, LUDOVIC, *Nelson and his Captains*, London 1970
KENNEDY, PAUL, *The Rise and Fall of British Naval Mastery*, London 1976
KORNGOLD, RALPH, *The Last Years of Napoleon*, London 1960
LAURENT DE L'ARDÈCHE, P.M., *Histoire de l'Empereur Napoléon*, Paris 1839
LENOTRE, G., *Napoléon, croquis de l'épopée*, Paris 1932
LEVENE, RICARDO, *A History of Argentina*, New York 1963
LEWIS, MICHAEL, *Napoleon and his British Captives*, London 1962
LEWIS, MICHAEL, *The History of the British Navy*, London 1957
LLOYD, CHRISTOPHER, *The Nation and the Navy*, London 1961
LLOYD, CHRISTOPHER, *The Nile Campaign*, Newton Abbott 1973
LLOYD, CHRISTOPHER, *Batailles navales au temps de la marine à voile*, Paris 1972
LONGFORD, ELIZABETH, *Wellington – The Years of the Sword*, New York 1969
LUCAS-DUBRETON, J., *Soldats de Napoléon*, Paris 1977
LUDWIG, EMIL, *Napoleon*, London 1927
MAHAN, CAPTAIN ALFRED, *The Influence of Sea Power upon History 1660-1805*, London 1980
MACKSEY, PIERS, *The Wars in the Mediterranean, 1803–1810*, London 1957
MARCHANT, LESLIE, *France Australe*, Perth 1982
MAURO, FRÉDERIC, *L'expansion européenne (1600-1870)*, Paris 1967
MCEVEDY, COLIN, *The Penguin Atlas of Modern History (to 1815)*, London 1972
MCEVEDY, COLIN AND HONES, RICHARD, *Atlas of World Population History*, London 1972
MELCHIOR-BONNET, BERNARDINE, *Dictionnaire de la Révolution et de l'Empire*, Paris 1965
MEREJKOVSKY, DMITRI, *Napoléon – La Gloire et l'Ombre*, Paris 1968
MISLER, JEAN (edited by), *Napoléon*, Verviers 1968
MITCHELL, DONALD W., *A History of Russian and Soviet Sea Power*, New York 1974
MOOREHEAD, ALAN, *The Fatal Impact*, London 1966
MOOREHEAD, ALAN, *The Blue Nile*, New York 1972
MORDAL, JACQUES, *25 siècles de guerre sur mer*, Verviers 1959
MURRAY, CAPTAIN A., *Memoirs of the Naval Life and Services of Admiral Sir Philip C.H.C. Durham, GCB*, London 1846
NAIPAUL, V.S., *The Loss of El Dorado*, London 1978
New Cambridge Modern History, The (vol. ix), Cambridge 1965
NORMAN, C.B., *The Corsairs of France*, New York 1929

OMAN, CAROLA, *Britain Against Napoleon*, London 1942

O'MEARA, DR BARRY EDWARD, *A Voice from St. Helena*, London, 1821

OUDARD, GEORGES, *La Louisiane au temps des Français*, Paris 1931

PAKENHAM, THOMAS, *The Year of Liberty*, London 1973

PALACIO, ERNESTO, *Historia de la Argentina*, Buenos Aires 1965

PALMER, ALAN, *Napoleon in Russia*, London 1967

PALMER, ALAN, *Alexander I, Tsar of War and Peace*, London 1974

PALMER, ALAN, *An Encyclopedia of Napoleon's Europe*, London, 1984

PALMER, R. R. (edited by), *Atlas of World History*, New York 1957

PARKINSON, C. NORTHCOTE, *War in the Eastern Seas*, London 1954

PARKINSON, WENDA, *'This gilded African' – Toussaint L'Ouverture*, London 1978

PARRY, J. H., *Trade and Dominion*, London 1974

PARRY, J. H. AND P. M. SHERLOCK, *A Short History of the West Indies*, London 1971

PIVKA, OTTO VON, *Navies of the Napoleonic Era*, London 1980

PORTER, ADMIRAL DAVID, *Memoirs of Commodore David Porter*, Albany (N.Y.) 1875

PRATT, FLETCHER, *The Navy – A History*, New York 1938

PRENTOUT, HENRI, *L'Ile de France sous Decaen*, Paris 1901

PURYEAR, VERNON, *Napoleon and the Dardanelles*, Berkeley (Calif.) 1951

RECOULY, RAYMOND, *Bonaparte à Toulon*, Paris 1929

REILLY, ROBIN, *William Pitt the Younger*, New York 1979

REMOND, RENÉ, *Les Etats-Unis devant l'opinion française*, Paris 1962

ROMAND, LOUIS-JACQUES, *Mémoires de ma vie militaire 1809-1815*, Besançon 1981

ROSCOE, THEODORE AND FREEMAN, FRED, *Picture History of the US Navy*, New York 1956

ROSE, J. H., *Life of Napoleon I*, London 1902

ROSNY, J.-H., *Les folles passions de Pauline Borghese*, Paris 1933

SAINTE-CROIX DE LA RONCIÈRE, *Victor Hugues le Conventionnel*, Paris 1932

SAINTE-CROIX DE LA RONCIÈRE, *Le Général Richepanse*, Paris 1933

SAINTOYANT, J., *La colonisation française pendant la Révolution*, Paris 1930

SAINTOYANT, J., *La colonisation française pendant l'Empire*, Paris 1931

SAINT-RUF, GERMAIN, *L'épopée Delgrès*, Paris 1977

SASSENAY, MARQUIS DE, *Napoléon et la fondation de la République Argentine*, Paris 1892

SAVANT, JEAN, *Napoléon*, Paris 1974

SAXE-WEIMAR, GERARD, DUC DE, *Précis de la campagne de Java*, Leipzig 1821

SCHALCK DE LA FAVERIE, A., *Napoléon et l'Amérique*, Paris 1917

SEARS, STEPHEN W. (edited by), *The Horizon Book of the British Empire*, New York 1973

SEN, S. P., *The French in India*, Calcutta, 1958

SHERWIG, JOHN M., *Guineas and Gunpowder*, Cambridge 1969

SIX, GEORGES, *Dictionnaire biographique des généraux et amiraux de la Révolution et de l'Empire*, Paris 1934

SMYTH, CAPTAIN W. H., *The Life of Captain Philip Beaver*, London 1839

SOCIÉTÉ DE MILITAIRES ET DE GENS DE LETTRES, *Résumé des victoires et conquêtes des Français (1792-1823)*, Paris 1826

SOUTHEY, CAPTAIN THOMAS, *Chronological History of the West Indies*, London 1827 (reissued 1968)

TAILLEMITE, ETIENNE, *Dictionnaire des marins français*, Paris 1982

TAILLEMITE, ETIENNE, *L'Histoire ignorée de la Marine française*, Paris 1988

THOMAZI, AUGUSTE, *Marins batisseurs d'empire*, Paris 1946

THOMAZI, AUGUSTE, *Les marins de Napoléon*, Paris 1978

THORN, MAJOR WILLIAM, *A Memoir of the Conquest of Java*, London 1826

THRASHER, PETER ADAM, *Pasquale Paoli*, London 1970

TOMBE, CH., *Voyage aux Indes Orientales*, Paris 1811

TOUSSAINT, AUGUSTE, *History of the Indian Ocean*, London 1966

TOUSSAINT, AUGUSTE, *Histoire des Corsaires* (Collection Que sais-je?), Paris 1971

TOUSSAINT AUGUSTE, *Histoire de l'Ile Maurice*, (Collection, Que sais-je?), Paris 1971

TRAMOND, JOANNES, *Manuel d'Histoire Maritime de la France*, Paris 1916

TREVELYAN, G.M., *British History of the 19th Century and After (1782-1919)*, New York 1966

TRIEBEL, L.A. AND BATT, J.C., *French Exploration of Australia*, Sydney 1943

TUCKER, GLENN, *Poltroons and Patriots*, New York 1954

TULARD, JEAN, *Napoléon*, Paris 1977

TULARD, JEAN (edited by), *Dictionnaire Napoleon*, Paris 1987

TULARD, J., FAYARD, J.F., FIERRO, A., *Histoire et dictionnaire de la Révolution française*, Paris 1987

TURNBULL, ARCHIBALD DOUGLAS, *Commodore David Porter 1780-1843*, New York 1929

VAISH, DEVI CHARAN LAL, *The Rise of British Power in India and the Fall of the Marathas*, Lucknow 1972

VANDERCOOK, JOHN W., *Majesté Noire*, Paris 1930

VAN DEVANTER, M.L., *Raffles*, London 1894

VANNIA, HELIO, *Historia do Brasil*, Sao Paulo 1963

VAUCAIRE, MICHEL, *Bolivar*, Paris 1928

VIGNON, LOUIS, *L'expansion de la France*, Paris 1892

WAKEHAM, ERIC, *The Bravest Soldier – Sir Rollo Gillespie*, Edinburgh 1937

WARNER, OLIVER, *Trafalgar*, London 1959

WARNER, OLIVER, *Great Battle Fleets*, London 1973

WEINER, M., *The French Exiles 1789-1815*, London 1965

WHIPPLE, A.B.C., *Fighting Sail*, Amsterdam 1979

WHITWORTH, LORD (Despatches of), *England and Napoleon in 1803*, London 1887

WILLIAMS, GLYNDWR, *The Expansion of Europe in the 18th Century*, New York 1966

WILSON LYON, E., *Louisiana in French Diplomacy (1959-1804)*, Norman (Oklahoma), 1974

WISNES, ARMEL DE, *Ainsi vivaient les marins*, Paris 1971

WURTZBURG, C.E., *Raffles of the Eastern Isles*, London 1954

ZWEIG, STEFAN, *Brazil, Land of the Future*, New York 1943

Index